THE IDEAS OF MAN AND WOMAN IN RENAISSANCE FRANCE

The Ideas of Man and Woman in Renaissance France provides the first comprehensive comparison of the printed debates in the 1500s over the superiority or inferiority of woman – the *Querelle des femmes* – and the dignity and misery of man. Analysing these writings side by side, Lyndan Warner reveals the extent to which Renaissance authors borrowed commonplaces from both traditions as they praised or blamed man or woman and habitually considered opposite and contrary points of view. In the law courts reflections on the virtues and vices of man and woman had a practical application – to win cases – and as Warner demonstrates, Parisian lawyers employed this developing rhetoric in family disputes over inheritance and marriage, and amplified it in the published versions of their pleadings. Tracing these ideas and modes of thinking from the writer's quill to the workshops and boutiques of printers and booksellers, Warner uses probate inventories to follow the books to the households of their potential male and female readers. Warner reveals the shifts in printed discussions of human nature from the 1500s to the early 1600s and shows how booksellers adapted the ways they marketed and sold new genres such as essays and lawyers' pleadings.

Women and Gender in the Early Modern World

Series Editors:
Allyson Poska, The University of Mary Washington, USA
Abby Zanger

The study of women and gender offers some of the most vital and innovative challenges to current scholarship on the early modern period. For more than a decade now, Women and Gender in the Early Modern World has served as a forum for presenting fresh ideas and original approaches to the field. Interdisciplinary and multidisciplinary in scope, this Ashgate book series strives to reach beyond geographical limitations to explore the experiences of early modern women and the nature of gender in Europe, the Americas, Asia, and Africa. We welcome proposals for both single-author volumes and edited collections which expand and develop this continually evolving field of study.

Titles in the series

Imagining Women's Conventual Spaces in France, 1600–1800
The Cloister Disclosed
Barbara R. Woshinsky

Women, Imagination and the Search for Truth in Early Modern France
Rebecca M. Wilkin

English Printing, Verse Translation, and the Battle of the Sexes, 1476–1557
Anne E.B. Coldiron

Early Modern Women and Transnational Communities of Letters
Edited by Julie D. Campbell and Anne R. Larsen

Guardianship, Gender and the Nobility in Early Modern Spain
Grace E. Coolidge

Women Religious Leaders in Japan's Christian Century, 1549–1650
Haruko Nawata Ward

Women, Identities and Communities in Early Modern Europe
Edited by Stephanie Tarbin and Susan Broomhall

The Ideas of Man and Woman in Renaissance France

Print, Rhetoric, and Law

LYNDAN WARNER
Saint Mary's University, Canada

Routledge
Taylor & Francis Group
LONDON AND NEW YORK

First published 2011 by Ashgate Publishing

2 Park Square, Milton Park, Abingdon, Oxfordshire OX14 4RN
711 Third Avenue, New York, NY 10017

Routledge is an imprint of the Taylor & Francis Group, an informa business

First issued in paperback 2018

British Library Cataloguing in Publication Data
Warner, Lyndan.
The ideas of man and woman in Renaissance France: print, rhetoric, and law. – (Women and gender in the early modern world)
1. Women – France – History – Renaissance, 1450–1600 – Sources. 2. Women – Legal status, laws, etc. – France – History – 16th century – Sources. 3. Sex role – France – History – 16th century – Sources. 4. Oral pleading – France – History – 16th century. 5. Legal literature – Publishing – France – History – 16th century. 6. Booksellers and bookselling – France – History – 16th century.
I. Title II. Series
840.9'3522'09031–dc22

Library of Congress Cataloging-in-Publication Data
Warner, Lyndan.
The ideas of man and woman in Renaissance France : print, rhetoric, and law / Lyndan Warner.
p. cm. – (Women and gender in the early modern world)
Includes bibliographical references and index.
ISBN 978-1-4094-1246-5 (hardcover : alk. paper)
1. Women – France – History – Renaissance, 1450–1600. 2. Men – France – History – Renaissance, 1450–1600. 3. Women – France – Legal status, laws, etc. – History. 4. Men – France – Legal status, laws, etc. – History. 5. Women in literature – History. 6. Men in literature – History. I. Title. II. Series.

HQ1149.F8W37 2011
305.30944'09031–dc22

2010044260

ISBN 978-1-4094-1246-5 (hbk)
ISBN 978-1-138-37970-1 (pbk)

To Lorna

Contents

List of Figures

Notes on the Text

Translation

Each book title is translated into English on its first appearance in a chapter with the original language in parentheses or noted below in the footnotes. Translations from French are my own unless indicated in the footnotes where I have referenced any widely accessible translations. For Montaigne's *Essays*, I followed the 1603 translation of John Florio but modernised the spelling and sometimes adapted it with help from Michael Screech's translation of the *Complete Essays* (Harmondsworth, 1991).

Transcription

In the text and footnotes I have preserved the original French spelling and punctuation except to clarify the text or when I have substituted j for i, and v for u, and expanded contractions such as 'on' or 'om' for õ and 'an' for ã.

Dates

I have treated the year as beginning on 1 January, but noted these occasions by indicating the dates in square brackets.

Names

All Greek and Roman authors are identified in known single-name form in both the text and Bibliography.

For French authors I have used the international form of the author's name listed in the Catalogue général of the Bibliothèque nationale, France.

Bibliography and footnotes

For books printed in the 1400s to 1600s, I have kept the details of the printers and publishers in the footnotes as their identities and networks are central to the argument. For modern works, the details of the publishers can be found in the Bibliography. As early modern printers and booksellers tended to be a bit longwinded in promoting their works, I have used short titles in the footnotes and longer versions in the Bibliography.

For Montaigne's *Essais*, I have referenced Villey and Saulnier's print edition, the text of which appears online through the Montaigne Project hosted by the University of Chicago with the layers of Montaigne's writing indicated by colour.

http://www.lib.uchicago.edu/efts/ARTFL/projects/montaigne/

This website connects the Villey and Saulnier edition to the digital images of the entire Exemplaire de Bordeaux, so that the reader can see Montaigne's handwritten amendments to the 1588 Parisian edition of his *Essais* published by Abel L'Angelier. For the controversy over editions of the *Essais*, see John O'Brien, 'État présent: Are We Reading what Montaigne Wrote?', *French Studies* 58:4 (2004): 527–32.

Abbreviations

Montaigne, *Essais*	Michel Eyquem de Montaigne, *Les Essais de Michel de Montaigne* [1595], eds Pierre Villey and V.L. Saulnier (Paris, 1965)
Montaigne, *Essays*	Michel de Montaigne, *The Essayes of Michael Lord of Montaigne* [1603], trans. John Florio, 3 vols (London, 1910)

Acknowledgements

This book has been many years in the making so I need to start at the beginning and thank two undergraduate professors, Jim Tully and Pierre Boulle, who first captured my attention with the history of ideas and the society of early modern France. Quentin Skinner and Keith Wrightson sustained and shaped these co-existing interests in Renaissance rhetoric and ideas as well as social history during my graduate years.

In France many thanks are due to the staff and *magasiniers* of the Bibliothèque de l'Arsenal; the Bibliothèque nationale Réserve; the Bibliothèque nationale manuscripts room, especially Charlotte Denoël, *conservateur*; the Bibliothèque Mazarine; the Bibliothèque Sainte Geneviève; the Bibliothèque municipale de Lyon; and the Archives nationales. In the UK, I am grateful to the staff at the British Library; the Cambridge University Library; Emmanuel College, Cambridge; Trinity College, Cambridge; the Bodleian Library, Oxford; and the Taylor Institute, Oxford. In Canada, the Centre for Reformation and Renaissance Studies and the Fisher Rare Books Room both at the University of Toronto have provided access to valuable resources. At Saint Mary's University, Sandra Hamm's efforts to track down interlibrary loans have been nothing short of heroic.

I would like to express my appreciation to the Bibliothèque de Genève; the Houghton Library at Harvard University; Special Collections at the University of Glasgow; the Master and Fellows of Trinity College, Cambridge; and the National Library of the Netherlands, for graciously allowing me to reproduce images from their collections.

I owe a debt of gratitude to Jérôme Delatour for sharing his knowledge of the Dupuy family and for his extreme kindness in checking some documents in the BN manuscripts room. The late Michel Simonin generously shared portions of the then-unpublished L'Angelier catalogue with me and discussed the Palais de Justice book trade. The School of Politics and History at the University of Adelaide, Australia gave our family a generous welcome in 2008 and shared their interlibrary loan budget; and so special thanks to David Lemmings, then Head of School, and Claire Walker.

The Bibliographical Society, UK supported the early research on inventories. The Faculty of Graduate Studies and Research at Saint Mary's University provided several grants to fund the research necessary for the completion of this book. Conference participants in New Zealand, Germany, Canada, France and the UK have contributed to this book with their questions and comments. In the History Department at Saint Mary's we have created a collegial group, for which I am thankful.

Geraldine Thomas has helped with classical references when a Renaissance lawyer perplexed me. George F.W. Young, Lynn Martin, Hugh Stretton, all retired, had the leisure to read and comment on drafts, and help me whittle my argument, when I was often reluctant to ask harried colleagues, though Mark Houlahan willingly took time out from academic life to give me feedback. Every few years Neil Kenny resurfaces with his good humour and advice. The perpetually busy Tim Stretton has read and commented on the book from start to finish and has been subjected to many developing theories. I appreciate all their help.

For my sanity, I thank Helen Groth and Gary Evans as well as my early morning running girlfriends and our neighbours the Fords, Amy Crowley and the Wallworth clan, and Jan Leonard and the Drohan family.

An anonymous reader for Ashgate Publishing provided wise and invaluable advice and I hope he or she will see my gratitude in the much-improved version. I am grateful to Abby Zanger and Allyson Poska for welcoming this book into the Women and Gender in the Early Modern World series and I have been more than lucky to work with the wonderful Erika Gaffney, who gently guided my progress and the project with Ashgate.

A huge thank you to Pat and Hugh Stretton for lending us a house with doors leading onto a sunny garden during the Australian leave when I finished the bulk of the writing, and also to Tim for taking on most of the childcare when we were there, helped by aunts and uncles. In Canada, my mother and sister Alison have on many occasions accepted the challenge of caring for an ever-expanding brood when I travelled to research or give a conference paper, and my brother Glenn often provided the lakeside venue.

There is no greater paradox of misery and dignity than giving birth to another human being, except perhaps writing a book. Charlotte, Ella and Victor did not hasten the completion of this monograph, but they have tolerated far too many times when Mommy was busy at her desk. They have taught me more about the human experience than any book, dialogue or lawyer's pleading I have ever read. I shall be so happy to answer the next innocent query – 'Is your book finished yet?' – from a child who could produce several high-quality, colour-illustrated literary works over the course of a rainy afternoon.

This book is dedicated to my mother, Lorna Kingston, who introduced me to Paris and many other things.

Chapter 1
Introduction

The Ideas of Man and Woman in Renaissance France

One of the values we hold most fundamental in modern life is the dignity of the human condition. The preamble to the 1948 Universal Declaration of Human Rights refers to the 'inherent dignity' of all humans and the first article of the declaration states that '[a]ll human beings are born free and equal in dignity and rights'. In the Renaissance, only certain persons of noble blood possessed dignity through birth. For most in sixteenth-century France dignity or *dignitas* was a status to be achieved or an honour to be earned, often through a virtuous life carrying out a public duty or office. The Renaissance idea of the dignity of man also drew upon the story of God's creation of Adam and his place in the universe. Renaissance writers engaged in a vigorous debate about whether Eve, as a woman created from Adam's rib, shared in this dignity and questioned the role she played in the introduction of human misery to the world. From the moment God expelled Adam and Eve from Paradise for sinning, the potential of humans to attain dignity was constantly threatened by a weakness – perhaps a penchant – for vice. This oscillation between dignity and misery, between virtue and vice, was ever present in Renaissance culture. Moral literature and 'histories' written in the early modern period dwell on the contradictions and paradoxes in the lives of men and women. While dignity might be taken for granted as a human right in the modern world, Renaissance moral treatises constantly reminded male and female readers of their precarious grip on dignity because of this shared human tendency to vice.

These Renaissance debates pondered man's capacity to recover his dignity through virtuous effort or challenged whether Adam and his descendants would be forever mired in vice, misery and folly. The reflections on man's position relative to the heavens and to the creatures of the earth and the seas were major preoccupations of Renaissance literature printed in the 1500s. And just as Adam had a companion in Eve, 'Renaissance man' was often accompanied by a woman, a *femme*, which in French carries the double meaning of both woman and wife. Numerous books questioned the relationship of woman to man. Was she inferior, superior or his equal? This Renaissance quarrel of the sexes, now known as the *Querelle des femmes*, spurred numerous bestsellers for the bookstalls in Paris and Lyon from the 1530s through to the 1550s and persisted in various printed genres to the end of the century.

The academic disciplines of intellectual history and women's and gender history have tended to separate the study of the dignity and misery of man from the debate on the nature of woman called the *Querelle des femmes*. This book, by contrast, underlines the continuities between the Renaissance ideas of man and woman. Considering man at the height of his dignity or suffering in abject misery or contemplating woman as the most excellent of all creatures or as frail, weak and inferior, reveals the sixteenth-century mental habit of exploring both sides of an argument, the *pro et contra* or pros and cons. We begin to understand the texts of the *Querelle des femmes* considering the superiority or inferiority of woman not as separate entities to be weighed by their 'feminism' or their 'misogyny' but as contiguous with contemporary writings on the excellence and frailty of man. This comparison shifts our understanding when we recognise how in the early sixteenth century there was a two-way street between the *Querelle des femmes* and the debate on the dignity and misery of man. It changes the parameters of the discussion when we begin to understand how many writers such as Agrippa, Champier or Boaistuau crossed over from, imitated or borrowed examples from one side to the other.

The *Querelle des femmes*, like the debate on the dignity and misery of man, did not remain static. In the mid- to late sixteenth-century writers such as Louise Labé or Montaigne moved beyond the usual approaches to the debates on man and woman to focus on the vagaries of human nature. The second half of this book traces the durability of the ideas of man and woman and their evolution through to the end of the 1500s in a range of printed formats from dialogues, to moral lessons, essays and the speeches of lawyers.

Relating the Renaissance Dignity and Misery of Man to the *Querelle des femmes*

Most landmark studies of the idea of human dignity centred on the Italian Renaissance and therefore tended to ignore the abundant sixteenth-century French satires, dialogues, paradoxes and essays on the misery of the human condition.[1] The religious civil wars, which broke out intermittently in France from 1562 to the mid-1590s, contributed to sixteenth-century preoccupations with human misery and concerns about the diversity of opinion.[2] Some scholars have recognised how

[1] Paul Kristeller, *Renaissance Thought: The Classic, Scholastic and Humanist Strains* (New York, 1961); Charles Trinkaus, *In Our Image and Likeness: Humanity and Divinity in Italian Humanist Thought*, 2 vols (London, 1970); Charles Trinkaus, *The Scope of Renaissance Humanism* (Ann Arbor, MI, 1983).

[2] Readers interested in the events of the civil wars could consult Mack P. Holt, *The French Wars of Religion, 1562–1629*, 2nd edn (Cambridge, 2005); Jean-Marie Constant, *Les Français pendant les guerres de religion* (Paris, 2002); for more specific studies on the civil wars and the milieu of the Parlement de Paris see Sylvie Daubresse, *Le Parlement de Paris ou 'la voix de la raison' (1559–1589)* (Geneva, 2005) and Nancy Lyman Roelker, *One King, One Faith: The Parlement of Paris and the Religious Reformations of the Sixteenth Century* (Berkeley, CA, 1996) among many other titles.

the focus on optimism and human potential distorts our picture of the Renaissance world-view and have balanced these statements of the 'philosophy of man' with the many sources of pessimism in early modern thought.[3] An exceptionally clear account of Renaissance moral philosophy managed to trace the *de dignitate et miseria hominis* tradition across Europe and its collective origins in classical, biblical, patristic and medieval sources.[4]

Meanwhile the study of dignity-of-man literature in Renaissance France began in earnest in the 1970s.[5] By the early 1980s, critical editions of the sixteenth-century French 'bestsellers' on human misery and dignity, known as the 'ample discourse on human miseries' and the 'brief discourse on the excellence and dignity of man' opened up a discussion of how Renaissance writers could both praise and blame the human condition.[6] The way French sixteenth-century writers considered both dignity and misery in turn has been interpreted as a Christian humanist 'meditation on man'.[7] None of the studies by these distinguished scholars of Renaissance Europe, however, nor a group of scholars meeting for a colloquium on the theme of the Renaissance dignity of man in the 1990s, thought to make the leap to early modern ideas about woman.[8] There have been intermittent attempts to highlight the idea of woman within the tradition of the history of ideas, most notably by Maryanne Horowitz's conceptual work in the 1970s and 1980s, Prudence Allen's

---

[3] Charles Nauert, *Agrippa and the Crisis of Renaissance Thought* (Urbana, IL, 1965), pp. 2–3; Hiram Haydn, *The Counter-Renaissance* (New York, 1967). For a later corrective, see Marilyn Migiel, 'The Dignity of Man: A Feminist Perspective', in M. Migiel and Juliana Schiesari (eds), *Refiguring Woman: Perspectives on Gender and the Italian Renaissance* (Ithaca, NY, 1991), pp. 212–13, 231–2.

[4] Jill Kraye, 'Moral Philosophy', in Charles Schmitt and Quentin Skinner (eds), *The Cambridge History of Renaissance Philosophy* (Cambridge, 1988), pp. 303–86.

[5] Lionello Sozzi, 'La "dignitas hominis" chez les auteurs lyonnais du XVIe siècle', in *Actes du colloques sur l'humanisme lyonnais au XVI*[e] *siècle* (Grenoble, 1974), pp. 295–338; Lionello Sozzi, 'La "dignitas hominis" dans la littérature de la Renaissance française', in A.H.T. Levi (ed.), *Humanism in France at the End of the Middle Ages and in the Early Renaissance* (Manchester, 1970), pp. 176–98; Lionello Sozzi, *La dignité de l'homme à la Renaissance* (Turin, 1982).

[6] Pierre Boaistuau, *Le Théâtre du monde où il est faict un ample discours des misères humaines* [1558], ed. Michel Simonin (Geneva, 1982); Pierre Boaistuau, *Bref discours de l'excellence et dignité de l'homme* [1558], ed. M. Simonin (Geneva, 1982).

[7] Jerry Nash, 'The Christian–Humanist Meditation on Man: Denisot, Montaigne, Rabelais, Ronsard, Scève', *Bibliothèque d'Humanisme et Renaissance* 54:2 (1992): 353–71.

[8] Pierre Magnard (ed.), *La Dignité de l'homme: actes du colloque tenu à la Sorbonne-Paris IV* (Paris, 1995); Jean-Luc Martinet, *Montaigne et la dignité humaine: contribution à une histoire du discours de la dignité humaine* (Paris, 2007); Charles Nauert, *Humanism and the Culture of Renaissance Europe*, 2nd edn (Cambridge, 2006); Angelo Mazzocco, *Interpretations of Renaissance Humanism* (Leiden, 2006); Marie-Luce Demonet (ed.), *Montaigne et la question de l'homme* (Paris, 1999).

meticulous chronological research in the 1980s and 1990s, and more recent work on the 'woman question' as it relates to early modern scepticism.[9]

In the 1970s, 'second-wave' feminism renewed interest and scholarship on the *Querelle des femmes* as an early form of 'feminism'.[10] Since the 1980s the proliferation of books on Renaissance woman has compensated for the lack of attention to 'woman' within discussions of the philosophies of 'Renaissance man'. Scholars of 'Renaissance woman' have scoured the sources for early sparks of 'feminism' or passages and texts that defended and promoted women as virtuous or as heroines.[11] Renaissance defences of women written by men and women have benefited now from several decades of scholarship on women's history and restoring the 'other voice in early modern Europe'.

In the late 1980s feminist theorists, literary critics and historians began to reassess the categories of man, woman, sex and gender identities and in 1989 scholars established the *Journal of Women's History* as well as the journal *Gender & History*.[12] Social and cultural historians began to investigate the processes and

---

[9] Maryanne Horowitz, 'The Image of God in Man: Is Woman Included?', *The Harvard Theological Review* 72 (1979): 175–206; Maryanne Horowitz, 'The Woman Question in Renaissance Texts', *History of European Ideas* 8 (1987): 587–95; Prudence Allen, *The Concept of Woman*, 2 vols (Grand Rapids, MI, 1997–2002); Rebecca Wilkin, *Women, Imagination and the Search for Truth in Early Modern Europe* (Aldershot, 2008), pp. 97–139, 141–82.

[10] For first-wave feminism see Georges Ascoli, 'Essai sur l'histoire des idées féministes en France: du XVIe siècle à la Révolution', *Revue de synthèse historique* 13 (1906): 25–42; Lula McDowell Richardson, *The Forerunners of Feminism in French Literature of the Renaissance from Christine de Pisa to Marie de Gournay* (Baltimore, MD, 1929). For second-wave feminism see Maïté Albistur and Daniel Armogathe, *Histoire du féminisme français du moyen âge à nos jours* (Paris, 1977); Marc Angenot, *Les Champions des femmes: examen du discours sur la supériorité des femmes 1400–1800* (Montréal, 1977). The sweeping and comprehensive compilation of conduct literature in English, French, German and Italian and the outline of the war of the sexes in Ruth Kelso's *Doctrine for the Lady of the Renaissance* (Urbana, IL, 1956) was reissued in 1978 and again in 1996.

[11] Constance Jordan, *Renaissance Feminism: Literary Texts and Political Models* (Ithaca, NY, 1990); Pamela Joseph Benson, *The Invention of the Renaissance Woman: The Challenge of Female Independence in the Literature and Thought of Italy and England* (University Park, PA, 1992); Gaia Servadio, *Renaissance Woman* (London, 2005); Éliane Viennot, 'La diffusion du féminisme au temps de Louise de Labé', in Béatrice Alonso and Éliane Viennot (eds), *Louise Labé 2005* (Saint-Étienne, 2004), pp. 21–35; Helen Swift, *Gender, Writing, Performance: Men Defending Women in Late Medieval France, 1440–1538* (Oxford, 2008).

[12] Gisela Bock, 'Women's History and Gender History: Aspects of an International Debate', *Gender and History* 1:1 (1989): 7–30; Judith Butler, *Gender Trouble: Feminism and the Subversion of Identity*, 2nd edn (London, 1999), pp. 10–11; Karen Offen offers a clear account of the relationship between women's history and gender history in the 1980s and 1990s in 'History of Women', in Bonnie Smith (ed.), *The Oxford Encyclopedia of Women in World History*, 4 vols (Oxford, 2008), vol. II, pp. 463–71.

ideas that contributed to identifying 'masculinity' and 'femininity' or 'manhood' and 'womanhood'. For the early modern period studies of masculinity have focused on ideas of sexuality, the body, hermaphroditism or how to establish oneself from youth to manhood rather than on the concept of man in relation to his fellow beings in the heavens, the seas and on earth.[13]

In the early 1990s careful, comparative research on the literature of the woman question across Renaissance England, France and Italy began to emerge.[14] A monumental work placed women of the French Renaissance in the context of existing laws, socially stratified roles and access to education.[15] More recently, the *Querelle des femmes* has been studied in the context of the invention of the Salic law requiring a male heir to the French royal throne and thereby analysing female access to political power in the early modern period.[16]

Each of these approaches has informed and shaped the research for this book, but it remains evident that the Renaissance ideas of man and woman could benefit from a comparative approach. Books on 'Renaissance woman' and on early forms of 'feminism' – although vital and necessary amendments to the historical picture – have continued to isolate the debate on the nature of woman from the rest of moralist literature on human nature.[17] A recent conference proposing to 'revisit the *Querelle des femmes*' set as its theme the 'Discourses on the inequality/equality of men and women between 1400 and 1600'. Yet despite the theme inviting a comparison, the programme focused exclusively on aspects of the debate about woman.[18] This is not to ignore the fact that there were some treatises restricted to a discussion of the nature of woman, the texts known collectively as the

---

[13] Philip Ford and Paul White (eds), *Masculinities in Sixteenth-Century France: Proceedings of the Eighth Cambridge French Renaissance Colloquium 5–7 July 2003* (Cambridge, 2006); Todd Reeser, *Moderating Masculinity in Early Modern Culture* (Chapel Hill, NC, 2006); Elizabeth Foyster, *Manhood in Early Modern England: Honour, Sex, and Marriage* (London, 1999); Alexandra Shepard, *Meanings of Manhood in Early Modern England* (Oxford, 2003); John Tosh, *Manliness and Masculinities in Nineteenth-Century Britain: Essays on Gender, Family, and Empire* (New York, 2005); Lewis Seifert, *Manning the Margins: Masculinity and Writing in Seventeenth-Century France* (Ann Arbor, MI, 2009).

[14] Jordan, *Renaissance Feminism*; Benson, *The Invention of the Renaissance Woman.*

[15] Evelyne Berriot-Salvadore, *Les femmes dans la société française de la Renaissance* (Geneva, 1990).

[16] Eliane Viennot, *La France, les femmes et le pouvoir*, 2 vols (Paris, 2006–2008): on the Renaissance period see esp. vol. I, pp. 452–569; and for the early seventeenth century, see vol. II, pp. 61–112.

[17] Madeleine Lazard, *Images littéraires de la femme à la Renaissance* (Paris, 1985); Ian Maclean, *The Renaissance Notion of Woman* (Cambridge, 1980).

[18] At http://www.siefar.org, accessed 18 November 2010. 'Revisiter la Querelle des femmes: Les discours sur l'égalité/inégalité des femmes et des hommes de 1400 à 1600', Société Internationale pour l'Etude des Femmes de l'Ancien Régime, Paris, France, 19–20 November 2010.

Querelle des femmes. Yet it is important to remember how these books were sold, how purchasers often arranged to have several works of moral philosophy bound together,[19] and how the *Querelle* texts draw on and imitate the dignity and misery-of-man examples and commonplaces. Like the dignity and misery-of-man commonplaces, in the early years of the sixteenth century the *Querelle des femmes* rarely escapes the creation story as an interpretation of man and woman's place in the world. Likewise man or *homme* often means human or *humain* and the moralists describe the human condition rather than specific ideas about the masculine sex, and so it is essential to remain on the lookout for a female presence in these texts. Comparing the techniques and aims of these two bodies of literature reveals the extent to which they overlapped.

Pioneers in the field of gender history, including Gisela Bock and Margarete Zimmermann, have acknowledged the need for more comparative research specific to the ideas of man and woman in the early modern period. They note that the 'concept' of the *Querelle des femmes* refers to 'an all-encompassing gender debate in which not only women but – and that has been insufficiently realised – men are an issue as well'. Bock began to make this connection between the dignity of man and the dignity of woman in the Renaissance, but a book-length study has never been attempted.[20]

Attention also needs to be paid to the negative aspects of human life so prevalent in French Renaissance writing – the misery and frailty of the human condition. Discussions of Renaissance humanism tend to underplay the abundant reading material on human weakness, folly and vice that flooded the book market in the 1500s. Yet aspiring merchants, legal professionals, nobles and their wives living in a topsy-turvy world could read as much advice about the dangers of ruin, misery and misfortune as they could about the pursuit of dignity, virtue and nobility.

If we fail to compare the debate on the nature of woman with the contiguous debate on the dignity and misery of man, then we risk misinterpreting the Renaissance idea of human nature. Without the context and comparison, one might find misogyny in places where a simple lament on human weakness or a satire on the human condition was intended. To separate the 'Renaissance man' from his female counterpart misleads the modern reader about how these concepts occur in the sixteenth-century sources.

Some scholars believe that misogyny provides the key to understanding Renaissance 'feminist' literature. '[I]n the beginning was the word, and the word was misogynist. This is the ideological, literary, and cultural context for reading

---

[19] Nancy Vickers, 'The unauthored 1539 volume in which is printed the *Hecatomphile, The Flowers of French Poetry*, and *Other Soothing Things*', in Margreta de Grazia, *et al.* (eds), *Subject and Object in Renaissance Culture* (Cambridge, 1996), pp. 166–7.

[20] Gisela Bock and Margarete Zimmermann, 'The European *Querelle des femmes*', *Disputatio: An International Journal of the Late Middle Ages* 5 (2002): 133; Gisela Bock, *Women in European History* (Oxford, 2002), pp. 2–14.

and appreciating virtually every early modern feminist work'.[21] One does not have to look too far to find 'misogynistic' utterances in Renaissance texts such as the ironically entitled *The Praise of Women* or *La Louenge des femmes*, 1551, playfully featuring the writer 'André Misogyne'. Under the pseudonym Hélisenne de Crenne a woman penned a series of fictional letters first published in the late 1530s. In these letters she took positions attacking the female sex and defending it. She wrote one of the letters as if a husband replied scornfully to his wife: 'What miserable creatures you are, you and those like you – there are so many of your kind! For the seed of fidelity has been sown so little in this fickle female sex. O fraudulent womankind! … Surely there is no more proud or perilous enemy of man than woman'. In another letter Hélisenne de Crenne addressed a man opposed to the education of women: 'You inveigh against womankind in particular, and speaking in general terms, you say that women are rough and benighted people; and you conclude that their only pastime should be to spin'.[22] Women writers, including Hélisenne de Crenne, voiced the attacks and came to the defence of their sex, in part, because debating both sides of a question was so prevalent in early modern culture.

It seems that we are in danger of perpetuating a double standard. If we ignore early modern lamentations of the weaknesses of man, we might make the mistake of misinterpreting *Querelle des femmes* writing about the weaknesses of woman as pure misogyny. A variation on this theme occurs when the defences of woman by women writers come to be identified as 'sincere' while male defences of woman 'lack credibility' or must be 'rhetorical'.[23] If there is some doubt about whether any pro-woman statements in the early modern period are 'sincerely' feminist, then why should one assume that anti-woman statements are 'sincerely' misogynist? To limit the scope of the investigation to the question of feminism or misogyny overplays the early *Querelle des femmes* and fails to underline the more subtle forms of opposing voices or multiple voices in the mid- to late sixteenth-century dialogues, collections of moral lessons and essays. This narrow choice between feminism and misogyny also diminishes the extent of borrowing and intertextual

---

21 Jerry Nash, 'Renaissance Misogyny, Biblical Feminism, and Hélisenne de Crenne's *Epistres familieres et invectives*', *Renaissance Quarterly* 50:2 (1997): 379.

22 Hélisenne de Crenne, *A Renaissance Woman: Helisenne's Personal and Invective Letters*, eds and trans. Marianna Mustacchi and Paul Archambault (Syracuse, NY, 1986), pp. 91, 99; Hélisenne de Crenne, *Les Œuvres de ma Dame Helisenne de Crenne. A Sçavoir, les Angoisses douloureuses qui procedent d'amours. Les Epistres familières et invectives & Le songe de ladicte dame. Le tout reveu & corrigé de nouveau par elle* (Paris: Estienne Groulleau, 1560), facs. edn (Geneva, 1977), sigs Nv^{r-v}, Oiiij^{v}. See also Jacques Tahureau, *Les dialogues: non moins profitables que facetieux* [1565], ed. Max Gauna (Geneva, 1981), p. 60.

23 Pierre Darmon, *Mythologie de la femme dans l'Ancienne France* (Paris, 1983), pp. 64–6, 56–7; Ilana Zinguer, *Misères et grandeur de la femme au XVIe siècle* (Geneva–Paris: Slatkine, 1982), pp. 16–17, 19–20, 60–65; Swift, *Gender, Writing, Performance*, pp. v, 5, 8, 184, 188–9.

play from a wider range of sources that marked the writing on the nature of woman from the 1500s into the 1600s.

This book assesses the ideas of woman and man in terms of the *pro et contra* practices in the Renaissance, but it also charts how these discussions shifted over the course of the sixteenth century. A paradox 'exploit[s] … competing value systems', so by positing both the *pro* and the *contra* a writer could recast and challenge fixed truths or judgements and present a neglected truth. As Rosalie Colie reminds us in *Paradoxia Epidemica*, whether the writer believed in an argument is not in question, but the audience representing 'received opinion' had to believe its dialectical opposite.[24] Paradox exposed multiple truths. A writer might express several competing truths, but this does not discount the conflicting statements; rather it indicates how each counterpoint might be a partial representation of truth. The *Querelle des femmes* or the expression of statements for and against women was not merely 'rhetorical' or a schoolboy's exercise in rhetoric; the story does not end there.[25] Writers could pursue rhetorical arguments using any topic, such as the exaltation of the dignity of salt by Jean de Marconville in 1574. The sheer volume of published texts and poems in the French sixteenth century does disclose an unrelenting interest in the nature of woman and her potential as a wife. The economic contribution of a wife or her management of household resources and the importance of the social and professional or trade connections of her family in early modern France were of immense importance to the fate of her husband and their children.[26] The only comparable topic of moral philosophy competing for as much space on sixteenth-century bookshelves was rank, that is, the roles of fortune or virtue, birth or merit in determining a family's social position. And of course these topics were inextricably linked.

---

[24] Rosalie Colie, *Paradoxia Epidemica: The Renaissance Tradition of Paradox* (Princeton, NJ, 1966), p. 10.

[25] Margarete Zimmermann, '*The Old Quarrel*: More than Just Rhetoric', in Wolfram Aichinger, *et al.* (eds), *The* Querelle des Femmes *in the Romania* (Vienna, 2003), pp. 30–31; Joan Kelly, 'Early Feminist Theory and the *Querelle des Femmes*, 1400–1789', in J. Kelly, *Women, History and Theory: The Essays of Joan Kelly* (Chicago, IL, 1984), p. 74: 'The static quality of the genre should not mislead us into accepting the commonly held notion that the *querelle* was a kind of literary game, however'.

[26] 'Introduction', in Suzanne Desan and Jeffrey Merrick (eds), *Family, Gender and Law in Early Modern France* (University Park, PA, 2009), p. xiv; Suzanne Desan, 'Making and Breaking Marriage: An Overview of Old Regime Marriage as a Social Practice', in ibid., pp. 2–3, 12; James Collins, 'The Economic Role of Women in Seventeenth-Century France', *French Historical Studies* 16:2 (1989): 436–70.

The Social Mobility of the Renaissance Man and his Wife

The fascination with ideas of man and woman in sixteenth-century France resulted from a growing obsession with the status of individuals, families and households. Although today the term 'Renaissance man' conjures up an image of an individual capable of a range of achievements, in sixteenth-century France the effort required to achieve 'dignity' was a family affair. The individual accomplishments of father or husband might reflect on his person, just as his social status defined the place of his family, but the collective efforts of his household stood behind each success or failure. An honourable wife, and the social networks she provided access to, contributed to the possible rise of a man's fortune, whereas a dishonourable wife lacking moderation almost certainly created misery – one reason why books debating the nature of woman and her virtues and vices were an ever-popular choice for Renaissance booksellers and their customers. To understand the early modern desire for 'dignity' and the ever-present anxiety about 'misery' it is therefore necessary to sketch the social structure as well as some of the political developments in sixteenth- to early seventeenth-century France.

The status of the father or husband defined the position of most households and their occupants within the social hierarchy of early modern France. A wife or mother could enrich the household, literally through the financial contribution of her dowry or sometimes more significantly through access to her family's networks for opportunities to advance sons and daughters, but once married a woman's dignity was not independent of her husband.[27] A wife's honour, her ability to conduct herself and to govern her children and servants reflected on the household. She could harm it or she could enhance it – one reason why the *Querelle des femmes* was so entangled in the nature and potential of woman as a wife – but neither her actions nor her birth determined the status of the household.

It often took several generations for a bourgeois or merchant family to achieve the dignity conferred by noble status as each generation made an incremental gain or simply maintained its station. Indeed in the transition from merchant to noble, the first investment was likely to be an office – a position in the royal administration. This office might confer *dignitas* and the privilege of 'personal nobility' to its holder. The second investment was some form of landed property such as a country estate suitable for 'living nobly'.[28] A strategic marriage usually boosted prospects as well. According to custom, nobility could be achieved gradually after three generations or a hundred years, although officeholders practised 'living nobly' long

[27] Robert Descimon, 'Un langage de la dignité. La qualification des personnes dans la société parisienne de l'époque moderne', in Fanny Cosandey (ed.), *Dire et vivre l'ordre social en France sous l'Ancien Régime* (Paris, 2005), pp. 90–91.

[28] Barbara Diefendorf, *Paris City Councillors in the Sixteenth Century: The Politics of Patrimony* (Princeton, NJ, 1983), p. 69.

before that.[29] Merchants and the *noblesse de robe* – nobles who held purchased offices – stood to gain from the dignity-of-man ethos of self-improvement and the humanist emphasis on the achievement of virtue through study and civic service. Men like Michel de Montaigne, who just slipped into the *noblesse de robe*, may have had some military experience, but their 'nobility' was based on learning, a purchased office, the long gown or *robe* associated with their position, and a seigneurial estate. On the other hand, many of the traditional military nobility – the *noblesse d'épée* – such as Philippe du Plessis-Mornay or Pierre de la Primaudaye were also men of great learning.[30]

The sale of positions in the royal administration, known as venality of office, began to increase rapidly in the sixteenth century. These sales raised revenue for the crown and so the practice continued despite concerns about the capacity of a purchaser to fulfil the duties of his office.[31] It has been calculated that in 1515 there were at least 4,041 officeholders. By the mid-seventeenth century that figure had expanded to 46,047 officeholders.[32] The most controversial purchases and the most prized offices were in the judiciary. During Francis I's reign and the reign of his son Henri II, the Parlement de Paris, the highest sovereign court in the land, expanded by naming new presiding judges (*présidents*), hundreds of judges or magistrates (*conseillers*), and through the creation of two entirely new *chambres des enquêtes* as well as several other council and criminal chambers.[33]

In the fourteenth and fifteenth centuries the king nominated persons to the sovereign courts with new members added by 'election' or appointment. At that time these offices were viewed as a 'lifelong endowment'.[34] During the Valois reigns of the sixteenth century, the purchase of an office became an investment in property to pass on to the next generation. From 1541 certain offices held the possibility of resignation *en survivance* – when an officeholder designated his child or relative as his successor. When a *conseiller* in Parlement retired, he was

---

29 Robert Descimon, 'The Birth of the Nobility of the Robe: Dignity versus Privilege in the Parlement de Paris, 1500–1700', in Michael Wolfe (ed.), *Changing Identities in Early Modern France* (Durham, NC, 1997), pp. 107–9; J.H. Shennan, *The Parlement of Paris* (London, 1968), pp. 120–21.

30 James Supple, *Arms versus Letters: The Military and Literary Ideals in the 'Essais' of Montaigne* (Oxford, 1984), pp. 3–4, 69, 263–4.

31 Roland Mousnier, *La Venalité des offices sous Henri IV et Louis XIII*, 2nd edn (Paris, 1971), pp. 113–15; John Dawson, *The Oracles of the Law* (Ann Arbor, MI, 1968), pp. 350–62; J.H.M. Salmon, *Society in Crisis: France in the Sixteenth Century* (London, 1979), pp. 221–3.

32 Emmanuel Le Roy Ladurie, *The Royal French State 1460–1610* (Oxford, 1994), p. 17.

33 Roelker, *One King, One Faith*, pp. 34, 41; Félix Aubert, 'Recherches sur l'organisation du Parlement de Paris au XVIe siècle (1515–1589)', *Nouvelle revue historique de droit français et étranger* 36 (1912): 52–63.

34 Shennan, *Parlement of Paris*, pp. 116–17.

able to resign his position in favour of another person provided a tax on the value of the office was paid to the king for the privilege and the designated person was deemed fit to carry out the responsibilities of office. If the officeholder died within 40 days of the transfer, however, the office reverted to the king, who was then able to sell it for its full value. Michel de Montaigne obtained his first officeholding position through his paternal uncle Pierre Eyquem, later moving to the Parlement de Bordeaux. When he eventually resigned his post as judge (*conseiller*), Montaigne had no male heir so Florimond de Ræmond purchased his office.[35] In 1604, Henri IV introduced the *paulette*, an annual tax of about one-sixtieth of the value of an office, which allowed an officeholder to bequeath his office to an heir without the worry of the 40-day rule.[36] Once the inheritance of an office became a certainty, the price inflated quickly from approximately £6,000 for a judgeship in the Parlement de Paris in 1523 to £64,500 in 1615.[37]

The increasingly widespread practice of the sale of offices and the inflation of the price for some of these offices produced social tensions and fuelled an outpouring of reflective moral literature on the nature of dignity, virtue and nobility. The 'language of dignity' or the designated titles for each rank changed quite swiftly in the 1500s and early 1600s for blood nobles by birth and for those whose office conferred a personal nobility, for the families attached to a landed estate as well as for the bourgeois and the merchant classes.[38] Some lawyers and attorneys (*procureurs*) maintained themselves in the liberal professions and alongside merchants; many of these bourgeois never sought or obtained a royal or civic office as the first step to nobility.[39] The attorneys and their clerks who dealt with court officials and shuffled the legal papers for the advocates could languish at this level, for the most part self-employed and outside of the venal officeholding system. Francis I squeezed their opportunities for advancement as he began to limit the number of attorneys allowed to practise in the Parlement de Paris and in the provincial courts, part of a long process, lasting well into the seventeenth century, to turn these positions into venal offices raising revenue for

35 Fleury Vindry, *Les parlementaires français au XVIe siècle*, 2 vols (Paris, 1910–12), vol. II, pp. 27, 100; Almquist, 'Writing Pluralist Biography', p. 63.

36 Shennan, *Parlement of Paris*, p. 118; Étienne Pasquier, *Lettres familières*, ed. Dorothy Thickett (Geneva, 1974), p. 414.

37 Robert Descimon, 'The "bourgeoisie seconde": Social Differentiation in the Parisian Municipal Oligarchy in the Sixteenth Century, 1500–1610', *French History* 17:4 (2003): 397, Table 3; Dawson, *Oracles of the Law*, p. 360; Mousnier, *La Venalité*, pp. 342–3, 356–69.

38 Descimon, 'Un langage de la dignité', pp. 99–107.

39 Historians have long debated whether the sale of offices helped create the religious tensions of the civil wars: see Descimon's review of the debate in 'Bourgeoisie seconde', pp. 388–93; on the differentiation between bourgeois and officeholders, see Descimon, 'Bourgeoisie seconde', pp. 400–401, 421 and contributions to the debate in *French History* 17:4 (2003) by Sara Beam, Hilary Bernstein and Mack Holt.

the crown.[40] So much expansion of the French state took place in the sixteenth century that lawyers and officeholders in the Palais de Justice in Paris struggled to comprehend how much their social and professional world had changed in living memory. In the *Lawyers' Dialogue* set in 1602 against the background of a strike by the lawyers in the Parisian sovereign courts, Antoine Loisel recreates a fictional version of a conversation with his real-life friends Étienne Pasquier and François Pithou and their sons.[41] The group looks back with nostalgia on the legal profession and the milieu of the Parlement de Paris. 'The calling of a lawyer was the seedbed of dignities and the route to attain the offices of councillors, king's attorneys, presidents and others.'[42] The character Étienne Pasquier tells his friends and their sons that in 1549 when he was admitted to the Palais de Justice at the beginning of Henri II's reign the calling or 'Estate of a lawyer was principally held in honour, as the ladder by which one rose to greater Estates and Dignities of the Kingdom'.[43] Étienne Pasquier's son Nicolas suggests that 'choices and advancements' will be limited 'as long as the venality and dearness of offices last, which we see growing and increasing from one day to the next'. His elder son Théodore Pasquier suspects he 'would stay perpetually in the Hall of the Palais, if my father did not relinquish his estate as King's Attorney in the Chambre des comptes, that he has resigned to me *en survivance* … I believe we no longer live in a time where one seeks men for their merit and value, but they must advance through the ranks on their own, and by money'.[44] In 1604, Pasquier actually did resign his position as *avocat général* in the Chambre des comptes in favour of his son Théodore.

Fathers took risks not only to enhance personal dignity but also to advance the family name. In a letter, the real life Étienne Pasquier exhorted his friend Monsieur de Basmaison, a lawyer in a provincial presidial court, to forsake his ambition to become a provincial judge: 'poor unhappy [man] that you are, what new conceit of ambition has caught you unawares'? For 30 years Basmaison had served as a lawyer cherished by the great nobles and respected by the 'common people'. 'It is to obtain some peace in my old age (say you) and to advance my family'. Instead of the relative free rein of the lawyer 'in which you are king in your city' and 'your fortune depends on you', if Basmaison obtains a judgeship

40 Sara Beam, *Laughing Matters: Farce and the Making of Absolutism in France* (Ithaca, NY, 2007), pp. 94–5, 201–2.

41 Miriam Yardeni, 'L'ordre des avocats et la grève du Barreau parisien en 1602', *Revue d'histoire économique et sociale* 44 (1966): 481–507.

42 Antoine Loisel, *Pasquier ou dialogue des advocats*, in M. Dupin (ed.), *Lettres sur la profession d'avocat et bibliothèque choisie des livres de droit qu'il est plus utile d'acquérir et de connaître*, 4th edn, 2 vols (Paris, 1818): 'Car auparauant l'Estat d'Advocat estoit la pepiniere des dignitez, et le chemin de paruenir aux Offices de Conseillers, Aduocats du Roy, Presidens et autres', vol. I, p. 203.

43 Loisel, *Dialogue des advocats*, p. 267.

44 Ibid., p. 256.

he will enslave himself to the will of others.[45] As we shall see when we examine the French Renaissance writing on human nature, misery-of-man literature discouraged ambition as a vice and often urged the reader to be content with his or her lot in life. The dignity-of-man ethos, on the other hand, promoted a humanist drive for self-improvement. And yet once the dignity of office or a noble rank had been achieved, a family had to be on guard against fortune and the possibility of ruin. In sixteenth-century Parisian *bourgeois* families, stagnation and decline were just as evident as social elevation into the nobility of the robe. Even within families, branches that stayed in trade without any investment in offices might sink into obscurity, while an investment in an office for an able son could pay off in social stability or upward mobility.[46]

Training for Dignity, Preparing for Misery

For the families that embarked on the path to personal nobility, or that wanted to remain there, the training for an office began in childhood. Boys and girls would be schooled at home, learning to read several years before they learned to write. The Renaissance male reader often began his humanist education at a municipal school or college in the provinces. Although open to all boys in the community, these provincial feeder schools also prepared the wealthier children of the region for higher colleges in Paris or other cities. The schoolboy's curriculum consisted of grammar, rhetoric, poetry, history and moral philosophy with an emphasis on the importance of reading history in order to learn how to live well. The study of rhetoric worked in tandem with the study of history and moral philosophy as the child weighed up the virtues and vices that governed personal conduct. Pupils absorbed the histories of great men and their examples of conduct in private life as well as public conduct in battle and in government.

In his textbook on rhetoric, *On the Abundance of Words and Ideas* (*De duplici copia verborum ac rerum commentarii duo*), 1512, Erasmus shows the schoolboy how to acquire a supply of *exempla* by organising the material from fables, maxims, histories, allegories, anecdotes or strange cases into sections or categories of subjects in a commonplace notebook.[47] He suggests drawing on the customs of various nations in order to play on the differences, between say Greeks and

---

45 Étienne Pasquier, 'A Monsieur de Basmaison, Advocat au siege Presidial de Rion. Il dissuade un sien amy, de quitter l'estat d'advocat pour prendre un office de Iudicature', in *Lettres d'Estienne Pasquier* (Paris: Abel L'Angelier, 1586), Bk VII, letter 9 [hereafter as VII: 9], fo. 210r.

46 Descimon, 'Bourgeoisie seconde', pp. 399–401, 412; Robert Descimon, 'Élites parisiennes entre le XVe et XVIIe siècle: du bon usage du Cabinet des titres', *Bibliothèque de l'École des chartes* 155 (1997): 644; Diefendorf, *Paris City Councillors*, p. 88.

47 Desiderius Erasmus, '*Copia*: Foundations of the abundant style' [*De duplici copia verborum ac rerum commentarii duo*], ed. Craig R. Thompson, *Collected Works of Erasmus*,

Romans, the Spartans and the Athenians, or between ancient and modern living. The writer or orator should also remark on the 'quality' of the actions described in each example; what does the example reveal about the persons concerned? Erasmus asks his reader to consider differences in status, wealth or age; how the actions of a prince might differ from those of a slave; how the behaviour of a rich man differs from a poor man's; how his conduct differs from a woman, boy or girl. These illustrative examples play a 'leading role' in entertaining and convincing the reader. A description of the 'circumstances' further magnifies the deed or diminishes it.[48]

Erasmus counsels his future orator to build up a storehouse of 'expressions lined up ready for action'. Not only will these help the schoolboy when he enters the realm of public speech, but these tools will also be of great assistance for 'commenting on authors', translation and 'writing verse' – the very activities that sixteenth-century financial, political and judicial officeholders engaged in for self-promotion and to advertise their talents.[49] To help the student hone the skill of inventing propositions he will need exposure to 'moral philosophy, history, and a wide range of authors in speeches intended to urge a course of action or do someone honour'.[50]

Readers and writers could then use these examples in a variety of contexts, addressing moral issues of praise and blame, in political rhetoric meant to persuade or dissuade or in the forensic rhetoric of the lawyer pleading before a court. Erasmus guides the reader on how to elaborate on the qualities of each virtue or its opposite vice. To define a virtue, one should explain 'how it differs from other virtues', describe what is 'particular' to the virtue, what activities demonstrate the virtue, 'what nourishes, or destroys it', and the advantages or 'profit' (*utilitas)* it brings to man.[51] As Erasmus carefully indicates, some examples belong under more than one heading because they can 'serve not only diverse but contrary uses', in short, to prove both the *pro et contra*.[52] Erasmus instructs his schoolboy to read widely because '[n]o discipline is so remote from rhetoric that you cannot use it to enrich your collection'.[53]

As we turn to the French literature, moral thought and lawyers' pleadings of the sixteenth century, it is helpful to bear in mind Erasmus' instructions to the pupil on the commonplace book. French writers such as Jacques Tahureau, Jean

86 vols (Toronto, 1978), vol. XXIV, pp. 607, 635; Ann Moss, *Printed Commonplace-Books and the Structuring of Renaissance Thought* (Oxford, 1996), ch. 5, esp. pp. 108–9.

48 Erasmus, *De copia*, p. 607.

49 Ibid., p. 302.

50 Ibid., p. 604.

51 Ibid., p. 636.

52 Ibid., p. 639; John Lyons, *Exemplum: The Rhetoric of Example in Early Modern France and Italy* (Princeton, NJ, 1989), pp. 16–19; Thomas Sloane, 'Schoolbooks and Rhetoric: Erasmus's *Copia*', *Rhetorica* 9:2 (1991): 116.

53 Erasmus, *De copia*, p. 638.

de Marconville or Montaigne and lawyers such as Étienne Pasquier, Antoine Loisel or Anne Robert would certainly have been familiar with it from their schooldays.[54] Most of all they would have been familiar with the mode of thinking about associated virtues and the contrast of their opposite and related vices, how to control vice and promote virtue, how to argue on both sides of a question, and how to govern one's conduct in the world.

Of course not all Renaissance writers were trained at school in humanist rhetorical practice. We know less about how girls or the sons of merchants of modest means were trained to read or how they learned the separate skill of writing, but post-mortem inventories reveal a number of easy-to-read grammar, writing and spelling manuals while evidence from notaries' records shows parents buying books for children or hiring tutors for girls.[55] When these more humbly educated readers turned their efforts to the pen they still engaged in the practice of imitation and compilation. And without a schoolboy's training in rhetoric, female writers still expressed attitudes about vice and virtue, and how to govern one's self and one's household; this was not the exclusive preserve of lawyers and Renaissance moral philosophers. Even the authors of reading and writing manuals emphasised how to follow the 'path to live well' and organised their precepts in such a way that humble readers could learn moral lessons of virtue as they learned the ABCs.[56]

A young man's training for a profession was refined at university in Paris or one of the larger regional cities such as Orléans, Tours or Toulouse.[57] After study of the liberal arts, a young man might also obtain a degree in law, usually Roman or civil law. But years of study did not fully prepare him for practice in the legal world of the sovereign courts or for the fact that each region of France had its own customs and laws – about 65 'general' regions of customary law.[58] So it is

[54] On Montaigne's education see Zachary Schiffman, 'Montaigne and the Rise of Skepticism in Early Modern Europe: A Reappraisal', *Journal of the History of Ideas* 45:4 (1984): 503–7, especially nn. 9, 18 and 19. On school training, see Moss, *Printed Commonplace-Books*, ch. 6.

[55] Susan Broomhall, *Women and the Book Trade in Sixteenth-Century France* (Aldershot, 2002), pp. 13–16.

[56] Pierre Habert, *Le Miroir de vertu et chemin de bien vivre, contenant plusieurs belles histoires par quatrains et distiques moraux, le tout par alphabet, avec le stile de composer toutes sortes de lettres missives, quittances et promesses, la punctuation et acens de la langue françoise, l'instruction et secrets de l'art d'escriture* (Paris: Claude Micard, 1571–72).

[57] George Huppert, *Les bourgeois gentilhommes: An Essay on the Definition of Elites in Renaissance France* (Chicago, IL, 1977), pp. 62–4, 81, 98; George Huppert, *Public Schools in Renaissance France* (Urbana, IL, 1984), pp. 35–6, 45, esp. n. 44; on girls' schools see Berriot-Salvadore, *Les femmes*, pp. 90–98.

[58] Jonathan Dewald, *The Formation of a Provincial Nobility: The Magistrates of the Parlement de Rouen 1499–1610* (Princeton, NJ, 1980), pp. 23–7; Dawson, *Oracles of the Law*, p. 266; Catherine Holmès, *L'éloquence judiciaire de 1620 à 1660: reflet de problèmes sociaux, religieux et politiques de l'époque* (Paris, 1967), pp. 18, 20–21.

no wonder that, even after his 'reception' in the Parlement de Paris, a young man like Pasquier spent years just listening to the proceedings and lawyers pleading their cases, taking notes and furthering his training before he finally argued his first case?[59]

The career of a son was a multi-generational family concern. Officeholders embarked upon their careers around the same time as marriage because a marital alliance brought in-laws who expanded their networks of influence. When the practice was allowed, fathers frequently retired from their posts in favour of their sons. In the absence of a father, a guardian such as an uncle took up this role as mentor.[60] Parents weighed the talents of their sons with the needs of the family when setting their vocations. They also weighed the needs of the family with the wishes of a daughter when marrying her into a new family network. Pasquier deplores the behaviour of contemporaries hell-bent on advancing the next generation regardless of their progeny's talents. 'Not wishing to resemble some others of our city, who seeing themselves advanced to a particular estate, [they] cannot imagine anything else but how to promote their children to higher estates'. Pasquier recounts how he sent his eldest son to school and then to college to prepare him for the law profession, all the while aware that children should be 'inclined' to their vocation 'because above all, their natural disposition should not be forced'. Although there was some tension between the *noblesse de robe* and the *noblesse d'épée*, there were several routes to success and noble status in the ancien régime and Pasquier's five sons headed in different directions. Théodore, the eldest, followed his father as a lawyer in the Parlement de Paris while Nicolas, the second son, became a judge (*conseiller*) and master of requests (*maître des requêtes*). The middle child Pierre 'whom I destined … to succeed in the courts' was not so compliant and fled to Italy, where he eventually served in the military like his younger brother Guy. The youngest son René died in battle at the hands of the Catholic Leaguers during the siege of Melun in the early 1590s.[61]

---

[59] Paul Bouteiller, 'Étienne Pasquier avocat au Parlement de Paris (1549–1585)', *Bulletin de la Société de l'histoire de Paris et de l'Île de France* 117 (1990): 47; Roland Delachenal, *Histoire des avocats au Parlement de Paris 1300–1600* (Paris, 1885), pp. 25–6; Bernard de la Roche Flavin, *Treize livres des Parlemens de France esquels est amplement traicté de leur origine et institution* (Geneva: Matthieu Berjon, 1621), pp. 298, 322.

[60] Diefendorf, *Paris City Councillors*, p. 84.

[61] Pasquier, 'A Theodore Pasquier, son fils [Sur la profession d'advocat]', in *Lettres familières*, IX:6, p. 156. Pasquier frequently wrote to Antoine Loisel and other friends about his sons. In a letter unpublished in Pasquier's lifetime he proudly wrote of Théodore's progress when his son began a career in Parlement in March 1582: 'tout va bien *et in re publica et privata*', in ibid., VII, Lettres inédites A, p. 107; Pasquier, 'A Monsieur de Foix, Conseiller du Roy au Conseil d'Etat et Ambassadeur au Sainct Siege', in ibid., VII:1, pp. 90–91. On Pierre, see Pasquier's letter 'A Monsieur de Tolet, Abbé de Plimpié', in ibid., IX:2, pp. 149–50, and 'A Monsieur Morin', in ibid., X:2, p. 179. On René's death see the letter to Madame de Ferrière, ibid., XIV:6, pp. 213–16. On Pasquier's son Guy see 'Au Capitaine de la Ferlandière, Pierre Pasquier, son fils', ibid., XVI:5, pp. 254–5.

Mothers also participated in decision-making about the education of sons and their eventual vocations. Madeleine de l'Hôpital wrote to her four sons to remind them of the importance of study. To her eldest Charles, apparently considered not as 'fit for study as [his] brothers', she advises that he must educate himself throughout his youth 'according to the capacity of his mind and [do] the best he can'. Then his parents will consider which occupation they wish for him. 'Your father and I are satisfied enough to bestow a calling without giving you pain'. As for Michel, who had not 'as much capacity', his mother says 'if you are wise you will take pains to become learned' as 'we resolutely wish for you to follow the path of Monsieur your grandfather' (the Chancellor Michel de l'Hôpital). She urged him to 'conform yourself to the [intention] of your kin … and not to complain of a little labour in your youth to learn'.[62] By 1581, Michel had obtained a post as a judge (*conseiller*) in the Parlement de Paris; his younger brother Paul would follow suit in 1588.[63]

The path to advancement, the maintenance of honour and dignity, and the way to keep misfortune and misery at bay, were all closely tied to the marital alliance. Madeleine de l'Hôpital reminds her sons of her own father's legacy and reputation. She values her connections, as would her husband the opportunities offered by his in-laws. When Pasquier advises his son Nicholas on the choice of a husband for his granddaughter, he weighs the pros and cons of arms versus letters. Pasquier suggests that Nicholas might choose a man who had impoverished himself to buy an office so that he may appear in public in the red robes of a judge in Parlement but as a result needs to marry for money. On the other hand, Nicholas could choose a *gentilhomme* of arms who would probably turn out to be a 'casanier' or sluggard. But Pasquier suggests that his son Nicholas choose the profession of arms for a son-in-law rather than the robe or 'robbe longue' because his two grandsons by Nicholas had taken the path of arms and family bonds preferred a military profession in a brother-in-law.[64]

The choice of a husband or wife mattered because the couple – each with his or her assigned role – worked on behalf of their household and their extended families. Both the husband and wife had a duty to maintain the family honour and each needed to learn a self-control that served as an example to the rest of the household, and that the husband could be expected to carry into public life in his political or administrative duties. As one mid-sixteenth-century treatise *On the Dignity of Marriage* explained:

---

[62] BN, MS Collection Dupuy 194, letter 20, Madeleine de l'Hôpital to her sons, 5 May [no year].

[63] Édouard Maugis, *Histoire du Parlement de Paris*, 3 vols (Paris, 1913–16), vol. III, pp. 262, 272.

[64] Pasquier, 'A mon fils Maistre Nicholas Pasquier, Conseiller et Maistre des requetes ordinaire du Roy', in *Lettres familières*, XXII:11, p. 413.

> There is a certain resemblance between a republic and an economy [of the household], in which the father of the family in the first place is like a king, and the wife, mother of the family, is the mistress and companion and afterward in their empire and government are the children and other servants, as citizens, over whom they preside and rule, who when well governed and maintained in constant discipline, preserve and increase the family things.[65]

In the French Renaissance world, this philosophy saturated the culture of 'learned people', nobles and officeholders while those lower down the social scale shared the pragmatic desire for a stable and well-ordered family.[66] Moral philosophy combined ethics – that is, the government of one's self through the promotion of virtue and rejection of vice – with economics or the government of the family and household, and with politics or the government of the state and its citizens.[67] An anonymous sixteenth-century female writer suggested to her readers in *Des saines affections* or *On the Healthy Passions* how even those 'used to actions of virtue' could draw some benefits from unfortunate circumstances.[68]

> All this might not be as difficult as it might seem if by frequent practice you acquire the habit of living 'content'. You can't live in the great households of princes and lords? Be content with your own. You don't feel capable of government [of the state]? Be a good citizen. In this manner you make easy, what one makes difficult in life.[69]

The Renaissance man and woman were encouraged to cultivate their dignity, but to prepare themselves for misery. They were to preserve and improve the family's

---

[65] Claude Baduel, *Traicté trèsutile et fructueux de la dignité de mariage et de l'honneste conversation des gens doctes, & lettrez*, trans. Guy de la Garde (Paris: Arnoul L'Angelier, 1548): 'Car il y a certaine similitude d'vne Republique a l'Economye, en laquelle le pere de famille en premier lieu est cõme vn roy, & la femme mere de famille est la maistresse, & cõpagne, & en leur empire & gouuernement sont en apres les enfans & autres domesticques, comme citoyens, esquelz ils president & commandent, lesquelz quant bien sont gouuernez, & entretenus en toute constante discipline & conseruent, & amplifient leurs choses familieres', sig. E^{r}.

[66] Julie Hardwick, 'Between State and Street: Witnesses and the Family Politics of Litigation in Early Modern France', in Desan and Merrick (eds), *Family, Gender*, pp. 126–35.

[67] Kraye, 'Moral Philosophy', pp. 303–6.

[68] On the identification of this anonymous writer as Madeleine de L'Aubespine and recent scholarship on her background, see Chapter 7, note 41.

[69] [Madeleine de L'Aubespine], *Des saines affections* (Paris: Abel L'Angelier, 1593), fos 17v–18r: 'Tout cela ne sera point si difficile, comme il semble, si par frequent exercice vous prenez habitude de viure cõntent. Ne pouuez-vous demeurer éz maisons des princes & seigneurs? Contentez vous de la vostre. Ne vous sentez-vous pas capable de gouuernement? Soyez bon citoyen. En ceste maniere vous rendrez aisé ce qu'on fait difficile en la vie'.

place, but be careful not to climb too far up the ladder. One had to learn to be content with whatever fortune might bring, because the chances for social decline were just as real as the opportunities for social advancement.[70]

Print, Rhetoric and Law

Against the background of these social tensions and the culture of Renaissance humanism, this book sets out to explore the ideas of man and woman in France over the course of the 1500s through the three interwoven themes of the subtitle: print, rhetoric and law.

Print

The form of ideas can be as important as their content. Throughout its pages this book investigates the sixteenth-century networks of printers and booksellers in Paris and Lyon who promoted the circulation of ideas on the nature of man and woman. It traces the editorial policies of certain print workshops and booksellers whose steady income from legal manuals and ordinances funded their more speculative literary ventures.[71] It also follows the trail of texts produced from the 1500s to the early 1600s from the booksellers' stock to the personal libraries of potential readers.[72] Turning from production to reception, household inventories, letters, reading notes and lawyers' pleadings are used to investigate the book collections of officeholders and lawyers and to consider what reading material may have been available to their wives, daughters and sisters.[73] The final chapter examines how the new practice of printing lawyers' pleadings in the late 1500s and early 1600s shaped the presentation of notable judicial decisions and enhanced the lawyers' practices of imitation and citation so that their speeches began to read more like the moral literature and essays of their era. And as we shall see in a moment, the booksellers who sold these legal titles at their boutiques in the Palais de Justice also stocked works on the nature of man and woman.

Rhetoric

In an age of paradox and contradiction, few Renaissance writers argued exclusively in favour of the dignity of man or against it by pointing to the ubiquity of human misery from birth to death in every occupation and region. A writer might

---

70 Descimon, 'Bourgeoisie seconde', pp. 388–424; Julie Hardwick, *The Practice of Patriarchy: Gender and the Politics of Household Authority in Early Modern France* (University Park, PA, 1998), pp. 10–13.

71 See Chapter 2, pp. 29–42, Chapter 7, pp. 171–5.

72 See Chapters 2, 3 and 7, pp. 42–8, 58–9, 63, 66, 70, 72, 79, 82, 167–71.

73 See Chapter 7, pp. 176–86.

emphasise the pursuit of dignity through virtue and yet underline the futility of striving for social position because in the end all are equal in death. Or a defender of woman might argue for the equality of woman in terms of her soul and yet argue for woman's superiority over man because of her capacity for virtue. It is a mistake to dismiss these Renaissance writing patterns as 'just rhetoric' as often happens when the *Querelle des femmes* is characterised as 'static' or simply a literary game. As we shall see, the study and practice of rhetoric, and the compilation and imitation of examples, were fundamental aspects of Renaissance culture.[74] Similarly, later discussions will demonstrate how the forensic rhetoric at work in the highest sovereign court in France, where lawyers pleaded on behalf of their clients, was intimately connected to the rhetoric of praise and blame prevalent in sixteenth-century literature.[75]

Understanding the centrality of rhetoric in the humanist curriculum helps us interpret the ideas of man and woman found in the commonplaces demonstrating dignity and misery, human superiority or inferiority, vice and virtue, that a Renaissance reader encountered in the books of moral philosophy, history and rhetoric printed in the 1500s.[76] Chapters three through six place the *Querelle des femmes* and the dignity- and misery-of-man debates in context by demonstrating the Renaissance preoccupation with the contrary aspects of human nature throughout the 1500s. Very few sixteenth-century *Querelle des femmes* writers dared to attack woman in print without providing a 'Champion' to come to her defence. The reluctance of Renaissance writers to defame the female sex in print without any redeeming praise requires some explanation about the strength of the *pro et contra* and the essential social roles of women as wives and mothers.[77] The early modern attraction to contradiction and the interest in articulating a contrary opinion is further examined through the 'back and forth' sixteenth-century dialogues where the ideas of man and woman, initially so closely tied to the creation story of Genesis, began to evolve in a broader context of human civilisations much as sixteenth-century historians began to reconsider the biblical timelines of the origins of Europe.[78] Finally it is important to examine how writers collected commonplaces and applied these examples of human nature in new forms of prose writing such as wide-ranging collections of 'lessons', *discours* or essays to explore the ambiguities and contradictions of life.[79]

---

[74] See Chapters 3 to 6, pp. 66–70, 90–91, 95–100, 111–14, 117–19, 144–52.

[75] See Chapter 5, pp. 131–2, Chapter 8, pp. 191–6, 203–6, 210–12, 221–2.

[76] See Chapter 3, pp. 55–66, 74–87.

[77] See Chapter 4, esp. pp. 104–11, 117–19.

[78] Chapter 5; Anthony Grafton, *What was History? The Art of History in Early Modern Europe* (Cambridge, 2007).

[79] See Chapter 6.

Law

In the law courts of early modern France the ideas about man, woman, marriage, family and inheritance were vigorously tested and disputed as lawyers formulated their pleadings to persuade the judges and win victory in court. The legal battles between family members explored in the concluding chapter provide a glimpse of the ideals and virtues of man and woman that lawyers used to represent their clients as well as the transgressions and vices helpful when characterising the opposing parties in the case.

Lawyers collected classical anecdotes and tales of virtuous ladies or heroic men in their reading notebooks to be 'ready for action' in a pleading before the Parlement de Paris where they put these examples to work in disputes over inheritance or parental authority. Chapter eight compares the lawyers' pleadings as recorded by clerks in the registers of the highest court of appeal to the versions of these deliberations circulating in print. The comparison of the registers, manuscript and printed speeches exposes the impact of print in amplifying and intensifying the lawyers' representations of man and woman in their roles as husbands, fathers, brothers, sons, wives, mothers, sisters or daughters. Moreover the printed versions of lawyers' pleadings and collections of notable decisions were often promoted, produced and sold by the same booksellers distributing the works of moral philosophy and literature considering the highs and lows of the human condition. Through these three lenses of print, rhetoric and law, we begin to understand the circulation of ideas of man and woman in Renaissance France.

* * *

The Ideas of Man and Woman in Renaissance France shows how writers borrowed and imitated examples to support one view and then overturned and inverted these examples to argue the opposite view. Once the writer's manuscript went into production, the merchant printers and some booksellers shaped these works for sale by packaging texts and images together. The woodcut reproduced here and on the book jacket provides a visual example of this practice of borrowing and reworking examples across a range of literary works implemented at the production stage in the printer's workshop.

This image of a woman writing at a desk first appeared in a book produced by Denis Janot's printing workshop in 1537 and offered for sale by Charles L'Angelier at his stall in the Palais de Justice in Paris. It resurfaced on many occasions in books produced and sold by Denis Janot in the late 1530s and early 1540s such as the guidebook called the *Spur of Discipline* or *L'Esperon de discipline* that developed some dignity-of-man themes to 'stimulate' a love of 'doctrine', knowledge (*science*) and 'good, virtuous and moral works'.[80] Janot

[80] Stephen Rawles, 'Denis Janot Parisian printer and bookseller, 1529–1544. A bibliographical study', 3 vols, PhD thesis, University of Warwick (1976), vol. II,

used this woodcut repeatedly in the editions of the *Controversies of the Masculine and Feminine Sexes* in 1538 and 1540, identified by many commentators as a 'misogynist' text because it argues for the inferiority of woman to man. Janot also inserted this image concurrently from the late 1530s and early 1540s into several of the works of Hélisenne de Crenne considered one of the earliest 'feminist' voices to defend her sex.[81] Looking at this image within Hélisenne de Crenne's works alone, such as the *Dream of Helisenne* (*Songe d'Hélisenne*) or *Les Epistres familieres et invectives* where it is the opening woodcut, a reader might be

Figure 1.1 'A man approaches a woman at her writing table', Gratien Dupont, *Controverses des sexes masculin et fœmenin* (Paris: Denis Janot, 1540), woodcut also printed in several works of Hélisenne de Crenne from Janot's press, courtesy of the Bibliothèque de Genève (BGE Hf324).

cat. no. 266, Claude de Cuzzi, *Philologue d'honneur* (Paris, Denis Janot for Charles L'Angelier, no date but after 15 November 1537); cat. nos. 67, 81, Clement Marot, *La suyte de l'adolescence clementine* (Paris: Denis Janot, 1537 and 1538); cat. no. 130, Michel d'Amboise, *Les contrepistres d'Ovide* (Paris: Denis Janot, 1541); cat. no. 135, Giovanni Boccaccio, *Complaincte tres piteuse de Flamette* (Paris, Denis Janot, 1541); cat. no. 99, Antoine du Saix, *L'Esperon de discipline* (Paris: Denis Janot, 1539).

81 See Chapter 4, p. 107; Rawles, 'Denis Janot', cat. nos. 73, 118, Gratien Dupont, *Controverses des sexes masculin et fœmenin* (Paris: D. Janot, 1538 and 1540); Stephen Rawles, 'Corrozet's *Hecatomgraphie*: Where Did the Woodcuts Come From and Where Did They Go?', *Emblematica* 3:1 (1988): 33.

tempted to identify the woman as Hélisenne writing at her desk.[82] This woodcut was frequently recycled in works of contemporary literature whether to incite discipline and virtue in the humanist style of the dignity of man or to illustrate the 'misogynist' and 'feminist' sides of the *Querelle des femmes*. Just as this image was borrowed and imitated and put to various and sometimes paradoxical uses in printed works, so too were many of the commonplaces and ideas relating to man and woman. Placing these ideas in their proper context therefore entails investigating their derivation and publication history, beginning with the print workshops and booksellers responsible for commissioning, producing, printing, reissuing and selling these original or imitated ideas in a range of different texts. It is to the booksellers and book markets of the sixteenth century that we must now turn.

[82] Rawles, 'Denis Janot', cat. nos. 116, 142, Hélisenne de Crenne, *Le songe de Madame Helisenne* (Paris: Denis Janot, 1540 and 1541); cat. no. 265, Hélisenne de Crenne, *Les Epistres familieres et invectives* (Paris: Denis Janot, no date but after 18 October 1539), sig A3v; Diane Wood, *Hélisenne de Crenne: At the Crossroads of Renaissance Humanism and Feminism* (London, 2000), p. 153.

Chapter 2
Booksellers and the Market to the 1550s

And so there are more books than readers,
More readers than virtuous doers,
More writers and more eloquent pleaders
Than listeners and do-gooders.

Et que plus sont de livres que lecteurs,
Plus de lecteurs que vertueux facteurs,
Plus d'escripvains & plus de bien disantz
Que d'auditeurs & que de bien faisantz.[1]

Gilles Corrozet, *Hecatomgraphie* (Paris: Denis Janot, 1540)

As Gilles Corrozet, the Parisian bookseller and author of the moral emblem book *Hecatomgraphie* knew all too well, the writers of books had more enthusiasm in dispensing advice than readers did in listening to it or acting upon it – 'plus sont de livres que de lecteurs'.[2] Like Corrozet, the historian faces the uncertainty of knowing about bookowners and their reading practices and is sometimes left to wonder whether once these books were printed, sold and found their place in a busy household, they sat collecting dust until a notary or bookseller came along to record their titles and value in an inventory of the goods belonging to an estate.

This chapter follows these 'books of the humanities', of history, moral philosophy and literature – offering examples of how to live virtuously and avoid vice – from the printers and booksellers who produced them to the customers who purchased, obtained or may have read them. It examines the networks of the book trade in Paris and Lyon in the first half of the sixteenth century in order to understand the editorial policies of the merchant printers and booksellers who distributed and promoted the literature of the dignity and misery of man and the *Querelle des femmes* on the nature of woman. At times printers and booksellers collaborated to produce these literary titles for sale. At times they packaged dialogues for niche markets such as the *Querelle des femmes* and vigorously

---

1 Gilles Corrozet, 'Gilles Corrozet Parisien aux bons espritz & amateurs des lettres', in *Hecatomgraphie: C'est a dire les descriptions de cent figures & hystoires, contenantes plusieurs appophtegmes, proverbes, sentences, & dictz tant des anciens que des modernes* (Paris: Denis Janot, 1540), sig. Aii^v. 'French Emblems at Glasgow' website, University of Glasgow, at http://www.emblems.arts.gla.ac.uk/french/index.php, accessed 4 December 2010.

2 Elizabeth Hodges, 'Representing Place in Gilles Corrozet's *Antiquitez de Paris*', *French Studies* 62:2 (April 2008): 143.

marketed their versions of the text over those of their rivals. Along the way this chapter will pause to mention and trace the distribution of some of the titles that will be analysed in chapters three to six. The concluding section considers the clientèle of certain Parisian booksellers on the Île de la Cité by looking in detail at the personal library amassed in the first half of the sixteenth century by a Parisian notary and his wife who possessed many titles of the *Querelle des femmes* and the dignity and misery of man.

The Book Markets of Paris and Lyon

Although Lyon and Paris were both major printing centres in the sixteenth century, there were noticeable differences in their book markets. The Parisian printers and booksellers installed themselves close to two literate groups: the university crowd near rue St Jacques, and the officeholders around the Palais de Justice on the Île de la Cité. The print industry in Lyon, by contrast, flourished through book fairs held four times a year and was ready to ship books to eager booksellers in Paris as well as over the border to Geneva or Italy.[3] After the 1530s, Lyon probably benefited from its distance from Paris, where the Faculty of Theology began to put censorship into practice. This regulation of the print industry began in earnest in the wake of the 1534 *Affaire des placards* when the edict of 13 January 1535 temporarily prohibited printing and ordered the closure of all bookstores.[4]

Within the walls of the Palais de Justice on the Île de la Cité in Paris could be found the Chambre des comptes (a sovereign court of the Exchequer), the Cour des aides (a sovereign court for cases concerning the levy of taxes such as *aides* and *tailles*), the Chancellerie (the offices and residence of the Chancellor), a prisoners' block, the thirteenth-century Sainte Chapelle (which still stands there today) and, probably of most importance for this study, the Parlement de Paris. Working within the highest sovereign court and court of appeal, the magistrates in the Parlement de Paris had obvious judicial powers but they also acted as a political 'frein' or bridle on the monarch, possessing the power to register royal edicts and laws and the right to remonstrate against the policies of the king. The Palais de Justice was more than the judicial and administrative centre of the kingdom; it was also a marketplace where pedlars and market-stall vendors vied to attract a wealthy clientèle of lawyers, royal officeholders and magistrates. Parisian booksellers often advertised their locations on the title pages of books available at their stalls. As an edition of the *Roman de la Rose* announced, the L'Angelier brothers had a 'boutique at the first pillar of the Great Hall of the Palais' in front of the judges' chapel. The luxury wares on sale at the Palais de Justice ranged from books and paintings to silks and linens. The bookseller Gilles Corrozet shared a bench in the

[3] Annie Charon [Parent], *Les métiers du livre à Paris au XVIe siècle (1535–1560)* (Geneva, 1974), p. 150.

[4] Ibid., p. 49.

Grand'Salle or Great Hall in the 1560s with his second wife, a *lingère*.[5] An Italian traveller in 1596 described how the river Seine encircles the Île de la Cité full of houses and boutiques, Nôtre Dame Cathedral and the Palais de Justice, a former king's palace:

> In this Palais [de Justice] can be found a Great Hall paved with black and white marble 112 paces long and 45 wide. In the middle of this room one notices a stone colonnade and all around [the room] are stone statues of all the kings of France ... Close by there is another room, wainscoted in gold, where every day the Parlement meets [as well as] the Chambre des comptes and the other magistrates of the city. In this Palais there are two more galleries, three staircases and finally the square where there are 224 boutiques selling all sorts of pretty things. It is there where men and women, nobles and others, at any hour of the day come to make their purchases.[6]

The pedlars, booksellers and linen suppliers were not the only ones selling their wares. Lawyers hoping to find a client also hustled for courtroom business. In the mid-sixteenth century an ordinance from the Parlement aimed to prevent lawyers from loitering in front of the first pillar by the 'consultation room'. Galiot du Pré's bookstall was situated in this prime location, and instead of obstructing his business the lawyers and counsellors were ordered to 'modestly' wait 'each one at his bench' for the 'parties' to a lawsuit to seek a consultation.[7]

Who influenced the types of books produced for a sixteenth-century reading public? The *marchand libraire* or merchant bookseller sold books printed to order or books purchased from printers or booksellers. A quick, although not foolproof, identifier of the merchant bookseller is the *pour* (for) rather than *par* (by) on a title page. A merchant bookseller might obtain a royal privilege, which gave exclusive reproduction rights to a work for a designated period of time – usually 5 to 10 years – using the printers of his choice. The *maître imprimeur* or master printer ran the atelier, struggling with a not-always-compliant workforce of journeymen and apprentices. These master printers had to contend with the maintenance of

[5] Philippe Renouard, *Imprimeurs parisiens, libraires, fondeurs de caractères et correcteurs d'imprimerie: Depuis l'introduction de l'imprimerie à Paris (1470) jusqu'à la fin du XVIe siècle* (Paris, 1898), p. 82; Philippe Renouard, *Documents sur les imprimeurs, libraires ... ayant exercé à Paris de 1450–1600* (Paris, 1901), p. 60; Jérôme Pichon and Georges Vicaire, *Documents pour servir à l'histoire des libraires de Paris, 1486–1600* (Paris, 1895), p. 125.

[6] Henri-Jean Martin, *Livre, pouvoirs et société à Paris au XVIIe siècle (1598–1701)*, 2 vols (Geneva, 1969), vol. I, pp. 32–3; Annie Charon, 'Le monde de l'imprimerie humaniste: Paris', in Roger Chartier and Henri-Jean Martin (eds), *Histoire de l'édition française*, 4 vols (Paris, 1984), vol. I, *Le livre conquérant*, p. 246.

[7] Roland Delachenal, *Histoire des avocats au Parlement de Paris 1300–1600* (Paris, 1885), p. 58, n. 2.

their presses, expensive typefaces, ink supplies and ornate letters.[8] Some of the merchant booksellers were more akin to the 'publishing houses' of today. Arnoul L'Angelier and his brother Charles, the Parisian booksellers, represented their relationship with their typographic mark of two angels intertwined or 'anges liés' and they often provided printers with this mark and ornamentation for books for their boutique.[9] Natalie Davis has shown that in Lyon the merchant end of the business was much more profitable than the 'dirty work' of printing.[10] So the Palais de Justice booksellers probably had an easier time mingling with their clientèle of royal administrators and king's counsellors than men who still engaged in the mechanical art of printing.

Certain individuals, such as Jean de Tournes or Denis Janot, managed to combine the talents of both the humanist world and the print workshop to act as *marchands imprimeurs* or merchant printers producing books and selling them at a stall, boutique or book fair. Like the bookseller who obtained a privilege or the reproduction rights to a work and ordered books to be printed for his boutique, these merchant printers interest us because they too sought royal permission to print certain texts, making it easier to identify an editorial policy. Sometimes a printer would keep some copies of a text for his own mark – in Denis Janot's case a thistle. On extra copies he or she probably placed a colophon or 'imprimé par' on the last page and left some blank pages for a bookseller such as L'Angelier to add his mark. In these cases the bookseller had no association with the printer and editorial choices cannot be gleaned, but it is still valuable to know which booksellers distributed which books. Printers frequently sold off extra copies of books in the 'public domain'.[11] Annie Charon explains how a writer could have a book printed in return for some copies or might assume some of the printing costs on the understanding that distribution would be shared. Sometimes a writer would underwrite the costs of printing in return for all of the copies and determination of distribution, as in the case of François de Billon's *Impregnable Fort of the Honour of the Feminine Sex*, 1555.[12]

Some printers concentrated on biblical and spiritual works, which formed the basis of even the most modest library. If a family was to own a single book it

[8] Minutier central des notaires de Paris, Archives nationales, Paris [hereafter MC, AN, Paris], post-mortem inventory of Jehan le Blanc, printer, 11 August 1601, XI, 114.

[9] P. Renouard, *Imprimeurs parisiens*, p. 209; Jacques Renouard, 'L'Officine des L'Angelier, libraires parisiens 1536–1562', Mémoire présentée par Jacques Renouard candidat au diplôme supérieur, University of Paris (1916), p. xxxi.

[10] N.Z. Davis, 'Le monde de l'imprimerie humaniste: Lyon', in Chartier and Martin (eds), *Histoire de l'édition française*, vol. I, p. 259.

[11] Renouard, 'L'Officine des L'Angelier', pp. xxiv–xxvi.

[12] Charon, 'Le monde', p. 239; On Jean Dallier see Georges Lepreux, *Gallia typographica*, 5 vols (Paris, 1909–14), vol. V, pp. 177–88.

was probably a book of hours or a Bible.[13] The evangelical printers who rose to prominence in the first half of the sixteenth century engaged in the humanist enterprise of editing and interpreting works in Latin and Greek.[14] Our focus, however, concerns the printers and booksellers who dealt primarily in French texts; particularly after the 1539 Edict of Villers-Cotterêts boosted publication in French by declaring it the official language.

Networks of Book Distribution and Editorial Policies

Many workers in the book trade intermarried and formed family and business alliances, making it necessary to unravel the relation of one printer as son-in law, brother, daughter or parent to another printer, binder or bookseller. Women as wives, daughters or widows of book trade workers were essential for the survival of these businesses, though surprisingly not all the women in book trade families were literate.[15]

A few minutes' walk from Nôtre Dame Cathedral, where Denis Janot established himself as a merchant printer, the L'Angelier brothers set up shop together as merchant booksellers in 1529 at the first pillar in the Grand'Salle of the Palais de Justice. The notarial records on Arnoul and Charles L'Angelier bear witness to Natalie Davis' point about the comfortable wealth of merchant booksellers relative to printers. The L'Angeliers spent their money buying property in the country, on the construction of houses, renovations and improvements to their gardens.[16] So if their business was profitable, how did they place themselves in the market?

The L'Angeliers obtained privileges for many of the books they stocked in their boutiques and contracted the print runs with numerous printers.[17] The printer François Girault lived at the sign of the 'Ange lié' on rue d'Ablon owned by Arnoul L'Angelier. Poncet le Preux, another Palais bookseller, and the L'Angelier brothers contracted Girault to print some royal ordinances. Similarly, a contract between Pierre Trepperel and the printer Girault shows that when Girault vacated

---

13 Roger Chartier, 'Stratégies éditoriales et lectures populaires', in *Lecteurs & lectures dans la France d'Ancien Régime* (Paris, 1987), pp. 89, 93.

14 Charon, *Métiers*, pp. 49–50.

15 Sylvie Postel-Lecocq, 'Femmes et presses à Paris au XVIe siècle: quelques exemples', in H. Martin (ed.), *Le Livre dans l'Europe de la Renaissance: Actes du XXVIIe colloque international d'études humanistes de Tours* (Paris, 1988), p. 257; Annie Charon, 'A propos des femmes et des métiers du livre dans le Paris de la Renaissance', in D. de Courcelles and C. Val Julián (eds), *Des femmes et des livres: France et Espagnes, XIVe–XVIIe siècle* (Paris, 1999), pp. 137–48; Susan Broomhall, *Women and the Book Trade in Sixteenth-Century France* (Aldershot, 2002), pp. 67–8.

16 Davis, 'Le monde', p. 268; P. Renouard, *Documents*, p. 148; J. Renouard, 'L'Officine des L'Angelier', p. xxi.

17 J. Renouard, 'L'Officine des L'Angelier', p. xxvii.

Arnoul's property for new premises the new tenancy contract specified that the 30 *livres tournois* in rent would be paid in 'books and print' – 'livres et impressions'.[18] L'Angelier and the printer may have had a similar arrangement.

After three years sharing a boutique, Charles settled at the first pillar and Arnoul moved to the second pillar outside the Grand'Salle within the Palais de Justice. Although the L'Angelier brothers separated their businesses, they still entered into association with each other and with the many other booksellers at the Palais de Justice and in the vicinity of Nôtre Dame Cathedral on the Île de la Cité to share editions. In 1554 Charles became a *libraire juré* (a master of the book trade sworn under oath before the Faculty of Theology of the University of Paris) and stayed at the first pillar until 1557 when he installed his boutique within the Palais at the Salle des Merciers (Hall of Pedlars). Arnoul never left the Grand'Salle where his son-in-law Claude Gaultier would practise and where his son Abel L'Angelier would eventually establish his boutique and sell Montaigne's *Essais*.[19]

When Arnoul L'Angelier died in 1557 it was over a decade before his son Abel entered the trade under his own name. Abel L'Angelier's mother, Girarde Roffet, ended her widowhood with a marriage to Lucas Breyer, a merchant printer, so that Abel's sometime colleague Lucas II Breyer was his half-brother. Early in his career Abel L'Angelier had even shared a fourth edition of Homer's *Iliad* with his mother as Widow Lucas Breyer.[20] Abel L'Angelier married a woman already established in the book trade as the widow of the elder Pierre du Pré and ex-daughter-in-law of Galiot du Pré, one of the first Palais de Justice booksellers. The first traces of Abel L'Angelier's activity as a bookseller began after his marriage to Françoise de Louvain in 1573 and the books on sale 'at the first pillar of the Grand'Salle of the Palais' started to appear in 1574.[21] Another success story, Abel became a *libraire juré* in 1584 and a *Syndic de la Communauté* (an officer of the self-regulating book trade) in 1596. He died in January 1610.[22] After her second husband died, Françoise de Louvain continued the business until her death in 1620 and procured privileges as the Widow L'Angelier, playing on the respect granted to

---

18 Ibid., pp. 434, 462, 465.

19 Ibid., p. xxiv.

20 Girarde Roffet was the daughter of bookseller–binder Pierre Roffet. From Lucas Breyer's death in 1581, she ran the business alone until 1587 when she transferred her stock of books to her son Lucas II Breyer: Postel-Lecocq, 'Femmes et presses', p. 261; Philippe Renouard, *Imprimeurs et libraires parisiens du XVIe siècle. Fascicule Breyer* (Paris, 1982).

21 Jean Balsamo and Michel Simonin, *Abel L'Angelier et Françoise de Louvain (1574–1620). Suivi du catalogue des ouvrages publiés par Abel L'Angelier (1574–1610) et la Veuve L'Angelier (1610–1620)* (Geneva, 2002), pp. 36–7.

22 P. Renouard, *Imprimeurs parisiens*, pp. 209–21; on L'Angelier see Michel Simonin, 'Abel L'Angelier: Le politique du Palais', in *Politique et littérature en France au XVIe et XVIIe siècles* (Paris, 1997), pp. 53–86.

Abel in royal and printing circles.[23] We shall return to the role of Abel L'Angelier and his widow in chapter seven, but for the moment we shall focus on some of the other prominent book-trade families who were contemporaries and associates of his father Arnoul and uncle Charles.

Jean Janot, a merchant printer and *libraire juré*, married Macée Trepperel, and after his father-in-law's death became an associate of his mother-in-law, Widow Jean I Trepperel.[24] Jean Janot, active in the neighbourhood of Nôtre Dame Cathedral from 1508 until his death in 1522, aimed his stock of books at the 'grand public' by printing almost exclusively in the vernacular.[25] Two of Janot's sons, Simon and Denis, also entered the book trade.[26] Denis began his business in 1529 in the Grand'Salle of the Palais de Justice, working with Alain Lotrian for the first few years. He struck out on his own in 1534 and would eventually establish himself as a merchant printer back on rue Neuve Nôtre Dame where his father and mother had run the family printing business. Like his grandmother and his mother, Denis Janot's widow Jeanne de Marnef took over the business at the sign of St John the Baptist across from the little church of Ste Geneviève des Ardents, which stood beneath the towers of Nôtre Dame Cathedral.[27] Jeanne de Marnef was not a newcomer to the trade. She was the daughter of Geoffroy de Marnef, himself a *libraire juré* active from 1481 to 1518. Her uncles Jean I de Marnef and Enguilbert were printers at the sign of the Pelican in both Paris and Poitiers, and her late husband had carried some of her uncles' stock in his boutique.[28] Jeanne's sister Denise de Marnef, widow of the printer Ambroise Girault, entered into association with their brother Jerome at the sign of the Pelican in 1548.[29]

After a year-and-a-half running the printing business as a widow, Jeanne de Marnef married Estienne Groulleau, who practised as a merchant printer at the same location – the sign of St John the Baptist on rue Neuve Nôtre Dame

23 On L'Angelier's reputation see the royal privilege in *Les Images ou tableaux de platte peinture des deux Philostrates sophistes grecs et des statues de Callistrate* (Paris: Veuve Abel L'Angelier and Veuve M. Guillemot, 1615), fo. 921v; Michel Simonin, 'Trois femmes en librairie: Françoise de Louvain, Marie L'Angelier, Françoise Patelé (1571–1645)', in Courcelles and Val Julián (eds), *Des femmes et des livres*, pp. 149–61.

24 Roger Doucet, *Les bibliothèques parisiennes au XVIe siècle* (Paris, 1956), p. 13.

25 Ibid., p. 14.

26 Pichon and Vicaire, *Documents*, pp. 48–9. Henri Omont, *Catalogue des éditions françaises de Denys Janot, libraire parisien (1529–45)* (Paris, 1899), cat. no. 86, p. 19.

27 Stephen Rawles, 'Denis Janot Parisian printer and bookseller, 1529–1544. A bibliographical study', 3 vols, PhD thesis, University of Warwick (1976), p. 17; P. Renouard, *Imprimeurs parisiens*, p. 191.

28 Omont, *Catalogue*, pp. 17–18.

29 Renouard, *Imprimeurs parisiens*, p. 262; Philippe Renouard, *Imprimeurs & libraires parisiens du XVIe siècle. Fascicule Cavellat, Marnef, Cavellat* (Paris, 1986), pp. 163, 172; Charon, *Métiers*, p. 149.

– until 1561.[30] Groulleau adopted the same typography, the same printer's mark of thistles and continued, like Jeanne de Marnef, the same business associations that Janot had established with Vincent Sertenas and Jean Longis, booksellers at the Palais de Justice. The trio of Denis Janot, Jeanne de Marnef and Groulleau ran the printing business under the twin towers of Nôtre Dame in succession from about 1529 to 1561.

Stephen Rawles comments that, in 1534/35, already a lean year because of the *Affaire des placards* and subsequent prohibition of printing, Denis Janot concentrated on 'safe, saleable volumes.'[31] Like his father, Denis Janot dealt almost exclusively in vernacular books, but with more of a slant to the *studia humanitatis*: poetry, moral philosophy and history. In 1543 Francis I granted Janot the title of *Imprimeur du roi en langue française*, official king's printer in the French language. This favour only entailed an automatic five-year privilege on his printed books, but Janot published a catalogue of his stock shortly thereafter, which enables us to trace some of his activities. The catalogue lists only 14 books in Latin out of 163 titles.[32] Janot's stock reflects the policy of Francis I to require laws, edicts and ordinances to be printed in French. The king also commissioned translations into French of classical authors such as Thucydides, Plutarch and Xenophon and Janot's catalogue demonstrates a heavy emphasis on translation, an editorial policy that served him well.[33]

In the 1530s he printed Hélisenne de Crenne's translation of parts of Virgil's *Æneid*, a collection of Seneca's 'sentences' and 'particular teachings', Cicero's *Familiar Letters* (reprinted twice) and his *On Duties*, four *Satires* from Juvenal, Jean Parmentier's translation of Sallust's *Catalina* (reprinted twice), Ovid's *Letters*, and in the 1540s the seventh and eighth books of Pliny's *Natural History*, which Janot shared with Jean Longis. For the reading public of lawyers there were Justinian's *Institutes* in French translation as well as many style and protocol manuals to assist royal and civic officeholders in carrying out their judicial and administrative duties. And of course many of the titles of the *Querelle des femmes* emerged from Janot's press, often enjoying a reprint a year or two later. Janot and Vincent Sertenas, a Palais de Justice bookseller, are probably most famous

---

30 Groulleau and Marnef married by 14 August 1546 as a privilege granted in Marnef's name indicates: 'Privilège accordé pour 6 ans à Jeanne de Marnef, veuve de Denis Janot, épouse d'Estienne Groulleau, le 14 août 1546'. See [Jean Maugin], *Les Figures de l'Apocalypse de Saint Ian apostre et dernier evangeliste exposées en latin et vers francoys* (Paris: De l'imprimerie d'Estienne Groulleau, 1547). On 3 August 1547, Estienne Groulleau with Pierre Trepperel (the printer grandson of Jean I Trepperel), Widow Macée Trepperel and others opposed the sale price of two houses belonging to Jean Trepperel, a silk merchant, so Groulleau was acting on Marnef's behalf alongside her in-laws from her first marriage; see P. Renouard, *Documents*, p. 291.

31 Rawles, 'Janot', p. 26; P. Renouard, *Documents*, p. 138.

32 Rawles, 'Janot', p. 35; Omont, *Catalogue*, p. 13.

33 Charon, *Métiers*, p. 41.

for their collaboration on the popular romance translations of the adventures of *Amadis de Gaule*.

Some of Janot's most noteworthy contributions to French printing, however, were illustrated moral guidebooks, known as emblem books, such as Guillaume de la Perrière's *Theatre of Good Understanding* (*Théâtre des bons engins*) printed in 1540 as the first emblem book in the French language. From 1532 Janot entered into association with Gilles Corrozet, the historian, writer and bookseller who played a part in several of the key successes of his business. Janot produced Gilles Corrozet's *Hecatomgraphie* as the second French emblem book in 1540, 1541 and 1543, with a fourth printing in later 1543 or early 1544.[34] The title page of the book explains the concept of the emblem book and the meaning of Hecatomgraphie: *That is to say Descriptions of One Hundred Images and Stories, Containing Several Apophthegms, Proverbs, Sentences, & Sayings from the Ancients as well as Moderns*. Corrozet explains how 'every story is illustrated by an image' and guides the reader on how to consult the book.[35]

> When you are at your leisure …
> When you would like to learn an example
> Of moral speeches of philosophy
> Which is often necessary.
> Read this Hecatomgraphie.
>
> *Quand vous serez à vostre bon loisir …*
> *Quand vous vouldrez scavoir quelque exemplaire*
> *Propos moraulx de la philosophie*
> *Et ce qui est maintesfoys necessaire*
> *Lisez dedans cest Hecatomgraphie.*[36]

Janot's book stock thus reflects a heavy emphasis on contemporary French moral literature and translations of the classics. Rawles notes that, of the 30 editions accounted for in Janot's stock for the publication year 1541, Janot printed 29 himself. Twenty-seven of these imprints are in French and 22 are illustrated.[37]

---

34 Alison Adams, Stephen Rawles and Alison Saunders (eds), *A Bibliography of French Emblem Books of the Sixteenth and Seventeenth Centuries*, 2 vols (Geneva, 1999), vol. I, pp. 367–78; Alison Saunders, *The Sixteenth Century French Emblem Book: A Decorative and Useful Genre* (Geneva, 1988), pp. 294–5. Guillaume de la Perrière's *Théâtre des bons engins* was printed four times by Janot in 1539 [1540], by de Tournes in Lyon and the Trepperel family in Angers in 1545, again by de Tournes in 1546, 1547, 1549 and 1553, and by Estienne Groulleau in 1554.

35 Corrozet, *Hecatomgraphie*, sig. Aiii^{v}.

36 Corrozet, 'Huictain', in *Hecatomgraphie* (1541), sig. Aiiii^{r}.

37 Rawles, 'Janot', p. 32.

When Janot died in December 1544, Jeanne de Marnef continued her husband's associations, printing or sharing at least seven books with either Jean Longis or Vincent Sertenas, such as the sixth and seventh *Amadis de Gaule* installments. However, Marnef seems to have procured few privileges for new works and altered her husband's business by dropping the merchant side to concentrate entirely on printing. The emphasis on the title page of her books changes from her husband's 'On les *vend* à l'enseigne Sainct Jehan Baptiste' or 'sold at the Sign of Saint John the Baptist' to 'De l'*imprimerie* de Jeanne de Marnef, demourant en la rue Neuve nostre Dame, à l'enseigne Sainct Jean Baptiste' – 'from the printing press of Jeanne de Marnef dwelling on rue Neuve Nôtre Dame at the sign of Saint John the Baptist'.[38] It is interesting that she did not try to present herself as Widow Janot, the practice of many widowed female printers, as her surname Marnef was already prominent enough in the book trade. In fact, she printed books under privilege to another printer. In 1546 she copied the posthumous *Rymes* of Pernette du Guillet from the first edition that the merchant printer Jean de Tournes had just published in Lyon. Marnef's title page boasts that it has been expanded by 'new compositions'. Jean de Tournes would only publish his second edition of Pernette du Guillet in 1552. Marnef even reproduced the letter from 'Printer to Reader' written by Jean de Tournes just as it had appeared in his edition, but with no mention of his name, and she also reprinted the inspirational letter of dedication 'To the Ladies of Lyon' by de Tournes' editor, Antoine du Moulin. Her edition is not as beautifully produced as Jean de Tournes', but it demonstrates the exchange of books and ideas between Paris and Lyon even if only in pirated editions.[39] In the same year Marnef copied from de Tournes a translation of *Five Short Works of Plutarch* (*Cinq Opuscules de Plutarque*). When she printed Plutarch's *Virtuous and Illustrious Deeds of Women of Antiquity* (*Des vertueux et illustres faitz des anciennes femmes*), she copied a Lyon edition of Guillaume Rovillé complete with his dedicatory letter to a lady of Lyon. She also continued some of the practices of her husband when in 1545 she printed Plutarch's *Precepts of Marriage* first translated by Jean Lodé in 1499, produced by Janot in 1535 and reprinted the following year.[40]

---

[38] My emphasis. Pernette du Guillet, *Les Rithmes et poesies de gentile, et vertueuse dame D. Pernette du Guillet Lyonnoise. Avecq'le triumphe des Muses sur Amour: et autres nouvelles compositions* (Paris: De l'imprimerie de Jeanne de Marnef, 1546). Other titles use the term 'En l'imprimerie de Jeanne de Marnef'; see Plutarch, *Opuscules de Plutarque, des vertueux et illustres faitz des anciennes femmes* (Paris: Jeanne de Marnef, 1546) or *Cinq opuscules de Plutarque Cheronne* (Paris: Jeanne de Marnef, 1546).

[39] Du Guillet, *Rithmes*; see for example, 'Antoine du Moulin Aux dames lyonnoises, S.', sig. Aij^{r}.

[40] Philippe Renouard, Imprimeurs et libraires parisiens: Jeanne de Marnef [Veuve Janot], Paris: Bibliothèque nationale imprimés réserve, MS, nos. 293, 308–9; Robert Aulotte, *Amyot et Plutarque: La tradition des moralia au XVIe siècle* (Geneva, 1965), pp. 73–6; Rawles, 'Janot', cat. nos. 42, 56.

In Lyon, Jean de Tournes had paid his dues as a journeyman in the workshop of Sebastien Gryphius. De Tournes finally managed to achieve master printer status in his late thirties when his wife inherited a house where he could establish his business on the rue Mercière between the Rhône and Saône rivers. Lyon did not share Paris's extensive reading market of officeholders in the sovereign courts, nor was it a university town. Instead the Lyon printers and booksellers relied on book fairs in Lyon and Frankfurt and networks with Paris and cities outside of France, utilising Lyon's advantageous proximity to Italy, Switzerland and the Mediterranean Sea.

There are shared themes in the types of works that Janot, de Tournes, Sertenas and the L'Angelier brothers were producing in the 1540s. If imitation is the sincerest form of flattery, then de Tournes would compliment Denis Janot when he copied the illustrated moral book format that had worked so successfully for Janot. In 1547, de Tournes copied Janot and Corrozet's popular translations of *Aesop's Fables*, but added his own exclusive touch – a *Life of Æsop* by Antoine du Moulin. Obviously the *Fables* sold well in French because de Tournes reprinted them in 1549 and 1551.[41] On four occasions before 1553 de Tournes copied Guillaume de la Perrière's original French emblem book *Théâtre des bons engins*, which Denis Janot brought to light for the first time in 1539.[42] In 1547 de Tournes copied the *Three New Goddesses: Pallas, Juno and Venus* [*Les Trois Nouvelles Déeses Pallas, Iuno, Venus*] shared by Jeanne de Marnef with Michel Fezandat in 1546.

Although de Tournes copied formats and ideas, he does not seem to have pirated any editions under privilege to another person. De Tournes actually appealed to his fellow printers not to breach the privileges granted in the name of the king, imploring these printers to 'diligently observe' the privileges so each would earn the profits that 'belong to him'.[43] It is important to distinguish, then, between piracy or breach of privilege and the copying of a work in the public domain that was no longer under privilege. Initially, the privilege system was an optional source of protection for a new book. As David Pottinger explains, after the problems of the religious reform movement emerged, Francis I imposed the requirement of a royal privilege on books of a religious nature and shortly thereafter extended the

---

41 A. Cartier, M. Audin and E. Vial (eds), *Bibliographie des éditions des de Tournes, imprimeurs lyonnais*, 2 vols (Paris, 1937–38), vol. I, cat. nos. 71, 128, 184. The edition is by Jean de Tournes and Guillaume Gazeau.

42 See also Alison Saunders, 'Paris to Lyon and Back Again: Trends in Emblem Publishing in Mid-Sixteenth Century France,' in Philip Ford and Gillian Jondorf (eds), *Intellectual Life in Renaissance Lyon: Proceedings of the Cambridge Lyon Colloquium 14–16 April 1991* (Cambridge, 1993), pp. 63–79. The 1553 Jean de Tournes edition has no privilege.

43 [Jean de Tournes], 'L'Imprimeur aux imprimeurs', in Bonaventure des Periers, *Recueil des œuvres de feu Bonaventure des Periers* (Lyon: Jean de Tournes, 1544), sig. n3v; Cartier, *et al.* (eds), *Bibliographie*, vol. I, p. 181.

measure to all books.[44] The owner of the privilege arranged for the printing and distribution of the work. To do so entailed investment and possible loss, so it was common practice for the printer or bookseller to share an edition with a colleague and divide the books according to financial contribution to the printing costs. Booksellers frequently shared the cost of an edition or simply split the print run with their merchant printer. The close-knit community of Palais de Justice and Île de la Cité booksellers worked together through family and business networks but also because of internal competition.[45] To attract customers, keep their clientèle and probably as a measure against piracy, booksellers often stocked a bestseller also available in the neighbouring boutique.

In order to ensure access to popular works, booksellers and printers shared distribution between Paris, Lyon and other trade centres. Jean de Tournes, for instance, conducted business with the L'Angelier brothers. In the summer of 1561 Charles L'Angelier, 'merchant bookseller', settled a debt for over 60 *livres tournois* worth of 'merchandise' from Jean de Tournes 'printer bookseller in Lyon'.[46] Their association seems to have begun very early in Jean de Tournes' solo career as a printer. In January of 1543, for example, Charles L'Angelier obtained a three-year privilege for Anthoine Alaigre's translation of Antonio Guevara's *On Contempt for the Court and On the Praise of 'Rustic' Life* or the *Mépris de la court* dedicated to Guillaume du Prat, the son of Francis I's Chancellor.[47] Jean de Tournes and Charles L'Angelier produced copies of the *Mépris de la court* in the same year with the same translator and same letters of dedication, and yet each bookseller sold his copies with his own mark. It is possible that L'Angelier arranged for Jean de Tournes to act as his printer in return for a share in distribution.

Although Denis Janot's prominence led him to the title of *imprimeur du roi*, he died in 1544 before the privilege system took a firm hold in the publishing community. However, his colleague and sometime collaborator at the Palais de Justice, Vincent Sertenas, became a leading procurer of royal privileges. Michel Simonin states that, by about 1540, with the success of the *Amadis de Gaule* romance series, Sertenas was sitting comfortably in the middle of a 'solid network' even if he practised 'in the shadow of Janot'.[48] In 1552 Sertenas obtained an invaluable royal monopoly for official acts, edicts and ordinances, an advantage renewed in

---

[44] Elizabeth Armstrong, *Before Copyright: The French Book Privilege System 1498–1526* (Cambridge, 1990); David Pottinger, *The French Book Trade in the Ancien Regime, 1500–1791* (Cambridge, MA, 1958), pp. 210–16.

[45] Charon, *Métiers*, p. 49.

[46] Cartier, *et al.* (eds), *Bibliographie*, vol. I, p. 143; Pichon and Vicaire, *Documents*, p. 115.

[47] P. Renouard, Imprimeurs et libraires parisiens: L'Angelier, Paris: Bibliothèque nationale imprimés réserve, MS; Cartier, *et al.* (eds), *Bibliographie*, vol. I, cat. no. 8 and pp. 168–9.

[48] Michel Simonin, 'Peut-on parler de politique éditoriale au XVIe siècle: le cas de Vincent Sertenas libraire parisien', in Martin (ed.), *Le livre dans l'Europe*, p. 265.

1554, that guaranteed him an income and a steady clientèle. With apparently easy access to royal privileges for many works, Sertenas was in a position to decide upon distribution *and* choose whether or not he would share editions. He could keep all profits to himself or share the profits or a potential loss if the book was not popular. As Simonin points out, Sertenas continued to share editions and form alliances even from this position of relative security. From the early 1550s he managed to introduce many new literary titles. In November 1553, for example, he acquired a ten-year privilege for printing and selling the lawyer Étienne Pasquier's *Le Monophile*, a dialogue on love and woman. Sertenas shared the distribution of a second edition of the *Monophile* among the familiar group: Jean Longis and Charles L'Angelier, booksellers like himself within the Palais de Justice walls, and Groulleau operating just a block away by Nôtre Dame Cathedral.[49]

In 1552 Sertenas the Palais bookseller employed his privilege for Pero Mexia's *Diverse Lessons*, translated for a French audience by Claude Gruget, printed by Groulleau, and distributed by Sertenas, Longis and Groulleau. In Mexia's popular collection, reprinted in 1554, 1556, 1557 and revised and expanded by Gruget in 1560, the themes range from the ages of man to the nature of woman, to tales of Emperors and Amazons, to marriage, the invention of letters and the first library in the world.[50]

Sertenas offered his clientèle the *Dialogues* of Louis Le Caron in 1555 and Pierre Boaistuau's *Prodigious Tales* appeared in 1556. Simonin calls 1558 the 'year of Boaistuau' because Sertenas published Boaistuau's *pro* and *contra* twin publications: the *Théâtre du monde* on human misery and the *Bref discours de l'excellence et dignité de l'homme*. Two works of compilation, they explore both the glory and the wretchedness of the human condition and will be examined in chapter three. Sertenas' editorial policy steered towards this public taste for dialogues, prodigious and amorous tales, the *pro* and *contra* and collections of diverse opinions and topics. With a steady income from 'official' and legal publications, Sertenas' literary stock in the 1550s reflects a taste for moral lessons, dialogues and collections of diverse topics.

Packaging and Selling the *Querelle des femmes* and the Dignity and Misery of Man

As a group, these booksellers fostered the *Querelle des femmes* and the dignity-and misery-of-man debates. For example, Claude Gruget, the Parisian translator, editor and a frequent collaborator of Vincent Sertenas, adapted Sperone Speroni's

49 The title pages for the four booksellers are facsimile reproduced in Avenir Tchemerzine, *Bibliographie d'éditions originales et rares d'auteurs francais des XVe, XVIe, XVIIe, et XVIIIe siècles*, 10 vols (Paris, 1927–33), vol. IX, p. 79.

50 Pero Mexia, *Les Diverses leçons*, trans. Claude Gruget (Paris: Estienne Groulleau, 1552), sig. PPiii^{r}; to be analysed in Chapter 6, pp. 143–4, 146–52.

Dialogues from Italian for a French audience in 1551. Printed by Estienne Groulleau, and under the royal privilege granted to Vincent Sertenas, the title page for the bookseller reads, 'For Vincent Sertenas at the Palais in the gallery where one goes to the Chancellerie and at the hôtel d'Albret at Mont Saint Hilaire'. Sertenas' mark appears on the last page. On separate copies, Groulleau placed his mark of thistles on the title page, advertising his boutique at the sign of St John the Baptist. Speroni's *Dialogues* provide one example of a shared edition from the same print run as the copies sold by Sertenas and Groulleau both indicate, 'End of the *Dialogues* of Sperone Speroni, printed at Paris 15 July 1551, by Estienne Groulleau'.[51] The dialogue on the 'dignity of women' had already been translated into French, as Claude Gruget acknowledges twice in his translator's letter. He concedes that the French versions of Speroni's *On the Dignity of Women* and the *Care of the Household* stemmed from a source printed in Lyon. Gruget explains how he has not touched these translations so as 'not to harm another's labour'.[52]

The story, however, is not that straightforward, because these collaborating printers and booksellers at times switched roles to become rivals, by producing the same or similar works in different configurations or editions. Speroni's dialogues *On the Dignity of Women* and the *Care of the Household* had already appeared in print both in Lyon *and* in Paris for sale at the Palais de Justice. From 1546 Jean de Tournes in Lyon sold Speroni's two dialogues on woman and the household, accompanied by a translation of Plutarch's *Precepts of Marriage*.[53] Arnoul L'Angelier apparently sold Speroni's *Care of the Household* and *On the Dignity of Women* packaged with Plutarch's essay on marriage at his boutique in Paris in 1548 in the same size and format as Jean de Tournes' edition. In this case, it is possible that the interests of the Lyon merchant printer, Jean de Tournes and the Parisian bookseller Arnoul L'Angelier intersect.[54] The Speroni dialogues on woman and the household, which de Tournes produced in Lyon and

---

[51] See Sperone Speroni, *Les Dialogues de Messire Speron Sperone Italien, traduitz en françoys, par Claude Gruget, Parisien* (Paris: Vincent Sertenas, 1551), fo. 229v: 'Fin des dialogues de Speron Sperone, imprimez à Paris le 15 de Iuillet 1551, par Estienne Groulleau'.

[52] Claude Gruget, 'A Monseigneur, Monsieur de Maupas, Abbé De Saint Ian De Laon, & Aumosnier Ordinaire du Roy. C.Gruget, S.', in Speroni, *Dialogues* (1551) [not foliated]; on Claude Gruget and his translations see Paul Chavy, *Traducteurs d'autrefois: Moyen Âge et Renaissance*, 2 vols (Paris, 1988), vol. I, pp. 650–52.

[53] Cartier, *et al.* (eds), *Bibliographie*, vol. I, cat. no. 65; *De la cure familIere avec aucuns preceptes de mariage extraicts de Plutarque, aussi un dialogue de la dignité des femmes, traduit des dialogues de M. Speron, italien* (Lyon: Jean de Tournes, 1546); Aulotte, *Amyot et Plutarque*, pp. 58–9.

[54] Antoine du Verdier, *Les Bibliothèques françoises de La Croix du Maine et de Du Verdier*, ed. Jean-Antoine Rigoley de Juvigny, 6 vols (Paris: Saillant and Nyon, 1772–73), vol. I, p. 436: 'De la cure familière avec aucuns Préceptes de Mariage, extraits de Plutarque: aussi un Dialogue des femmes, traduit des Dialogues de M. Speron Italien (imprimés à Paris in-16, par Arnoul L'Angelier.)'.

Arnoul L'Angelier distributed in Paris, packaged with the guaranteed attraction of Plutarch, obviously corresponded to an interest in selling a popular *Querelle des femmes* title: ideas about woman within marriage and about woman in relation to man. We shall discuss these dialogues further in chapter four on the *Querelle des femmes*.

The focus of Claude Gruget's, Sertenas' and Groulleau's efforts, however, has a much broader interest and points to the wider base for this literature on the dignity or status of woman. Sertenas' and Gruget's book reproduces the same two dialogues on woman's nature, but packaged in a much broader format. In his translator's letter Gruget explains the contents of the *Dialogues* on 'love and jealousy', on 'pregnancy and childbirth' and on usury (Gruget praises Speroni's skill at making the most despicable act in the world seem good). Gruget also translates Speroni's dialogue of Jupiter and Discord, 'in which can be found the great forms of natural and moral philosophy' and the seventh dialogue on language, and Gruget recommends for 'every studious man' the Speroni piece on rhetoric. In his letter of dedication the translator Gruget highlights the dialogue as a means of presenting several sides to a story and suggests that the paradoxical nature of the *Dialogues* will interest the reader, a theme we shall consider in chapter five. 'Knowing how much you take pleasure in debating and upholding paradoxical opinions to sharpen and test the minds of young people who sometimes endeavour to resist your invincible reason, and in the dialogues at hand, you shall find many speeches which seem, at first, to be against common and ordinary opinion'.[55]

These booksellers competed to get their version of a text to market. An essay or dialogue, like Speroni's the 'dignity of women', might appear in a *Querelle des femmes* collection or as part of a *recueil*, a moral anthology, considering everything in human life from usury to rhetoric. They promoted the exclusivity of their editions by including letters from the translators such as Gruget and from the editors such as Antoine du Moulin who had shaped the edition. As we shall see in the cases of the merchant printer Jean de Tournes or the bookseller Jehan André, these businessmen might also appeal directly to the prospective buyer.

Editorial Policy: Pleasing the Eye, Selling the Idea, Promoting the Book

Increasing commercial demands made Jean de Tournes aware of the need to please the reader with both content and presentation. Promoting his 'revised' and 'corrected' version of a popular and often reprinted work, the merchant printer Jean de Tournes explained why he chose to print in 'good, clear letters, and in a small volume as you can see, so that it is more portable. Because so great are the benefits and delights of reading such a book that for nothing in the world would

55 Gruget, 'A … Monsieur De Maupas', in Speroni, *Dialogues* (1551) [not foliated].

I have been dissuaded from doing it'.[56] Jean de Tournes left traces of his editorial policy in the prefaces he wrote to promote the books from his press.[57] He offers his reader both 'utility' and extravagant attempts to regale their eyes in order to encourage the mind or 'spirit'. De Tournes reminds the reader of 'the desire that I have always had to revive all useful Authors and Works that the injury of time has forgotten or corrupted' when he introduces his edition of the *Illustrations de Gaule* by Jean le Maire de Belges.[58] But de Tournes was always eager to present contemporary works of French literature or *nouveautés* such as the *Rymes* of Pernette du Guillet, Louise Labé's *Œuvres* or Maurice Scève's *Microcosme* for his esteemed customers: 'The affection, benevolent Reader, that I have always borne and still bear for the public good, bids me to share with you something new and profitable'.[59] One of these novelties was an emblem book of the New Testament, which he recommended as a 'memory aid' offering 'recreation to the eye' and 'contentment to the soul'.[60] De Tournes prints this 'representation of the Holy Bible' for the reader without 'the leisure to read and enjoy [the written word]'. He hopes the reader will 'cover the walls of your memory chambers' with these religious images rather than 'pagan histories'.

The Lyon printer also stressed the importance of the French language for his enterprise, 'always performing the duty of bringing honour to our Gallic

---

56 [Jean de Tournes], 'L'Imprimeur au lecteur', in Johann Boemus, *Recueil de diverses histoires, touchant les situations de toutes regions & pais, contenus es trois parties du monde: avec les particulières mœurs, loix, & ceremonies de toute nations & peuples y habitants. Reveu & verifié jouxte le vray exemplaire Latin* (Lyon: Jean de Tournes, 1544), fo. title page verso: 'Car tant est de grand profit & delices la lecture d'un tel Livre, que pour rien, du monde ie ne me fusse destourné de ce faire'; Cartier, *et al.* (eds), *Bibliographie*, vol. I, cat. no. 17.

57 Eugene Vial in Cartier, *et al.* (eds), *Bibliographie*, vol. I, p. 126, n. 31. I have added the locations of several letters: *Recueil de diverses histoires*, 1544; *Le Livre de Marc Aurele Le Empereur*, 1544; *Il Petrarca,* 1545 (to Maurice Scève in Italian); *Œuvres* de Clément Marot, 1546; *De la vraye tranquilité de l'esprit*, 1546; Dante, 1547 (to Maurice Scève in Italian); *Epistres famileres de Cicero*, 1549; Marot, *Œuvres*, 1549; *Illustrations de Gaule*, 1549; *Opuscules de divers autheurs medecins*, 1552; *Juvanei sedulii sacra poesis*, 1553 (to Cardinal d'Armagnac in Latin); *Choréide* (Aux Dames); *Quadrins historiques de la Bible*, 1555; Pontus de Tyard, *Solitaire second ou prose de la musique*, 1555; Suetonius, *La vie des XII Césars*, 1556; *Mantice*, 1558; Ausonius, 1558; *Figures du Nouveau testament*, 1558; *Les hymnes du temps*, 1560.

58 [Jean de Tournes], 'L'Imprimeur au lecteur salut … de Lyon ce quatriesme de Septembre MD.XLIX', in Jean Lemaire de Belges, *Les Illustrations de Gaule et singularitez de Troye* (Lyon: Jean de Tournes, 1549), verso of the *Couronne Margueritique* title page; Cartier, *et al.* (eds), *Bibliographie*, vol. I, cat. no. 145.

59 [Jean de Tournes], 'L'Imprimeur au lecteur', in Suetonius, *De la Vie des XII Césars* (Lyon: Jean de Tournes, 1556); Cartier, *et al.* (eds), *Bibliographie*, vol. II, cat. no. 347.

60 [Jean de Tournes], 'L'Imprimeur aux lecteurs salut', in Charles Fontaine, *Figures du Nouveau testament* (Lyon: Jean de Tournes, 1556).

language'.[61] Like Janot, he too achieved status as the *Imprimeur du roi en langue française* and many of the titles of the *Querelle des femmes*, such as the ironically entitled *Praise of Women*, or *Louenge des femmes* of 1551, appeared for the first time from de Tournes' press in Lyon. De Tournes featured translations in French, such as Juan Luis Vives' *Instruction of the Christian Woman* in 1543, reprinting the work in 1545, 1547 and 1549. Apart from a family association with his son-in-law for Latin imprints, de Tournes did not seem to engage in the systematic collaboration of sharing privileges common to the Parisian Palais de Justice booksellers. Instead he seems to have printed and sold his wares at the Lyon book fair or directly to these booksellers.[62]

In 1546 de Tournes addressed the reader of Isabella Sforza's *On the True Tranquility of the Soul* (*De la vraye tranquilité de l'esprit*), explaining how all 'illustrious' persons of their time have attempted to comfort 'our human misery.' Some counsel the 'utility' of misery, others lean towards honour, others to 'sensual pleasures' in order to find a remedy for the diversity of miseries that continually assault us in this tumultuous life. These persons have discovered, however, that there is no 'felicity' in the human body apart from a 'tranquility of spirit'. De Tournes adds that, for each person attempting to achieve this goal of tranquility, 'it was necessary to read many diverse Authors in Greek and Latin, ancients as well as moderns'. The Lyon merchant printer explains to his 'Reader Friend' that he had contemplated bringing together a collection of these authors for publication and to this end he had already accumulated a fair number of entries when he received Isabella Sforza's treatise. '[A]fter having read, re-read, and savoured it, [it] seemed to me to be the only one in which the Author had reached the mark, where so many good souls (so I believe) would have worked in vain but [would] still not have known how to find or untie the knot that bound and held this rich treasure for us; so carefully have they searched and for so long'. Moreover, he praises the work of this virtuous lady who succeeds where so many 'learned' [men] had failed. As a merchant printer de Tournes sought to bring into the market a novelty: a collection of ancient and modern precepts translated into French exclusively for his press. De Tournes presents Sforza's book to the reader as beneficial not just in his judgment alone but also according to the 'gentz doctes', or learned people, he consulted before publication 'who had seen it and read it and corrected it for your utility and profit'.[63]

---

61 [Jean de Tournes], 'L'Imprimeur au lecteur', in Claude Paradin, *Quadrins historiques de la Bible* (Lyon: Jean de Tournes, 1555), sigs A5r–v.

62 For Jean de Tournes' participation in Lyon book fairs see 'Pièces justificatives', 1 June 1560 in Cartier, *et al.* (eds), *Bibliographie*, vol. I, pp. 142–3.

63 [Jean de Tournes], 'L'Imprimeur au Lecteur Benivole Salut … De Lyon ce 28. de Iuin, M.DXXXXVI', in Isabella Sforza, *De la vraye tranquilité de l'esprit* (Lyon: Jean de Tournes, 1546), pp. 2–4. On the possible authorship of this text by Ortensio Lando and his frequent use of female impersonations see Meredith Ray, 'Textual Collaboration and

One of the 'learned men' frequently consulted by Jean de Tournes was the editor and translator Antoine du Moulin, who entered the Lyon printer's employ in 1544 from a position as *valet de chambre* to Francis I's sister, the Queen of Navarre. Her circle extended to a number of literary men such as Pierre Boaistuau, Claude Gruget, Jacques Peletier du Mans and Nicolas Denisot (Le Conte d'Alsinois).[64] Claude Gruget provided regular translation services for the Parisian bookseller Vincent Sertenas. These writers, editors, translators, printers and publishers operated within a literate elite with strong connections of trade between Paris and Lyon, the two leading centres of French print. Antoine du Moulin, Gruget, Boaistuau and the merchant printers and booksellers Sertenas, Groulleau, the L'Angeliers and Jean de Tournes died in the 1550s and early 1560s carried off, in part, by a wave of the plague.[65] At times these learned men and printers competed with one another; at times they collaborated in order to secure the widest possible distribution and sale of their books.

Bookowners as Customers of Île de la Cité Booksellers

In 1536, working in the shadow of Nôtre Dame Cathedral, Denis Janot printed and sold *The Great Style and Protocol Manual of the Chancellerie of France* (*Le grant stille et prothocolle de la chancellerie de France*) following his father and grandmother the widow Jean Trepperel, who had collaborated to produce this style manual with the added attraction of the *Guide for Clerks* (*Guidon des sécretaires*) in the 1520s.[66] Janot also helped produce *Le grant coustumier de France* – a collection of French customary law. His 1544 catalogue advertised his printing of the 1539 *Royal Ordinances*.[67] Professionals such as lawyers (*avocats*) and attorneys (*procureurs*) working closely with the royal and judicial administration

Spiritual Partnership in Sixteenth-Century Italy: The Case of Ortensio Lando and Lucrezia Gonzaga', *Renaissance Quarterly* 62:3 (2009): 699–710.

[64] On Du Moulin's position see Lemaire de Belges, *Illustrations de Gaule*, title page; A. Cartier and Adolphe Chennevière, 'Bibliographie d'Antoine du Moulin', *Revue d'histoire littéraire de la France* 4 (1895): 475; on the editing of Marguerite de Navarre's *Heptaméron*, see Nicole Cazauran, 'Boaistuau et Gruget éditeurs de l'*Heptaméron*: à chacun sa part', *Travaux de littérature* 14 (2001): 149–69.

[65] Arnoul L'Angelier died in 1557; Sertenas' house was cleaned for the 'peste' after his death, 30 March 1562 [1563]; see Pichon and Vicaire, *Documents*, p. 128. De Tournes died of the plague in 1564. Gilles Corrozet died in 1568.

[66] Hélène Michaud, 'Les bibliothèques des secrétaires du roi au XVIe siècle', *Bibliothèque de l'Ecole des chartes* 126 (1968): 344, n. 13; Hélène Michaud, *La Grande Chancellerie et les écritures royales au seizième siècle (1515–1589)* (Paris, 1967), pp. 296–7, nn. 4–7.

[67] See Omont, *Catalogue*: *Coustumier de France*, cat. no. 19; *Les Ordonnances royaulx sur le faict de la justice*, cat. no. 69; *Guidon*, cat. no. 70; *Pratique*, cat. no. 37.

purchased these tools of the trade alongside the judges, masters of requests and notaries who held royal or civic offices.[68]

A typical example of a bookowner is Gilbert de Hodic, a notary at the Châtelet de Paris, a regional court. He owned the ordinances of the city of Paris, the 'first printing' of royal ordinances such as the one later advertised by the printer Denis Janot, the style guide to the 'chancellerie', the 'first printing' of the 'grand coustumier general' by Galiot du Pré and two 'prothocolles' for notaries.[69] We find these style and protocol guides among the books in the personal libraries of lawyers, legal clerks and judges (*conseillers*) in Parlement who died in the 1540s like Hodic.[70] Hodic was on the lower to middle rungs of the ladder to dignity above the wealthy merchants but below the officers in the sovereign courts. His 'professional' library was representative of this range of 'gens de justice' who tended to possess larger collections of books than any other occupational or social group.[71] Lawyers and judicial officeholders had school and university education and were more likely to own legal and classical texts in Latin. Notaries had school and some vocational training, while merchants probably had some schooling and training from a 'master writer'.

Apart from the titles useful to help him carry out his office, Hodic's collection indicates an interest in religious questions and many of the 'theology' titles are in Latin. Of more importance for our study, in October 1549 when the Palais de Justice bookseller Galiot du Pré was asked by the notaries to assess the worth of Hodic's substantial library of 400 volumes, he found many of the books of 'grammar', 'humanities' and 'histories' and others in 'vulgar French' that we shall encounter throughout this book. Hodic must have perused the boutique of Corrozet in the marketplace of the Palais de Justice or Janot's shop on rue Neuve Nôtre Dame to buy Corrozet's moral emblem book the *Hecatomgraphie* as well as Corrozet's guidebook to the French capital the *Antiquitez de Paris*. On questions of human nature, Hodic could have read his copy of Philippe Béroalde's *On Human Felicity* (*De la felicité humaine*), which Janot published in an in-octavo edition in 1543, or the *Livre de la police humaine* published by Charles L'Angelier.[72]

---

68 Robert Descimon, 'Les notaires de Paris du XVIe au XVIIe siècle: office, profession, archives', in Michel Cassan (ed.), *Offices et officiers 'moyens' en France à l'époque moderne: Profession, culture* (Limoges, 2004), p. 22.

69 MC, AN, Paris, post-mortem inventory of Gilbert de Hodic, notary, 21 October 1549, III, 300, fo. 32v.

70 See for example MC, AN, Paris, the post-mortem inventories of Nicole Duvivier, lawyer at the Parlement, 19 March 1543/44, LXXXVI, 89; Jehanne Charpentier, wife of Pierre Boucher, a clerk in the Cour des aides, 2 October 1544, VI, 68; Damoiselle Gabrielle Coutel, wife of Jean Texier, judge (*conseiller*) at Parlement, 18 August 1546, LXXXVI, 92.

71 Albert Labarre, *Le livre dans la vie amiénoise du seizième siècle: l'enseignement des inventaires après décès, 1503–1576* (Paris, 1971), pp. 112–15, 139–42.

72 Gilles d'Aurigny, *Le livre de police humaine contenant briefve decription de plusieurs choses dignes de memoire: si comme du gouvernement d'un Royaume, & de toute*

For a conduct book of advice on how to live and die well, Hodic could turn to *The Ship of Princes* or *La Nef des princes* first published in Lyon in 1502 and later in Paris in 1525.[73] Several popular titles by Pierre Gringore exploring tales of vice and virtue such as the *Short Speeches of Mother Fool* (*Menus propos de la mere sotte*), the first book printed by Denis Janot circa 1529, the *Fantasies of Mother Fool* as well as the *Adages* were all available from Janot's rue Neuve Nôtre Dame address and could be found in multiple copies in Hodic's library. Hodic also possessed other 'popular' versions of classical works sold by Janot and advertised in his catalogue such as the two copies Seneca's *Golden Words on the Four Cardinal Virtues* known as the *Mots dorez* as well as an abridged version of Valerius Maximus, the 'epitome de Valere'.

The inventory listed two copies of *On the True Tranquility of the Soul* (*De la vraye tranquilité de l'esprit*) on human nature and moral questions, a translation from Italian recommended and sold by Jean de Tournes in Lyon in two editions in 1546 and 1549 and perhaps available at the stall of Charles L'Angelier who stocked some of de Tournes' titles. Other translations from Italian included Castiglione's *Courtier*, as well as Speroni's dialogue *On the Care of the Household* packaged with the 'dialogue on the dignity of women' and Plutarch's precepts of marriage available from Arnoul L'Angelier at the Palais de Justice or Jean de Tournes in Lyon.[74]

Hodic's collection was rich in *Querelle des femmes* literature, comprising Boccaccio's 'des cleres dames', the collection of tales of famous women published by Antoine Verard in Paris in 1493 or in a new octavo edition available from the L'Angelier brothers from 1538.[75] Other titles included a *legende des femmes*, a *Praise of Women* (*Louange des femmes*) and *The Book of Distaffs* or *Le livre des quenouilles* in which a group of old women tell old wives' tales and discuss marriage, husbands, children and remedies among other things.[76] His copy of 'les

---

administration de la Republique, ou son assemblés par un receuil succinct, maintes belles sentences d'historiens & philosophes divers propos & faictz d'hommes prudens qui est une œuvre veritablement beau noble & excellent fort necesaire à toutes gens (Paris: Charles L'Angelier, 1544), and again 1546, 1549; Hodic inventory, 1549, III, 300, MC, AN, Paris, fos 30v–31r.

[73] Symphorien Champier [and Robert de Balsac], *La Nef des princes et des batailles de noblesse ... et aultres enseignemens utilz et proffitables à toutes manières de gens pour congnoistre à bien vivre et mourir ... Le régime d'ung jeune prince et les proverbes des prïnces et aultres petitz livres très utilz et proffitables, lesquelz ont esté composez par maistre Simphorien Champier* (Paris: Le Noir, 1525) or (Lyon: Guillaume Balsarin, 1502); MC, AN, Paris, Hodic inventory, 1549, III, 300, fo. 30r.

[74] MC, AN, Paris, Hodic inventory, 1549, III, 300, fos 30v, 31v, 32v.

[75] Giovanni Boccaccio, *Le Livre de Jehan Bocasse de la louenge et vertu des nobles et cleres dames* (Paris: Antoine Vérard, 1493); Giovanni Boccaccio, *Le plaisant livre de noble homme Jehan Bocace, poète florentin, auquel il traicte des faictz et gestes des illustres et cleres dames* (Paris: Arnoul and Charles les Angelliers frères, 1538); MC, AN, Paris, Hodic inventory, 1549, III, 300, fo. 31r.

[76] MC, AN, Paris, Hodic inventory, 1549, III, 300, fos 30v, 31r, 32v.

louenges de marraige' was probably a work by Erasmus entitled the *Declamation of Praises of Marriage* published in Lyon in 1525 or it might have been Pierre de Lesnauderie's *Praise of Marriage and the Collection of Histories of Good, Virtuous and Illustrious Women* printed in Paris in the 1520s by Denis Janot and Galiot du Pré among others.[77] Hodic also owned the translation from Latin of Juan Luis Vives' *Instruction of the Christian Woman*, which he could have purchased from a number of sources, including the four editions printed by Jean de Tournes in the 1540s or the copies produced by Denis Janot's print workshop (managed by his recently bereaved widow) for the Palais de Justice bookstall of Galiot du Pré in 1545.[78] Hodic collected two copies of the *Familiar and Invective Letters of Madame Helisenne* available from Janot's press in 1539 in which the female writer Hélisenne de Crenne takes up the *Querelle* with a fictional male foe.[79] Among Hodic's possessions the bookseller Galiot du Pré found the classic *Querelle des femmes* text – the *Roman de la Rose* – stocked by many booksellers including the L'Angelier brothers and du Pré himself. Hodic also seems to have been a fan of Rabelais as he owned *Gargantua* as well as the *Third Book of Pantagruel* (*Le Tiers livre*) in which Panurge debates whether or not he should marry. Hodic owned two copies of La Borderie's *Amye de Court*, shared by Janot with Vincent Sertenas and Gilles Corrozet in 1542. He possessed the *Anatomical Praises* or *Blasons anatomiques*, a book in praise of all the parts of the body with accompanying woodcuts, first published in 1543 under privilege to Charles L'Angelier, and advertised by Janot in his catalogue. A book noted in the inventory rather ambiguously as 'le sexe feminin' could be Agrippa's groundbreaking work on the *Nobility and Pre-Excellence of the Feminine Sex* printed by Denis Janot in the 1530s and advertised in his catalogue.[80]

Hodic could have purchased his copy of Bouchet's *Triumphs of the Noble Lady* (*Triumphes de la noble dame*) from any of this circle of Palais de Justice or Île de la Cité printers and booksellers including the L'Angelier brothers.[81]

---

[77] Desiderius Erasmus, *Déclamation des louenges de mariage* [attribution to Paris: Simon Dubois, 1525]; Pierre de Lesnauderie, *La Louenge de mariage et recueil des hystoires des bonnes, vertueuses et illustres femmes* (Paris: F. Regnault, 1523) or (Paris: Pierre Sergent, 1523) or (Paris: Denis Janot, no date) or (Paris: Galiot du Pré, 1527); Hodic inventory, 1549, III, 300, MC, AN, Paris, fo. 31r.

[78] Juan Luis Vives, *L'Institution de la femme chrestienne. Tant en son Enfance, que Mariage, & Viduité. Avec l'office du Mary* (Paris: Denis Janot for Galiot du Pré, 1545), in-16; Cartier, *et al.* (eds), *Bibliographie*, vol. I, cat. nos. 15 (1543), 45 (1545), 106 (1547), 155 (1549); MC, AN, Paris, Hodic inventory, 1549, III, 300 fo. 31v.

[79] MC, AN, Paris, Hodic inventory, 1549, III, 300, fos 31r, 32v.

[80] S.M. Bouchereaux, 'Recherches bibliographiques sur Gilles Corrozet', *Bulletin du bibliophile* (1948): 324, 326; Omont, *Catalogue*, p. 1; MC, AN, Paris, Hodic inventory, 1549, III, 300, fos 30r, 31r, 32r.

[81] MC, AN, Paris, Hodic inventory, 1549, III, 300, fo. 31r, J. Renouard, 'L'Officine des L'Angelier', p. 344.

Similarly, the notary's copy of Antonio Guevara's *On Contempt for the Court and On the Praise of Rustic Life* (*Mépris de la court*) or his *Orloge des princes* could have been purchased from several booksellers including Denis Janot or Charles L'Angelier.[82]

Gilbert de Hodic entrusted his widow Geneviève Bureau with the role of executor of his will and she became tutor to their five children. Although she did not sign the inventory, midway through the sixteenth century it was customary for notaries but not for witnesses to affix their signatures to the document.[83] The couple lived on the rue du Mouton near the Hôtel de Ville, a short walk from Châtelet de Paris where Hodic held his office. In one of the rooms the inventory takers found on a little table 50 volumes of books in French worth more than five *livres tournois* or almost 2 *écus* that Hodic's widow 'declared to be for her use'. Thus in their city residence she owned about one-tenth as many books as her husband. The titles of Bureau's books remain unspecified, but the 50 books in her Parisian home were not the only ones available to her. The widow owned another residence in her own name – 'appartenant de son propre' – in the village of Courcelles where she showed the notaries which goods and possessions belonged to 'the said inheritance'. Here she had access to another 30 books of various kinds. In Geneviève Bureau's country house the couple could read second copies of the *Roman de la Rose*, Rabelais' *Gargantua*, Guevara's *Mépris de la court* and the *Adages of Mother Fool* printed by Denis Janot and sold in front of Nôtre Dame Cathedral. As a good housewife, Geneviève Bureau might consult the manual for grafting vines and trees or a second manual on the 'art' of sowing and making a garden nursery. For more serious study she might read Erasmus' *Complaint of Peace* of 1525 or turn her attentions to the family's third copy of Marguerite de Navarre's *Mirror of the Sinful Soul*.[84] In Bureau's country residence the couple could read the *Art of Living Well and of Dying Well*.[85] Coquillart's *The New Laws with the Debate of Ladies and of Arms*, published in the 1490s by Denis Janot's grandmother and several decades later by one of Janot's collaborators on the rue Neuve Nôtre Dame, provided some satirical and pseudo-legal advice on a variety of matters including whether a wife was allowed to take revenge on an abusive

82 MC, AN, Paris, Hodic inventory, 1549, III, 300, fo. 29r.

83 Florence Greffe and Valérie Brousselle, 'Introduction', in F. Greffe and V. Brouselle (eds), *Documents du Minutier central des notaires de Paris: Inventaires après décès (1547–1560)* (Paris, 1997), p. 10.

84 Desiderius Erasmus, *Complainte de la paix*, trans. Louis de Berquin (Lyon: P. de Vingle, c. 1531); MC, AN, Paris, Hodic inventory, 1549, III, 300: 'Le mirouer de l'ame pecheresse, fo. 27v, 'Le mirouer de la Royne de Navarre', fo. 28r, also 'Le mirouer dor de l'ame pecheresse', fo. 28v.

85 Guillaume Tardif, *Le livre intitulé l'art de bien vivre et de bien mourir* (Paris: for Antoine Verard, 1496) and (Lyon, no date).

husband.[86] By the time that the widow Geneviève Bureau died in 1556, only 24 books could be found at the Courcelles property, about six fewer than when her husband died, but no titles are given apart from the mention of two pairs of books of hours.[87]

Geneviève Bureau was one of the many wives of officeholding administrators who were potential readers and consumers at the bookstalls on the Île de la Cité in the courtyard of the Palais de Justice and in front of Nôtre Dame Cathedral. Booksellers were not unaware of this target market of female readers. In Christine de Pisan's *Treasure of the City of Ladies*, which Denis Janot printed for Jehan André in 1536, André the bookseller exhorts his female readers – the 'Virtuous hearts of feminine grace' – to appreciate this treasure of 'praiseworthy sentences'. Then he adds a bit of publicity for his shop:

> You now have in your view
> A great treasure on sale for you
> For little money Jehan André presents it
> To every one who comes and opens it.
>
> *Or avez vous en veue maintenant*
> *Ung grand tresor qui vous est mis en vante*
> *Pour peu d'argent Iehan André le presente*
> *Qui l'a ouvert à ung chascun venant.*[88]

Geneviève Bureau's social circle and family included a lawyer brother in the Parlement de Paris. Two of her sons held offices at the Châtelet de Paris, another became a clerk in the prévôté of Meaux, and a fourth entered the clergy. Her daughter Madeleine married a lawyer in Parlement who also held an office as the deputy or substitute to the *procureur général du roi* in the Parisian Cour des aides. For this type of family the inventories typically reveal a husband with a 'cabinet' or 'study' full of professional books for his office and some books for leisure or devotion.

Yet there are some clues that Geneviève Bureau may have had access to the books in her husband's study beyond the titles she declared to be for her own use.

---

86 Guillaume Coquillart, *Les droitz nouveaulx, avec le débat des dames et des armes* (Paris: Veufve Jehan Trepperell, c. 1499) and (Paris: Alain Lotrian, no date).

87 MC, AN, Paris, Post-mortem inventory of Geneviève Bureau, widow of Gilbert de Hodic, 15 September 1556, III, 307.

88 'Advertissement Aux Lecteurs', in *Le Trésor de la cité des dames, selon dame Christine de la cité de Pise, livre tresutile & prouffitable pour l'introduction des roynes, dames, princesses, & autres femmes de tous estatz, auquel elles pourront veoir la grande & saine richesse de toute prudence, saigesse, honeur, & dignité dedans contenues* (Paris: Denis Janot for Jehan André, 1536).

Nestled in with Xenophon's *Economy*, a treatise on governing the household,[89] could be found a translation of Plutarch's treatise on the education of children entitled 'la nourriture des enfans' and available from the boutique of Vincent Sertenas in the late 1530s.[90] There was a manual on jam-making, the 'Manière de faire confiture', and a cookbook, a 'livre de cuisine'. Among the books in Hodic's study, the inventory listed some intriguing manuals on making women's cosmetics and lotions (with recipes and advice on medical treatments for children) such as the *Source of Honour to Maintain Corporal Elegance for Ladies*[91] *and the Decoration of Human Nature and the Ornament of Women.*[92] Without annotations on a copy of a book owned by the Hodic–Bureau household or the rare find of a commonplace notebook or reading journal we can never really know what books the couple may have read, but it is tempting to imagine Hodic or his wife with access to these *Querelle des femmes* books, debates on marriage and moral guides to leading a virtuous life and fleeing vice, advice on achieving dignity and avoiding misery. Someone in the Hodic–Bureau household wandered through the bookstalls in front of Nôtre Dame Cathedral and in the marketplace of the Palais de Justice in the 1530s and 1540s and took home many of these titles on human nature.

Tracing the distribution networks of merchant printers and booksellers in Paris and Lyon creates an understanding of the alliances by which those working in the print trade ensured the widest possible circulation of their books. The editorial policies and marketing strategies of Denis Janot and Vincent Sertenas active in Paris or Jean de Tournes in Lyon become evident from their stock, their promotional catalogues or their acquisition of royal privileges to print and distribute certain texts, and their attempts to reach the potential customer directly with a prefatory letter. At times the holder of the royal privilege associated with other printers and booksellers to disseminate a title; at times these collaborators became rivals when they packaged dialogues for the niche *Querelle des femmes* market or placed these

---

89 Xenophon, *Science pour senrichir honnestement et facilement, intitulee Leconomic Xenophon* (Paris: Geoffroy Tory, 1531).

90 Plutarch, *Le liure de plutarche de leducation & nourriture des enfans* (Paris: Vincent Sertenas, [1537]), or it might possibly have been the second half of a treatise on discipline and moral behaviour available from Denis Janot, which included a translation of Plutarch's treatise on the upbringing of children and featured the woodcut in Figure 1.1. Antoine Du Saix, *L'Esperon de discipline pour inciter les humains aux bonnes lettres ... en laquelle est traicté de la nourriture et instruction des enfans* (Paris: Denis Janot, 1538), see Introduction, p. 22; MC, AN, Paris, Hodic inventory, 1549, III, 300, fo. 31r.

91 Olivier de la Marche, *La Source d'honneur, pour maintenir la corporelle élégance des dames en vigueur fleurissant et pris inextimable, avec une belle épistre d'une noble dame à son seigneur et amy* (Lyon: Romain Morin, 1531); MC, AN, Paris, Hodic inventory, 1549, III, 300, fo. 31r.

92 Andre Le Fournier, *La décoration d'humaine nature, et aornement des dames. Compile et extraict des tres excellens docteurs et plus expers medecins* (Paris: Jehan Sainct Denys and Jehan Longis, 1530); MC, AN, Paris, Hodic inventory, 1549, III, 300, fo. 32r.

same dialogues within a broader context of moral philosophy as the translator underlined their interest for those wishing to argue on both sides of a question.

Turning from distribution to content, chapters three and four examine the ideas, examples and commonplaces of literature of the dignity and misery of man and the *Querelle des femmes*. Some of the titles, such as *De la vraye tranquilité*, Speroni's *De la dignité des femmes*, the works of Hélisenne de Crenne, Mexia's *Diverses leçons*, Boaistuau's treatises on the dignity and misery of man, traced through the printing networks in this chapter or found among the hundreds of volumes in the households of the notary Gilbert de Hodic and his wife in the late 1540s to 1550s, will be examined in more detail in chapters three through six.

Chapter 3
The Dignity and Misery of Man … and of Woman

This chapter compares the literature of the *Querelle des femmes* with the printed works on the dignity and misery of man and examines how these debates borrowed, imitated and exchanged many of the same commonplaces. By investigating both dignity and misery, we overcome the tendency of intellectual historians to present the Renaissance as a period of optimism with opportunities for the man of greatness.[1] This juxtaposition also allows for a consideration of the *Querelle des femmes* outside of the usual framework of early feminism rising against misogyny. Renaissance writers were quite comfortable shifting from praise to blame and back again, emphasising contradictions and paradoxes. When the debates are understood as part of a rhetorical tradition accentuating both positive and negative sides of an argument and exploring opposing voices, we emerge with a much better-rounded understanding of ideas of both man and woman in Renaissance France.

These ideas had roots in the social realities of sixteenth-century France, in particular the concerns with rank and marriage. The printed works on the pursuit of virtue and the avoidance of vice, on the dignity and misery of man and of woman, resonated with and played on the tensions about status and reputation in the 1500s. The *Querelle des femmes* has been acknowledged as an airing of anxieties about women, especially women as wives.[2] The woman discussed in the *Querelle* is often a wife, whether the ideal woman providing the comfort one might desire in a companion or the adulterous woman a groom might fear. A bachelor like Rabelais' Panurge in the *Tiers livre* debates whether or not he should marry. 'But what if my wife … made me a cuckold … this would be enough to make me exceed the bounds of patience'. When his friend Pantagruel therefore advises Panurge not to marry, the bachelor begins to wonder what he might miss if he gives up the possibility of marriage. 'But surely, in my state, freed [of any obligations] and unmarried … I have no one to care for me so and to bear me such love, that one calls conjugal love'. And so Pantagruel changes his advice. Owners of the *Tiers livre* such as the Parisian notary Gilbert de Hodic and his wife Geneviève Bureau, who obtained the book at some point between its initial publication in 1546 and

---

1 Gene Brucker, 'The Italian Renaissance', in Guido Ruggiero (ed.), *A Companion to the Worlds of the Renaissance* (Oxford, 2002), pp. 23–6.

2 Evelyne Berriot-Salvadore, *Les femmes dans la société française de la Renaissance* (Geneva, 1990), pp. 15–16, 30; Constance Jordan, *Renaissance Feminism: Literary Texts and Political Models* (Ithaca, NY, 1990), p. 12.

Hodic's death in 1549, could follow Panurge's debate with Pantagruel weighing the ups and downs of marriage and the probability of making a good match.[3] The *Querelle des femmes* raised questions about a wife's conduct, her ability to run the household, educate virtuous children and enhance the family's reputation, honour and social networks.

By contrast there has been little recognition that the dignity- and misery-of-man literature reflected a similar concern about the male head of the household whose status defined the place of his family in the social hierarchy. The humanist ethos aimed at achieving dignity or nobility by 'working ceaselessly for virtue', as one scholar phrased it in the sixteenth century when dedicating an edition to a prince of the blood.[4] Whether in learning or through actions and deeds, an effort to improve one's self was encouraged for the prince, the noble head of household or the aspiring *bourgeois*. Conversely, not everyone managed to improve the rank of the family and household, some stagnated and simply maintained their positions or watched those around them rise or fall. Heads of household attempted to protect their posterity against misfortune, while manoeuvring to improve the status of the next generation.

The Social Consequences of Dignity and Misery

As we saw in the Introduction, the early Valois kings Francis I and Henry II expanded the officeholding opportunities in the royal administration. Several generations of merchants could purchase their way into the nobility of the robe through investment in an office, a landed estate and education to ensure the success of their children in the next generation. A strategic marriage was as important at the level of the artisan, such as a journeyman in a print workshop hoping to become a master printer, as it was to the *bourgeois* who hoped to enter the service of king and state with a venal or purchased office.[5] It could be argued that marriage

[3] François Rabelais, *Le Tiers livre des faicts et dicts héroïques du bon Pantagruel*, in Guy Demerson (ed.), *Œuvres complètes* (Paris, 1973), pp. 400–401; Minutier central des notaires de Paris, Archives nationales, Paris [hereafter MC, AN, Paris], post-mortem inventory of Gilbert de Hodic, notary, 21 October 1549, III, 300, fo. 32r.

[4] Antoine du Moulin, 'À tresillustre, treshaut et tresvertueux prince, Monseigneur Antoine de Bourbon duc de Vendosme, Antoine [du Moulin] son treshumble & tresobeissant serviteur, salut & prosperité', in Jean Lemaire de Belges, *Les Illustrations de Gaule et singularitez de Troye* (Lyon: Jean de Tournes, 1549), sig. * 2v. An alternative interpretation suggests that the 'dignité de l'homme commande le discours politique qui justifie et légitime la hiérarchie' – Jean-Luc Martinet, *Montaigne et la dignité humaine: contribution à une histoire du discours de la dignité humaine* (Paris, 2007), pp. 108–9.

[5] Jonathan Dewald, *The Formation of a Provincial Nobility: The Magistrates of the Parlement de Rouen 1499–1610* (Princeton, NJ, 1980), esp. ch. 6; Barbara Diefendorf, *Paris City Councillors in the Sixteenth Century: The Politics of Patrimony* (Princeton, NJ, 1983).

alliances became even more crucial to chances for success and advancement once the opportunities to purchase an office began to diminish in the mid- to late sixteenth century. While city councils or municipal offices might remain open as paths to service and power, fewer families had access to the highest royal offices from the 1540s because of the possibility of resigning a post and passing it on to a son, son-in-law or nephew to keep it within the family. If sons could not advance family fortunes, they might be able to maintain the status of their fathers or fathers-in-law or after 1604 inherit a post, subject to the annual fee called the *paulette*.[6] Even at the apex of *parlementaire* power, the combination of blood and marriage enhanced chances for success. In 1582 Achille de Harlay, the son of a former *premier président* or Chief Justice of the Parlement de Paris, replaced his father-in-law Christophe de Thou as *premier président*.[7] A good marriage might provide riches as well as status. As a seventeenth-century presiding judge at the Parlement of Rouen wrote of his predecessor: 'He was very wealthy, both in his own right, through his mother and paternal grandmother, and by right of his two wives, and he enjoyed great credit in Rouen in the minds of the populace'.[8]

But it was not all onward and upward to the top of the pyramid. Some judges had to sell their positions to cover debts, while other officeholding families were ruined by the debts incurred to obtain royal office and the expenditure on household servants, education of children, dowries and land required to maintain that social position.[9] Others preferred to remain in a liberal profession as lawyers or *procureurs* (attorneys), or keep the free status of a merchant without ever seeking office. Some never managed to get a foothold with a royal or civic office and stagnated as the situation changed over the course of the century. Entry to the Parlement de Paris as a lawyer had been considered a 'social trampoline' in the mid-sixteenth century, but by the early 1600s the opportunities for jumping from lawyer to officeholder in the judiciary or administration were limited, expensive and mostly gained through inheritance.[10] Nobles from birth who served the king in the traditional military

---

6 Dewald, *Provincial Nobility*, pp. 157–8; Sara Beam, 'The "basoche" and the "bourgeoisie seconde": Careerists at the Parlement of Paris during the League', *French History* 17:4 (2003): 372–5; see the debate in *French History* 17:4 (2003), articles by Hilary Bernstein, Mack Holt, Robert Descimon and Beam.

7 Étienne Pasquier, 'A Monseigneur de Harlay Conseiller d'Estat, & premier President en la Cour de Parlement de Paris. Il congratule Monsieur le Premier president de sa promotion en cest estat', in *Les Lettres d'Estienne Pasquier conseiller et advocat general du roy en la Chambre des comptes de Paris* (Paris: Abel L'Angelier, 1586), VII:7, fo. 206r. Achille de Harlay (1536–1616), son of a previous president Christophe de Harlay, had married Catherine the daughter of his predecessor Christophe de Thou; see also Étienne Pasquier, *Lettres familières*, ed. Dorothy Thickett (Geneva, 1974), p. 403.

8 Dewald, *Provincial Nobility*, p. 246.

9 Ibid., pp. 157, 241–3.

10 Marie Houllemare, 'Un avocat parisien entre art oratoire et promotion de soi (fin XVIe siècle)', *Revue historique* 306:2 (2004): 301.

capacity and high-ranking royal officers such as Admiral Chabot and Chancellor Poyet experienced spectacular falls from grace.[11] Those in royal service seem to have been more immune to the vagaries of fortune than the merchant branches of families who did not seek the patronage of the king or a place in his administration and subsequently experienced bankruptcy and decline.[12] Consequently, there were several paths to power, to ruin or to stagnation.

Descimon has noted how the 'different concepts of civil nobility were not mutually exclusive' and has likened them to the 'voices of a musical composition'.[13] Families stressed both virtue and the hereditary qualities of *race* or bloodline in the *livres de raison* and genealogies kept by the male head of the household to record births and deaths of kin. Davis argues that families probably held 'contradictory' beliefs in virtue through effort and the inherent qualities of their stock – a tension between an ethos of upward mobility and the 'defense of position and privilege'.[14] This sense of overlapping concepts, or 'contradictory' beliefs, might help us to understand how Renaissance writers could argue for both the misery and the dignity of man and of woman.

As we know from the discussion in the Introduction, the Renaissance idea of dignity was a status to be achieved through virtue and duty, but *dignitas* in sixteenth-century France also contained the 'ambiguous' and perhaps 'conflictual' notion of place within the social hierarchy.[15] For those not born near the top of the hierarchy, the dignity of noble status conferred to a husband or son by a purchased or venal office was then maintained or improved by family efforts or through marriage alliances over several generations. Husbands or wives could tarnish family honour, but the loss of status held by a male head of household could affect the entire family. The consequences of the dignity of social position or misery of a loss of fortune for the family provide a further reason why we need to examine

[11] Félix Aubert, 'Le Parlement de Paris au XVIe siècle', *Nouvelle revue historique de droit français et étranger* 29 (1905): 747–51; Étienne Pasquier, 'Du procez extraordinaire fait, premierement à Messire Philippe Chabot Admiral de France, puis à Messire Guillaume Pouyet Chancelier', in *Des recherches de la France*, in *Les Œuvres d'Étienne Pasquier*, 2 vols (Amsterdam, 1723), vol. I, Bk VI, ch. 9, cols. 549–52.

[12] Robert Descimon, 'The "bourgeoise seconde": Social Differentiation in the Parisian Municipal Oligarchy in the Sixteenth Century, 1500–1610', *French History* 17:4 (2003): 399, 406, 412, 414; on the 'social decline' of lawyers and the resulting tensions with royal officeholders, see Miriam Yardeni, 'L'ordre des avocats et la grève du Barreau parisien en 1602', *Revue d'histoire économique et sociale* 44 (1966): 490–93.

[13] Robert Descimon, 'The Birth of the Nobility of the Robe: Dignity versus Privilege in the Parlement de Paris, 1500–1700', in Michael Wolfe (ed.), *Changing Identities in Early Modern France* (Durham, NC, 1997), pp. 95, 115.

[14] See N.Z. Davis, 'Ghosts, Kin and Progeny: Some Features of Family Life in Early Modern France', *Dædalus* 106 (1977): 98.

[15] Robert Descimon, 'Un langage de la dignité. La qualification des personnes dans la société parisienne de l'époque moderne', in Fanny Cosandey (ed.), *Dire et vivre l'ordre social en France sous l'Ancien Régime* (Paris, 2005), pp. 75–6.

the commonplaces, contradictions and paradoxes of the nature of man alongside the discussion of woman's nature in the *Querelle des femmes*.

The Dignity of Man

The dignity of man assumed man's natural superiority to animals and the rest of creation. Isabella Sforza explains in her chapter 'On the Excellence and Dignity of Man' how God made man surpass all other animals in worthiness and 'subjected everything to him by means of [human] reason'.[16] Yet there was room for man to strive for perfection, reach for the heavens and share with God in the divine. The reader of French Renaissance dignity-of-man literature repeatedly encounters the idea that, although every person possesses a human form, some do not develop to a level of dignity or wisdom. Worse still, others become less than human and, through idleness or pursuit of their appetites, they descend to the level of beasts. Each person has the capacity to ascend the chain of being to the level of the divine or descend to the base level of the earth.

The *Ship of Princes*, first published in 1502, advertised on its title page that it contained 'many useful and profitable teachings for all sorts of people to know how to live and die well'. The book explains that God created man to be capable of virtue, prudence and learning. In the section on the 'government and regime of a young prince', Symphorien Champier suggests that 'imprudent and willfully malicious men, incorrigible and without learning are not at all true men – *vrays hommes* – rather [they] are almost monsters of nature'. Champier argues that some individuals 'are more capable of virtue and wisdom than others', but it is rare to find one so 'depraved' that he is not capable of some knowledge or learning. Champier emphasises the effort required by each human. It is the 'exercise' or practice of one's learning combined with one's gifts from nature that allow one to achieve the 'perfection of our souls and eternal happiness'.[17] Charles de Bovelles' *Of Wisdom* (*Liber de sapiente*), written in 1509, explains how Nature provides every human (*homini*) with being, life, sensation and reason (*substantia, vita, sensus, ratio*). Hence every human has the capacity to exist, live, feel and

---

16 Isabella Sforza, *De la vraye tranquilité de l'esprit* (Lyon: Jean de Tournes, 1546), p. 6; on Ortensio Lando as the possible author and his connection to the *Querelle des femmes*, see Meredith Ray, 'Textual Collaboration and Spiritual Partnership in Sixteenth-Century Italy: The Case of Ortensio Lando and Lucrezia Gonzaga', *Renaissance Quarterly* 62:3 (2009): 699–710, and Francine Daenens, 'Isabella Sforza: Beyond the Stereotype', in Letizia Panizza, (ed.), *Women in Italian Renaissance Culture and Society* (Oxford, 2000), pp. 35–7.

17 Symphorien Champier [and Robert de Balsac], *La Nef des princes et de batailles de noblesse avec aultres enseignemens utilz et profitables a toutes manieres de gens pour cognoistre bien vivre et mourir* (Lyon: Guillaume Balsarin, 1502), fos xii^{v}–xiii^{v}; MC, AN, Paris, Hodic inventory, 1549, III, 300, fo. 30r.

Figure 3.1 'The levels of being', Charles de Bovelles, *Of Wisdom* (*Liber de sapiente*) (Paris: Henri Estienne, 1510), courtesy of the Houghton Library, Harvard University (Houghton f FC5 B6624 510q).

understand.[18] Despite sharing the same exterior form, some men only manage to realise a fraction of the capabilities at their disposal; some men simply exist and never reach the level of reason or understanding. At the lowest level of being man exists in sloth, inert like a rock. If he proceeds to the next step of life, man reaches a vegetable or plantlike state or, as we might say today, he becomes like a 'couch potato', absorbing food and drink without restraint or thought. If man adds sensation and feeling, he reaches the level of being of beasts and might be so tempted by luxuries or sensual pleasures that he never reaches the ultimate state of reason. Not surprisingly, Bovelles' book depicts the third level of being as a woman staring into her mirror and therefore in danger of revelling in her vanity and sensuality.

To be fully human was an act of self-perfection and it was through self-knowledge, or knowledge of the soul, that man came to know all things in the world. He encompassed all the lesser states of being – mineral, vegetable and animal – and through his reason and intellect man could also 'embrace' the higher states of being such as the divine, the angels, the heavens.[19] As a result, man – the sum of all the elements in the universe – represented a *microcosm*, a little world or *petit monde*.[20] In Étienne Pasquier's dialogue the *Monophile*, published from the 1550s through to the 1570s, one of the speakers suggests that man is a 'little world' as if an 'image of the universe'.[21]

Not only did man 'contain' or 'comprise' all the elements in the world, his very existence made him the *vinculum mundi* or link between the heavenly world and the earthly world. God's breath of the soul into Adam uplifted the body He had created from the vile dust of the earth. Through his divine spirit God linked man to the heavens.[22] In the *Institutes of the Christian Religion* Jean Calvin suggests

---

18 Charles de Bovelles [Carolus Bovillus], *Liber de sapiente*, in *Que hoc volumine continentur: Liber de intellectu; Liber de sensu; Liber de nichilo; Ars oppositorum insuper mathematicum opus quadripartitum: De numeris perfecti* (Paris: Henri Estienne, 1510); Charles de Bovelles, *Liber de sapiente / Le livre du sage*, ed. P. Magnard (Paris, 1982), p. 57.

19 Bovelles, *De sapiente*, pp. 160–61, 165; Emmanuel Faye, 'De la dignité de l'homme selon Charles de Bovelles', in Pierre Magnard (ed.), *La dignité de l'homme* (Paris, 1995), pp. 132–3.

20 Pierre de la Primaudaye, *Academie françoise, en laquelle il est traité de l'institution des moeurs et de ce qui concerne le bien & heureusement viure en tous estats & conditions: Par les preceptes de la doctrine & les exemples de la vie des anciens sages, & hommes illustres*, 4th edn (Lyon: Jean Veirat, 1591), fos 10r–v or sigs b2r–v; Jill Kraye, 'Moral Philosophy', in Charles Schmitt and Quentin Skinner (eds), *The Cambridge History of Renaissance Philosophy* (Cambridge, 1988), pp. 312–14. Kraye traces the topos from its Aristotelian origin in the phrase mikros kosmos through to its use by fifteenth-century Italian humanists Marsilio Ficino and Pico della Mirandola when Pico gave the topos a new slant by allowing that because man had no particular being he was free to fashion himself.

21 Pasquier, 'Le premier livre du Monophile', in *Œuvres*, vol. II, 713C–D.

22 Eugene Rice stresses that the Greek Church Fathers Gregory of Nyssa, Nemesius of Emesa and Origen encouraged the themes of man as a microcosm and as *vinculum*

that the ancient philosophers had good reason to call man a 'petit monde', because he is the 'chef-d'œuvre' through which 'one contemplates the power, goodness and wisdom of God'.[23]

According to Charles Trinkaus and Eugenio Garin, the Italian dignity-of-man tradition dropped the notion of man as a microcosm in favour of the Old Testament story of man's creation in God's image and likeness.[24] Vernacular writers in France continued to popularise the topos of man as the little world, often combining it with the story of the creation of man in God's image or man's redemption in Christ. Maurice Scève, the Lyon poet, combined these elements in his long poem about the creation of Adam and Eve entitled the *Microcosm*, printed posthumously by his friend Jean de Tournes in 1562. Adam, the microcosm, narrates a dream about the future to his companion Eve and foresees how God will forgive their sin by sending His son to the world. Christ's life of faith will 'restore' man to God.[25]

In *The Week or Creation of the World* (*La sepmaine ou creation du monde*), first published in 1578, Guillaume Saluste, Sieur du Bartas, remarks: 'Within us can be seen fire, air, earth and the waves of the sea / In brief, man is nothing but an abridgement of the world'.[26] The Palais de Justice bookseller Abel L'Angelier obtained the privilege for *La sepmaine* and issued it six times in the early 1580s. The editor of the stunning 1583 in-quarto edition remarked that the copy in the reader's hands counted as the twentieth in three years – an exaggeration, but the work was undoubtedly popular.[27] Indeed the *Sepmaine*, often twinned with Du Bartas' epic poem on Judith's triumph over Holofernes, can be found in large and small formats in many Parisian private libraries at the end of the sixteenth century. Two men frequenting the Palais de Justice, one as a lawyer and the other as an officeholder in the Chambre des comptes, possessed in-quarto editions of the type sold by L'Angelier.[28] Due to the book's warm reception, the editor Simon

---

mundi – see 'The Renaissance Idea of Christian Antiquity: Humanist Patristic Scholarship', in Albert Rabil (ed.), *Renaissance Humanism: Foundations, Forms, and Legacy*, 3 vols (Philadelphia, PA, 1988), vol. I, pp. 23–4; Kraye, 'Moral Philosophy', p. 311, n. 60.

23 Jean Calvin, *Institution de la religion chrestienne* (Geneva: François Perrin, 1566), Bk I, v, 3.

24 Charles Trinkaus on Eugenio Garin in *In Our Image and Likeness: Humanity and Divinity in Italian Humanist Thought*, 2 vols (London, 1970), vol. I, pp. 187–8; Genesis I:26; Martinet outlines a range of commonplaces, *Montaigne*, pp. 92–111.

25 Maurice Scève, *Microcosme*, ed. Enzo Guidici (Paris, 1976), p. 242, Bk III, lines 983–7: 'Qui restituera son Homme à Dieu, son père'.

26 Guillaume de Saluste du Bartas, *La sepmaine* [1581], ed. Yvonne Bellenger, 2 vols (Paris, 1981), vol. I, p. xxi; ibid., vol. II, p. 269, lines 405–6: 'En nous se void le feu, l'air, la terre, & l'onde: En bref l'homme n'est rien qu'un abregé du monde'.

27 François Rouget, 'Quelques éléments nouveaux sur les éditions anciennes de Du Bartas', *Bibliothèque d'Humanisme et Renaissance* 66 (2004): 133–49.

28 MC, AN, Paris, post-mortem inventories of Damoiselle Ysabeau Marron, formerly wife of Jehan de la Robertière, Doctor Regent in the Faculty of Law at the University of Paris and lawyer in the Chambre des comptes, 31 October 1585, XLIX, 215, and Vincent

Goulart wished to 'make the reading of this *Sepmaine* a bit easier' for those who might not have understood its more difficult passages. For the humble reader, Goulart schematises the L'Angelier edition of the *Sepmaine* with 'a general argument, summaries at the beginning of each book, annotations in the margin, and especially a very ample index at the end, where I clarified in alphabetical order, all things that could hinder the less practised reader, whom I principally had in mind'.[29] The title page of this edition, shown in detail in Figure 3.2, portrays each day of creation, depicting God's shaping of Eve from Adam's rib and a cherub distracted by Eve's beauty.

The humble reader might have had difficulty with the Greek references, but these concepts became less remote when placed within the biblical tradition – the idea of man as a microcosm overlapped with and reinforced the Christian idea of man as a marvel to be admired. In the *Institutes*, Calvin suggests that man is the means through which God reminds us of His power. Calvin saw the human body and human capacities as possible subjects of study for the 'common' or more 'rustic' people – the 'vulgaires' and the 'plus rudes'.[30]

Telling the creation story of Adam allowed an author to exalt man's dignity and praise God's work by dwelling on the perfection of each body part. In the *Brief Discourse of the Excellence and Dignity of Man*, published by Vincent Sertenas in 1558, Pierre Boaistuau glorifies the body and the margins announce: 'Praise of the excellence of the eyes', 'Praise of eyebrows', 'Praise of the nose', 'Praise of the tongue', 'Praise and use of teeth', 'Praise of the chin and the beard', 'Praise of the ears' and so on.[31] These commonplaces reappear in the *Sepmaine* where Du Bartas extols the virtues of the nose, for example, because it is 'the gutter by which the excrements of heavy substance empty below'.[32] Boaistuau repeats the idea of the Church Father Lactantius that the beard, an 'ornament of virility and strength', acts as an 'interpreter' to assess the 'maturity of the body' as well as determine sex difference. In Pierre de La Primaudaye's *French Academy*, first published in 1580 and owned by a Parisian lawyer before his death in 1584, the dialogue begins with

---

Gelée, king's counsellor and controller in the Chambre des comptes, 7 October 1603, XXIV, 142.

29 [S.G.S] Simon Goulart, 'Au lecteur', in *Commentaires & annotations sur la sepmaine de la creation du monde de Guillaume de Saluste, seigneur du Bartas* (Paris: Abel L'Angelier, 1583), sig. e ij^r. See Jean Balsamo and Michel Simonin, *Abel L'Angelier et Françoise de Louvain (1574–1620). Suivi du catalogue des ouvrages publiés par Abel L'Angelier (1574–1610) et la Veuve L'Angelier (1610–1620)* (Geneva, 2002), p. 76 and cat. nos. 67 (1582), 81 (1583), 82 (1583), 105 (1584), 134 (1585), 159 (1585–6); L'Angelier held the privilege from 1582 with the printer Timothée Jouan.

30 Calvin, *Institution*, Bk I, v, 2; Charles Trinkaus, 'Renaissance Problems in Calvin's Theology', in *The Scope of Renaissance Humanism* (Ann Arbor, MI, 1983), pp. 320–21.

31 Pierre Boaistuau, *Bref discours de l'excellence et dignité de l'homme* [1558], ed. M. Simonin (Geneva, 1982), p. 51.

32 Du Bartas, *La sepmaine*, ed. Bellenger, vol. II, p. 276, lines 545–7.

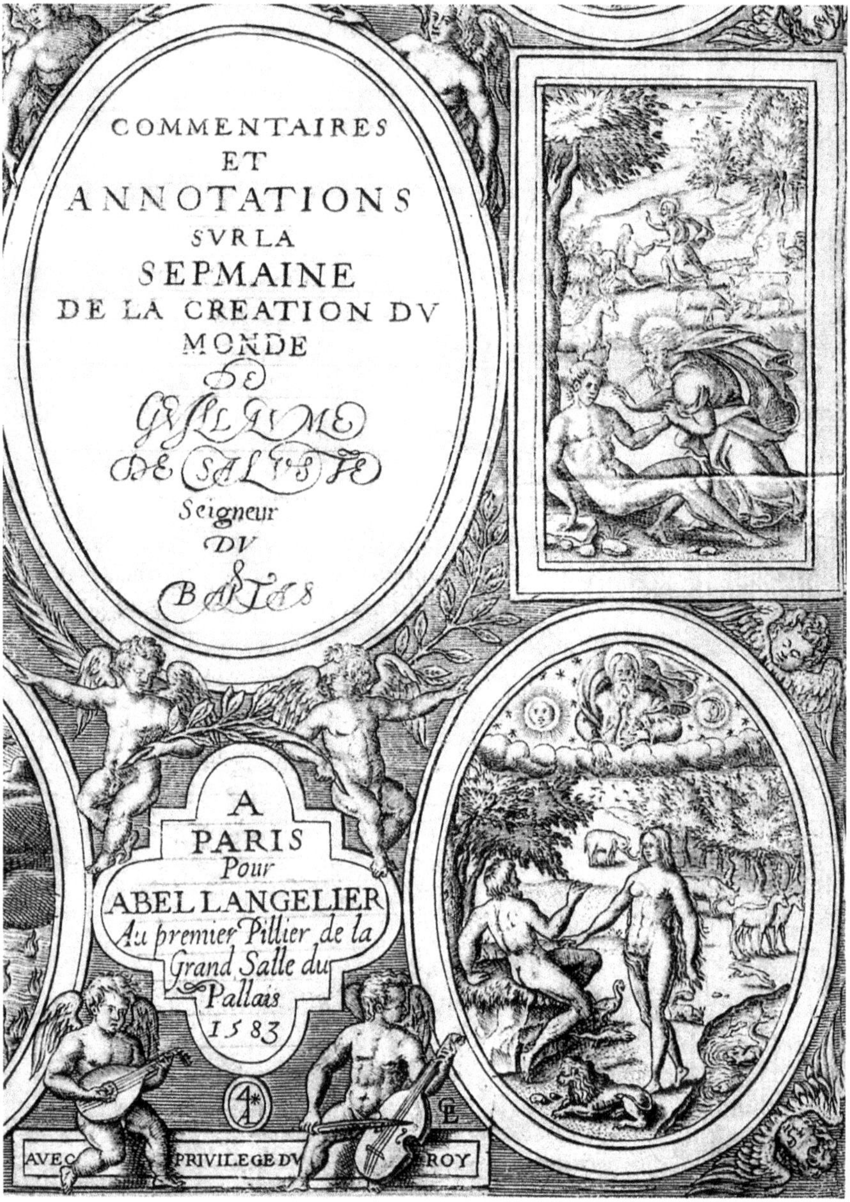

Figure 3.2 Title page detail of the creation of Adam and Eve, Guillaume du Bartas, *La Sepmaine* (Paris: Abel L'Angelier, 1583), courtesy of the Master and Fellows of Trinity College Cambridge (G.23.4[1]).

the creation of Adam and the group marvels at the ability of hands to write the letters of the alphabet, to produce words on paper, and how each person has their own individual style of handwriting.[33]

One of the prominent features of man's creation was his upright posture. Boaistuau praises the head as the 'tower and rampart of reason and wisdom' enabling man to contemplate the heavens as the place of his origin and in recognition of God his creator. When Adam opens his eyes in Maurice Scève's *Microcosme*, his first action is to admire the heavens.[34] Adam in Du Bartas' *Sepmaine* also lifts his eyes to the heavens and the editor Simon Goulart explains the idea to the reader in Christian terms but also traces the commonplace to Ovid's *Metamorphoses*:

> Whereas other animals hang their heads and look at the ground,
> he made man stand erect,
> bidding him to look up to heaven,
> and lift his head to the stars.
>
> *Pronáque cùm spectent animalia cetera terram,*
> *Os homini sublime dedit cœlúmque tueri [videre]*
> *Iussit, & erectos ad sydere tollere vultus.*[35]

According to dignity-of-man commonplaces, God granted to humans alone the privilege of contemplation of the heavens. Symphorien Champier suggests that man looks to the heavens because he has an immortal soul.[36] Yet only a few individuals, such as Charles de Bovelles' wise man, pursue this opportunity to become the true and fullest representations of humankind. All men have the same form, 'they all walk with their heads held high', but only the wise man contemplates the heavens.[37] Du Bartas stresses to the French reader that whereas animals gaze at

---

[33] La Primaudaye, *Academie françoise*, 1591 edn, fo. 10v or sig. b 2v; MC, AN, Paris, post-mortem inventory of Claude Amelot, lawyer, 20 January 1584, LXXXVII, 66.

[34] Boaistuau, *Bref discours*, p. 49, line 300; Scève, *Microcosme*, p. 151, line 134.

[35] Guillaume du Bartas, *Les Œuvres de Guillaume de Saluste, Seigneur du Bartas* (Paris: Michel Gadouleau, 1583), n. 44, fos 280v–281r or sigs AAiiij^{v}–AAv^{r}; Ovid, *Metamorphoses*, trans. and ed. Mary Innes (Harmondsworth, 1986), Bk I, 84–6, p. 31; see also Bovelles, *De sapiente*, pp. 66–7; Lionello Sozzi, 'La "dignitas hominis" dans la littérature de la Renaissance française', in A.H.T. Levi (ed.), *Humanism in France at the End of the Middle Ages and in the Early Renaissance* (Manchester, 1970), pp. 186–7; Kraye, 'Moral Philosophy', p. 311, n. 55; C.A. Patrides, *Premises and Motifs in Renaissance Thought and Literature* (Princeton, NJ, 1982), p. 85, nn. 5, 6.

[36] Champier, *Nef des princes*, 1502 edn, fo. xiii^{v}.

[37] Bovelles, *De sapiente*, pp. 86–7; Eugene Rice, *The Renaissance Idea of Wisdom* (Cambridge, MA, 1958), pp. 118–19.

their bellies to mark their bestial appetites – 'qui n'ont soin que du ventre' – Adam looks up to the heavens so that he may 'contemplate the place of his birth'.[38]

The erect human posture also serves to underline man's creation in the image and likeness of God. Moreover, his upright stance establishes him as the ruler over God's creatures on earth:[39]

> The Animals, perceiving [man] walk
> With his head held high, like their dear Lord
> Fearful, and amazed gathered around him
> And all, the head lowered, humble, greeted him:
> Recognising in him the hand of their maker.
>
> *Les Animaux divers l'appercevant marcher*
> *Ainsi la teste en haut, comme leur Seigneur cher*
> *Craingnans, et estonnés autour l'environnerent,*
> *Et tous, la teste en bas, humbles le saluerent:*
> *Reconnoisans en luy la main de leur facteur.*[40]

Bovelles' wise man lives 'like a God on earth'.[41] Scève describes how at the time of creation the animals 'waited in peace for the one who, like God in Heaven, [would be] their master here on earth'.[42] In the *Sepmaine* the 'King of animals' displays the traces of 'Divinity' on his face.[43]

The role as 'Seigneur' or Lord on earth stems from the idea that God created the world as man's dominion available for his exploitation.[44] Jean Parmentier, a merchant from Dieppe, marvels at the scope of God's creation in the *Treaty in the Form of an Exhortation Containing the Wonders of God and on the Dignity of Man*, 1530, which he wrote on a voyage to Sumatra. Parmentier describes how God elected man as 'sovereign admiral' of the sea and as 'great captain' and 'great chief general' of the earth and air. Parmentier reminds this 'king' of the gifts of his

---

38 Du Bartas, *Œuvres*, fo. 280v or sig. AA iiij^{v}; Du Bartas, *La sepmaine*, ed. Bellenger, vol. II, p. 274, lines 493–8.

39 Champier, *Nef des princes*, 1502 edn, fo. xiii^{v}.

40 Scève, *Microcosme*, p. 151, Bk I, lines 141–5.

41 Bovelles, *De sapiente*, p. 93 and n. 8, p. 323.

42 Scève, *Microcosme*, p. 150, Bk I, lines 101–2: 'attendoyent en paix celuy, qui devoit estre / Comme Dieu est au ciel, ici bas leur seul maistre'. Scève also refers to Adam as 'Dieu terrestre, et humain'. At this point Eve has already been created but there is no mention of her sharing in the image of this God on earth – p. 153, line 210.

43 Du Bartas, *La sepmaine*, ed. Bellenger, vol. II, p. 273, lines 282–3. Du Bartas also refers to man as the 'chef de l'univers' (line 476), 'un second Dieu' (line 460), 'Le terrestre Empereur' (line 490), 'Seigneur de ce bas Univers' (line 520).

44 Jean Calvin, *Institutes of the Christian Religion* [1559], ed. John McNeill (London, 1960), pp. 161–2, 181–2.

Creator, and because nothing is possible without divine grace, exhorts his reader to 'praise God, to love Him and to serve Him'.[45]

Adding another commonplace of the dignity of man tradition, Champier collects the 'fleur des princes', a bouquet or collection of exemplary men: Alexander the Great, Lycurgus the lawgiver, Julius and Augustus Caesar, David and Solomon who 'by their virtue attained honour and triumph'.[46] Similarly, Boaistuau's *Bref discours* demonstrates human 'perfection' with a series of examples of 'illustrious persons'. Boaistuau seeks 'the things particular to man, [in] each of which, I shall make evident what is the dignity and wit of man.' He highlights the military accomplishments of Alexander, Caesar and Pompey, Archimedes for his knowledge of mathematics and the accomplishments of artists whose work rivals the beauty of Nature. Switching from ancients to moderns, Boaistuau salutes the inventor of the printing press and Leonardo da Vinci's invention of flying.[47]

From Dignity to Misery and from Praise to Blame

Most commonplaces on the dignity of man could be easily overturned and employed to prove the absurdity and misery of man. Many sixteenth-century writers questioned the very notion of human superiority. In the opening decade of the century, Champier would suggest that man's body was more fragile than other terrestrial creatures.[48] Sforza's book on the tranquility of the soul also assessed human strengths and weaknesses. 'I desire to know of these haughty [people] who believe they have in hand the key to Heaven and Hell, what is this thing that most especially bids and exhorts them to be so high and mighty? … [I]t seems to me infinitely foolish [for] almost any animal is more robust and full of life than man. Who surpasses the elephant in strength? Who exceeds the deer in speed? Who sees more sharply than the eagle?' Gilbert de Hodic and Geneviève Bureau, the notary and his wife living near the Hôtel de Ville in Paris, could have read about these human weaknesses in either of their two copies of Sforza's book or in their copy of Champier's moral advice to the prince.[49]

---

[45] Jean Parmentier, *Traicté en forme d'exhortation contenant les merveilles de Dieu et de la dignité de l'homme*, in *Œuvres poétiques* [1531], ed. Françoise Ferrand (Geneva, 1971), pp. 99–100, stanza XXIV, lines 237–47, and p. 103, lines 321, 334.

[46] Champier, *Nef des princes*, 1502 edn, fo. xxv^{v}.

[47] Boaistuau, *Bref discours*, pp. 55–62, 65. Simonin comments that Boaistuau's emphasis on invention strays from the *dignitas* genre of the Italian humanist Manetti. As Maurice Scève and Guillaume du Bartas similarly focus on human reason and ingenuity perhaps this approach separates French dignity- and misery-of-man treatises from the Italian tradition.

[48] Champier, *Nef des princes*, 1502 edn, fos xii^{v}–xiii^{r}.

[49] Sforza, *Vraye tranquilité*, pp. 53–4; MC, AN, Paris, Hodic inventory, 1549, III, 300, fos 30r, 31v.

In his pioneering essay on dignity-of-man literature in France, Lionello Sozzi outlined the shift from dignity-of-man to misery-of-man themes by focusing on the evolution of the topos describing man's upright posture. Initially man's face pointing to the heavens indicates his superiority and reminds him of his Creator, but as Sozzi outlines inverting the topos became a way to mock worldly ambition and human presumption.[50] Two versions of the topos can be found in Jacques Tahureau's mid-sixteenth-century *Dialogues, Not Less Profitable than Facetious Where Each Person's Vices are Very Fiercely Rebuked to Encourage Us to Flee Them and Follow Virtue*. One speaker known as the Cosmophile follows Ovid and asserts that man, as the only creature of reason, naturally extends his gaze to the heavens. His companion the Democritic ridicules this ideal and tells the story of the astronomer who gazed attentively at the stars one evening 'and raising his nose in the air like an aggravated sow, fell suddenly into a pit'. An old man nearby mocked the astronomer for wanting to know what was in the sky when he was unable to perceive what was under his very feet.[51] The Democritic derides the contemplation of the heavens and draws attention to a biblical passage in which God reserved the heavens for His domain and gave the earth to man, 'where it was made plain enough that they should be content with their allotted place, without undertaking to fly higher and to gain knowledge of what is uncertain to them'. The Democritic speaks directly against the humanist self-improvement ethos and replaces it with the maxim that each person should be content with his or her station in life.[52] Sozzi maintains that Tahureau's dialogue indicates a 'new orientation', and other French writers began to employ the story of the stumbling scholar to mock human presumption.[53] Later Montaigne would ridicule the idea that 'our upright stature' affirms superiority over animals. Some beasts look directly to the sky, while others such as ostriches or camels stretch their necks so that Montaigne finds them 'much more raised and upright, than ours'. Or as Montaigne later wrote in the margins of his 1588 edition of the *Essais*: '[w]hat beasts have not their face aloft' and 'see as much of heaven and earth as man (*l'homme*)'?[54]

---

50 Sozzi, 'Littérature française', p. 188; Lionello Sozzi, *La dignité de l'homme à la Renaissance* (Turin, 1982), pp. 94–5.

51 Jacques Tahureau, *Les Dialogues ... non moins profitables que facetieux, ou les vices d'vn chacun sont repris fort aprement pour nous animer dauantage à les fuir, & suiure la vertu* (Paris: Gabriel Buon, 1570); Jacques Tahureau, *Les Dialogues: non moins profitables que facetieux* [1565], ed. Max Gauna (Geneva, 1981), pp. 163–4; Trevor Peach, *Nature and Reason: étude critique des Dialogues de Jacques Tahureau* (Geneva, 1986), pp. 28–30.

52 Tahureau, *Dialogues*, ed. Gauna, p. 164.

53 Sozzi, 'Littérature française', p. 190.

54 Montaigne, *Essais*, II:12, 'Apologie de Raimond Sebond', pp. 483–4; Montaigne, *Essays*, vol. II, p. 181; Montaigne Project, http://artfl.uchicago.edu/images/montaigne/0209.jpg; see also Sozzi, 'Littérature française', p. 191.

Sozzi is certainly correct to identify a changing pattern, but he gives the impression of a steady, linear progression to rationalism whereas the reality was jagged and uneven. By trying to determine a precise turning point, he risks ignoring earlier formulations mocking the topos of man's upright posture. The image of the stumbling astrologer had already appeared in Gilles Corrozet's emblem book the *Hecatomgraphie* printed by Denis Janot in Paris in 1540, 1541, twice in 1543–44 and again by Janot's successor Estienne Groulleau in 1548. Mockery of the wise man contemplating the heavens could also be found in Corrozet's popular translation of *Æsop's Fables* that Denis Janot printed in 1542 and again in 1544, while Jean de Tournes in Lyon printed three further editions in 1547, 1549 and 1551.[55]

In Corrozet's version of the tale, a philosopher 'raising his eye to the sky ... fell into a pit'. Figure 3.3 shows the philosopher taking the perilous step into the hole at his feet in Corrozet's emblem 'Contre les astrologues'. The philosopher waits in the ditch until his servant comes to pull him out and asks his master why he troubles to know the secrets of the heavens when he cannot see what is before his eyes. As Corrozet summarises: 'With this speech [the servant] rebukes the folly of

Figure 3.3 Emblem 'Against the philosopher', Gilles Corrozet, *Hecatomgraphie* (Paris: Denis Janot, 1540), courtesy of University of Glasgow, Special Collections (SMAdd385).

[55] Alison Adams, Stephen Rawles and Alison Saunders (eds), *A Bibliography of French Emblem Books of the Sixteenth and Seventeenth Centuries*, 2 vols (Geneva, 1999–2002), vol. I, pp. 367–78; Paola Cifarelli, 'Introduction', in Gilles Corrozet, *Second livre des fables d'Ésope* [1548] (Geneva, 1992), p. 15.

the philosopher and his astrology'. This philosopher had forgotten that it is more important to know oneself – 'Qu'il fault avoir de soy la cognoissance' – than to acquire knowledge of the secrets of God and the heavens.[56]

Corrozet's *Hecatomgraphie* and *Æsop's Fables* were circulating widely at the time when Jacques Tahureau composed his *Dialogues*. A book collector like Gilbert de Hodic, we observed in chapter two, could have encountered woodcut as well as textual versions of the 'facing the heavens' topos in his copies of Ovid's *Metamorphoses*, Erasmus' *Praise of Folly*, Alciati's emblems, *Æsop's Fables*, or Gilles Corrozet's emblem book the *Hecatomgraphie*.[57] As Hodic died in 1549 it was not necessary to wait, as Sozzi suggests, until the posthumous 1565 edition of Tahureau's *Dialogues* to find a mockery of the contemplative man looking to the heavens.[58]

More importantly, Sozzi's emphasis on the long term leads to a neglect of Renaissance *pro et contra* techniques; the switch from dignity to misery and back could occur within the same text.[59] By shifting from praise to blame and back again an author showed his prowess at conducting an *argumentum in utramque partem* – arguing both sides of a question. The author's opinion might reside either in the excellence of man or in human misery, but perhaps the truth, if there was a truth, lay somewhere between these two extremes.

From Praise to Blame and Back Again

In the *Brief Discourse on the Excellence and Dignity of Man* published by Vincent Sertenas in 1558, Boaistuau turns from the 'the sea of miseries with which I had burdened man from his birth to his grave' to a demonstration of man's excellence and dignity.[60] He tells his dedicatees that he wishes to counter the tragic picture

---

56 Gilles Corrozet, *Hecatomgraphie* (Paris: Denis Janot, 1540), the emblem 'Contre les astrologues', sigs K vi^{v}–K vii^{r}.

57 MC, AN, Paris, Hodic inventory, 1549, III, 300, fos 30v, 31v, 32r.

58 Sozzi, 'Littérature française', p. 190. Sozzi notes this story also appears in Erasmus' *Praise of Folly*, but he still seems to see Tahureau's *Dialogues* as a turning point. See also Peach, *Nature and Reason*, p. 28; and on the origin of the story in Diogenes Lærtius' *Lives*, I, xxxiii–xxxiv, see Tahureau, *Dialogues*, ed. Gauna, n. 26, p. 165.

59 Sozzi acknowledges the accent on *miseria hominis* yet he does not emphasise the Renaissance practice of arguing on both sides of a question. Champier's many excerpts on the vanity of worldly existence 'risque de transformer son chapitre consacré à l'"*excellentia hominis secundum Trimegistum*" en un tableau nettement clairobscuré, où, sur une quinzaine de passages choisis, presque la moitié mettent l'accent sur les côtés négatifs et les limites de l'homme, plutôt que sur son excellence et sa dignité' – Lionello Sozzi, 'La "dignitas hominis" chez les auteurs lyonnais du XVIe siècle', in *Actes du colloques sur l'humanisme lyonnais au XVIe siècle* (Grenoble, 1974), pp. 311–12.

60 Boaistuau, *Bref discours*, pp. 35–6.

of his *Theatre of the World Where There is Made an Ample Discourse of Human Miseries* in order to 'soften' and 'moderate' its criticism for the benefit of readers who might find his comments about the 'works of God' to be 'too harsh'.[61] Boaistuau was not alone in providing opposing arguments, and although *in utramque partem* reasoning has captured the attention of Renaissance scholars for some time now, it will do no harm to look at the function of opposing voices in Boaistuau's treatises on the dignity and misery of man because some modern commentators continue to confine early modern authors to the expression of one particular viewpoint.[62] Moreover, it will help us in our comparison with the *Querelle des femmes*.

The *Théâtre du monde où il est faict un ample discours des misères humaines* and the *Bref discours de l'excellence et dignité de l'homme* were initially published as two separate books by Vincent Sertenas and his son-in-law Gilles Robinot based at the Palais de Justice in Paris. Within three years the two books were published, sold and bound together as a unit.[63] In a preface to the reader of his *Théâtre du monde* Boaistuau considers the 'ingratitude of man' – 'mescognoissance de l'homme'. 'Man reforms, rules, measures and ponders that which can be seen under the cope of heaven and [yet] is so confused and stubborn [about] himself'. Boaistuau explains to his reader, 'for this reason … I have fashioned this Théâtre in which he can contemplate and consider his infirmity and misery so that looking into all parts of the body and reviewing all the parts of his life, he would be moved to detest his vileness'. Boaistuau explains that the world is like a theatre in which some play roles of 'low birth' (*basse condition*) while others take on the roles of kings or dukes. Yet in the end, when the actors take off their masks, all are men.[64] In the conclusion to the treatise on the excellence and dignity of man Boaistuau acknowledges that he must respond briefly to the allegations made in 'our book of human miseries'. 'God did not create him subject to such miseries at first, considering that he had raised him to the highest degree of all the dignities in the world'. Man brought this wretchedness upon himself and if man had not strayed from the path of obedience, God would have kept him in 'perpetual happiness'. The Lord designed man's creation from such 'vile and abject matter as the slime of

---

[61] Pierre Boaistuau, *Le Théâtre du monde où il est faict un ample discours des misères humaines* [1558], ed. M. Simonin (Geneva, 1982), p. 43.

[62] On reasoning *in utramque partem* see Victoria Kahn, *Rhetoric, Prudence and Skepticism in the Renaissance* (Ithaca, NY, 1985), pp. 20–22; Zachary Schiffman, *On the Threshold of Modernity: Relativism in the French Renaissance* (Baltimore, MD, 1991), pp. 54–7, 59, 62; Quentin Skinner, 'Thomas Hobbes: Rhetoric and the Construction of Morality', *Proceedings of the British Academy* 76 (1991): 3, 22, 45.

[63] See the lists of editions in Boaistuau, *Théâtre*, pp. 27–9, and Boaistuau, *Bref discours*, p. 27. The separate 1558, 1559 and 1560 editions were shared between Sertenas, Robinot and Sertenas' frequent collaborator Jean Longis; see Boaistuau, *Théâtre*, pp. 35–8, and Boaistuau, *Bref discours*, pp. 29–31.

[64] Boaistuau, *Théâtre*, pp. 42–3.

the earth' to humble man and instil obedience but not to diminish human glory.[65] 'Our God wanted to create us from two substances, one earthly and the other celestial to this end; if we puff ourselves up or swell with pride, the vileness of the creation of our body, which is nothing but earth, ash and rottenness, will tame and restrain us'.[66] Boaistuau accounts for the apparent opposite perspectives of his two works by highlighting the differences in the human condition before and after the Fall. In his 'general conclusion' Boaistuau considers man (*l'homme*) created by God as the *chef d'œuvre* of the universe. Yet, corruption infects all of Adam's posterity – man is reduced from the 'Lord of all creatures' to the 'slave of sin'. Then Boaistuau reflects on man's redemption through the incarnation of Christ: '[B]ut if we wish to consider him as repaired, as if brand new, by the immortal seed of the word of God, one will see him restored not only to his first honours and favours, but to much greater ones'.[67]

To suggest that one view prevails over the other contradicts the practice of Renaissance reasoning and the structure of these texts that argue on both sides of a question. The paradoxes, dialogues or collections of stories are meant to accentuate – and this cannot be stressed enough – these oscillations from dignity to misery and back again. Of all the cases of *argumentum in utramque partem*, commentators seem most likely to accept that a writer such as Boaistuau might describe both the dignity and misery of man because this vision of human nature coincides neatly with Adam before and after the Fall.[68] When attention shifts to weighing the *pro et contra* for the inferiority and superiority of woman in the *Querelle des femmes*, the Renaissance writers suggesting more than one possibility for the position of women are labelled 'inconsistent' or not 'sincere', thus dismissing the possibility of multiple truths.[69] The interpretation of the debates of the dignity and misery of man and the *Querelle des femmes* are worth dwelling on further because many writers thrived on contradiction and these opposing voices in the ideas of man and woman are fundamental to the Renaissance understanding of human nature. This chapter parallels the themes and commonplaces of the dignities and miseries of man alongside woman to show how crisscrossed and intertwined these concepts were.

When Guillaume de la Perrière introduced one of his emblem books in 1553 he explained his choice of a paradoxical title. 'I named my said work, MOROSOPHIE,

65 Boaistuau, *Bref discours*, pp. 80–81.

66 Ibid., p. 42.

67 Ibid., pp. 82–3.

68 Martinet, *Montaigne*, pp. 88–9, 125; Richard Carr, 'Introduction', in Pierre Boaistuau, *Histoires tragiques* [1559] (Paris, 1977), pp. xxx, xxxii, xxxiv; Richard Carr, *Pierre Boaistuau's Histoires tragiques: A Study of the Narrative Form and Tragic Vision* (Chapel Hill, NC, 1979), p. 250; Pierre Villey, *Les sources et l'évolution des Essais de Montaigne*, 2 vols (Paris, 1908), vol. II, p. 34; Simonin, 'Introduction', in Boaistuau, *Théâtre*, p. 23; Simonin, 'Introduction', in Boaistuau, *Bref discours*, pp. 20–21.

69 See Chapter 4, pp. 96–100.

a compound Greek saying signifying in Greek the same as foolish-wisdom in French ... I have no doubt that among the many follies will be found some wisdom, among many thorns a rose, among many shells a pearl and among many fables a truth'.[70]

Maurice Scève's *Microcosme* honours 'man' with the title role in his epic poem on the creation of the world, the animals, Adam and Eve. Yet Scève does not simply dwell upon human dignity because he also considers the human condition outside Paradise. 'The misery and horror of this frail life / Subject to hunger, thirst, cold and heat pell-mell'.[71] Fallen man looks to God to recover some measure of human dignity: 'Then, man humbled by his punishment and his trespass / Reassures himself by raising his thought to higher [things]'.[72] Scève alternates between dignity and misery when he underlines how human creativity also destroys:

> After discovering thousands and thousands of beautiful things,
> And as many torments and all sorts of cruelty
> Man can act as God to fellow man, and act as a wolf as well
> He who can help so much, can also [do] a lot of harm.
>
> *Apres avoir trouvé mille, et mille beautés,*
> *Et autant de tourmens à toutes cruautés*
> *L'homme à l'homme estant Dieu, et l'homme à l'homme loup*
> *Qui peut gramment [grandement] aider, et peut nuire beaucoup.*[73]

Pierre Dampmartin, former *procureur général* of the Duc d'Alençon the younger brother of Henri III, addresses both the dignity and misery of man in *On the Knowledge and Marvels of the World* (*De la Conoissance et merveilles du monde et de l'homme*) published in 1585.[74] Dampmartin recalls for the reader a series of conversations in the company of the Duc d'Alençon in which he was asked to 'tell us about the blame of the world as well as its praise' – 'nous dire le blasme du monde aussi bien que la louange'. Dampmartin explains that the Greeks could argue 'for and against' – 'pour & contre' – and practised 'this custom of contradiction'

---

70 Guillaume de la Perrière, *La Morosophie de Guillaume de la Perrière, Tolosain, contenant cent emblèmes moraux, illustrez de cent testrastiques latins, reduit en autant de quadrins françoys* (Lyon: Macé Bonhomme, 1553), in *Le Théâtre des bons engins & La Morosophie*, facs. edn Alison Saunders (Aldershot, 1993), sig. A 4v.

71 Scève, *Microcosme*, p. 159, Bk I, line 389: 'La misere et horreur de cette vie fraisle / Sujette à faim, et soif, froid et chaud pellemesle'.

72 Ibid., p. 160, Bk I, line 441: 'Lors l'homme humilié en sa peine, et sa faute / Se r'assure eslevant sa pensee plus haute'.

73 Ibid., pp. 240–41, Bk III, lines 937–40.

74 François Berriot, 'Pierre de Dampmartin vu à travers sa *Conoissance et merveilles du monde et de l'homme* entre Plutarque et Montaigne', in *Prose et prosateurs de la Renaissance* (Paris, 1988), pp. 279–80.

– 'ceste accoustumance a ce contredire'.[75] When Dampmartin listed the possible miseries faced by humans the duke 'told me that I had given him great pleasure in sparing nobody … having never thought so deeply about the misery of men'. Nevertheless the duke wished the next discussion to consider 'the excellence that God has placed in us'.[76]

The dignity- and misery-of-man literature, like a collection of essays or a dialogue, demonstrates two or more perspectives on man. It represents the human potential for greatness and fragility. It praises and it blames. The rhetorical practice of *pro et contra* considers how each topic, each idea, is reversible. This tactic had the effect of bringing an accepted truth into doubt in order to propose in its stead a neglected truth. In paradox, too, the apparently unpraiseworthy becomes praiseworthy and has the effect of bringing the original assumption into doubt.[77]

The Misery of Downward Mobility

When Lothario Segni, later Pope Innocent III, wrote *On the Contempt for the World with the Misery of the Human Condition* in 1195 he intended to follow it up with a treatise on the dignity of man and present a dual vision of humanity.[78] The notary Gilbert de Hodic owned a copy of this medieval treatise on the misery of the human condition in Latin, which circulated in a number of editions in print from the 1470s, but the first printed French adaptation was Guillaume Alexis' *The Past-Time of Every Man and Every Woman* published in 1505 and sold at Antoine Verard's Parisian boutiques on rue Neuve Nôtre Dame and at the first pillar of the Palais de Justice – one of seven sixteenth-century French editions.[79] Alexis' adaptation of the *Passe temps* for a French audience dwells upon the 'misery of human relations' so that each person will consider 'his estate and condition' in order to 'maintain humility'. The *Passe temps* features the three aspects of the misery-of-man theme prevalent in the 1500s – the lifecycle shared by all humans, the thorns, discomforts and miseries of each estate or occupation, and the constant presence and temptation of vice.[80] While the first section of the *Passe temps* focuses on the

---

75 Pierre de Dampmartin, *De la Conoissance et merveilles du monde et de l'homme* (Paris: Thomas Perier, 1585), sig. G^{v} or fo. 25v.

76 Ibid., fo. 48r or sig M iv^{r}.

77 Skinner, 'Thomas Hobbes', p. 20; Rosalie Colie, *Paradoxia Epidemica: The Renaissance Tradition of Paradox* (Princeton, NJ, 1966), p. 10.

78 MC, AN, Paris, Hodic inventory, 1549, III, 300, fo. 26r; Kraye, 'Moral Philosophy', pp. 306–7. A French adaptation circulated in manuscript from the late 1490s; see Eustache Deschamps, *Double lay de la fragilité humaine*, in *Œuvres complètes*, 11 vols (Paris, 1878–1903), vol. II, pp. 37–305.

79 'Bibliographie', in Guillaume Alexis, *Œuvres poétiques*, 3 vols (Paris, 1896–1908), vol. II, pp. 79–94.

80 Alexis, *Le Passe temps de tout homme et de toute femme*, in *Œuvres*, vol. II, p. 110.

universal lifecycle from birth to death and the inevitable misery found in all walks of life, in the second part biblical figures such as Nebuchadnezzar, Herod and Samson serve to warn against the vices of covetousness, gluttony, drunkenness, sensuality, ambition and pride.

As we discussed in the Introduction and earlier in this chapter, the idea of the dignity of man in the sixteenth century involved working 'ceaselessly for virtue' to achieve upward mobility or maintain one's place in the social hierarchy. The misery-of-man theme reflected the anxieties of the hereditary *noblesse d'épée* and the established *noblesse de robe* about the possibility of downward mobility. A change of fortune lurked in waiting for the man of a certain stature – the prince, the emperor, the noble, the magistrate – especially if he gave in to pride or *outrecuidance*, in which he literally believes in himself too much and overestimates his worth relative to God. The misery-of-man literature stresses that, despite a variation of rank, wealth and status, all humans share an 'equality' in the misery of the human condition. Of course, these aspects of the misery-of-man theme – the universal lifecycle from birth to death, the misery of each estate or occupation, and the human penchant for vice – often intertwined and played off one another. By emphasising the cycle of the 'ages of man' – fragile birth, adolescence, the thorns of marriage, the varied miseries of each rank, trade or profession, the senility of old age, and finally the universal reality of death – misery-of-man themes highlighted the shared human experience.

Gilles Corrozet's emblem book the *Hecatomgraphie* illustrates these common experiences with emblems such as 'In the end, we are all equal' – 'La fin nous faict tous egaulx'. The verse accompanies an illustration of a chess game where the king, queen, knights and pawns, each piece 'seated in its place' – 'assis en son lieu' – waits ready for the game to begin. When the game is over and the player tidies away the pieces the kings and queens are 'Placed in a pouch, without rank or degree / And with no one beholden to another'. Corrozet reminds his reader: 'We all play chess in this world'. Some are dukes, some are emperors, but when the game of life is over all humans finish in the grave. Corrozet describes how the earth rots the bodies of princes just as easily as it decomposes 'the bodies of the common poor'.[81]

Isabella Sforza's late-1540s treatise on the 'tranquility of the soul' suggests that 'there is nothing in the world more abominable before God nor more odious than pride, which caused the most beautiful creature ever created to fall from Heaven like a thunderbolt'. By cultivating humility before God, or through Stoic preparation focused on self-knowledge, constancy and tranquility, the man of dignity could detach himself from a dependence on worldly goods and status. Sforza outlines to her reader her method to combat the pride by which man elevates himself 'to the

---

[81] Corrozet, *Hecatomgraphie* (Paris: Denis Janot, 1540), sigs D iv^{v}–D v^{r}: 'Mis dans ung sac, sans ordre ne degré / Et sans avoir l'ung plus que l'aultre à gré'; see 'French Emblems at Glasgow' website, at http://www.emblems.arts.gla.ac.uk/french/facsimile.php?id=sm385-d4v, accessed 3 November 2010.

Heavens'. Whenever tempted by this 'malignant thought' she reminds herself that she is 'mortal, fragile, with poor resistance to any little mishap whatsoever', and exposed to a 'thousand chances of fortune'.[82] To achieve the tranquility of mind Sforza promotes, each person needs to rid themselves of the passions of private gain, greed and the 'excessive love' for 'fortune's blessings, worldly reputation, children and life'.[83]

The notary Hodic or his wife Geneviève Bureau obtained a copy of Corrozet's *Hecatomgraphie* at some point in the 1540s because the 1549 inventory of their household near the Paris Hôtel de Ville lists Corrozet's emblem book next to their two copies of Sforza's treatise.[84] Corrozet borrowed the chess game emblem from Guillaume de la Perrière's *Theatre of Good Understanding*, which had also been printed by Denis Janot in Paris in 1540 a few months earlier. During a game of chess the king holds 'grande preference' or a place high above his subjects, La Perrière suggests, yet after the 'game of transitory life' the kings are no longer 'greater than vassals' because until the players begin again, kings and pawns 'are equal in honour'.[85]

As Boaistuau clarifies, 'the philosophy of human misery' acts as a mirror to humble princes and other great lords when they indulge in 'vainglory'. Princes who place too much confidence in their 'dignity and grandeur' need to ponder the nature of man – 'que c'est que de l'home' – and 'how many miseries and calamities to which our miserable life is subject'.[86] Boaistuau echoes how every king experiences the same process of birth as his subjects. 'We all have therefore the same beginning and the same end'.[87] This need to remain humble acted in opposition to the self-improvement ethos of the dignity of man, which was a breeding ground for the vices of ambition and pride. In the *Théâtre du monde*, Boaistuau repeats how the 'miserable condition of our humanity' culminates in death. If in any estate, age, country, kingdom or century a man could be found daring to boast that he had never tasted death, the living would be pleased to meet him. All humans experience frustration. Every human has 'complained', 'bemoaned' or become 'vexed' about his or her 'estate' or 'way of living'.[88] All

---

82 Sforza, *Vraye tranquilité*, pp. 51–2, see Ch. 3 above, p. 55 n. 16.

83 Ibid., pp. 10–11.

84 MC, AN, Paris, Hodic inventory, 1549, III, 300, fo. 31v.

85 Guillaume de la Perrière, *Le Théâtre des bons engins* (Paris: Denis Janot, 1544), Emblem XXVII, sig. E^{r}.

86 Pierre Boaistuau, *Institution du royaume chrestien, extraictes de plusieurs fameux autheurs Grecz et Latins, sacrés & prophanes, mise en langue francoise* (Paris: [Gilles Robinot], 1559), fos 77v, 71r. Original edition as *L'Histoire de Chelidonius Tigurinus* (Paris: Vincent Sertenas, 1556).

87 Boaistuau, *Institution*, fos 77v–78r.

88 Boaistuau, *Théâtre*, pp. 121–2: 'Qui est celuy d'entre les humains qui ne soit jamais adonné à quelque estat ou à quelque autre matière de vivre qui ne l'ait en fin accusé, et duquel il ne soit plainct, ennuyé et fasché.'

estates and occupations suffer misery; it is a shared condition of humanity from popes to beggars, sailors, farmers, labourers, merchants and soldiers.[89]

Dampmartin's *De la Conoissance et merveilles du monde et de l'homme* recounts the pains of labourers, vineyard-keepers, common people or the 'menu peuple', merchants, bankers, those who practise the 'vocation of letters and the sword', the clergy and princes. In the dialogue the Duke d'Alençon interrupts Dampmartin because he has been too 'respectful' and suggests that his servant should not be afraid to offend him. In talking of the life of princes, the duke reminds the audience that 'we are not more happy than you are … we have the same ills and inconveniences as other men'.[90]

The idea of shared human experience aimed to prevent what Ruth Mohl has termed the 'defection of estate' or social mobility.[91] Not every family managed to better its fortunes through education or the purchase of an office, so the literature discussing the miseries of each estate or vocation helped the individual to accept his or her lot in life. When Barbara Diefendorf charts the careers of sixteenth-century Paris city councillors, ranging from merchants to low, middle and high officeholders, her tables demonstrate occupational stability as well as mobility. Over half of the men beginning their careers in a low office or a liberal profession remained at this level at the peak of their careers. Most of the councillors in Diefendorf's study who rose to high office also tended to have fathers who had occupied posts at this level, although several had risen from merchant origins to high office in one generation.[92] It is not surprising, then, that some treatises tended to reinforce the maintenance of the status quo and to disapprove of 'vainglory' and ambition.

In the later sixteenth century *Des saines affections*, a moral commonplace book, addressed the 'calling' or vocation of each [estate] in the *Vacation d'un chacun*. '[M]an is born subject to all sorts of miseries', hence we are all 'prisoners of fortune' because there is no difference between a chain of gold and a chain of iron. If low rank and humble lineage torment you – 'si la bassesse & obscurité de race t'afflige' – consider how the 'nobility and grandeur' possessed by social superiors 'bestows a thousand worries'. If you are subject to the 'command and will of another', remember that this person experiences many 'discontents and anxieties that you don't see'.[93] The probable author of the anonymous *Saines affections* was Madeleine de L'Aubespine, a daughter, sister and wife of three secretaries of state serving several kings in the second half of the sixteenth century and early

89 Ibid., pp. 122–62.

90 Dampmartin, *De la Conoissance*, fos 35r–37r, 41r, 43v or sigs Iiij^{r}, I v^{r}, K^{r}, L^{r}, Liij^{v}.

91 Ruth Mohl, *The Three Estates in Medieval and Renaissance Literature* (New York, 1933), pp. 6–7, 324–5.

92 Diefendorf, *Paris City Councillors*, pp. 84, 86–7, 88–9, 139–40.

93 [Madeleine de L'Aubespine], *Des saines affections* (Paris: Abel L'Angelier, 1593), fos 15r–v or sigs Ciij$^{r–v}$.

seventeenth century.[94] She reminds her reader that one should never envy persons of a higher station because often what we think of as a great 'height' is in fact a 'precipice.' The most 'heureux' or fortunate governed their conduct and life course according to their circumstances; they 'prudently knew [how] to conduct themselves in the estate that they had once chosen'.[95] If all humans experienced the same life process then 'grandeur' was no guarantee against fortune's powers.

The misery of man in each estate allowed each group to perform different functions according to their social roles. The capricious nature of fortune worked against the humanist idea of endeavouring to achieve a social dignity and maintain it. Why strive for a higher social position if it only offered the same certain miseries and ultimately the same death? The themes of the misery of man crisscrossed and intersected and so the messages were mixed and pointed to a range of truths about the human condition. Writers in the sixteenth century pondered the human condition with a series of *pro et contra* debates: praising the dignity-of-man virtues of invention or working for self-improvement while blaming the misery-of-man vices such as ambition and pride. The dignity- and misery-of-man themes were often interdependent with praise in response to blame or vice versa. Advocating the possibility of dignity while reminding the reader of the realities of misery was a frequent practice in Renaissance moral treatises.

This chapter focuses more on the opposing voices in the *Querelle des femmes* such as the arguments emphasising the excellence and dignity of woman or pointing to how she participated in the misery of man. Chapter four will pay more attention to how the contradictions or 'inconsistencies' in the commonplaces and arguments about the nature of woman parallel the interwoven and overlapping concepts we have just noted in the dignity- and misery-of-man literature.

Borrowing from the Dignity of Man to Praise Woman

When we juxtapose the *Querelle des femmes* texts with the Renaissance literature of the dignity and misery of man, the extent of the borrowing of commonplaces, overlap and intertextuality becomes obvious. The *Querelle des femmes* debated the nature of woman in the same manner as writers discussed the nature of man by encouraging virtue through praise and discouraging vice with blame and vituperation. These treatises on man and woman were not produced, written or sold in isolation from one another. A reader of a *Querelle des femmes* text would have encountered many of the same commonplaces he or she might have found in a work of moral philosophy on the dignity and misery of man.

---

94 On the authorship of the anonymous *Des saines affections* and its attribution to Madeleine de L'Aubespine see Chapter 7 below, p. 172, note 38.

95 Ibid., fo. 16v or sig. Ciiij^{v}.

Like the dignity- and misery-of-man literature, with its roots in the creation story of Genesis, the *Querelle des femmes* grew out of the tale in Paradise.[96] For the *Querelle* defenders of women, the crowning achievement of God's work was the creation of woman. As early as the 1440s manuscript, and through to the printed versions from 1485 to 1530, Martin Le Franc's *Champion of Ladies* suggested that 'woman' as the last creation contained everything in the world.

> And so woman is the last work
> Because she contains all the world
> As perfect and sovereign.
>
> *Ainsi fut femme œuvre darraine [dernière]*
> *Pource tout le monde contint*
> *Comme parfaicte & souveraine.*[97]

Woman was the summit of all of God's works, bringing harmony to the world: 'She is the peace and the end / Where all of this world is comprised / When things are made in an order / The last one encompasses them all'.[98] Within her she 'contained and consummated all the wisdom and power of the Creator'.[99] As 'the last one created of all other creatures' woman was 'the final and most perfect accomplishment of all of God's works, and the perfection of the universe' – 'la fin et le plus parfaict accomplissement des œuvres de Dieu, et la perfection de l'Univers'. Just as dignity-of-man writers like Boaistuau recall that the Lord 'mettait la main' or sculpted Adam with His own hands, Eve was the *chef d'œuvre* of creation and the ultimate accomplishment of God. Henricus Cornelius Agrippa, the German humanist doctor and friend of Charles de Bovelles and Symphorien Champier, announces in his treatise *On the Nobility and Pre-excellence of the*

---

96 Gisela Bock and Margarete Zimmermann, 'The European *Querelle des femmes*', *Disputatio* 5 (2002): 137.

97 Martin Le Franc, *Le Champion des dames. Livre plaisant copieux & habondant en sentences. Contenant la deffence des dames contre Malebouche & ses consors, & victoire d'icelles. Compose par Martin Franc, secretaire du feu pape Felix V & nouvellement imprimé a Paris* (Paris: Galiot du Pré, 1530), fo. lxxix^v; Martin Le Franc, *Le Champion des dames* [c. 1440], ed. Arthur Piaget (Lausanne, 1968), p. 148; Helen Swift, *Gender, Writing Performance: Men Defending Women in Late Medieval France, 1440–1538* (Oxford, 2008), Appendix 2; Lula McDowell Richardson, *The Forerunners of Feminism in French Literature of the Renaissance from Christine de Pisa to Marie de Gournay* (Baltimore, MD, 1929), p. 38.

98 Le Franc, *Champion*, 1530 edn, fo. xciii^r: 'Selle fust la paix & la somme / Ou tout cestuy monde est compris / Quant les choses font en ung ordre / La derniere toutes enclost'.

99 Henricus Cornelius Agrippa, *De la noblesse & preexcellence du sexe fœminin* (Paris: Denis Janot, c. 1535), sig. B v^v: 'Car le createur venant à la creation de la femme, se reposa en icelle comme non ayant devant soy chose plus honorable à créer, & en icelle à esté terminée & consummée l'œuvre de la sapience, & puissance du createur'.

Feminine Sex, written in Latin in 1509 and printed at least four times in French in the 1530s: 'Now woman is God's last chef d'œuvre that he placed in this world'. Without her, God's six-day-old world '(now well supplied with all its needs) would be imperfect'.[100]

Admiring the creation of Eve, Le Franc presents her as the 'mirror of the world': 'Bien vint le vray miroir du monde'.[101] Eve is rarely described in vernacular texts using the Greek term *microcosm* or its alternate 'little world', which had been the source of dignity for Charles de Bovelle's wise man.[102] Antoine Dufour's manuscript 'The Lives of Famous Women' given to Anne de Bretagne in 1504, however, describes Queen Zenobia as a 'true microcosm, which is a little world' – 'vray microcosme, qui est ung petit monde'.[103] Dufour combines several of the dignity-of-man commonplaces to praise Zenobia: 'Because her eyes were in her head as if set upon the heavens, [they] yielded a shining, infused light, that is to say she was not only illuminated but through an honest look of her eye, she illuminated all others'.[104]

In the *Champion of Ladies*, printed in Paris in 1530, the eponymous hero explains how man and woman share identical souls and accuses those who denigrate women of misinterpreting the Scriptures. 'As for their souls they [man and woman] are of one being and one excellence: perpetual images of God'. Only the exterior body misleads humans into ascribing difference between the sexes.[105] Both man and woman share 'remembrances' or marks of divinity because God created humans in his image and likeness. As two different sixteenth-century French translations of Agrippa's *On the Nobility and Pre-excellence of the Feminine Sex* phrased the concept, God created 'deux hommes à son image et semblance' or 'deux creatures humaines semblables l'une à l'aultre'.[106] The two

---

100 Henricus Cornelius Agrippa, *Traité de l'excellence de la femme* (1578), in Luce Guillerm, *et al.* (eds), *Le miroir des femmes*, 2 vols (Lille, 1983–84), vol. II, pp. 99–100; Agrippa, *De la noblesse*, sigs B v^{v}–B vi^{r}; Boaistuau, *Bref discours*, pp. 38–9.

101 Le Franc, *Champion*, 1530 edn, fo. lxxx^{r}; Le Franc, ed. Piaget, p. 149, line 4600.

102 Bovelles discusses the relative positions of Adam, Eve and Abel as *homines* sharing the same form – *De sapiente*, pp. 175–7; Joseph Victor, *Charles de Bovelles, 1479–1553: An Intellectual Biography* (Geneva, 1978), p. 122.

103 Antoine Dufour, *Les vies des femmes célèbres* (1504), ed. G. Jeanneau (Geneva, 1970), p. 117.

104 Ibid., pp. 117–18. 'Car ses yeulx estoyent en son chief comme au ciel atachez, qui rendoyent lumière infuse et transfuse, c'est-à dire elle non seulle estoit enluminée, mais par la bonne contenance de son œil toutes autlres_enluminoit'.

105 Le Franc, ed. Piaget, p. 189, lines 5929–44:
Pas n'entant ceste difference
Quant a leurs ames, pour ce qu'elles
Sont d'ung estre et d'une excellence
Ymages Dieu perpetuelles.

106 Agrippa, *Traité* in Guillerm, *et al.* (eds), *Miroir*, p. 99; Agrippa, *De la noblesse*, sig. Bv^{v}.

sexes are the same except for the 'different situation of some parts of the human body' required for reproduction.[107] A century later Marie de Gournay based her 1622 treatise, *The Equality of Men and Women*, on the same premise. She allows for a differentiation between the sexes only for the purposes of procreation. 'Man and woman are so much one that if man is more than woman, woman is more than man'.[108]

Agrippa shared the notion, put forward by his friend Charles de Bovelles in *On Wisdom* and echoed by his friend Champier in the *Nef des princes*, that each human possesses the same form. Some fulfil their potential while others stagnate at the level of beasts. In the *Three Books of Occult Philosophy* (*De occulta philosophia libri tres*) written shortly after his treatise on the excellence of woman, Agrippa acknowledges, like Bovelles before him, that human accomplishment occurs 'according to our capacity' or '*secundum capacitatem*'.[109] Agrippa's wise man seizes his dignity that enables him to attain great power and virtue – '*et ipsa est dignificatio homini ad hanc tam sublimem virtutem ac potestatem*'.[110] This man of dignity rebuffs the sensual world and masters virtue through intelligence and self-knowledge. He must feel the dignity of his soul and rise above his physical self.[111] This stress on the capacity of the soul resurfaces in Agrippa's defence of woman. He emphasises that the soul – not the body – mirrors the image of God. He insists that man and woman share the divine spiritual image, and asserts that women share the same potential as men. The Lord 'gave to woman as to man the same form of soul, utterly without difference. Between these souls could not be found any difference of sex. Woman received equal [capacities of] understanding, reason, speech and language as man and [she] inclines to the same end of blessedness and felicity as man, where there will be no difference or domination of one sex over the other'. Agrippa concludes that 'in both is a same liberty of judgement and will and equal dignity' – 'en tous deux est une mesme liberté de arbitre & volunté, & pareille dignité'.[112] Self-determination brings dignity to Adam in Pico

---

107 Agrippa, *De la noblesse*, sig. B^{r}.

108 Marie de Gournay, *L'Égalité des hommes et des femmes* (1622), in *Œuvres complètes*, eds. Jean-Claude Arnould, *et al.*, 2 vols (Paris, 2002), vol. I, pp. 978–9: 'L'homme et la femme sont tellement uns, que si l'homme est plus que la femme, la femme est plus que l'homme'.

109 Henricus Cornelius Agrippa, *De occulta philosophia libri tres*, ed. V. Perrone Compagni (Leiden, 1992), p. 520; Henricus Cornelius Agrippa, *Trois livres de la philosophie occulte ou magie*, trans. J. Servier, 3 vols (Paris, 1981–82), vol. III, pp. 142–3.

110 Agrippa, *De occulta*, p. 407; Agrippa, *Trois livres*, vol. III, pp. 24–5: 'c'est la prise de conscience de la dignité de l'homme qui doit lui permettre d'atteindre ce pouvoir si grand et de produire en lui une si haute vertu'. He continues: 'L'homme doit avoir au plus haut point le sentiment de cette dignité'.

111 Agrippa, *De occulta*, pp. 506–13, 539; Agrippa, *Trois livres*, vol. III, pp. 128–31, 163.

112 Agrippa, *De la noblesse*, sig. B^{r}: 'a donne a la femme comme a l'homme une mesme forme d'ame, & totallement indifferente, entre lesquelles n'est trouvée nulle diversité de

della Mirandola's 1486 *Oration on the Dignity of Man*, allows Bovelles' wise man to raise his intellect to the level of the divine, and empowers Agrippa's wise man in the *De occulta philosophia*. The woman of Agrippa's *De la noblesse et preexcellence du sexe feminin* must also seize the potential of the soul to overcome passions and the body.

Boaistuau, Jean Parmentier, Maurice Scève, Guillaume du Bartas and other dignity-of-man writers describe the world as waiting for Adam's creation so that he could reign as the King or Lord over all creatures on earth. Pierre Boaistuau opens his *Bref discours de l'excellence et dignité de l'homme* with God's creation of man in His image and likeness 'so that he would be King and Emperor of everything contained in the universe'. In return man was meant to marvel at the excellence of God's work, revere God, and recognise His generosity towards man.[113] Similarly Agrippa promotes the dignity of woman when he recounts how God introduces Eve as the Queen with the whole world as her palace – the 'Roine et dame d'ycelui en son palais'.[114] Agrippa reinforces the notion of the world created as her kingdom – a 'royaulme' at her obeisance and under her dominion. 'It is not without cause if all creatures love and honour woman, and for good cause all creatures are subject and obedient to her, she who is the Queen and the end of all creatures, the perfection and glory in all manner' of things.[115] In his *Impregnable Fort of the Honour of the Feminine Sex*, sold in the 1550s by Jean Dallier on the Pont St Michel connecting the university quarter to the Île de la Cité, François de Billon compares Eve's arrival to the pageantry of a royal entry: 'Woman … introduced by Him … as a Queen in her royal territory, already decorated and furnished in all places for her Entry'.[116]

Because woman shared the divine image of God and because she was the *chef d'œuvre*, *Querelle* defenders exalted the beauty of the female body and her body parts: her face, neck, eyebrows, teeth, fingers and so on. Early Renaissance writers valued facial beauty as the most noble because the erect human stature pointed the face to the heavens, reflecting God's divinity. '[W]oman is more capable of and more often filled with the divine splendour than man as one can see by her purity and marvellous beauty … this beauty is nothing other than the splendour of the

---

sexe, la femme a receu egal entendement, Raison, Oraison, & parler comme l'homme, & tend à la mesme fin de beatitude que l'homme, la ou n'y aura nulle difference de domination d'ung sexe sus l'aultre'; Agrippa, *Traité*, in Guillerm, *et al.* (eds), *Miroir*, p. 99.

113 Boaistuau, *Bref discours*, pp. 38–9.

114 Agrippa, *Traité*, in Guillerm, *et al.* (eds), *Miroir*, p. 100.

115 Agrippa, *De la noblesse*, sig. Bvi^{v}: 'Ce n'est point sans cause, si toute creature ayme & honore la femme, & a bonne cause luy est toute creature subiecte, & obeissante, la quelle est la Royne & la fin de toutes creatures, la perfection, & la gloire perfaicte en toutes manieres'.

116 Francois de Billon, *Le Fort inexpugnable de l'honneur du sexe femenin* (Paris: Jean Dallier, 1555), fo. 125r: '[L]a Femme … Introduyte par luy … comme Royne en son royal Possessoire, ia paré & fyny de tous pointz pour son Entrée'.

face and divine light joined unto created things [and] shining through the beautiful bodies of [women]'.[117] There was no competition for which sex possessed superior beauty. In the *Discourse on the Beauty of Ladies*, sold in Paris by Abel L'Angelier in the Palais de Justice from 1578, Agnolo Firenzuola argues that God granted man an erect posture not only that he might look to the heavens, but also to appreciate the beauty of woman and the proportions of her body.[118]

In 1543 and again in 1550 Charles L'Angelier, the bookseller in the Palais de Justice, published the *Anatomical Praises of the Feminine Body* featuring the collected poems of several well-known figures such as Maurice Scève and Clément Marot. The Parisian merchant printer Denis Janot on rue Neuve Nôtre Dame advertised these *Blasons anatomiques du corps feminin* in his 1544 catalogue. These *blasons* or praises appropriate a feature of the dignity-of-man tradition: the praise of all of the body parts ranging from the innocent to the lewd: hair, the eyebrows, the eye, the tear, the cheek, the tooth, the nipple, the *con* or cunt and the *cul* or 'arse'. The *blasons* and their companion woodcuts had initially been published in 1536, again within a year and for a third time in 1539 as part of a popular collection of texts known as the *Hecatomphile*.[119] The notary Gilbert de Hodic and perhaps his wife seem to have enjoyed these verses in praise of the body in the 1530s and 1540s because a copy of the *Blasons anatomiques* could be found in their household along with two copies of the *Hecatomphile*.[120] The praise of the body provides an example of the possible two-way traffic in dignity-of-man and *Querelle* commonplaces. Scève's participation in the *Blasons anatomiques du corps feminin* may have led him to praise Eve's body parts in his *Microcosme*, published posthumously in 1562. Eve's hair is 'spun gold' flowing down over a plump and curvy body and Adam can do nothing but admire her rose-tinted cheeks and the rest of her enticing qualities.[121]

---

117 Agrippa, *De la noblesse*, fo. Bviii^v: 'Et pourtant et que la femme est plus capable de la divine splendeur, que l'homme, & plus souvent est remplie, ce que aussi l'on peut veoir par la purité, & merveilleuse beaulté d'icelle, Car comme il soit que ceste beaulté nest aultre chose que la splendeur de la face & lumiere divine inserée es choses crées, reluysante par le beaux corps d'icelles'. On beauty in pro-woman treatises, see Marc Angenot, *Les Champions des femmes: examen du discours sur la supériorité des femmes 1400–1800* (Montréal, 1977), pp. 117–21.

118 Agnolo Firenzuola, *Discours de la beauté des dames*, trans. Jean Pallet (Paris: Abel L'Angelier, 1578), fos 18r–19v.

119 See 'L'imprimeur aux lecteurs', in *Blasons anatomiques du corps feminin* (Paris: Charles L'Angelier, 1543), fo. 60v; Nancy Vickers, 'The unauthored 1539 volume in which is printed the *Hecatomphile, The Flowers of French Poetry*, and *Other Soothing Things*', in Margreta de Grazia, *et al.* (eds), *Subject and Object in Renaissance Culture* (Cambridge, 1996), p. 176.

120 MC, AN, Paris, Hodic inventory, 1549, III, 300, fos 30v, 31r, 32r.

121 Scève, *Microcosme*, Bk I, pp. 152–4, lines 173–87, 195–205; V.L. Saulnier, *Maurice Scève*, 2 vols (Paris, 1948–49), vol. I, p. 144, and vol. II, p. 192.

Exempla, or stories of famous and infamous women, were one of the standard devices of the *Querelle des femmes* just as examples of illustrious men or weak and vicious men helped to demonstrate the dignity and misery of man. In 1502 and 1503 the companion treatises the *Ship of Princes* or *Nef des princes* subtitled 'to understand how to live and die well' and the *Ship of Virtuous Ladies* or *Nef des dames vertueuses* included examples of men and women.[122] *The Nef des dames* opens with the 'Fleur des dames' – a list of famous women in the tradition of Boccaccio and Christine de Pisan.[123] These famous women might be drawn from the Old Testament or from among female saints or historical figures such as Joan of Arc.[124] The 'Fleur des princes' in the *Nef des princes* gathers examples of virtuous princes such as Philip of Macedon, as we discussed above. Champier's prologue to the *Nef des dames vertueuses* addresses 'the heap of people' who recount the sins of women with the 'malice of a venomous tongue'. The attackers of women remind their readers of Medea killing her children, Bathsheba misleading David, Delilah betraying Samson, Sarah killing her seven husbands, and the destruction of the city of Troy for the beauty of Helen. In all these incidents, however, Champier traces the 'principal cause' back to men. He compares women to 'sheep in front of the wolf'; without access to the Scriptures they don't know how to defend themselves. 'I ask you, who say such things, why do you not repeat the good as well as the bad'? Why not recall instead the virginity and humility of Mary, Suzanne's chastity, Lucretia's purity, Judith's wisdom, the 'prowess' of Penthasilea, the prophecies of the Sybils, and the valour of Queen Semiramis?[125] Typical of the genre, Champier complains about the malicious *exempla*, repeats them, and then provides his own illustrious examples in defence of woman, demonstrating his ability to argue *in utramque partem* – on both sides of an argument. The *Querelle* writers needed attacks on women in order to come to their defence.[126]

---

[122] Symphorien Champier, *La Nef des dames vertueuses* (Paris: Jehan de la Garde, 1515). In the first Lyon edition of 1503, dedicated to Anne de France, all Latin quotations were accompanied by a French translation, but the Latin was dropped in the later edition sold in Paris.

[123] Lionello Sozzi, 'Boccaccio in Francia nel cinquecento', in Carlo Pellegrini (ed.), *Boccaccio nella cultura francese* (Florence, 1971), p. 231.

[124] Boccaccio's *De claris mulieribus*, 1360–62, first became available in French print as *De nobles et clères femmes* at the Parisian bookseller Antoine Vérard in 1490. Two other collections of famous women that alter Boccaccio's tone – Antoine Dufour's *Les vies des femmes celebres*, 1504, written for Anne de Bretagne, and Christine de Pisan's *Cité des Dames*, 1399 – were never printed. See Dufour, *Femmes célèbres*, 'Introduction', pp. xxvi–xxxix, and 'Index générale des femmes illustres', pp. 208–11.

[125] Champier, *Nef des dames*, sig. b ii^{v}.

[126] Floyd Gray, *Gender, Rhetoric and Print Culture in French Renaissance Writing* (Cambridge, 2000), p. 13.

Treatises in defence of women drew attention to examples of female ingenuity in imitation of dignity-of-man commonplaces on the inventions of great men.[127] Jean de Marconville's paradox *On the Goodness and Badness of Women*, 1564, devotes a whole chapter to the 'Excellence of women and their ingenious inventions'. He starts out by praising life in a community, the invention of letters, the creation of law and the invention of the clock. He isolates the invention of letters as the most important one because it allowed the preservation of ideas: 'things that happened a thousand years ago are present to us'. He asks: 'But who was the inventor of such a great benefit to humankind? Was it the philosophers and wise men of times past?' Marconville singles out Carmenta, also known as Nicostraté, as the inventor of letters and writing.[128] Ceres receives credit for the invention of law and 'without [law] no households, no cities, republics or communities nor the world itself' could exist at all. Isis invented agriculture, Pallas invented spinning and making cloth. Marconville ponders the 'singularité', excellence or peerlessness, of 'their great minds' and claims that 'celestial favours' were more 'excellently granted' to women than to men. 'Because who is the man who was ever the inventor of a thing better for the adornment of the mind than letters, learning (*les sciences*) and law, and than wheat, wool-working and weaving (*textrine*) for the maintenance of the human body, and yet these are all feminine inventions?'[129]

To demonstrate the excellence of woman, *Querelle des femmes* writers drew upon the Scriptures, the histories of ancient Greece and ancient Rome, and on contemporary examples of women or royalty in the same way dignity-of-man writers compiled lists of exemplary warriors, kings, scholars and inventors.[130] Hélisenne de Crenne's letters cite a long list of learned ancient women such as Cornelia, the noble mother of the Gracchi brothers who 'taught them eloquence', and Aspasia, 'who was filled with such great knowledge that Socrates did not blush at learning anything from her'. But Hélisenne also praises her contemporary, the 'queen of Navarre', who combines 'Plato's godlike wisdom, Cato's prudence, Cicero's eloquence, and Socrates' wisdom' and so 'her brilliance enhances all of

---

127 Du Bartas, *Œuvres*, fos 305v–311r; Boaistuau, *Bref discours*, pp. 61–2; Billon, *Fort inexpugnable*, fos 22r, 24r, 26r.

128 Jean de Marconville, *De la bonté et mauvaistié des femmes* (Paris: Jean Dallier, 1564), sigs Bij^v– Biij^v or fos 10v–11v; Jean de Marconville, *De la bonté et mauvaistié des femmes*, ed. Richard Carr (Paris, 2000), p. 49. See also Sieur de Cholières [Jean Dagoneau], *La Guerre des masles contre les femelles: représentant en trois dialogues les prérogatives et dignitez tant de l'un que de l'autre sexe. Avec les meslanges poétiques du sieur de Cholieres* (Paris: Pierre Chevillot, 1588), fos 70v–72v.

129 Marconville, *De la bonté*, 1564 edn, fo. 13r or sig. Bv^r; Marconville, *De la bonté*, ed. Carr, p. 53.

130 Berriot-Salvadore, *Les femmes*, p. 355; Dufour, *Femmes célèbres*, ed. Jeanneau, 'Introduction', p. xxvii; Étienne Pasquier, *Le Monophile* [1554], ed. E.H. Balmas (Milan, 1957), p. 134.

womankind'.[131] As we have seen, two copies of Hélisenne de Crenne's familiar and invective letters, printed and sold by Denis Janot and his successors in front of Nôtre Dame Cathedral from the late 1530s through to 1560, could be found in the household of the notary Hodic and his wife by 1549.[132] Later in the century, writers such as Charles Estienne, Jean Marconville or Marie de Romieu listed Hélisenne de Crenne alongside Marguerite de Navarre or Christine de Pisan as examples of the excellence of woman.[133] But there was a catch to these exempla: the misogynist camp could claim that a learned woman such as Christine de Pisan was an exceptional case.[134] Defenders of women argued that these illustrious examples represented women's potential, given access to education and without the oppressive restrictions of custom. Women writers such as Louise Labé, Marie de Gournay and Charlotte de Brachart argued that once women did have the opportunity for education they should use their new skills to demonstrate the wrong men have committed by denying women access to it.[135]

In *The War of Males Against Females: Representing in Three Dialogues the Prerogatives and Dignities of One as well as the Other Sex*, published in 1588, the character Nicogène notes that to catalogue exemplary women and their inventions actually weakens their defence because it merely emphasises the fact that these

---

[131] Hélisenne de Crenne, *A Renaissance Woman: Helisenne's Personal and Invective Letters*, trans and eds Marianna Mustacchi and Paul Archambault (Syracuse, NY, 1986), pp. 100–101; Hélisenne de Crenne, *Les Œuvres de ma Dame Helisenne de Crenne. A sçavoir, les angoisses douloureuses qui procedent d'amours. Les Epistres familières et invectives & Le songe de ladicte dame. Le tout reveu & corrigé de nouveau par elle* (Paris: Estienne Groulleau, 1560), facsimile edn (Geneva, 1977), sigs O v^{r}–O vi^{r}.

[132] MC, AN, Paris, Hodic inventory, 1549, III, 300, fos 31r, 32v.

[133] Charles Estienne, 'Pour les femmes: Declamation XXIIII. Que l'excellence de la femme est plus grande que celles de l'homme', in *Paradoxes ce sont propos contre la commune opinion: debats, en forme de declamations forenses: pour exerciter les ieunes advocats en causes difficiles* (Poitiers: Jean de Marnef, 1553), pp. 183–4; Marconville, *De la bonté*, ed. Carr, p. 92; Marie de Romieu, 'Brief Discours: Que l'excellence de la femme surpasse celle de l'homme, autant recreatif que plein de beaux exemples', in *Les premières œuvres poétiques*, ed. Andre Winandy (Geneva, 1972), pp. 20–21, lines 296–306; Evelyne Berriot-Salvadore, 'Les héritières de Louise Labé', in Guy Demerson (ed.), *Louise Labé, les voix du lyrisme* (Lyon, 1991), p. 94.

[134] Ian Maclean comments that contemporaries question whether 'famous women are exceptional or whether they are an indication that all their sex possesses such virtue which is repressed by law and custom' – see *Woman Triumphant: Feminism in French Literature 1610–1652* (Oxford, 1977), p. 22; Ian Maclean, *The Renaissance Notion of Woman* (Cambridge, 1980), p. 63.

[135] Louise Labé, 'A M.C.D.B.L.', in *Oeuvres complètes*, ed. François Rigolot (Paris, 1986), pp. 41–3; Gournay, *Égalité*, pp. 970–73; Charlotte Brachart, *Harengue faicte par damoiàselle Charlotte de Brachart surnommée Arétuze qui s'adrese aux hommes qui veuillent deffendre la science aux femmes* (Chalon-sur-Saône: Jean Des Preyz, 1604), p. 5.

women are exceptions.[136] But then he turns the spotlight back on his own sex. Nicogène asks: 'Are all men like Lycurgus?' It is one thing to consider the actions or lives of exemplary women, 'but to hope to encompass the whole feminine sex, would be as well argued as to say that because there was a Solon and Lycurgus that all males are worthy of meddling with such excellent offices and employments'.[137] Exemplary men attain an excellence unparalleled by the rest.

The *Querelle des femmes* often overlapped with the discussion of the potential and excellence of man to highlight the dignities of woman, but the comparison did not end there. Discussions of the nature of man and woman entwined to ridicule the follies of both sexes.

Grands hommes and their Foibles in the *Querelle des femmes*

Comparing the relative merits and weaknesses of man with those of woman was a dominant feature of the *Querelle des femmes* because it could serve to humble man and his pride while promoting female virtue and achievement. Highlighting the vices of the great men of history reminded the male or female reader how even those in positions of power were not exempt from vice. Man or woman, from the lowly to the nobility, needed to govern the self.

In the late fifteenth century Guillaume Alexis, a cleric, translated Innocent III's treatise on human misery and vice into French verse as *The Past-time of Every Man and Every Woman*, which we examined as part of the misery-of-man tradition. To accompany his translation and to focus more specifically on the relations between the sexes Alexis wrote a dialogue entitled the *Debate of Man and Woman* – one of the few dialogues in which a female voice defends her sex. Alexis' Man attacks female vices while the representative Woman points to male vice and demonstrates the abundance of female virtue. In the 1493 edition, produced in the Paris workshop of Denis Janot's grandfather, Woman points out the sins of men: Cain's murder of Abel, Judas' betrayal of Jesus, how the Apostles denied him and how men crucified him.[138] She surveys the crimes of vicious male leaders such as Herod and Nero. Men hide the vices of their sex and try to distract attention from their sins by blaming women: 'Of [their own] great excesses and misdeeds / Men never speak'.[139] She contrasts male sin with the virtue of Mary, Hester and Judith. Even a wise man like Abraham was instructed by the Lord to listen to his wife Sarah. 'There are more men in prison', Woman asserts, '[a]nd

---

136 Cholières, *Guerre*, fo. 72v.

137 Ibid., fos 75v–76r.

138 Guillaume Alexis, *Le débat de l'omme et de la femme*, in *Œuvres*, vol. I, pp. 144, 134–6 on Joseph, David, Solomon, Virgil, Samson, Priam, Paris and Hector – see lines 25–7, 33–5, 41–2, 57–9, 65–7.

139 Ibid., p. 142, lines 165–6: 'Des grans oultrages et meffais / Des hommes ne parlent jamais'.

more women at sermons'.[140] The Woman even takes the counteroffensive with a 'reply' (*replique*) to close the debate. Men defame all women, she claims, when they overlook the good, which outweighs any sin.

> Men show themselves to be infamous
> In wanting to defame women
> Some evil has come from [women]
> But has been exceeded by many good things.
>
> *Les hommes se monstrent infames*
> *En voulant diffamer les femmes*
> *Aucun mal en est procedé;*
> *Mais les grans biens ont excedé.*[141]

She advises that the practice of vituperation should be suppressed: 'No one wins through reproach'.[142]

By highlighting male weakness an author could serve two purposes: to dissuade the reader from vice, because even great men needed to be vigilant about their moral conduct, and to indicate the path of virtue. Agrippa, for example, parodies the *hommes illustres* tradition by referring to the examples of famous women who duped the best of men. Adam was the best and most noble man created by God, but a woman brought him down – a 'femme l'a abaissé'. Samson was a strong man, but a woman exceeded his force; Lot was provoked to incest by his daughters; and it was a woman who challenged David's saintliness. With periphrastic speech, Agrippa suppresses the women's names in all of these examples. None of the women were to blame; these illustrious men merely succumbed to their own wretched vices.[143]

Turning Man's Dignity into Female Fragility

Defenders of women, such as Agrippa, publicise male vice to amplify female virtue, whereas the 'assailants' of the female sex use examples of female weakness to establish man's dignity. Again, these attacks on woman adapt many commonplaces from the debate on the dignity and misery of man and, as always,

---

140 Ibid., on Mary, p. 134, lines 29–31; on Hester, p. 136, lines 53–5; on Judith, p. 136, lines 61–3; on Abraham and Sarah, p. 140, lines 125–7; on pious women and wicked men, p. 143, lines 197–8.

141 Ibid., p. 142, lines 161–4.

142 Ibid., p. 144.

143 Henricus Cornelius Agrippa, *De nobilitate et præcellentia fœminei sexus* (1529), eds R. Antonioli, *et al.* (Geneva, 1990), p. 101; E.V. Telle, *L'Œuvre de Marguerite d'Angoulême Reine de Navarre et la querelle des femmes* (Toulouse, 1937), p. 49.

the creation story provided the starting point. Man is more worthy (*digne*) than woman – 'L'homme est plus digne que la femme' – for five reasons stemming from the creation story: order, form, matter, authority and degree. First of all man had 'priority' – he came before Eve. Secondly, woman has an inferior 'form' because she was made from the bone of Adam's rib, from only a part of man, not the whole. Dwelling on woman as the 'imperfect man' or 'half a man' highlighted male perfection. Thirdly, woman was made from 'roigneures' – the leftovers after the creation of Adam.[144] Fourthly, God never gave any authority to woman, for as Genesis makes clear, woman was subject to man. Adam alone was given dominion over the earth, and as ruler he names the animals. The fifth factor is the question of degree. Defenders of women liked to draw dignity from Mary's conception of Jesus, but attackers of women pointed to Adam as the father of woman.[145]

The best retort to a characterisation of the sexes – based on male physical perfection and female debility as the imperfect male or 'homme demy' – can be found in an anonymous dialogue of 1516. In the *Apologetic Dialogue Excusing or Defending the Devout Feminine Sex* the character Badmouther (*Bouche maldisant*) asks Defending Woman (*Femme deffendant*) how she can compare 'feminine strength with virile virtue' because it is known that 'the feminine sex' is by 'nature frail and weak'. In her reply Defending Woman draws on Aristotelian notions of conception, which claimed that a change in the direction of the wind or sexual position might determine whether a child was male or female. Just as writers on the misery of man reduce a man's status to the fortune of his birth, Defending Woman reduces the significance of the body to the role of fortune at conception. She retorts that 'the circumstance of sex is in the body not the mind, because there is no difference between man and woman in the soul, but as the natural philosophers say, sex is a bodily and accidental condition'.[146] Defending Woman, like her misery-of-man counterparts who question rank and status, suggests that all humans are the same and therefore equal, with only fortune or accident introducing difference. Misery-of-man writers often used this commonplace to reinforce the role of each estate, maintain the status quo, and to remind the noble and the prince to be on guard against a misplaced pride.

Writing on the dignity of man played on the wonder of his creation – with praise of all man's body parts including his face, which looked up towards the heavens.

---

144 Gratien Dupont, *Les Controversses des sexes masculin et femenin* (Toulouse: Jacques Colomiés, 1534), fo. xxxix; Le Franc, *Champion*, 1530 edn, fo. lxxxvi^{r-v}.

145 For these five reasons of male superiority, see Dupont, *Controverses*, 1534 edn, fos xxxvii^{r}–xlii^{r}; Gratien Dupont, *Controverses des sexes masculin et fœmenin* (Paris: Denis Janot, 1540), Bk II, fos 15v 25r or sigs B vii^{v}–DD^{r}; ; see below, pp. 87, 89; these reasons might be overturned to prove female superiority, see C. Estienne, 'Pour les femmes', in *Paradoxes*, 1553 edn, pp. 177–9.

146 *Dialogue apologétique excusant ou deffendant le dévot sexe fémenin, introduict par deulx personnaiges, l'un a nom Bouche maldisant, l'autre Femme deffendant* (Paris: [attributed to Frédéric d'Egmont], 1516), fo. lvii^{r}.

Eve shared in this praise; her face was widely assumed to be more beautiful. Of course every point of praise could be overturned and in this titillating manner a writer could focus on the base parts of a woman's body and bring her down from the heights of dignity. The response to the *Blasons anatomiques du corps feminin*, entitled the *Counterpraises* or *Contreblasons*, denigrates all of the female body parts. A short poem of ten lines within the *Contreblasons* offers an explanation to the reader. Although the body is 'well formed' a more 'beautiful creature', the 'celestial soul', lives inside. 'The soul is divine and the body rottenness', which is why each person should disdain the body.[147] Following the editions of the *Hecatomphile*, which contained the *Blasons*, and the separate editions of the *Blasons* from 1536 to 1550, a further response entitled *The Praise of Woman* or *Le Blason de la femme* appeared in an anonymous collection distributed by the Lyon merchant printer Jean de Tournes. This poem pretended to present the best case for female beauty by suggesting that a woman's fading beauty seeks refuge in artifice.[148] Woman's hair is like the serpents of Medusa, her body is 'fardé' or powdered, and underneath her rouge a woman's flesh is gnawed away by the pox – 'rongee de verole'. She appears to have skin like alabaster, but really she coats it with plaster. She hides her sagging breasts because she is a golddigger. Perhaps the bawdiest section is the description of woman's 'stinking hole' – the author's method of ensuring that woman could not share in man's dignity. The rest of woman is useless – 'ne sert à rien' – except to deprive man of all his worldly goods.[149] Each point of dignity could be overturned to show fragility or worse. But this could apply to man and to woman.

The *Poetic Judgement of Feminine Honour and Sojourn of Illustrious, Shining and Honest Ladies*, sold in front of the Palais de Justice in Poitiers from 1536, balances dignity with misery by assessing man's and woman's roles in the household and in society. In the opening pages Jean Bouchet reminds the reader that human creatures are 'nothing' or 'vanity'. All are 'sinners' and therefore Bouchet finds it 'absurd' that some men defame 'the noble feminine sex' in speech and in writing.[150] He opens his book in defence of woman with a section on the excellence of man. God fashioned Eve from Adam's rib, so man is the 'chief' or head of woman. Bouchet 'protests' he does not favour the 'honour of women' over

---

[147] Charles de la Hueterie, 'Dizain', in *Blasons*, fo. 85v; Billon, *Fort inexpugnable*, fo. 6v.

[148] 'Le Blason de la femme', in *La Louenge des femmes, Invention extraite du commentaire de Pantagruel, sus L'Androgyne de Platon* (Lyon: Jean de Tournes, 1551), facs. edn Ruth Calder (New York, 1967), pp. 9–15.

[149] Ibid., p. 13.

[150] Jean Bouchet, 'Apologie de l'autheur', *Le Jugement poetic de l'honneur femenin & sejour des illustres claires & honestes dames* (Poitiers: A l'enseigne du Pelican davant le Palais [Marnef brothers], 1536), sigs aa ii^{r}–aa ii^{v}. On Bouchet see Berriot-Salvadore, *Les femmes*, pp. 34–9; Richardson, *Forerunners of Feminism*, pp. 71–4.

men; rather, he intends to 'keep each one in his due place and quality'.[151] Bouchet then proceeds to a consideration of the excellence of woman over man using the creation story commonplaces about the material, place and order of creation. Man was created from the 'slime of the earth' – 'lymon de la terre' – whereas God fashioned woman from a 'rational creature', a 'creature raisonnable'. Woman came to life in Paradise, whereas man was created outside, and so on. He asserts with Agrippa and Le Franc that woman's soul, like man's, was created in the image of God. If men have prerogatives, such as the administration of the sacraments and public roles of government, they also have concomitant responsibilities and 'dangers' to their souls, bodies and 'goods', whereas women should be content 'to have been relieved' of these responsibilities.[152] At home, however, a wife might provide advice because the 'learning' [*science*] and 'prudence' of wives 'builds the household' – 'edifie la maison'. Like the misery-of-man treatises denouncing human presumption, Bouchet advises 'each person' to consider 'the end or reason [he or she] was created and placed on this earth' – to serve, honour and glorify God. He concludes that, if the feminine sex possesses some faults, 'I intend only to demonstrate' that there are also 'many excellences in this sex'. One sex should not extol itself over the other, because 'God is the only true judge of the goodness and the malice of men and women'.[153] Echoing the misery-of-man treatises that counsel the maintenance of estate and discourage the ambitious lower ranks from seeking the dizzy heights of dignity, Bouchet urges each sex to maintain its role.

Many writers weighed positive and negative aspects of each sex and intensified the goodness of one to exacerbate the damage to the other. Writers in Renaissance France acknowledged that there was no one truth and alluded to diverse possibilities. Sometimes writers emphasised dignity, sometimes misery, sometimes virtue, sometimes vice, sometimes man, sometimes woman.

Woman Shares the Misery of Man in Marriage

One of the themes of the misery of man was to accentuate the shared human experiences of people from all ranks and occupations from the lowly peasants, artisans and soldiers to nobles and princes.[154] There was a long tradition of including the miseries of husband and wife as a stage of adulthood in the lifecycle. Innocent III's medieval treatise on the misery of the human condition, *De miseria*

---

151 The margin announces 'De l'excellence de l'homme': Bouchet, *Le Jugement poetic*, sig. aa iii^{r}.

152 The margin indicates 'De l'excellence de la femme': ibid., sig. A iiii^{r}.

153 Ibid., sigs A iii^{v}–Aiiii^{r}.

154 Boaistuau, *Théâtre*, pp. 101–4, 113, 226–7, 230; Simonin, 'Introduction', in ibid., p. 19; Pope Innocent III [Lotario dei Segni], *De miseria condicionis humane*, ed. Robert Lewis (Athens, GA, 1978), Bk I, pp. 92–104; Deschamps, *Double lay de la fragilité humaine*, in *Œuvres completes*, vol. II, pp. 256–7.

condicionis humane, devoted the seventh chapter to the misery of the celibate and the married. When Guillaume Alexis' adapted and updated Innocent III's *De miseria* for a popular French version printed in 1505, he described how a wife hounds her husband.[155] Eustache Deschamps' translation of Innocent III's *De miseria*, which circulated only in manuscript, expanded the 'misery of marriage' chapter into an entirely separate treatise, the *Mirror of marriage*.

In the late 1500s Philippe Desportes and Nicole Estienne built on the misery of marriage theme with their literary exchange on the woes of married life from the perspectives of husband and wife. Philippe Desportes' *Stances on marriage* (1573) explains that no torment imposed on the world by the gods could equal the misery wrought by the 'law of marriage' upon a man, not 'bloody murder' nor 'worries', 'labour', 'hunger' or 'poverty'. He plays on the typical *Querelle des femmes* complaints about each type of wife a man might marry – whether she is rich, poor, beautiful or ugly.[156] Nicole Estienne's response in the 'Stanzas on marriage' initially circulated in manuscript, but was published in the 1580s under her married name Madame Liebault as *The Miseries of the Married Woman*. Estienne turns the tables by listing how a wife must suffer if she marries a poor man, a rich disdainful husband, or wastes her youth on a cruel old spouse. The daughter of the printer and writer Charles Estienne and a relative of the Estienne printing dynasty who published Desportes' poems, Nicole Estienne seeks in vain the so-called man of dignity and wisdom who would appreciate a learned, virtuous wife. She laments that all too frequently an 'unfit' husband (*malhabille*) marries a 'gentle woman' who is 'wise, of a rare mind, and of good judgment' – 'femme gentille, [s]age, de rare esprit & de bon jugement.' The ignorant husband invariably disregards his wife's learning, although a 'mindful person' (*discret personage*) would appreciate this precious gift. Estienne continues, 'But truly such a man is very rare around here' – 'Mais certes un tel homme est bien rare icy bas'. She recounts the tale of the Greek Cynic searching the city for wise men. Even with a lamp at high noon he could probably not find one in 10,000. Estienne laments the absence of men of reason because they would not prevent women from studying nor treat their wives as servants.[157] In their discussions of marriage as a stage in the

---

155 Alexis, *Le Passe temps*, in *Œuvres*, vol. II, pp. 135–40.

156 Philippe Desportes, *Stances du mariage*, in *Les premières œuvres* (Paris: Robert Estienne, 1573), fos 82v, 84r–v, Stance I:

> De toutes les fureurs dont nous sommes pressez …
> D'angoisseuses langueurs, de meurtre ensanglanté,
> De soucis, de travaux, de faim, de pauvreté,
> Rien n'approche en rigueur la loy de Mariage.

157 [Nicole Estienne] Madame Liebault, *Les misères de la femme mariée, où se peuvent voir les peines et tourmens qu'elle reçoit durant sa vie. Mis en forme de stances* (Paris: Pierre Menier, no date), sigs B ij^{r}–Biij^{v}; Jean-Antoine Rigoley de Juvigny (ed.), *Les Bibliothèques françoises de La Croix du Maine et de Du Verdier*, 6 vols (Paris: Saillant and Nyon, 1772–73), vol. III, p. 141; Hélène Cazès, 'Nicole Estienne à ses miroirs: les

lifecycle from the male and female perspectives, Desportes intertwines misery-of-man themes while Estienne defends the wife by satirising both the dignity- and misery-of-man literature.

Boaistuau's *Théâtre du monde* introduces marriage as part of the lifecycle or an age of man coinciding with adulthood. Yet in an aberration from the misery-of-man tradition Boaistuau expresses his reluctance to defame marriage and in stark contrast to the rest of the book he inserts a 'Praise of marriage to show the miseries that follow'.[158] This digression on the excellence of marriage is a curious sidestep in a treatise exploring the human misery of famine, war, plague and every occupation or trade. For all other aspects of life Boaistuau waits until the companion treatise, the *Bref Discours*, to rehabilitate human dignity and excellence.

Boaistuau praises the *femme* as a wife who grows into the 'treasurer and loyal guardian of the most intimate secrets'. In this 'friendship', the two become one. If the husband wishes to remain alone in his house, 'he has his wife who keeps him company' and 'comforts him'. In his absence his wife will 'desire and honour' him. When he comes back he is 'welcomed, cherished and favoured with the most delicate caresses that nature has taught her'. To 'speak the truth' woman is a 'gift of heaven granted to man as much for the refreshment and contentment of his youth as for the peace and comfort of his old age'. Marriage also provides an 'infinity of pleasures' in children, whose babbling, amusements and games help to 'circumvent' parts of 'our miserable life'. Boaistuau draws the reader's attention to his extensive praise of 'the excellence and dignity of marriage' in a 'mirror for prince' treatise already published by Vincent Sertenas, the Palais de Justice bookseller.[159] In fact, Boaistuau recycles whole sections of his 'mirror for prince' book in which he further elaborates many of the familiar *Querelle des femmes* commonplaces in praise of woman such as the place, order and material of creation.[160] Finally Boaistuau turns to the misery of marriage 'because my subject (which treats the miseries of all estates of our life) requires that I pardon this one no more than the others'. Boaistuau is careful to put any words against women and wives into the mouths of 'several authors', especially Guillaume de la Perrière, 'author of the *Political Mirror*' and, as we saw earlier, author of the moral emblem books *Théâtre des bons engins* sold by Denis Janot in the 1540s and the *Morosophie* of 'foolish wisdom'.[161] The complaints about women within marriage harp on their

"félicitéz" de mariage et les *Misères de la femme mariée*', in J. Lecointe, *et al.* (eds), *Devis d'amitié, Mélanges en l'honneur de Nicole Cazauran* (Paris, 2002), pp. 747–66.

[158] Boaistuau, *Théâtre*, pp. 162, 281, n. 269.

[159] Ibid., p. 164.

[160] Boaistuau, *Institution du royaume chrestien*, fos 132r–133v, Simonin, 'Introduction', in Boaistuau, *Théâtre*, p. 11; Michel Simonin, 'Notes sur Pierre Boaistuau', *Bibliothèque d'Humanisme et Renaissance* 38:2 (1976): 326, n. 7.

[161] Boaistuau, *Théâtre*, pp. 164, 166; Boaistuau conceals Erasmus as his source for the praise of woman possibly because Louis de Berquin was executed for his translation of Erasmus' work, see Telle's 'Introduction' to Erasmus, *Déclamation des louenges de*

'insolence' and 'arrogance'. Boaistuau points out how his sources wonder – 'they say' – how one could tolerate the 'yoke of such an imperfect sex'.

Boaistuau weighs up both sides of an argument. In placing his praise of marriage in the middle of a treatise on the misery of human life, Boaistuau reminds the reader that 'one will find among these roses many thorns' – there are two sides to the story.[162] He emphasises the opposing voices, but concludes that one might find much bitterness among the 'sweetnesses and delights' of marriage and to 'speak the truth' we must confess that 'if we wish to counterpoise the defects [*eclipses*] and miseries with the pleasures and delights ... one does not surpass the other'.

In the imitation, borrowing, and compilation of examples, we find a continual overlap and intertextuality of themes and commonplaces between the dignity and misery of man and the *Querelle des femmes*. As we saw in chapter two in the case of Speroni's dialogue on the 'dignity of women', this theme might be sold in a wide-ranging collection of his dialogues or packaged with a translation of Plutarch's advice on marriage and another dialogue on the care of the household.[163] In the case of Boaistuau in the 1550s, his praise of woman and marriage might appear in his 'mirror for princes' book or in the middle of his 'ample discourse of human miseries'.

The Dignity and Misery of Man ... and of Woman

Many of the commonplaces of the French dignity- and misery-of-man literature parallel and intersect with the debate on the nature of woman. The creation story and the Bible supplied abundant opportunities to dwell on the excellence of man and of woman, but the base human appetites and penchant for vice could not be ignored. The human condition lent itself to a *pro et contra* discussion. Man, the 'king of animals' and 'Lord of this lower universe', could easily be humbled. Similarly woman, despite her position as God's final creation and 'masterpiece', was considered to be fragile by nature and tempted by vice. Weighing human vice and virtue provided moral lessons in how to govern oneself – as necessary for the mighty prince as for the aspiring merchant, the officeholding noble and their wives. Pico della Mirandola's optimistic Renaissance vision of Adam as able to ascend to the level of the divine has helped to characterise this era as one of possibility, free choice and social mobility.[164] But for many *bourgeois* or low-level officeholders, sixteenth-century France was also an era of frustrated ambition and 'diminishing' expectations as families struggled to maintain their places in the social hierarchy.

marriage [attribution to Paris: Simon Dubois, 1525], facsimile ed. E.V. Telle (Geneva, 1976).

162 Boaistuau, *Théâtre*, p. 165.

163 See Chapter 2, pp. 37–9.

164 Charles Nauert, *Humanism and the Culture of Renaissance Europe*, 2nd edn (Cambridge, 2006), pp. 75–6.

One could easily stagnate at a lower level of being. Parents and bachelor sons knew the importance of a wife to a family's status: her social connections, her birth family's networks, the potential inflow of wealth from her dowry, as well as her abilities to govern the houschold and to 'preserve and increase the family things'.[165]

The review of the commonplaces of the dignity and misery of man alongside the *Querelle des femmes* commonplaces in this chapter establishes why it is essential to juxtapose these themes. While scholars have studied each of these debates separately, the shared rhetorical tradition of the dignity and misery of man and the *Querelle des femmes* has long been neglected. It is particularly important to emphasise the opposing voices of praise and blame as applied to the ideas of man and woman. Otherwise we fall into the assumption that praise of woman was an early form of feminism or dismiss it altogether as 'mere rhetoric'. Moreover, without an understanding of the practices of contradiction and opposing voices in Renaissance discussions of man and woman, we misconstrue the blame of the female sex as misogyny. The Renaissance idea of the dignity of man, too, was mitigated by the potential for vice and weakness. There is too much crossover to ignore how each debate overlapped with and borrowed from the other. By paying attention to the practices of imitation as well as the many shared and adapted commonplaces of the dignity and misery of man and the *Querelle des femmes*, the continuities of the debates emerge. This comparison of the Renaissance discussions of man and woman, husbands and wives, vices and virtues, also reveals the fundamental similarities of the social concerns for the place of the family and household in an era of upward social mobility for some and stagnation for others.

This chapter also continued to examine the theme, initially raised in chapter two, of how texts on man and woman and their vices and virtues were packaged and marketed by authors, merchant printers and booksellers. Chapter four examines the rhetorical practices of the printed *Querelle des femmes* and how and when the treatises were published and promoted by the merchant printers and booksellers separately from the dignity of man tradition, while chapter five focuses on how *Querelle des femmes* themes were integrated into dialogues and collections on the diversity of the human condition.

[165] Claude Baduel, *Traicté trèsutile et fructueux de la dignité de mariage et de l'honneste conversation des gens doctes, & lettrez*, trans. Guy de la Garde (Paris: Arnoul L'Angelier, 1548), sig. E^{r}.

Chapter 4
The *Querelle des femmes*

Like Renaissance dignity- and misery-of-man literature, the *Querelle des femmes* began in the late Middle Ages in manuscript. The *Querelle* gained momentum when Christine de Pisan queried why she seemed to encounter only malicious women in her reading of texts such as the *Roman de la Rose* when her acquaintances and women of the French court were modest, chaste and humble.[1] Three allegorical female figures – Ladies Reason, Right and Justice – appeared before Christine in a vision to compel her to build a *City of Ladies* to defend her sex. So she began to compile examples of illustrious and worthy women to counter the allegations about woman's nature found in writing by men. The sequel, the *Treasure of the City of Ladies*, was an advice manual of moral conduct for 'women of all estates' from princesses to prostitutes.[2] Martin Le Franc, the prévôt of Lausanne, came to the defence of woman with the *Champion of Ladies* in the 1440s. Le Franc's manuscript went into print around 1485 and Galiot du Pré, one of the first *libraire juré* of the University of Paris and a contemporary of Denis Janot's father, had the *Champion des dames* reprinted in 1530 to sell from his boutique at the first pillar in the Great Hall of the Palais de Justice.[3] The title page made clear both the adversarial nature of the text and the eventual victory of the Champion: *A Pleasant Book of Copious and Abundant Sayings. Containing the Defence of Ladies against Badmouth and his Consorts, and the Ladies' Victory*. Le Franc's champion, Free Will (*Franc Vouloir*), defends woman against a series of real and imagined adversaries such as Jean de Meun (co-author of the *Roman de la Rose*), Matheolus, Nasty Thought (*Vilain Penser*) and Badmouth (*Malebouche*).[4] The views of these medieval adversaries spread as booksellers turned manuscripts into

1 Margarete Zimmermann, 'The *Querelle des femmes* as Cultural Studies Paradigm', in Anne Jacobson Schutte, *et al.* (eds), *Time, Space and Women's Lives in Early Modern Europe* (Kirksville, MO, 2001), p. 20.

2 Christine de Pisan, *Le Trésor de la cité des dames, selon dame Christine de la cité de Pise, livre tresutile & prouffitable pour l'introduction des roynes, dames, princesses, & autres femmes de tous estatz, auquel elles pourront veoir la grande & saine richesse de toute prudence, saigesse, honeur, & dignité dedans contenues* (Paris: Denis Janot for Jehan André, 1536), title page.

3 For the manuscript and early printed versions of the *Champion des dames* see Helen Swift, *Gender, Writing, Performance: Men Defending Women in Late Medieval France, 1440–1538* (Oxford, 2008), Appendix 2.

4 Martin Le Franc, *Le Champion des dames. Livre plaisant copieux & habondant en sentences. Contenant la deffence des dames contre Malebouche & ses consors, & victoire*

print. In the late 1530s and early 1540s Denis Janot sold the *Roman de la Rose* as his father Jean had done. But the edition that the younger Janot sold in front of Nôtre Dame Cathedral and the L'Angelier brothers stocked in their boutique in the Palais de Justice had been updated and improved with roman and italic typefaces. These Île de la Cité booksellers were participating in a popular trend as the *Roman de la Rose* enjoyed 21 editions between 1481 and 1538.[5] Boccaccio's fourteenth-century manuscript collection of stories of 'famous' women circulated in a printed French translation in the last decade of the fifteenth century. By the late 1530s Boccaccio's 'pleasant book … in which he debates the feats and behaviour of illustrious … ladies' could again be found in the Palais de Justice at the stalls of the L'Angelier brothers. Versions in many European languages were popular in personal libraries both in manuscript and in print.[6] Some classical works on the subject of woman and the household such as Plutarch's treatise on the 'government of marriage' also began to appear in French translation for sale by Janot and the Palais booksellers.[7]

Not surprisingly, new contributions to the *Querelle* began to appear. New texts in print such as Pierre de Lesnauderie's 1523 *Praise of Marriage and Collection of Stories of Good, Virtuous and Illustrious Women* gathered classical and biblical examples of women's endeavours and actions, and like Boccaccio's collection of famous women, not all these stories were about female virtue.[8] In 1509, on his way to lecture in Italy, Henricus Cornelius Agrippa stayed in Lyon with Symphorien Champier, the doctor and author of the companion treatises the *Nef des princes* and the *Nef des dames vertueuses*.[9] In the autumn of that year, Agrippa delivered a lecture in Latin *On the Nobility and Pre-Excellence of the Feminine Sex* and circulated it in manuscript. When the lecture was published 20 years later at Antwerp with an imperial privilege *On the Nobility and Pre-Excellence of the Feminine Sex* altered the format of the *Querelle des femmes* in print because it

---

d'icelles. Compose par Martin Franc, secretaire du feu pape Felix V & nouvellement imprimé à Paris (Paris: Galiot du Pré, 1530), fos lxxiiii^{v}–lxxvi^{r}, cxvii^{v}–cxxiii^{r}.

5 Swift, *Gender, Writing, Performance*, p. 24.

6 Giovanni Boccaccio, *Le Livre de Jehan Bocasse de la louenge et vertu des nobles et cleres dames, translaté et imprimé novellement à Paris* (Paris: Antoine Vérard, 1493); Giovanni Boccaccio, *Le plaisant livre de noble homme Jehan Bocace, poète florentin, auquel il traicte des faictz et gestes des illustres et cleres dames* (Paris: Arnoul and Charles L'Angelier, 1538); Margaret Franklin, *Boccaccio's Heroines: Power and Virtue in Renaissance Society* (Aldershot, 2006), pp. 9–13.

7 Plutarch, *Plutarche de Cheroné, grec, ancien philosophe et historiographe, traictant entierement du gouvernement en mariage* (Paris: Denis Janot, 1536).

8 Pierre de Lesnauderie, *La Louenge de mariage et recueil des hystoires des bonnes, vertueuses et illustres femmes* (Paris: Pierre Sergent, 1523), fos iiii^{v}–v^{r}.

9 Charles Nauert, *Agrippa and the Crisis of Renaissance Thought* (Urbana, IL, 1965), pp. 20–24, 75–97; R. Antonioli, 'Préface', in Henricus Cornelius Agrippa, *De nobilitate et præcellentia fœminei sexus* [1529], eds R. Antonioli, *et al.* (Geneva, 1990), p. 11.

set out to prove the superiority of woman without repeating all the anti-woman commonplaces. Parisian booksellers stocked the first French translation of this treatise on the excellence of woman around 1530. From about 1535 Denis Janot sold two separate French editions on the rue Neuve Nôtre Dame in Paris and a Lyon bookseller printed another French translation in 1537.[10] Agrippa's approach inspired numerous sixteenth-century imitators, enjoyed translations into several European languages, and ushered in a new chapter in the *Querelle des femmes*.[11]

As we saw in chapter two, in 1549 the Parisian household of the notary Gilbert de Hodic and his wife Geneviève Bureau and Bureau's country house contained many of these *Querelle des femmes* texts. The couple had two copies of the *Roman de la Rose*, Boccaccio's collection of famous women and the 'book of Badmouth (*Malebouche*)', which could be the adversary Malebouche identified in the long title of the *Champion des dames* published by Galiot du Pré (who recorded the post-mortem inventory of their library), and a copy of a book entitled the *Praises of Marriage* ('louenges de marraige') possibly by Pierre de Lesnauderie or another work of the same name by Erasmus. The title on 'the feminine sex' ('le sexe feminin'), could be Agrippa's work on the excellence of the feminine sex or perhaps the verse form of Agrippa's treatise by François Habert.[12] As we shall see, the couple also owned many of the other titles discussed in this chapter.

To make sense of the *Querelle des femmes* texts we continue the examination of rhetorical practices begun in the previous chapter, evaluating the opposing and dissenting voices. We consider the problem of contradictory strategies and inconsistencies in arguments in praise of woman and confront the rare works that dared to attack the female sex in print without including any kind of defence of women. The role of the merchant booksellers and print distribution networks in

---

10 Henricus Cornelius Agrippa, *De la noblesse & preexcellence du sexe fœminin* (Paris: Denis Janot, c. 1535). The edition must date from 1535 when Janot had settled his business address because the title page indicates: 'On les vend à Paris par Denys Janot demourant en la rue Neuve nostre Dame à l'enseigne Sainct Iehan Baptiste, pres Saincte Geneviesue des Ardens'. For details of the editions see Stephen Rawles, 'Denis Janot Parisian printer and bookseller, 1529–1544. A bibliographical study', 3 vols, PhD thesis, University of Warwick (1976), bibliography nos. 227, 228. Janot probably copied the first French edition of the *De la noblesse & preexcellence du sexe fœminin* issued by the Parisian booksellers Gerard Morrhy and Jean Pierre c. 1530. See Philippe Renouard and Brigitte Moreau (eds), *Inventaire chronologique des éditions parisiennes*, 5 vols (Paris, 1972–), vol. II (1521–30).

11 Margarete Zimmermann, 'Querelle des Femmes, querelles du livre', in D. de Courcelles and Carmen Val Julián (eds), *Des femmes et des livres: France et Espagnes, XIVe–XVIIe siècle* (Paris, 1999), p. 88.

12 Minutier central des notaires de Paris, Archives nationales, Paris [hereafter MC, AN, Paris], post-mortem inventory of Gilbert de Hodic, notary, 21 October 1549, III, 300, fos 30v, 31r, 32r; see Chapter 2, pp. 42–9; Desiderius Erasmus, *Déclamation des louenges de mariage*, trans. Louis de Berquin [attribution to Paris: Simon Dubois, 1525], facs. edn E.V. Telle (Geneva, 1976).

packaging and perpetuating the *Querelle des femmes* and in promoting these texts remains under scrutiny as well.

The Archer's Strategy and the 'Problem of Inconsistency' in the *Querelle des femmes*

Most scholars have treated the *Querelle des femmes* separately from the rest of moral philosophy in part because they have scoured the defences of women to look for early sparks of 'feminism'. The terms 'feminism' and 'anti-feminism', although anachronistic, are often applied to the opposing sides of the *Querelle des femmes*.[13] These studies perform an essential service in assessing the place of women in early modern society and tracing the development of feminist thought, but as we have seen in the previous chapter they fail to recognise the extent to which the *Querelle des femmes* imitated and borrowed from the rest of moral philosophy – including commonplaces from the dignity- and misery-of-man tradition – to praise woman or to blame her.[14] More seriously, the anti-woman statements may be misconstrued as strictly 'misogynist' if we fail to compare them with the numerous attacks on man's vices and the descriptions of the miserable human condition.[15] In her groundbreaking studies in the late 1970s and early 1980s Joan Kelly characterised the *Querelle* 'defenses of women' as 'responses to specific published attacks upon [women]'. The 'defenders' or 'advocates' of women set out to 'reject misogynist claims'. Kelly saw the *Querelle* as a battle between 'the feminist side' and 'the misogynist side'.[16] While her essays introduced a new dimension to the theories about Renaissance man and woman and the relations between the sexes, decades later we are in a position to move beyond those parameters. Jerry Nash continues

---

[13] Georges Ascoli, 'Essai sur l'histoire des idées féministes en France: du XVIe siècle à la Révolution', *Revue de synthèse historique* 13 (1906): 25–42; Lula McDowell Richardson, *The Forerunners of Feminism in French Literature of the Renaissance from Christine de Pisa to Marie de Gournay* (Baltimore, MD, 1929); Maïté Albistur and Daniel Armogathe, *Histoire du féminisme français du moyen âge à nos jours* (Paris, 1977). Constance Jordan acknowledges that the term is 'open to question and especially when it is applied to Renaissance thought' – *Renaissance Feminism: Literary Texts and Political Models* (Ithaca, NY, 1990), p. 2.

[14] Gisela Bock discusses the dignity of man with the dignity of woman in *Women in European History* (Oxford, 2002), pp. 2–14.

[15] Lawrence Kritzman, *The Rhetoric of Sexuality and the Literature of the French Renaissance* (Cambridge, 1991), pp. 29, 37; Marc Angenot, *Les Champions des femmes: examen du discours sur la supériorité des femmes 1400–1800* (Montréal, 1977), p. 22; Pierre Darmon, *Mythologie de la femme dans l'Ancienne France* (Paris, 1983).

[16] Joan Kelly, 'Early Feminist Theory and the *Querelle des Femmes*, 1400–1789', in *Women, History and Theory: The Essays of Joan Kelly* (Chicago, IL, 1984), pp. 66–7, 71, 73–4, 87.

to view misogyny as the 'ideological, literary and cultural context' for women writers such as Christine de Pisan or Hélisenne de Crenne.[17]

Studies of the *Querelle des femmes* have devised a number of theories of 'gender identity' or models such as 'sex unity', 'sex polarity', 'complementarity' or 'profeminism' to classify the types of arguments one finds in the *Querelle*.[18] These classifications might help to organise the commonplaces, *exempla* and underlying assumptions of the *Querelle*, but for the most part *Querelle* texts do not conform to one specific typology and the models imposed by modern critics prove inadequate because they are insensitive to Renaissance rhetorical conventions.

Modern commentators also note that Renaissance writers exploring the relations between the sexes could be inconsistent in the application of the models of sexual equality, difference, superiority, inferiority or complementarity. In certain realms, such as wisdom or courage, woman might be held to possess capacities equal to man, and yet she also might possess feminine virtues such as piety and modesty, superior to her male counterpart.[19] Maclean notes that a writer might acknowledge the equal virtues between the sexes but also posit that a woman need exercise certain additional virtues such as silence and obedience to perform her social roles. He comments that this 'inconsistency' might reflect a conservatism, a fear of changing the social context and mere lip-service.[20] But what if this 'inconsistency' was actually a rhetorical strategy of adapting arguments for an audience? When an audience is uncertain, it might require several approaches to move or persuade it. In Quintilian's guidebook to classical rhetoric, the *Institutio oratoria*, he tells the orator: 'Different arguments move different people'. Quintilian advises the orator with doubts that 'as to being able to prove the stronger argument we should do well to rely on both'. He draws an analogy to an archer. If the archer is confident that he will hit the target he will be 'content with one shaft', but the archer who 'has no such confidence will do well to launch several and give fortune a chance to come to his assistance'.[21]

---

17 Jerry Nash, 'Renaissance Misogyny, Biblical Feminism, and Hélisenne de Crenne's *Epistres familieres et invectives*', *Renaissance Quarterly* 50:2 (1997): 379, 385.

18 Ian Maclean, *The Renaissance Notion of Woman* (Cambridge, 1980) pp. 55–6; Prudence Allen, *The Concept of Woman*, 2 vols (Grand Rapids, MI, 1997–2002), vol. I, p. 6, and vol. II, pp. 27–9; Jordan, *Renaissance Feminism*, p. 102. Pamela Joseph Benson alters the word 'feminist' to 'profeminist' because the treatises she studies defend women without a concomitant political reform – Benson, *The Invention of Renaissance Woman: The Challenge of Female Independence in the Literature and Thought of Italy and England* (University Park, PA, 1992), p. 2.

19 Maclean, *Renaissance Notion*, pp. 55–6; Allen, *Concept of Woman*, vol. II, p. 29.

20 Constance Jordan critiques Maclean, noting that works of protest were vigorous and heterodox with a diversity of concerns. See Jordan, *Renaissance Feminism*, p. 11, n. 1.

21 Quintilian, *Institutio oratoria*, ed. and trans. H.E. Butler, 4 vols (London, 1920–22), vol. II, p. 145, IV.v.13–17.

For the critics who ignore the Renaissance rhetorical practices of imitation and compilation, the internal inconsistency of the pro-woman line is felt to weaken the argument: the pro-woman writers could not possibly mean what they say if, for example, they present a case for woman as both equal and superior. Many have commented on the 'inconsistency' between Agrippa's opening claim in *On the Nobility and Pre-excellence of the Feminine Sex* that man and woman possess a spiritual equality and his subsequent claim to the pre-excellence of women over men based on the creation story, Nature, human laws and so on. Albistur and Armogathe remark that Agrippa's inconsistency confirms the impossibility of escaping from rhetorical conventions of proving the superiority of one sex over the other.[22] According to Agrippa 'there is no prerogative of excellence between man and woman, which can be claimed on the part of one or the other, because of his or her being or spiritual substance'.[23] However, Agrippa also notes that despite the equal capacities of their souls there may be other factors that allow for the pre-eminence of one sex over the other. Agrippa acknowledges that inequalities might arise because men have expropriated all the privileges for themselves and thus have deprived women of an education, a history, a political role and equal treatment before the law without an opportunity to improve their lot. 'But since the excessive tyranny of men prevails over divine right and natural laws, the freedom that was once accorded to women is in our day obstructed by unjust laws, suppressed by custom and usage, reduced to nothing'. He continues: 'And so these laws compel women to submit to men, as conquered before conquerors, and that without reason or necessity natural or divine, but under pressure of custom, education, chance, or some occasion favourable to tyranny'.[24]

Comments on 'inconsistency' habitually discredit the defences of woman because of an alleged lack of 'sincerity'; they dismiss the *Querelle* as a mere rhetorical exercise.[25] E.V. Telle assesses Agrippa's *De nobilitate* as an exercise

---

22 Angenot, *Champions des femmes*, p. 30; Albistur and Armogathe, *Histoire*, p. 92; Maclean, *Renaissance Notion*, p. 91; Madeleine Lazard, *Les avenues de Fémynie: les femmes à la Renaissance* (Paris, 2001), p. 31.

23 Agrippa, *De la noblesse & preexcellence*, sig. B^{v}: 'il n'i a point de prééminence de noblesse entre l'homme, et la femme, qui puisse estre pretendue de la part de l'un ou de l'autre, à cause de son essence et substance spirituelle'.

24 Henricus Cornelius Agrippa, *Declamation on the Nobility and Preeminence of the Female Sex*, trans. and ed. Albert Rabil (Chicago, IL, 1996), pp. 94–5; Agrippa, *Traité de l'excellence de la femme* (Paris, 1578), in Luce Guillerm, *et al.* (eds), *Le miroir des femmes*, 2 vols (Lille, 1983–84), vol. I, p. 101: 'Mais pour le jourd'huy la liberté qu'avoyent les femmes est reserrée par la tyrannie des hommes, qui se bandent contre tout droit et loix de nature'; Agrippa, *De la noblesse & preexcellence*, sigs Eviii^{r}, Gii^{v}: 'Parquoy les femmes sont contrainctes d'obéir à ces loix ici comme pauvres captives en guerre à leur vainqueurs: non point par aucune necessité ou raison divine ou naturelle, mais par je ne sçay quelle coustume, nourriture, et tirannique fortune et occasion qui cause cela'.

25 E.V. Telle, *L'Œuvre de Marguerite d'Angoulême Reine de Navarre et la querelle des femmes* (Toulouse, 1937), pp. 36–7; Madeleine Lazard, *Images littéraires de la femme*

in rhetorical paradox and quotes from Agrippa accordingly: 'Moreover, if I have placed the Beautiful Sex above our own ... I hope that the public will be gracious in favour of the august Princess in the honour of whom I have forwarded such a great paradox'.[26] Challenges to Agrippa's sincerity also cite his admission that, within the 'declamations of the sort he wrote in favour of women, there are many invalid arguments'.[27] Telle, Albistur, Armogathe, Maclean and Screech all challenge Agrippa's sincerity because of 'invalid' arguments or inconsistencies. And yet to do so seems to miss the point. As Screech himself comments: 'Despite the fact that the *De nobilitate* is a *declamatio*, the rules of which are given in his *Apologia calumnias propter declamationem de vanitate scientarium*, de Billon [the author of the 1555 *Impregnable Fort of the Honour of the Feminine Sex*] treats all the arguments as if they were of equal weight and solemnity'.[28] Floyd Gray comes closest to the mark when he suggests for *Querelle des femmes* writers that 'their strategy was less to pursue a consistent line of argument than to assemble all possible arguments in support of the case at hand'.[29] 'Invalid' arguments, mixed models, all of these were arrows for Quintilian's archer and as we saw in the previous chapter all of these can be found in equivalent writings about the nature of man.

In many of the modern commentaries on the *Querelle des femmes* we find ourselves coming dangerously close to a double standard. If a Renaissance male writer expresses how woman is inferior to man or lists a series of female flaws and vices he might be characterised as 'anti-feminist', or worse, 'misogynist'. If he writes about the superiority of woman, then his 'sincerity' is in question or his arguments 'invalid'.[30] Conversely, if a female writer defends her sex, she must be said to be an early feminist, whereas if she repeats any anti-woman commonplaces, utters a misogynist phrase or places anti-woman examples in the mouth of a fictional male character then she could not possibly have meant what she wrote.[31] These writings do not fit conveniently into modern models and we

---

à la Renaissance (Paris, 1985), p. 11.

[26] Telle, *L'Œuvre*, p. 46, n. 5.

[27] Maclean drawing on M.A. Screech in *Renaissance Notion*, p. 91. He further comments: 'As in the case of intellectual jokes, the humour may indicate the impossibility of discussing in serious terms the proposition of woman's equality, and therefore represents a strategy of discourse which is subversive in intention'.

[28] See Michael Screech, 'Rabelais, de Billon and Erasmus: A Re-examination of Rabelais's Attitude to Women', *Bibliothèque d'Humanisme et Renaissance* 13 (1951): 246.

[29] Floyd Gray, *Gender, Rhetoric and Print Culture in French Renaissance Writing* (Cambridge, 2000), p. 12.

[30] Swift comments on this type of analysis for the late medieval period: *Gender, Writing, Performance*, pp. v, 5, 8, 184, 188–9.

[31] Nash, 'Renaissance Misogyny', p. 387. Thus Nash explains some passages written in the 1530s by Marguerite Briet under the pseudonym Hélisenne de Crenne: 'Hélisenne, then proceeds, ironically, to instruct her husband in misogyny, which is obviously part of her strategy to preempt misogynist argument'. See Gray on how interpretations of the *Comptes*

risk 'anachronistic interpretation' if we ignore how the *Querelle des femmes* was shaped by Renaissance rhetoric, reading and writing.[32]

A more nuanced approach to Renaissance practices of imitation can be found in François Rigolot's reflections on 'misogyny' in Rabelais' *Pantagruel*. Rigolot focuses on an episode from *Pantagruel* involving the character Panurge and a lady of Paris. Rigolot demonstrates how Rabelais weaves passages from the Gospels of Matthew, in which Satan tempts Christ, into the scenes in *Pantagruel* where Panurge attempts to seduce a lady of Paris. As Rigolot explains, it is not sufficient to characterise Panurge as 'misogynist' or the passages as 'antifeminist'. Panurge is not an entirely dreadful figure and the Parisian lady, although Christ-like, is not beyond reproach. All the while Rabelais slips some misogynistic jokes into this 'feminist' rewriting of a biblical passage. The 'ambivalence' of Panurge's character and the ambivalence of the representation of an 'ideal woman' reflect, as Rigolot explains, 'the crisis of Renaissance exemplarity'.[33]

Ambivalence, mixed models, contradictory examples – these are the starting points for understanding the representations of woman in the *Querelle des femmes* and the ideas about human nature that we find in the debate on the dignity and misery of man. In trying to assemble proofs for the superiority of woman or even the equality of the soul, *Querelle* writers, like Quintilian's orator, pursued every means of persuasion available to them. Renaissance writers could claim both the equality of the sexes and the superiority of one sex over the other because they mixed, imitated and compiled from a variety of sources in order to persuade the reader. As we saw in chapter three, a writer might urge readers to raise their status *and* to accept their lot in life. One should attain rank, status and dignity through virtue and personal effort yet remember that fortune humbles even those of the highest rank, so ambition is futile. Although men and women possess different ranks by birth, everyone experiences the same lifecycle from birth to death. These ambivalent messages did not diminish the argument, but rather pointed to a wider complexity of competing truths.

Arguing for Female Superiority

In the 1550s Charles Estienne adapted Ortensio Lando's series of *Paradossi* from Italian for a French audience. The *Paradoxes Against Common Opinion Debated in*

---

amoureux (c. 1530s to 1540s) vary according to whether one considers the pseudonym Jeanne Flore to hide the identity of a female author, or whether the collected texts are 'exercises in male fantasy' or are 'the product of several authors' – *Gender, Rhetoric*, pp. 31–3; Ilana Zinguer, *Misères et grandeur de la femme au XVIe siècle* (Geneva, 1982), pp. 16–17, 19, 23–4, 63–6.

[32] Gray, *Gender, Rhetoric*, pp. 165–6.

[33] François Rigolot, 'Rabelais, Misogyny, and Christian Charity: Biblical Intertextuality and the Renaissance Crisis of Exemplarity', *PMLA* 109 (1994): 226, 234–5.

the Form of Declamations in place of Publique Censure: Onlie to Exercise Yoong Wittes in Difficult Matters offer the reader some 'bills of complaint' to help young lawyers practise difficult cases. Published and sold by Jean de Marnef at the sign of the Pelican in Poitiers, one of Estienne's paradoxes argues that it is better to be poor than rich and another suggests that it is better to spring from the 'bas lieu' or a low estate than from a great noble family.[34] Estienne parades Socrates, Euripides, Demosthenes, Horace and Virgil before his reader as examples of famous men of humble origin and satirises his contemporaries who tend to counterfeit their nobility and report that they issue from a very eminent lineage. Regardless of the 'nobility of the family' – the 'noblesse des maisons' – only 'toil and great pain' can render a poet, orator or philosopher 'noble and immortal for posterity'. Estienne hopes his paradox can 'bridle this vain and foolish passion' for noble titles because there is no location on earth without 'some seed of this miserable ambition'.[35]

Alongside his other paradoxes and commentaries on the social situation in early modern Europe, Estienne presents the case '[t]hat the excellence of woman is greater than that of man'. A generation later Marie de Romieu would imitate and adapt it in her *Brief Discourse that the Excellence of Woman Surpasses that of Man, as Delightful as it is Filled with Fine Examples* that Abel L'Angelier's mother and stepfather sold with Romieu's collection of poetry from their boutique at the second pillar of the Grand'Salle in the Palais de Justice in Paris.[36] Anne Larsen assesses Romieu's work as a 'feminist refashioning of Estienne's declamation and Lando's paradoxical encomium'.[37] Estienne presents his paradox as contrary to popular opinion, although by this point in the *Querelle*, thanks to the success of Agrippa's *De la noblesse & preexcellence du sexe fœminin*, these printed arguments for female superiority were coming to dominate. Female inferiority may have had a long tradition in areas of French law, in the biblical tradition and among Catholic clergy, in a society where the bulk of witchcraft accusations were against women, but in the bookselling circles of the Palais de Justice in the sixteenth century we cannot assume that devaluing woman or demeaning her everyday roles as a wife and mother was the acceptable opinion in print.[38] In interdisciplinary commonplace books, writers collected adages and *exempla* ready to hand for a demonstrative

---

34 Charles Estienne, *Paradoxes ce sont propos contre la commune opinion: debats, en forme de declamations forenses: pour exerciter les ieunes advocats en causes difficiles* (Poitiers: Jean de Marnef, 1553), pp. 160–69. For more editions see the 'Introduction' to Charles Estienne, *Paradoxes*, ed. Trevor Peach (Geneva, 1998), pp. 37–48.

35 Estienne, *Paradoxes*, 1553 edn, pp. 165–7.

36 Marie de Romieu, *Les Premieres œuvres poetiques de Mademoiselle Marie de Romieu Viuaroise contentant un brief discours, que l'excellence de la femme surpasse celle de l'homme non moins récreatif que plein de beaux exemples* (Paris: Lucas Breyer, 1581).

37 Anne Larsen, 'Paradox and the Praise of Women: From Ortensio Lando and Charles Estienne to Marie de Romieu', *Sixteenth Century Journal* 28:3 (1997): 768.

38 On assumed misogyny see Kelly, 'Early Feminist Theory', pp. 66–7, 71, 73–4, 87; Nash, 'Renaissance Misogyny', pp. 385, 405–7. On the legal and political inferiority of

argument. Ian Maclean notes that writers mostly collected commonplaces of female inferiority because even *Querelle* sections on 'heroic' women are belied by a context that reinforces these women as exceptional.[39] And yet if these commonplace books underline feminine weakness, why do writers repeatedly aim to prove female superiority or equality? One might jump to the conclusion that these treatises are declamations and paradoxes; demonstrations that the apparently unpraiseworthy is praiseworthy. There would probably be some truth in that conclusion. The *Querelle* has repeatedly been described as a series of exercises in the *genus demonstrativum* – that is, demonstrative or epideictic rhetoric, which seeks to praise (*in laudatio*) or to blame (*in vituperatio*).[40] Paradoxical *encomia* upheave convention or custom and point to a neglected truth by appearing to praise what cannot be praised, as when Estienne argues the advantages of poverty over riches and low birth over noble status.

In discussing 'woman' Estienne remarks that we often overlook the things that are most familiar and common to us and do not hold them in high enough esteem.[41] Marie de Romieu opens on a similar theme, but she focuses her gaze on the male sex. She acknowledges 'men of courage', 'men of knowledge' and the *grandeur* of men, but she wonders what her society values or prizes in such men. Is it their courage, *esprit*, 'magnificence', honour, virtue or excellence?[42] All of these virtues shine in the feminine sex so much that one might justly call women the more divine sex. Of course, as we saw in chapter three, Romieu includes a much more elaborate list of learned women than Estienne, and focuses on the shining examples of women among her contemporaries.[43] Romieu forcefully argues a point that is not found in Estienne's version: does her society value the virtue of these men or the mere fact that they are men?

Estienne addresses the 'complaints and objections' alleged by adversaries to 'contaminate' the honour of women and he alludes to male responsibility by deploring the 'troublesome importunity of men, their lascivious winks, tricks'. Men 'without any remorse in their conscience' will continue their pursuit of women even if they have to resort to force through some treason or with the help

women in early modern France, see Eliane Viennot, *La France, les femmes et le pouvoir*, 2 vols (Paris, 2006–2008), vol. I, pp. 452–569, and vol. II, pp. 95–125.

39 Maclean, *Renaissance Notion*, p. 84.

40 Angenot, *Champions des femmes*, pp. 152, 160.

41 Charles Estienne, 'Pour les femmes: Declamation XXIIII. Que l'excellence de la femme est plus grande que celles de l'homme', in *Paradoxes*, 1553 edn, pp. 177–8.

42 Marie de Romieu, 'Brief Discours: Que l'excellence de la femme surpasse celle de l'homme, autant recreatif que plein de beaux exemples', in *Les Premières œuvres poétiques*, ed. Andre Winandy (Geneva, 1972), p. 12, lines 9–16. English translation from Marie de Romieu, 'Brief Discourse: That Woman's Excellence Surpasses Man's', in Domna Stanton (ed.), *French Feminist Poems from the Middle Ages to the Present: A Bilingual Anthology* (New York, 1985), pp. 46–7.

43 See Chapter 3, p. 82.

of servants. Seduction is the only thing in which the 'excellence' of the minds of men demonstrates itself more firm and vigorous.[44] In her *Brief Discourse* Marie de Romieu expands Estienne's 20 or so lines of prose into 65 lines of verse, in part, using a male voice that shouts into Marie's ear:[45]

> 'Look here!' he says. 'Really, don't you know
> That we men fall only by your ways?
> Don't you know that the evil driving us
> Comes from your faces and your golden tresses?
> If Paris hadn't seen the eyes of Helen
> Wouldn't Troy still have its victorious heroes?'[46]

Like her predecessor Hélisenne de Crenne writing an invective letter to man in 1539, Romieu points out the folly of such words and asks the male voice: '[B]y this you clearly show / Your brain has no bridle nor restraint ... Why have you then a soul endowed with reason'?[47] Marie elaborates on all of the different types of male deception: men who cite the authority of God, men who pretend to act as protectors of female virtue, men who pretend to 'be your servant' or men who deceive with their 'honeyed words'. Like the husbands who envy the 'happiness' of the celibate, Marie mirrors their sighs: happy is the woman who is not on the receiving end of male 'importunity'.[48]

These demonstrations of the dignity and superiority of woman engage in a 'quarrel' with men within the text. Defenders of woman, including woman writers such as Romieu who came to the defence of their own sex, often included a male voice within their defences to stake out a misogynist perspective. The opposing voices and quarrels served to intensify the debate and to point to multiple truths even in titles that suggest a singular focus on the idea of woman. Margarete Zimmermann has noted how the early *Querelle* made way for a series of titles that preferred expressions such as 'apology', 'defence', 'grief' or 'complaint'.[49]

---

44 Estienne, 'Pour les femmes', in *Paradoxes*, 1553 edn, pp. 181–2.

45 Romieu, 'Brief Discours', pp. 15–17, lines 125–190; Estienne, 'Pour les femmes', in *Paradoxes*, 1553 edn, pp. 181–2.

46 Romieu, 'Brief Discourse', pp. 52–3.

47 Ibid.; Hélisenne de Crenne, *A Renaissance Woman: Helisenne's Personal and Invective Letters*, trans. and eds, Marianna Mustacchi and Paul Archambault (Syracuse, NY, 1986), pp. 94–5: 'Though men consider themselves rational they forsake reason for sensuality; then they blame women for making them succumb'; Hélisenne de Crenne, *Les Œuvres de ma Dame Helisenne de Crenne. A sçavoir, les angoisses douloureuses qui procedent d'amours. Les Epistres familières et invectives & Le songe de ladicte dame. Le tout reveu & corrigé de nouveau par elle* (Paris: Estienne Groulleau, 1560), facs. edn (Geneva, 1977), sig. Nviii^r.

48 Romieu, 'Brief Discourse', pp. 54–5 and pp. 16–17.

49 Zimmermann, 'Querelles du livre', p. 84; Zimmermann, 'Cultural Studies', pp. 22–3.

Alexandre de Pontaymeri presented his *Defensive Paradox Where it is Faithfully Demonstrated that Woman is a lot more Perfect than Man in all Virtuous Action* to the salon hostess Catherine de Clermont, Maréchale de Retz, distributed under Abel L'Angelier's privilege at the Palais de Justice in 1594 and again in 1596. The *Triumph of Ladies* was sold in the courtyard of the Palais de Justice in Rouen from 1599.[50] In the early seventeenth century, Marie de Gournay's *Equality of Men and Women* would focus on the equality of the sexes, rather than try to prove the superiority of one over the other. Gournay believed that 'the human animal is neither man nor woman'. She argues that the Scriptures tell us how 'Man was created male and female', counting these two as one. They are so much alike that 'Jesus-Christ is called the son of man' when it is known that he is only the son of a woman. Gournay concludes that all her examples and proofs demonstrate the equality between the sexes – 'indeed their very unity itself'.[51]

The Iniquity of Woman

It is essential to consider why, in the sixteenth-century *Querelle des femmes*, the opportunity to spread tales about female vice and the inferiority of women seemed to interest so few French writers. Most *Querelle* writers were only willing to blame woman once they had already confirmed their praise of the female sex. Writers safely took a stance against male 'adversaries' of woman and then repeated misogynistic commonplaces in order to refute them. Already by the 1440s the 'Champion of Ladies', in Le Franc's book of the same name, recounts a brief history of the *Querelle* when he responds 'to all the things that the adversary stated against marriage and ladies' and speaks of 'Jehan de Meun le villain', 'maistre Alain [Chartier]', 'Mathieu le bigame', Pierre Michault, the author of the *Malleus maleficarum* and other contributors to the debate for and against woman.[52] This early *Querelle* history would have been available to any reader of Le Franc in the beautifully produced 1530 edition sold by Galiot du Pré in Paris. Early *Querelle* titles in print such as the 1516 *Dialogue apologétique* continued fifteenth-century

---

50 Alexandre de Pontaymeri, *Paradoxe apologique, où il est fidèllement demonstré que la Femme est beaucoup plus parfaicte que l'Homme en toute action de vertu* (Paris: Abel L'Angelier, 1594); Jordan, *Renaissance Feminism*, pp. 210–11. See also Richard Carr's excellent analysis of paradox and this late sixteenth-century contribution to the *Querelle des femmes* in 'The Resolution of a Paradox: Alexandre de Pontaymeri's Response to the *Querelle des femmes*', *Renaissance Studies* 17:2 (2003): 246–56; Viennot, *La France, les femmes*, vol. II, pp. 60–61, 64.

51 Marie de Gournay, '*L'Égalité des hommes et des femmes* (1622), eds Jean-Claude Arnould, *et al.*, in *Œuvres complètes*, 2 vols (Paris, 2002), vol. I, pp. 978–9, 987.

52 Le Franc, *Champion des dames*, 1530 edn, fos cxvii^{v}–cxxiii^{r}; Martin Le Franc, *Champion des dames*, ed. Robert Deschaux, 5 vols (Paris, 1999), vol. II, pp. 111–13; on the debate format, Swift, *Gender, Writing, Performance*, pp. 105–10.

commonplaces and a *pro et contra* format as Badmouther (*Bouche maldisant*) disputed with Defending Woman (*Femme deffendant*).[53] On the other hand, when Agrippa challenged 'strong and tough men' to prove that 'the iniquity of man was better than a woman doing a good turn', very few responded.[54]

One of the few to take up the challenge was a provincial officeholder. Gratien Dupont, Seigneur de Drusac, wrote the *Controversies of the Masculine and Feminine Sexes* in 1533. It appeared in Toulouse in 1534 and was available in a roman type version by 1536 and again in 1537. Denis Janot must have seen an opportunity to sell a few books because he printed Dupont's *Controverses des sexes masculin et fœmenin* in 1538, issued it again with the date 1539 and reprinted a new edition in 1540. By 1541 Parisian bookselling rivals were selling copies of Dupont's *Controverses* on the rue Neuve Nôtre Dame and at the third pillar of the Grand'Salle in the Palais de Justice.[55] Dupont's *Controverses* was a rather unusual book because it set out to attack women and defend men, including trying to prove the idea 'that the iniquity of man is better than the woman who does a good turn' – 'Que l'iniquité de l'homme est meilleure que de la femme qui bien faict'.[56]

Dupont's *Controverses* was one of the few *Querelle* texts to suggest a thoroughgoing female wickedness without switching to a rebuttal in defence of woman. Because the *Controverses* catalogues the vices of women, Dupont had wanted to publish his work anonymously. His name did not appear on the title page but could be found in the 1534 text. He certainly had some justification for hiding his identity. Dupont's contemporaries were keen to abuse him just as he had heaped abuse on the female sex. Germain Colin Bucher the *sécretaire du grand maître de Malte* accused him of folly. Étienne Dolet wrote six Latin odes attacking Dupont and even suggested that the *Controverses* would be best used as toilet

---

53 *Dialogue apologétique excusant ou deffendant le dévot sexe fémenin, introduict par deulx personnaiges, l'un a nom Bouche maldisant, l'autre Femme deffendant* (Paris: [attributed to Frédéric d'Egmont], 1516).

54 Agrippa, *De la noblesse*, Janot edn, sig. Eiii^r: 'meilleure soit l'iniquité de l'homme que la femme bien faisant'; Ecclesiasticus 42:14.

55 Gratien Dupont, *Les Controversses des sexes masculin et femenin* (Toulouse: Jacques Colomiès, 1534) [hereafter spelled as *Controverses* like the later editions]; Gratien Dupont, *Controverses des sexes masculin et femenin* (no place, 1536); Gratien Dupont, *Controverses des sexes masculin et femenin* (no place, 1537); for details of the 1538, 1539 and 1540 Janot editions see Rawles, 'Denis Janot', bibliography nos. 73, 118; Gratien Dupont, *Controverses des sexes masculin et fœmenin* (Paris: Alain Lotrian, 1541); Gratien Dupont, *Controverses des sexes masculin et fœmenin* (Paris: Jean du Pré, 1541). See also Urban Nyström, *Poèmes français sur les biens d'un ménage depuis* L'Oustillement au villain *du XIIIe siècle jusqu'aux* Controverses *de Gratien Du Pont* (Helsinki, 1940), pp. 142–3, 145–52.

56 Dupont, *Controverses*, 1534 edn, sigs. xciii^v–xciiii^r; Dupont, *Controverses des sexes masculin et femenin* (Paris: Denis Janot, 1540), Bk II, fo. 103v.

paper.[57] Charles de Sainte-Marthe tells Dupont, the 'detractor of the feminine sex', that 'good people' (*gents de bien*) tossed his 'witless writing' into the fire.[58] In the 1580s Étienne Tabourot was rather disparaging about Dupont's poetic talent and described him as a 'rimailleur', which Cotgrave's dictionary translates quite delightfully as 'meane composer' or 'sorrie rimer'.[59] In the allegorical *Impregnable Fort of the Honour of the Feminine Sex* that François de Billon builds to protect women, the author imprisons three 'Captains of contempt', Boccaccio, Nevizanno and Dupont 'called Drusac'. Billon identifies Dupont, his only French prisoner, as a judicial officeholder and as a 'Robbe courte', indicating that Dupont wore the dress of the traditional sword-bearing nobility.[60] In 1564 Dupont's publisher in Toulouse brought to market the *Anti-Drusac or Little Book Against Drusac Made in Honour of Noble, Good and Honest Women.*[61] The hostile reception to Dupont's work may have set a precedent for anonymity. A collection of anti-woman writing, ironically entitled the *Louenge des femmes* or *The Praise of Women*, left Jean de Tournes' press in Lyon in 1551 bearing no trace of its authorship.

Modern commentators have expressed their dismay at the 'misogynist and extremely disparaging words of Gratien du Pont', describing the text as a 'misogynist handbook', 'a masterpiece of misogynist literature' and Dupont himself as 'one of the most vehement misogynists of the sixteenth century'.[62] Abel

---

57 Marc Chassaigne, *Étienne Dolet: portraits et documents inédits* (Paris, 1930), p. 68. The enmity between Dolet and Drusac traced to the *Jeux floraux* and Dolet feared Dupont had obtained an 'arrêt' of Parlement to exile him from Toulouse. Étienne Dolet, *Correspondance: Répertoire analytique et chronologique suivi du texte de ses letters latines*, ed. Claude Longeon (Geneva, 1982), pp. 49–50. See the letter of 22 June 1534.

58 Charles de Sainte-Marthe, *La Poésie francoise de Charles de Saincte Marthe* (Lyon: Le Prince, 1540), pp. 94–5. On these detractors see Charles Oulmont, 'Gratian du Pont Sieur de Drusac et les femmes', *Revue des études rabelaisiennes* 4 (1904): 5–6. See also La Croix du Maine's comment on Dolet's Latin odes in Jean-Antoine Rigoley de Juvigny (ed.), *Les Bibliothèques françoises de La Croix du Maine et de Du Verdier*, 6 vols (Paris: Saillant and Nyon, 1772–73), vol. I, pp. 252–3.

59 Étienne Tabourot, *Les Bigarrures dv Seigneur des Accordz* (Paris: Jean Richer, 1583), sig. D v[r] or fo. 29r; Randle Cotgrave, *A Dictionarie of the French and English Tongues* (London: Adam Islip, 1611).

60 François de Billon, *Le Fort inexpugnable de l'honneur du sexe feminin* (Paris: Jean Dallier, 1555), facs. edn Michael Screech (New York, 1970), fo. 18r.

61 Ascoli, 'Essai', p. 30; Telle, *L'Œuvre*, p. 55; *Biographie universelle ancienne et moderne* (Paris, 1814), tome XII, p. 594. The dialogue between Euphrates and Gymnisus was entitled *L'Anti-Drusac ou Livret contre Drusac, fait en l'honneur des femmes nobles, bonnes et honnêtes* (Toulouse: Colomiès, 1564). Unfortunately, I have not been able to locate a copy of this work.

62 Nash, 'Renaissance Misogyny', p. 380; Nancy J. Vickers, 'The unauthored 1539 volume in which is printed the *Hecatomphile*, *The Flowers of French Poetry*, and *Other Soothing Things*', in Margreta de Grazia, *et al.* (eds), *Subject and Object in Renaissance Culture* (Cambridge, 1996), pp. 178–9; Jean-François Courouau and Philippe Gardy,

Le Franc describes sections of the *Controverses* as 'obscene' and remarks that some of the play on words demonstrates a 'revolting vulgarity'.[63] Christie suggests that the poetry is in the 'worst possible taste'.[64] Richardson notes that the female 'sex could scarcely find a more inveterate enemy'.[65] Telle presents two explanations for the sixteenth-century outpouring of vituperation against Dupont. Firstly, Dupont's humanist contemporaries did not necessarily object to his statements against women, but they did oppose his scholasticism and a book that sounded 'trop son gothique et trop son rhétoriqueur'.[66] Secondly, Telle comments that the sixteenth-century public was more accustomed to praise than invective. If this had indeed been the case, Dupont's *Controverses* would have sunk without a trace rather than enjoy at least six editions in seven years. We would do well to remember that Denis Janot distributed Hélisenne de Crenne's *Familiar and Invective Letters* in 1539 alongside copies of Dupont's *Controverses* printed in 1538, issued again in 1539 and printed in 1540. Hélisenne de Crenne's invective letters were included in Janot's edition of her *Collected Works* in 1543. Janot's successor reprinted these *Œuvres* to sell in front of Nôtre Dame and for distribution by the Palais booksellers in 1551 and 1560. Readers were used to invective and blame whether it applied to the weakness and misery of man or to the imperfection of woman.[67] However, and here Telle is closer to the mark, in most instances blame was accompanied by praise in the form of a dialogue with characters such as *Franc Vouloir* defending woman against *Malebouche*, or the fictional Hélisenne defending woman in one of her invective letters while her fictional husband expressed his vituperation against women in another.[68] The expectation was for praise to weigh against blame.

Not all readers were offended by Dupont's *Controverses des sexes masculin et fœmenin*. After the first edition of Gratien Dupont's *Controverses* appeared, a small minority of supporters in Toulouse offered their congratulations. As the *lieutenant-général* of the local court (*sénéchaussée*), Dupont represented the king, sat as a judge, and held the right to sit with the presiding judges (*presidents à mortier*) in the Parlement of Toulouse. While Dupont held the position of lieutenant-général he had the privilege to occupy the former Palais de Justice in Toulouse, the

'Introduction', in *La Requeste faicte et baillée par les Dames de la ville de Tholose (1555)* (Toulouse, 2003), p. 59; Linda Timmermans, *L'accès des femmes à la culture (1598–1715): un débat d'idées de Saint François de Sales à la Marquise de Lambert* (Paris, 1993), p. 25.

63 Abel Lefranc, 'Le Tiers Livre de Pantagruel et la querelle des femmes', in *Rabelais, Étude sur Gargantua, Pantagruel, Le Tiers Livre* (Paris, 1953), p. 283.

64 Richard Copley Christie, *The Martyr of the Renaissance: A Biography* (London, 1880), pp. 110–11.

65 Richardson, *Forerunners of Feminism*, p. 70.

66 Telle, *L'Œuvre*, pp. 55, 57.

67 On models for invective writing see Janet Smarr, *Joining the Conversation: Dialogues by Renaissance Women* (Ann Arbor, MI, 2005), pp. 139–40.

68 Crenne, *Œuvres*, sigs M ij^{v}–O iij^{r}.

Chateau Narbonnais.[69] From about 1535 until his death sometime in 1544, Dupont was one of the dignitaries (*mainteneurs*) of the Floral Games, the annual literary competition in Toulouse, and indeed his only other known publication was a 1539 manual of rhetoric and poetry entitled the *Art and Science of Rhetoric in Verse*.[70]

Dupont's supporters were also local officeholders or notables. Bernard d'Estopinhan was a counsellor and solicitor to the King of Navarre. Guillaume de la Perrière, apparently a childhood friend of Dupont, held a degree in law and hailed from a lesser noble family in Toulouse.[71] La Perrière, author of the *Political Mirror* (*Mirouer politique*) and the emblem books *La Morosophie* and *Theatre of Good Understanding* (*Théâtre des bons engins*) discussed in chapter three, was perhaps a helpful contact in the Parisian bookselling world because his *Théâtre des bons engins* shared Denis Janot's Parisian press with Dupont's *Controverses* in the late 1530s. La Perrière's letter to Dupont in the 1534 Toulouse edition suggests that nothing could silence the 'feminine tongue' and 'usual babble' of women, but he assures Dupont not to fear feminine reprisals: 'your honour can not be diminished, nor your renown lessened ... if some women wish to argue that you should instead fashion your book on the praise of honest women over the vituperation of the infamous [you] could reply forgivingly, that by vituperating wicked women you commend the virtuous'. Then La Perrière compares Dupont to 'Cicero, upholder of Roman eloquence, in his invectives against Mark Anthony' and suggests that 'the wit or craft of the orator is more piercing and the style more flowing and copious in invective and stinging speech than in praising speech and panegyric'.

These prefatory letters support Dupont because he tells the 'truth' about female inferiority rather than circulate 'common opinions' about female honour and virtue. La Perrière congratulates Dupont on his 'honest enterprise' because he has 'written freely without fear and pursued his intent without flattery or adulation'.[72] D'Estopinhan echoes La Perrière when he tells Dupont: 'My lord, do not fear the insults of the envious, put behind you the fear of feminine fury [and] take the safeconduct of truth which will make you secure from the assaults of your adversaries'.[73] Estienne de Vignalz from Toulouse recalls the words of Socrates

---

69 Christie, *Martyr*, pp. 108–10.

70 Oulmont, 'Gratien du Pont', p. 9, n. 2; J.C. Dawson, *Toulouse in the Renaissance: The Floral Games, University and Student Life, Étienne Dolet (1532–34)* (New York, 1923), pp. 175, 180, 182.

71 *Dictionnaire de biographie française*, 20 vols (Paris, 1932–), fascicule CIX, vol. 19 (1995), p. 845.

72 'Guillaume de la Perriere, tolosain [sic] / A Gratian du Pont Escuyer / Seigñr de Drusac / Lieutenant layc en la Seneschaulcee de Tolose / Autheur du Present Livre. Salut', in Dupont, *Controverses*, 1534 edn, sigs ¢ v^{r-v}.

73 'Epistre a l'autheur. Bernard d'Estopinhan Conseiller & Solliciteur du Roy de Navarre de Tholose a son treshonnore seigneur Gratien du Pont escuyer se Seigneur de Drusac / Lieutenant layc du Seneschal de Tholose', in ibid., sig. ¢ viii^{r}: 'Ne crainctz doncq

'that of all the virtues a man should have, the principal one is that he be truthful and not a lying flatterer'.[74] Dupont's supporters praise him for writing openly about a 'truth' silenced by flattery. They tell the readers of the 1534 *Controverses* that the inferiority of woman was a suppressed truth.

Their words could not have been more accurate. The 1536 and 1537 editions were published without printers' marks, without locations, and without the letters by La Perrière, Vignalz and d'Estopinhan. The only piece left in the 1540 Paris edition printed and sold by Denis Janot is the verse by François de Chevallier of the College de Foix.[75] Denis Janot's 1538, 1539 reissue and 1540 editions of the *Controverses* omit Guillaume de la Perrière's letter at a time when the Parisian merchant printer would begin promoting La Perrière's *Théâtre des bons engins*, also distributed from Janot's rue Neuve Nôtre Dame press in 1540. Dupont dedicates his 1534 *Controverses* to Pierre du Faur, *maître des requêtes ordinaire du roi*. At that point Dupont's position as lieutenant-général of the *sénéchaussée* in Toulouse probably carried greater social weight than Du Faur's office. However, by 1538 Pierre II du Faur had risen to the post of fourth presiding judge of the Parlement of Toulouse with whom Dupont held the right to sit when he attended the sovereign court.[76] Surprisingly, the later Parisian editions drop the dedication signed by Dupont as a 'humble cousin' of Du Faur.[77]

In the *Controverses des sexes masculin et fœmenin*, as we see in Figure 4.1, the allegorical Masculine Sex approaches the Author to seek his help in a defence against women. Dupont's scenario mirrors Christine de Pisan's allegorical vision in the manuscript *City of Ladies* and its sequel the *Treasure of the City of Ladies* printed and sold by Denis Janot in 1536. Three allegorical virtues – Reason, Right and Justice – appear before her in the *City of Ladies* and again in its sequel to demand why she wasted 'the tool of her intelligence'. Christine kneels before the three Ladies who command her: 'Take up your quill and write'.[78]

Dupont later describes the battles between the sexes and an exchange of artillery and arrows ensues between the male sex and 'the soldiers of Venus'. Troops of 'femme muguettes' – courting women on the prowl for an unsuspecting man – wage a 'war' upon the masculine sex. The 1534, 1536 and 1540 editions further illustrate this battle and the arsenal of women in a series of woodcuts by different artists. In the 1534 edition these scenes are much more elaborate than the simplified versions of 1536 and 1540. The women assemble their weapons

---

mon seigneur les iniures des envieulx, mectz arriere la craincte de fureur femenine … prendz le saufconduit de verité qui te rend seur contre les assaulx de tes adversayres'.

74 'Estienne de Vignalz Tholosain à Gratian dupont escuyer Seigneur de Drusac, lieutenant layc en la Senechaulcee de Tholose, Autheur du present liure. Salut', ibid., sigs ¢¢$^{r-v}$.

75 Dupont, *Controverses*, 1540 edn, verso of the title page or sig. A i^{v}.

76 Christie, *Martyr*, pp. 108–9.

77 'Epistre de l'autheur', in Dupont, *Controverses*, 1534 edn, sig. ¢ii^{r}.

78 Christine de Pisan, 'Prologue', in *Le Trésor de la cité des dames*, sigs a iiii^{r}–a v^{r}.

such as 'les bonnes senteurs' or lovely scents, perfumes and herbs, powders and cosmetics, creating a situation in which men need protection from women.[79]

In the *Controverses*, the author Dupont takes up the challenge of the allegorical Masculine Sex and sets out to prove that female vice is no exception. He employs the conventional arguments derived from the creation of Adam and Eve. Man is superior to woman because of the order of creation, form, matter, authority and degree, as we discussed in chapter three.[80] Dupont laments the miseries of marriage and the woes posed by adulterous wives. He collects commonplaces of the various vices and sins committed by women such as pride, sensuality or a range of horrible deeds and crimes of incest, cruelty and murder. Accounts of Bathsheba, Clytemnestra, Cleopatra, Nero's mother, Messalina, Semiramis and others appear two or three times under different headings in his commonplace book. He allows the reader to judge the veracity of these stories, some of which are 'farfetched' and others 'true'.[81] Dupont's catalogue of vice mirrors the misery-of-

Figure 4.1 'Masculine Sex approaches the Author', Gratien Dupont, *Controverses des sexes masculin et fœmenin* (Paris: Denis Janot, 1540), courtesy of the Bibliothèque de Genève (BGE Hf324).

[79] Dupont, *Controverses*, 1540 edn, sigs BB ii^{v}–BB iiii^{r}, or Bk II, fos 10v–12r; Lefranc, 'Le Tiers Livre', pp. 283–4; Zimmermann, 'Querelles du livre', pp. 82–3; Zimmermann, 'Cultural Studies', p. 22.

[80] Dupont, *Controverses*, 1534 edn, fos xxxvii^{r}–xlii^{r}; Dupont, *Controverses*, 1540 edn, Bk II, fos 15v–25r or sigs B vii^{v}–DD^{r}; see Chapter 3, pp. 85.

[81] See Dupont, *Controverses*, 1534 edn, fos cxxx^{r}–clxxiii^{r}; Dupont, *Controverses*, 1540 edn, Bk III, sigs AAA iiii^{v} or KKKii^{v} or fos 4v–74v.

man commonplaces listed in books such as Guillaume Alexis' *Past-Time of Every Man and Every Woman* except that men in misery-of-man literature commit a wider variety of sins such as 'covetousness' and ambition. Moreover, Dupont's examples of feminine mischief are not new. His reader could have encountered them in *Querelle* texts such as the *Roman de la Rose*, Le Franc's *Champion des dames*, Alexis' *Debate of Man and Woman*, which he lists among the names of French authors 'brought forth [as evidence] in this book' – 'alleguez en ce livre'.[82]

A Literary Game?

Dupont's boldness is more apparent in the bawdy nature of the book and the lengthy discussion of the *con* – the cunt – in the vernacular. He does not hide this earthy section behind a veil of Latin but instead plays with the double meanings of the 'very perverse word' *con* in the 'Bourdons par equiuocques'. These lengthy passages of 'equivocal' verse – there are 442 of them – were a way of musing, or 'buzzing' as *bourdon* implies, on how many ways one could express this taboo word. Dupont denies any gratuitous 'pleasure' but claims he needs to warn men about the 'misfortunes' caused by a woman's 'filthy', 'stinking' and 'abominable beast'.[83] Here we see Dupont at work in the *rhétoriqueur* tradition popular at the end of the fifteenth century, using text and poetry in a visual fashion and engaging in '"artificial" language games'.[84] The word *con* appears in every line and in the extract below can be read as part of the verb *connaître*, 'to know', or it can be read as a variation of 'du con naître' meaning that all humans are 'born from the cunt', so that 'nous connaissons' can mean 'we know' or 'du con naissons' can mean 'from the cunt we are born'. If something is 'connu', it is 'known', but the 'con nu' is a 'naked cunt'. And so Dupont seems to delight in this opportunity for play on words and *double entendre*.

Ce non obstant que bien que nous (congnoissons
Quil est bien vray, que tous du con naissons
Petis & grans, telle chose (congnoissent
Que tous humains, il fault que du (con naissent
Tous lont congneu & tous les (congnoistront
Hommes & femmes, trestous (du con naistront
Tel dire vray, dung chascun est (congneu
Trestous naissons, de ce vilain (con nud
Point aultrement, null y ne (congnoistra
Car vrayement, chascun du (con naistra

---

82 Dupont, *Controverses*, 1540 edn, sigs KKK ii^{v}–KKK iiii^{v}, or Bk III, fos 74v–76v.

83 Ibid., Bk II, fos 53r–v or sigs GG v^{r-v}.

84 François Rigolot, '1493, The Rhétoriqueurs', in Denis Hollier (ed.), *A New History of French Literature* (Cambridge, MA, 1989), p. 131.

Figure 4.2 'Chessboard in the form of Eve', Gratien Dupont, *Les Controversses des sexes masculin et femenin* (Toulouse: Jacques Colomiés, 1534), courtesy of the National Library of the Netherlands (230 B 1).

De ce nous sommes, trestous bien congnoissans
Sages & folz, sommes du (con naissans

There is certainly some humour and a sense of play, which gives way to monotony as Dupont includes a canto from each of the following 'con' words: *confiance, contenir, controuuer, consentir, condescend, compassion, desconforter, condamner, convaincre, combattre, compartir, convenable, consoler, conduict, compenser, compasser, conprendre, converser, contenance, concord, connestable, comporter, contracter, composer, confondre, confermer, consommer, contrister, comparer, contourner, contenter, confesser.*[85] We begin to get a sense of why the book might be entitled the *Controverses*.[86]

His portrait of woman is not an entirely malicious one, but reveals itself as a game in the 1534 edition. Dupont constructed an 'Eschiquier' or chessboard of black and white rhyming squares with 'two endings' (*deux terminaisons*). Dupont suggests that one can play and move on the chessboard as a king, queen, knight, bishop or even a pawn to create the rhyme. The black squares jump diagonally from the 'Femme abuseresse' who was 'En sçavoir asnesse' or a 'Vraye diablesse' – an abusive woman, a real she-devil with the learning of an ass. The white squares reveal woman as 'De vice regente', 'Par trop deplaisante', and 'De l'homme servante' – Queen regent of vice, much too displeasing, and the servant of man.[87]

While this chessboard game appeared in the local 1534 Toulouse edition, by the time the 1536 and later Janot editions were circulating in Paris the 'eschiquier' only had white squares. The sense of play was still evident as a visual poem 'when you want to pass the time', but the literary game of chess strategy was gone.[88]

Dupont assembled each play with words and each variation on his theme of woman as part of his arsenal of rhetorical arrows against the female sex. Humour was certainly one of those weapons. In the preface to the 1534 edition of the *Controverses* François Chevallier was careful to point out Dupont's humour:

If your heart / is drawn to sadness
Read this book / which tells many satires
...To incite you / to laugh merrily.

85 Dupont, *Controverses*, 1534 edn, fos lxi^r–lxvii^r; Dupont, *Controverses*, 1540 edn, Bk II, fos 53r–63r or sigs GG v^r–HH vi^r.

86 Céline Goursolas-Marcy draws attention to the allusion to Seneca's *Controversiæ et suasoriæ* on presenting paradoxical cases or both the *pro et contra* while noting how Drusac simply presents the *contra* aspect: '"Controverses", "Jugement", "Requête" et *Querelle des femmes* (1534–55): Du droit de réponse dans un débat institué par les hommes', *Textuel* 49 (2006): 191–2.

87 Dupont, *Controverses*, 1534 edn, fos liiii^r–v; Zimmermann, 'Cultural Studies', p. 22.

88 Dupont, *Controverses*, 1540 edn, Bk II, fos 41v–42r or sigs FF i^v–FF ii^r.

> *Sy vostre cueur/a tristesse se attyre*
> *Lisez ce liure/qui dit maincte satyre ...*
> *Vous inciter/ gayement a bien rire.*[89]

Chevallier's 'rondeau' was the only introductory piece to set the tone of the *Controverses* in later editions published anonymously or available from Denis Janot's workshop near Nôtre Dame Cathedral. Gone were the accolades for Dupont speaking for truth over flattery, and gone was the praise for how he might preserve the 'liberty' of men by warning them against feminine wiles. Instead, once the reader had turned the title page, the work announced itself as a satire.

Word games, rhymes, humour and variety were powerful weapons and Dupont's contemporaries such as François de Billon took his games seriously enough to respond with counterattacks. Why? By omission Dupont had introduced something new into the sixteenth-century *Querelle*. Within the text of the 1534 edition, Dupont's negative portrayal of woman went unchallenged. The author of the *Controverses* envies the cleric (*homme d'eglise*) because he does not carry the heavy burden (*charge*) of a wife, whereas the man who wished to wed had a 'desire for great pain (*desir de grand mal*)'.[90] Dupont laments that a man must toil 'night and day' if he takes on a wife because he promptly requires a long list of household stuff starting with beds, a house, wheat and wine, chambermaids, grooms and wetnurses for his children and the revenue to pay for all of it.[91] He spouts the typical complaints about how carefully one must choose the 'age' and 'quality' of a wife because, whether young or old, rich or poor, ugly, beautiful or learned, each type had her own inconveniences.[92] The protests about the suffering of husbands, the verses about the female body and its functions and the examples of female sin and wickedness persist for hundreds of pages. In the first edition of his *Controverses* there was no rebuttal from a male 'champion of women' or a female character speaking in defence of her sex.

Dupont declares that he does not want to 'offend' (*meffaire*) noble Ladies, damoiselles or bourgeoises. He speaks only to those women not governed by reason and those guilty of 'abuses and treachery'. 'Good' women should excuse him and not be 'troublesome' if he reproaches arrogant, dishonest or sensual women.[93] Declarations about the malicious and sinful nature of women invariably appeared with a precautionary disclaimer in which the author excluded any good women.

---

89 'Francois Chevallier natif de Bourdeaulx, Collegie [sic] du College de Foix a Tholose. Rondeau au lecteur', in Dupont, *Controverses*, 1534 edn, fo. CCii^{v}; Dupont, *Controverses*, 1540 edn, verso of title page or sig. A i^{v}.

90 Dupont, *Controverses*, 1540 edn, Bk II, fos 96v, 126r.

91 Ibid., Bk II, fos 108v–109r.

92 Ibid., Bk II, fos 112v–126r.

93 Dupont, *Controverses*, 1534 Toulouse edn, fo. iiii^{v}; Dupont, *Controverses*, 1540 edn, 'L'autheur a toutes honnestes femmes, de quelque estat & condition quelles soient humble salut' – Bk I, sigs Aiii^{r}–Aiiii^{v} or fos 3r–4v.

A writer might also target a particular woman (whether real or imaginary) as the anonymous author(s) of the *Louenge des femmes* did in 1551. In the concluding poem *Aux dames* the *Louenge* writer admits that women have acquired some of their bad habits from men, 'but I speak to two, each one … [has] all the evils of the world gathered within her'. He adds that he also addresses any other woman who 'by chance, resembles these two'.[94]

By 1555, when François de Billon built his 'impregnable fort' to defend women, the 'assailants' he imprisoned such as Boccaccio and Nevizanno were actually few and far between. Billon mentions fewer than ten titles or authors. Many of the works attacking women had been translated for the French market from Italian and they earned Billon's disapproval because they were 'deceptive' – pretending to represent the honour of women while they actually disparaged the feminine sex. Hence, Billon objects to Ariosto's *Orlando furioso* because it is 'double'.[95] Billon complains about a French song circulating in print, *The Babble of Women* (*Le caquet des femmes*), as well as a little book of sayings and stories called *The Golden Words of Cato* (*Les motz dorez de Caton*) printed by Denis Janot and sold in the Palais de Justice.[96] Rabelais' *Third Book* of Pantagruel also comes under fire from Billon for its description of women. The *Tiers livre*, as we have seen, presented its critique of women as wives in the form of a dialogue, a banter or exchange between characters who debate whether or not Panurge should marry, and while many vices of women or wives are exposed, women are not bereft of virtue. The 'false book on the praise of women which still gads about the Palais de Paris' – the anonymous collection of anti-woman poems entitled *La Louenge des femmes* – irritated Billon because it contained no praise of women at all.[97]

François de Billon objects to Sperone Speroni's *Dignity of Women*, because it parades 'under colour of the name of dignity (which has some attraction as a thing of honour)'. The dialogue was more typical of *Querelle des femmes* literature like the *Tiers livre* in presenting a debate about the good and bad aspects of female nature.[98] In the *Dignity of Women* 'several learned persons' spend an evening debating whether 'woman is made by Nature in the service of man' or if 'man

94 'Aux dames', in *La Louenge des femmes, Invention extraite du commentaire de Pantagruel, sus L'Androgyne de Platon* (Lyon: Jean de Tournes, 1551), facs. edn Ruth Calder (New York, 1967), p. 54: 'Mais ie parle à deux, dont chacune … Tous maux du monde, en soy assemble. Et à autre aussi, si quelcune/ D'avanture à ces deux ressemble'.

95 As Pamela Benson clearly identified in *Invention of the Renaissance Woman*, pp. 91–155.

96 Pierre Grosnet, *Les Motz dorez de Cathon, en françoys et en latin, avecques bons et très utiles enseignemens, proverbes, adages, auctoritez et ditz moraulx des saiges, prouffitables à ung chascun* (Paris: Jean Longis, 1531); Alison Saunders, *The Sixteenth-Century Blason Poétique* (Bern, 1981), pp. 40–41.

97 Billon, *Fort inexpugnable*, fos 15v–21r.

98 Ibid., fo. 17r. See discussion on the sale and marketing of these dialogues in Chapter 2, pp. 37–9.

naturally submits to the authority of woman'.[99] The female representative Lady Beatrice suggests that the 'virtuous woman' does not feel her own appetites but seeks only to 'satiate the desires' of her husband. The 'natural condition' of woman is to 'serve her husband'. Without this 'servitude a woman is not a woman' and 'in other words her life should be called a living death'.[100] François de Billon takes particular exception to Lady Beatrice's conclusion that women are 'imperfect' by God's design and that it was 'convenient' or 'proper' for woman to serve because she was created for it.[101] And while Billon's point about the misleading nature of the title *De la dignité des femmes* is well taken, the characters speaking in 'defence of woman' do point out some 'positive' aspects of woman's nature.[102] A Count recalls the chivalric idea that the proper role or duty of the honourable man is 'to serve and honour women'. Woman not only rules man, he insists, but she governs herself better than the way in which man would wish to govern her. In contrast to man, whose soul is made of reason, the Count asserts that woman's soul is made of 'feelings' and 'love', suggesting that she might be more 'humane' or compassionate.[103] Speroni's dialogue on the dignity of women, its companion dialogue *On the Care of the Household*, packaged with the translations of Plutarch on marriage and sold in various formats in the 1540s and 1550s by Jean de Tournes in Lyon and Arnoul L'Angelier in the Palais de Justice in Paris, were far more typical of the printed *Querelle des femmes* texts in presenting the *pro et contra* than Dupont's *Controverses* or the anonymous *Louenge des femmes* that stressed the malicious nature of women. Billon's last prisoner was Dupont. Of the works listed by Billon, only Dupont's *Controverses* and the *Louenge des femmes* present thoroughgoing attacks on woman without any praise or characters who come to her defence.

Billon's list of 'assailants' attacking women in 1555 comes only a few years after the death of the Parisian notary Gilbert de Hodic, who owned numerous books on human nature and some texts specifically within the *Querelle*. In the inventory of the library in the household of Hodic and his wife we find several of the titles that earned Billon's ire, such as a translation of the *Orlando furioso* known in French as 'Roland le furieux', Rabelais' *Tiers livre*, several French translations of Boccaccio, a copy of a *Louenge des femmes*, as well as Speroni's *On the Care of the Household* packaged by Arnoul L'Angelier and Jean de Tournes together with Speroni's dialogue on the dignity of women.[104]

---

99 Sperone Speroni, *De la dignité des femmes*, in *De la cure famillere avec aucuns preceptes de mariage extraicts de Plutarque. Aussi un dialogue de la dignité des femmes* (Lyon: Jean de Tournes, 1546), p. 131.

100 Speroni, *Dignité des femmes*, p. 171.

101 Billon, *Fort inexpugnable*, fo. 17r; Speroni, *Dignité des femmes*, p. 176.

102 Speroni, *Dignité des femmes*, pp. 170–71.

103 Ibid., p. 146.

104 MC, AN, Paris, Hodic inventory, 1549, III, 300, fos 30r, 31r, 32r, 32v.

Concluding the *Querelle des femmes*

To proclaim the case for the inferiority of woman without the safety of a female defender was a rarity. Rosalie Colie reminds us that the subject of a rhetorical paradox is one disapproved of in 'received opinion'.[105] But what happens when the so-called paradox of the superiority of woman becomes the 'received opinion' in print? The most widespread printed ideas in the *Querelle des femmes* supported the dignity of woman.

But how can this be so? In many parts of French society in the 1500s the inferior female condition was clear. Few educational opportunities existed for women beyond some community schools and private tutors. For daughters there was no access to faculties of medicine, law or theology as there was to train sons for positions in the royal administration or the clergy. No female was allowed to succeed to the French throne or purchase and exercise a public office. A daughter marrying before the age of 25 left her father's power to live under the authority of her husband as the head of the household. A wife could not seek justice in the courts without the authorisation of her husband nor enter into legal contracts. A series of royal edicts in the second half of the sixteenth and early seventeenth centuries tended to favour paternal authority, while limiting rights to female inheritance and management of property as a widow. Listed in this point-blank fashion, the legal condition of woman was indeed grim. But the blend of royal edicts and numerous customary and written laws across early modern France meant that the application and interpretation of these laws in practice and in the court system was more mixed than uniformly bleak.[106] Individual wives managed to wield power in their households and in daily interactions with husbands, as many proverbs and 'misogynist' writers such as Dupont openly acknowledged: 'If you marry, you will be a slave for life' – 'Si tu maries, tu seras serf de vie'.[107] The social and economic contributions of a wife to the household were essential for the prosperity of the family. The connections and opportunities provided by marriage, the importance of in-laws for social or trade networks or for launching one's career as a royal officeholder, were not underestimated by the parents and sons and daughters carefully surveying their marriage prospects and those of their brothers and sisters.[108] The *Querelle des femmes* fed on this preoccupation with

105 Rosalie Colie, *Paradoxia Epidemica: The Renaissance Tradition of Paradox* (Princeton, NJ, 1966), p. 10.

106 Evelyne Berriot-Salvadore, *Les femmes dans la société française de la Renaissance* (Geneva, 1990), pp. 31–3, 42–3, 96–7; Clare Crowston, 'Family Affairs: Wives, Credit, Consumption, and the Law in Old Regime France', in Suzanne Desan and Jeffrey Merrick (eds), *Family, Gender, and Law in Early Modern France* (University Park, PA, 2009), pp. 63–7, 70–71.

107 *Controverses*, 1540 edn, Bk II, fo. 96v or sig. MM viii^{v}.

108 Julie Hardwick, *The Practice of Patriarchy: Gender and the Politics of Household Authority in Early Modern France* (University Park, PA, 1998), pp. 57–9, 107.

the choice and training of the wife who would enter into the domestic partnership needed for a household to flourish. The need for a 'good' wife was obvious; it was the 'received opinion', the 'common opinion'.

By the mid-sixteenth century, the defender of woman was the literal 'champion' of views acceptable for airing on the printed page; the poor 'misogynist' became the underdog. To argue the case of female inferiority in the printed *Querelle des femmes* required skill, daring and humour, if one attempted to flout the convention of coming to woman's defence.

Even Dupont, the first sixteenth-century vernacular writer to restrict his writing on the feminine sex to an 'attack', could not resist the eventual pull to a *pro et contra* argument. From as early as 1534 Dupont published a separate little book in the form of a civil lawsuit in which Masculine Sex, the complainant, submits a 'request' or petition against Feminine Sex. Judge Lady Reason has her clerk Just Duty write the referral of the case for a hearing. In 1536, 1537, 1538, 1539 reissue, 1540 and 1541 editions this petition or 'request' was included as part of the third book of the *Controverses*, although it was published separately again in Toulouse in 1542.[109] Masculine Sex chooses Lady Truth as his advocate, while Lady Strong Opinion defends Feminine Sex.[110] On several occasions in her reply or second pleading Lady Truth refers to the folios of the *Controverses* where Dupont excuses himself before honest and honourable women.[111] After the arguments presented by the advocates, Lady Reason retires to deliberate and confer with Good Right (*Bon Droict*) and Lady Discretion and pronounces her judgment in which she allows Masculine Sex's friend Dupont to name any women who badmouths him or his book and 'condemns' the defendant Feminine Sex to pay all the expenses.[112]

When pursuing an argument, a writer, like the archer in Quintilian's rhetorical guidebook *Institutio oratoria*, might resort to several shafts to hit the target. This multivalent strategy did not discredit the attempt, as some commentators we reviewed in this chapter have led us to believe by assessing *Querelle des femmes* texts as 'invalid', 'inconsistent', or lacking in 'sincerity'. Instead we need to acknowledge that a Renaissance writer might use several strategies to enhance the likelihood of persuading the reader. In Dupont's case these approaches included humour, visual and poetic games, plays on military imagery, titillating and bawdy language, profuse objections to marriage, an exhaustive compilation of examples

---

[109] J-F. Courouau and P. Gardy, 'Introduction', in *La Requeste*, p. 72; Dupont, *Controverses*, Janot edn, Bk III, fo. 79r. The courtroom was a popular setting for late medieval *Querelle des femmes* texts: Swift, *Gender, Writing, Performance*, pp. 131, 145, 148.

[110] Dupont, *Controverses*, 1536 edn, fos lxxvii^{r}–lxxxii^{v}; Dupont, 'Requeste du Sexe Masculin: contre le Sexe Femenin. A cause de celles et ceulx qui mesdisent L'autheur du liure intitule, les Controuerses, des Sexes Masculin & Femenin, baillee a Dame Raison: ensemble le plaidoye des parties: Et arrest sur ce intervenu', *Controverses*, 1540 edn, Bk. III, fos 77r–88r.

[111] Dupont, *Controverses*, 1540 edn, Bk III, fos 84v–85r.

[112] Ibid., Bk III, fo. 86v.

of female wickedness and eventually a parody of the law and procedures of the courts; all because he faced the formidable task of proving the inferiority of woman in a society that knew the value of a wife and in a culture that was used to arguing on both sides of a question.

With the exception of Dupont and the anonymous *Louenge des femmes*, few in the sixteenth century attempted the feat of arguing the inferiority of woman without a counterbalance in the form of a pro-woman character in dialogue, such as the Count in Sperone Speroni's *De la dignité des femmes*, a trend that continued into the second half of the century with some of the characters we shall meet in the next chapter – Charilée in Étienne Pasquier's *Monophile*, 1555; the Cosmophile in Jacques Tahureau's *Dialogues*, 1565; or Ginécophile in the *War of Males and Females* by Nicolas de Cholières, 1588. The alternative to the dialogue format was an argument *in utramque partem*, as in the case of Jean de Marconville's *On the Goodness and Badness of Women*, 1564. This pattern of opposing voices we find in the *Querelle des femmes* reflects a broad Renaissance interest in paradoxes, dialogues and 'other forms of argument lacking obvious closure'.[113]

The discussion of the nature of woman was not static and the practices of reading and compilation or *inventio* – the finding and assembly of proofs – as well as the ordering and style of presenting these arguments are important parts of the evolving story of the *Querelle des femmes*.[114] As we shall see in the next two chapters, the dominant paradigm of the creation story, which shaped the discussion of the dignity and misery of man as well as the *Querelle des femmes*, was to be displaced by reading beyond the Bible and the compilation of examples from a wider variety of literature.

---

113 Quentin Skinner, *Reason and Rhetoric in the Philosophy of Thomas Hobbes* (Cambridge, 1996), p. 99.

114 Gisela Bock and Margarete Zimmermann, 'The European *Querelle des Femmes*', *Disputatio: An International Journal of the Late Middle Ages* 5 (2002): 136, 142; Margarete Zimmermann, '*The Old Quarrel*: More than Just Rhetoric', in Wolfram Aichinger, *et al.* (eds), *The* Querelle des Femmes *in the Romania* (Vienna, 2003), pp. 30–34.

Chapter 5
The Dialogue: Beyond Dignity and Misery, Beyond the *Querelle des femmes*

Neither the *Querelle des femmes* nor debates on man's place in the world remained fixed in a world changed by exploration, reformation and civil wars. In the back-and-forth play of sixteenth-century dialogues, authors began to situate the ideas of man and woman in a broader context of human civilisations, less reliant on the story of Adam and Eve. Mid-sixteenth-century humanists and historical writers began to push aside the biblical timeline, while the dialogues of French writers such as Guy de Bruès, Jacques Tahureau and Louise Labé presented secular or pagan versions of a civilisation story at times adjoining with and sometimes instead of the account of creation from Genesis. The first part of this chapter examines how these mid-century writers rework the creation story commonplaces that had always provided the foundation for dignity, misery and *Querelle* treatises, and displace these topoi with alternative mythical or pagan accounts of the beginning of civilisation. By moving away from the creation story as a starting point, Tahureau, Bruès and Labé offer a broader idea of human excellence locating the conversations about the nature of man and woman among a myriad of other topics such as rank, nobility, medicine, philosophy, law, Nature or customs. The dialogue format continued to allow for a variety of perspectives, although some dialogues were more 'open' than others and throughout the chapter we pay attention to how 'open' or 'closed' a dialogue might be.

Many participants in the *Querelle des femmes* had training in the law, held positions as officeholders in the judiciary or set their debates about the nature of woman in a fictional courtroom setting. The second part of this chapter connects the legal and literary worlds of sixteenth-century France by evaluating how legally trained writers such as the lawyer, humanist and historian Étienne Pasquier, who argued many famous cases before the Parlement de Paris, or the Seigneur de Cholières might imitate, compile and argue the facets of female nature in dialogue format.

History and the Dialogue: From Creation Story to Civilisation Story

In sixteenth-century France, writing on human nature changed shape alongside the approach to the study of history. At the beginning of the sixteenth century universal histories such as Jean Lemaire de Belges' *The Illustrations of Gaul and Singularities of Troy*, first published in 1511, had traced human origins back to

Adam and Eve, Noah's family after the Flood and the origins of the French people back to the legend of Troy. The Lyon merchant printer Jean de Tournes published the last edition of Lemaire de Belges' *Illustrations de Gaule* in 1549 with a dedication praising the dignity of man and man's privileged role as a microcosm of the elements of the universe.[1] Pasquier's *Researches on France* (*Des recherches de la France*) first appeared at the boutique of Vincent Sertenas in the Palais de Justice in 1560 where Pasquier's dialogue on the nature of woman and love entitled the *Monophile* was already on sale. Pasquier's historical researches began not with God's creation of the world but with Cæsar's account of the civilisation of the Gauls. To research the history of France, Pasquier suggested that one should first 'cast a glance' at the old Gauls, and then look to the French 'before they were christianised'.[2] When François de Belleforest published his *Universal History Containing the Entire Description and Situation of the Four Parts of the Earth* in 1570, he expressed his disapproval of Lemaire de Belges' approach to French history and suggested 'leaving behind the fables and dreams of Troy'. Instead Belleforest was 'greatly overjoyed' by the methods of Pasquier's *Recherches de la France* and preferred to 'lean' on the 'authority of the ancients' who lived at the time of the Gauls.[3]

This shift to a historical 'civilisation story' did not lead to the sudden disappearance of the creation story tradition in the works on the dignity and misery of man and woman. François de Belleforest adapted and copied whole sections of Johann Boemus' *Recueil de diverses histories* (1529) when he published *L'histoire universelle du monde* in 1570, and so he still opened his universal history by comparing the biblical creation story with the pagan explanations of the origins of human life. These works co-existed on the shelves of booksellers and their customers. In the mid-1580s, for example, the Palais de Justice bookseller Abel L'Angelier sold Guillaume du Bartas' immensely popular *La Sepmaine* on the first week of creation, Nicolas Vignier's *La Bibliothèque historiale*, a history reference book with concurrent biblical and pagan chronologies, as well as Montaigne's

1 Antoine du Moulin, 'À tresillustre, treshaut et tresvertueux prince, Monseigneur Antoine de Bourbon duc de Vendosme', in Jean Lemaire de Belges, *Les Illustrations de Gaule et singularitez de Troye* (Lyon: Jean de Tournes, 1549), sig. *2r. On the many editions see Jacques Abelard, *Les Illustrations de Gaule et singularitez de Troye de Jean Lemaire de Belges* (Geneva, 1976).

2 Étienne Pasquier, *Des recherches de la France, livre premier et second* (Paris: Gilles Robinot, 1581), fo. 6v; George Huppert, *The Idea of Perfect History: Historical Erudition and Historical Philosophy in Renaissance France* (Urbana, IL, 1970), p. 154; Donald Kelley, *Foundations of Modern Historical Scholarship: Language, Law and History in the French Renaissance* (New York, 1970); Béatrice Sayhi-Périgot, 'À l'arrière-plan des *Recherches* I et II: le *Pourparler du Prince*', in *Étienne Pasquier et ses Recherches de la France* (Paris, 1991), pp. 63–77.

3 François de Belleforest, *L'histoire universelle du monde* (Paris: G. Mallot, 1570), fos 177v–178r; Huppert, *Perfect History*, pp. 93, 101.

Essais and its patchwork of classical, secular and theological accounts of human nature. Some Parisians might own both Belleforest's *Histoire universelle du monde* on the four parts of the world and a copy of Lemaire de Belges' *Illustrations de Gaule* or a copy of a *Histoire universelle du monde* and Du Bartas' *Sepmaine* on the first week of creation.[4]

It is not coincidental that this oscillation from creation to civilisation occurred from the 1550s to the end of the century when the dialogue – a genre that presents two or more perspectives – flourished in France.[5] The openness of a dialogue, Virginia Cox notes, depends on the effect of its 'fiction'. Use of a 'metaphor' for the dialogue, such as a banquet or some other social ritual, enhances its 'believability' by reminding the reader that no single speaker has a monopoly on the truth.[6] Writers of Renaissance dialogues were keen to distance themselves from the 'rigidity' of the medieval form of *disputatio* and were more likely to set a scene as a 'discussion among several speakers deemed to have actually taken place'.[7]

The debates about man's place in the world and woman's position relative to man feature throughout the dialogues of Tahureau, Bruès and Labé. Each dialogue develops a different scenario to explore an array of perspectives on human nature and all three venture outside of the familiar Garden of Eden.

Tahureau's *Dialogues* on Vices, Follies and Humanity

Jacques Tahureau, a friend of the poets Ronsard and Jean-Antoine de Baïf, focused on the human condition in the dialogues he wrote before his death in 1555 at the age of 27.[8] First published in 1565, the *Dialogues Not Less Profitable than Facetious Where Each Person's Vices are Strongly and [Bitterly] Rebuked to*

[4] Minutier central des notaires de Paris, Archives nationales, Paris [hereafter MC, AN, Paris], post-mortem inventory of Jacques Ligier, seigneur de Graville in Normandy, 19 June 1581, VIII, 426; MC, AN, Paris, post-mortem inventory of Damoiselle Ysabeau Marron, formerly wife of Jehan de la Robertière, Doctor Regent in the Faculty of Law at the University of Paris and lawyer in the Chambre des comptes, 31 October 1585, XLIX, 215.

[5] Jean-Claude Carron, 'The Persuasive Seduction: Dialogue in Sixteenth-Century France', in Marie-Rose Logan and Peter Rudnytsky (eds), *Contending Kingdoms: Historical, Psychological, and Feminist Approaches to the Literature of Sixteenth-Century England and France* (Detroit, MI, 1991), pp. 91–3.

[6] Virginia Cox, *The Renaissance Dialogue* (Cambridge, 1992), pp. 110–11.

[7] Eva Kushner, 'Renaissance Dialogue and Subjectivity', in Dorothea Heitsch and Jean-François Vallée (eds), *Printed Voices: The Renaissance Culture of Dialogue* (Toronto, 2004), pp. 229–30; Véronique Zaercher, 'Entre dispute et conciliation: stratégies et figures du "consensus" dans le dialogue de la seconde moitié du XVIe siècle', *Revue d'histoire littéraire de la France* 101 (2001): 1334.

[8] The *Dialogues* had 15 reprints from 1565 to 1602: see Max Gauna, 'Avant-Propos', in Jacques Tahureau, *Les Dialogues*: *non moins profitables que facetieux* [1565], ed. M. Gauna (Geneva, 1981), pp. vii, lvi.

Encourage Us to Flee Them and Follow Virtue had 15 reprints by the beginning of the seventeenth century. The character called the Democritic, whose name means 'the people's critic', wanders alone in the woods and muses aloud that philosophers have exaggerated the *grandeur* of man.[9] 'I firmly believe that if the philosophers who made the human condition (*la condition de l'homme*) so great and precious had known of the errors and follies of our age, instead of naming man the only participant of reason, over all the other animals, [they] would have given a whole other definition, or would have said that most among them have only the form and image of the rational creature'.[10] Another character, the Cosmophile or 'lover of the world', walking nearby in a grove of trees, overhears this complaint and seeks out the Democritic who holds 'men (*les hommes*) in such contempt'. He asks the Democritic to show him 'the path' to the happiness and wisdom achieved so rarely by humans – the 'grand contentement de l'homme de bon esprit'.[11] The Cosmophile and the Democritic's conversation meanders through many topics: the nature of women, court flattery, dancing, lawyers, the education of children, medicine, astrology, the issues of rank, nobility and justice, and poverty.[12] At times Tahureau presents women as creatures apart from men, but in the discussion between the Cosmophile and the Democritic women might share in human dignity and they certainly share in human misery and folly.

When the Cosmophile wonders if 'wise persons' (*les personnes de bon esprit*) could learn or improve themselves 'by making love to some gentle-woman', the Democritic responds that it is the 'silliest idea to have entered the minds of men' and so he launches into an attack on the female sex using some typical *Querelle des femmes* arguments. Women are imperfect creatures who exist merely for the purpose of human preservation, although if a man aspires to serve a woman (as her lover) then woman is no more to blame for her 'pride' or 'presumption' than those misguided members of the male sex 'not worthy to be called men'.[13] When the Democritic asks if women could govern as men do, the Cosmophile replies that the Amazons 'governed their republic' well. But the Democritic disapproves of the Amazons' cruelty to men and suggests that, if women had both strength of body and mind, the result would be a 'thousand inconveniences damaging to the

---

9 Jacques Tahureau, *Les Dialogues ... non moins profitables que facetieux, ou les vices d'vn chacun sont repris fort aprement pour nous animer dauantage à les fuir, & suiure la vertu* (Paris: Gabriel Buon, 1570).

10 Tahureau, *Dialogues* [1565], p. 15.

11 Ibid., pp. 16–17; Zaercher, 'Entre dispute', p. 1343.

12 See Barbara Bowen on the topics: 'Jacques Tahureau Revisited', *French Studies* 30:1 (1976): 20–21.

13 Tahureau, *Dialogues* [1565], pp. 23–4. See also Trevor Peach, 'Une source négligé de l'antifeminisme au XVIe siècle: le "Contra Amores" de Platina et les "Dialogues" de Jacques Tahureau', *Studi francesi* 19 (1975): 201–13; for the opposite view see Lula McDowell Richardson, *The Forerunners of Feminism in French Literature of the Renaissance from Christine of Pisa to Marie de Gournay* (Baltimore, MD, 1929), pp. 113–15.

preservation of our [male] sex'.[14] 'But to hear you speak,' protests the Cosmophile, 'God must have erred when he created woman' and he wonders how this is possible because 'according to God if woman is not even more perfect than man, she must at least be his equal'. The Democritic uses biblical examples to show that 'woman is more imperfect than man'. The New Testament, for instance, forbids women from preaching the word of God in public, which is permitted to men.

Undeterred, the Cosmophile recalls 'the powerful David, the wise Solomon, and the strong Hercules' who 'exceeded other men in riches, wisdom and strength', and still they did not disdain the love of women. The Democritic takes up the familiar *Querelle* stance about how even 'brave and valiant men' have been overcome by passion much to their 'great confusion and loss'. He complains that men have 'lost all understanding of perfection and good common sense'. In the early part of the century, Charles de Bovelles maintained that to be fully human was an act of self-perfection and how, through this knowledge of the self, man the microcosm could come to know all the things in the world. Tahureau's Democritic laments that, instead of contemplating 'the great things and the secrets of nature', men give themselves to the service of a 'thing so small and so vile as woman'. Citing the violence of Medea, Agrippina and Clytemnestra, the Democritic asks if there is 'a creature' more full of deceit, calumny and lies than the woman 'who wishes to govern herself badly' – 'qui se veut mal gouverner'?[15]

The Cosmophile, like a *Querelle* defender of women, turns the spotlight on male inconstancy and initially suggests that women are 'worthy of even greater praise' when men plead with them and pursue them in love. The Democritic confesses that the 'fickleness of men and their follies are great'. He admits his own foolish appetite in pursuit of women, but this widespread male folly doesn't mean that women are 'more wise or constant'. Women, too, participate in the 'folly and ignorance of men'.[16] In a disclaimer typical of the *Querelle des femmes*, the character Democritic reminds the reader 'as I have always said, I only intend to speak of foolish and presumptuous [women]'. He concedes that some women are full of 'a goodness, amiable sweetness and a gracious disposition', but they are so 'rare' and 'in such small number' that the presumptuous women can be said to represent them all.[17]

The dialogue continues back and forth with a long segment in which the Democritic complains about women as wives: how they spend their husbands' money, parade themselves in church, flirt with their servants and social inferiors,

---

14 Tahureau, *Dialogues* [1565], pp. 24–6.

15 Ibid., pp. 27–8, 30–31.

16 Ibid., pp. 27, 58–9. *Querelle* defenders of women would often accuse the attackers of holding a spurned lover's grudge against the entire female sex. Gratien Dupont, *Les Controversses des sexes masculin et femenin* (Toulouse: Jacques Colomiés, 1534), fos lxxvii–lxxxv; *La Louenge des femmes, Invention extraite du Commentaire de Pantagruel, sus L'Androgyne de Platon* (Lyon: Jean de Tournes, 1551), p. 6.

17 Tahureau, *Dialogues* [1565], p. 60.

and with a 'shameless will' make cuckolds of their husbands.[18] His long speech is so convincing that the Cosmophile is surprised when the Democritic justifies marriage as necessary for the perpetuation of the human species. Man's 'overly amorous extremity' leads him to foolish acts but also behaves according to the greatest wisdom and virtue in the world – 'les plus grandes sagesses et vertus du monde' – because the sexual instinct for human relations is more laudable than a 'lack of companionship' (*faute d'amitié*). Withdrawal from the community is 'worthy of even greater vituperation for being less human' than pursuing the follies of love or the bonds of friendship – 'digne de plus grande vitupere pour estre *moins humain* que l'autre'. Just when he has convinced the Cosmophile of the follies of marriage and the treacheries of women, the Democritic turns the conversation upside down and outlines how love, friendship and the marriage bond are the foundations of civil society.[19] Tahureau offers to his reader the increasingly familiar stance that being human means participating in civil society. Tahureau explains the origins of civilisation as the good will (*affection naturelle*) among humans. This secular civilisation story becomes the basis of human excellence.[20]

Turning to the nobility, the Cosmophile and the Democritic discuss men of 'dignities' who forget that their superior position stems mostly from fortune or circumstance and not from merit. These men 'swell up with such pride that they do not respect other men whatsoever, as if Nature had formed them from other stuff and expressly brought [them] forth to be heaped up with more riches than others'. The fictional Democritic admits his own noble pedigree: '[Y]ou would say I vituperated gentlemen indiscriminately (given that I would do wrong to myself) or other great lords, because in talking about each estate whether it be to blame or to mock, I judge only the vicious and the fools'.[21] In misery-of-man literature little attempt is made to apologise to virtuous 'good men' for drawing attention to examples of vicious or bestial humans. However, in the more contentious case of nobility, where not only virtue but rank and status were at stake, writers tread more warily. The Democritic warns how sumptuous garments add to the impressive demeanour of an *homme de bien* so that 'someone with a great train of valets or improved by clothing more rich and precious than the common people, is immediately judged by all as a great lord and gentleman'.[22] However, Tahureau's *Dialogues*, like Pierre Boaistuau's *Théatre du monde*, stress the role of fortune and the possibility of downward mobility by recalling the great kings and lords

---

[18] Ibid., pp. 36, 44.

[19] Ibid., pp. 77–80.

[20] Gauna, 'Introduction', in ibid., p. xlvii.

[21] Ibid., pp. 89–91. A posthumous dedication refers to Tahureau as a 'gentilhomme vivant de ses rentes', who served in the king's army against the emperor Charles V: see Maurice de la Porte, 'A Monsieur M. François Pierron Grand-Vicaire', in Tahureau, *Dialogues* [1565], pp. 2–3.

[22] Ibid., pp. 91–2, 98, 110.

reduced to an 'extreme misery and poverty'.[23] When the Cosmophile points to those of low estate such as Epaminondas of Thebes, who rose to great heights of power and riches, the Democritic counters: 'Do you think that there has never been a contrary [example] of mighty households of which the name is now forever erased'?[24] Tahureau's *Dialogues* mock a series of professions including medicine and the law, but he reserves particular disdain for the judicial officeholders, 'vultures disguised in long robes', who purchase their offices and dignities.[25]

Democritic laments the impossibility of finding an honourable man and quotes from 'our no less learned than facetious Rabelais': 'Honourable people, [may] God keep you safe and sound, where are you, I can't see you'.[26] Despite their different circumstances and stations in life, common people and nobles are essentially the same because all are foolish and lack judgment. Tahureau jettisons the notion that man is King or Lord on earth and instead the Democritic and the Cosmophile discuss a string of ancient and contemporary learned men including Plato, Aristotle, Solomon and Agrippa, only to find something to mock in each one.[27] Tahureau lambastes the *hommes illustres* tradition, points to human folly and yet very occasionally still supports the idea of the rare wise man – the 'homme de bon esprit' or 'personne de bon esprit' – found in dignity-of-man literature who acts through reason, force of will and liberty.[28] Democritic seeks the whereabouts of this man of dignity, the object of so much optimism, but he suggests that like Cicero's imaginary orator these 'personnes de si bon esprit' exist only as 'ideas', 'conceits' or 'fancies' of 'perfect men' (*hommes parfaits*).[29]

As Tahureau's Democritic states at the beginning of the second dialogue, his intent is to 'mock the follies of each and every one'.[30] The common person (*vulgaire*), the noble, man and woman share folly and presumption. A good, intelligent woman is a rare thing among her sex – 'femme de bon esprit (chose

---

23 Ibid., p. 90.

24 Ibid., pp. 172–5.

25 Ibid., pp. 108, 100–10.

26 Ibid., p. 97. These are the opening lines to the 'Prologue de l'Autheur' of Rabelais' *Quart livre* of Gargantua and Pantagruel in François Rabelais, *Œuvres complètes*, ed. Guy Demerson (Paris, 1973), p. 568: 'Gens de bien, Dieu vous sauve et garde, où estes-vous, je ne vous peus voir'.

27 Tahureau, *Dialogues* [1565], pp. 196, 201, 206. On Tahureau's mockery of *hommes illustres* see Gabriel Pérouse, *Nouvelles françaises du XVIe siècle* (Geneva, 1977), pp. 170–71; on the dignity-of-man commonplaces see Trevor Peach, *Nature and Reason: étude critique des Dialogues de Jacques Tahureau* (Geneva, 1986), p. 28.

28 Tahureau, *Dialogues* [1565], p. 132: for example, the Monirien, whom the Democritic describes as an 'homme de grand scavoir et de fort bon esprit', or as an 'homme de jugement de grande doctrine'. On Tahureau and the dignity of man, Trevor Peach, 'Another view of *Les Dialogues* of Jacques Tahureau', *French Studies* 33:3 (1979): 272–87.

29 Tahureau, *Dialogues* [1565], p. 96.

30 Ibid., p. 140.

toutefois rare en leur sexe)' in the same way that the virtuous man of judgment – 'homme de bon esprit' – is extremely scarce.[31] Although Tahureau reproduces some of the biblical examples of the early *Querelle*, gone is the obligatory reference to the creation story of Adam and Eve. Gone too is the arrival of human misery with original sin and the expulsion from Paradise. Tahureau's dialogues demonstrate how the discussion of the human condition moved away from the paradigm of the creation story. The dialogue format allows Tahureau to explore both sides of an argument, but by the end the Cosmophile is 'transformed' (*tout metamorphosé*) and tells the Democritic that henceforth he would hold in 'greater contempt' (*en plus grand mespris*) what had seemed 'the most perfect and the most pleasing' (*le plus parfait et le plus beau*).[32]

As we consider this literature it is helpful to bear in mind the potential audience. While the discussion of woman's nature shared space with a myriad of other human concerns in Tahureau's *Dialogues*, it was possible to promote the work as a *Querelle des femmes* text. In 1568, a bookseller in Antwerp packaged Tahureau's *Dialogues* for sale with Jean de Marconville's *De la bonté et mauvaistié des femmes*, aiming for the niche market of the *Querelle des femmes*.[33] The interest in the topic of the feminine sex continued and booksellers took their opportunities. Among the modest collection of books in the possession of a Parisian merchant Bobye and his wife in the late 1580s and passed on to their daughter by inheritance, can be found Tahureau's wide-ranging dialogues.[34] We shall discuss how Tahureau's *Dialogues* fitted into the rest of the Bobye family's book collection in chapter seven.

Guy de Bruès, Relativism and the Closed Dialogue

Guy de Bruès, a *noble de robe* from Languedoc, set his *Dialogues* as a series of conversations on three successive summer afternoons.[35] In this work, published in 1557, the poets Pierre de Ronsard and Jean-Antoine Baïf join two other companions: Jean Nicot, an ambassador for Henri II, and Guillaume Aubert, a lawyer in the Parlement de Paris. The four friends meet to discuss a question that has been troubling Baïf: whether one should prefer to be human or 'the most

31 Ibid., p. 62.

32 Ibid., p. 240; Zaercher, 'Entre dispute', p. 1347.

33 Sold in Antwerp in an in-16 format by Pierre Vibert from 1568; see Max Gauna, 'Note sur le texte', in Tahureau, *Dialogues* [1565], p. lxi.

34 MC, AN, Paris, Inventory [marital] community of goods, [between honourable Anne Bobye and] Jacques Malingre, lawyer at the Parlement de Paris, 20 February 1590, XXIII, 134; see Chapter 7, pp. 184–5.

35 On the publication of the dialogues, see Guy de Bruès, *Dialogues de Guy de Brués contre les Nouveaux Academiciens*, ed. Panos Morphos (Baltimore, MD, 1953), p. 83; Philippe Renouard, *Imprimeurs & libraires parisiens du XVIe siècle, Fascicule Cavellat, Marnef, Cavellat* (Paris, 1986), p. 3.

miserable of animals.'[36] The dialogue setting allows some of Bruès' characters to stray from the creation story and voice a competing secular, classical account of the beginning of civilisation. When Aubert sketches a vision of man in the state of Nature, Nicot shepherds the discussion back to a Christian context with the topos of man's erect posture by which man could admire the heavens and home of his Creator. As Nicot reminds Aubert, God moulded man, saying, 'let us make man in our image and likeness' and 'breathed life into Adam', to bear witness to the 'excellence and immortality of our soul'.[37]

At every opportunity in the *Dialogues* the sceptics Baïf and Aubert introduce the relativism of rank, age, custom, nation and gender to undermine the 'universal' definition of the excellence of man. Aubert turns to perceptions of women, familiar to a Renaissance reader of Plutarch, to any *Querelle des femmes* reader of Agrippa, or to any reader of Étienne Pasquier's 1550s dialogue the *Monophile*. Aubert outlines how his society shows little esteem for the female sex by limiting their public influence. but this practice was not universal. 'We don't want women to exercise any magistrate's office in a republic because they are too weak and gossipy and because their sex could not honourably permit it', but some ancient cultures as we read in Plutarch and Stobaeus 'often preferred [women] to men'.[38] He recognises that categories are flexible and unstable. Opinion, like law, is subject to change.

Despite the format, Bruès' *Dialogues* do not allow any suspension of judgment, but at the end of each of the three day-long discussions the four friends return to the Christian dignity of man. The title of the work reveals why each debate must reach this same resolution in favour of the creation-story dignity of man: *Les Dialogues de Guy de Bruès contre les Nouveaux Académiciens* subtitled *Que tout ne consiste point en opinion*.[39] These fictional dialogues between Aubert, Ronsard, Baïf and Nicot might have reflected salon conversations, or else Bruès employed the characters to act as a 'vehicle of truth'. As Cox notes, the use of historical figures in dialogue attempts to reproduce the effect of real conversation, but the 'muting effect of decorum' reduces the possibility for a 'frank exchange of ideas.'[40] As Véronique Zaercher has noted, from the outset the debate is 'conçue

---

36 Bruès, *Dialogues*, pp. 28–30, 97 for a fuller picture of how the dialogue setting unfolds. On Nicot, Ronsard, Aubert and Baïf see Thomas Greenwood, 'Guy de Bruès', *Bibliothèque d'Humanisme et Renaissance* 13 (1951): 173–6.

37 Bruès, *Dialogues*, p. 164.

38 Bruès, *Dialogues*, p. 191. See Henricus Cornelius Agrippa, *De la noblesse & preexcellence du sexe fœminin* (Paris: Denis Janot, c. 1535), sigs G iiii^v–G v^r; Étienne Pasquier, *Le Monophile* [1554], ed. E.H. Balmas (Milan, 1957), p. 136.

39 Jean-Claude Carron, 'Dialogical Argument: Scripting Rhetoric (The Case of Guy de Brues's *Dialogues*)', *South Central Review* 10:2 (1993): 22.

40 Cox, *Renaissance Dialogue*, pp. 32, 97; Carron notes that each interlocutor shares a belief in the 'truth' at the beginning of the dialogues, but that Baïf agrees to take the stance of the sceptic for the purpose of the debate: 'Persuasive Seduction', p. 104.

pour s'orienter vers un consensus'.[41] Bruès' dialogues were already 'closed', so although diversity and scepticism were allowed during the discussion, they were reined in by the conclusion. All the more remarkable, then, is the accomplishment of Louise Labé in playing with, opening up and expanding the ideas of human dignity and misery in the *Debate of Folly and Love*, 1555.

Louise Labé's Suspension of Judgment

Louise Labé's father was a wealthy ropemaker, active on the Lyon city council, who gradually lived from his investments rather than his trade. Labé was educated in Latin and Italian and frequented the circles of the humanist writers Maurice Scève and Pontus de Tyard and their mutual friend the merchant printer Jean de Tournes. She married a ropemaker of her father's status. The poet Jean-Antoine de Baïf and the lawyer Guillaume Aubert, fictionalised in Bruès' *Dialogues*, honoured Labé with odes for her *Works*.[42]

Louise Labé's *Debate of Folly and Love* (*Débat de Folie et d'Amour*) published by Jean de Tournes of Lyon in 1555 and again in 1556 opens with a banquet of the gods. At the entrance to Jupiter's palace Folly, determined not to be the last guest to arrive, tries to slip in before Cupid. An argument ensues and Folly, affronted by Cupid's arrogance, tears his eyes out and wraps a blindfold around his wounds so that Love is blind. When Venus complains to Jupiter of her son's injuries, Folly agrees to a hearing to settle the dispute. Apollo advocates the case of Cupid or Love, while Mercury, as the messenger who represents 'eloquence', counters with a 'praise of Folly' before Jupiter's court of banqueting gods.[43] The manner in which Labé sets the scene and lists the characters has led some critics to suggest she was outlining stage directions for a five-act play or a performance to be read aloud at a salon. It is even possible that the *Débat* was performed for a young Louis XIII in the early seventeenth century.[44]

In Apollo's praise of Love, Labé transfers the commonplaces of the dignity and misery of man to a pagan setting of many gods, suggesting for example that, 'as

---

41 Zaercher, 'Entre dispute', p. 1341.

42 Ann Rosalind Jones, *The Currency of Eros: Women's Love Lyric in Europe, 1540–1620* (New Haven, CT, 1990), pp. 156–8; for the odes and sonnets dedicated to Labé, see Louise Labé, *Oeuvres complètes*, ed. François Rigolot (Paris, 1986), pp. 141–200.

43 On the 'judicial eloquence' of Mercury and Apollo, see Christiane Lauvergnat-Gagnière, 'La rhétorique dans le *Débat de Folie et Amour*', in Guy Demerson (ed.), *Louise Labé, les voix du lyrisme* (Lyon, 1991), pp. 53–67.

44 Janet Smarr, *Joining the Conversation: Dialogues by Renaissance Women* (Ann Arbor, MI, 2005), pp. 168–72; Anne-Marie Bourbon, 'Introduction', in Louise Labé, *Debate of Folly and Love: A New English Translation with the Original French Text*, trans. Anne-Marie Bourbon (New York, 2000), p. 7; Aurore Evain, 'Introduction', in Evain, *et al.* (eds), *Théâtre de femmes de l'Ancien Régime: XVIe siècle* (Saint-Étienne, 2006), p. 21.

for their souls (*esprits*), humans (*hommes*) are made in our image and likeness'. Labé employs Apollo's speech on behalf of Cupid to put forth a variation on the civilisation story. The foundation of human society stems from Love and a 'benevolence' or affection that 'makes [humans] wish to do good to one another'. Labé avoids the creation story version of excellence that confuses the dignity of man with his physical image as a male. She offers an alternative to the human excellence defined through contemplative study and generally restricted to the male scholar or male professional. The advocate for Love underlines the importance of caring, community and humanity to others. 'This love, generally borne for one's (*semblable*) fellow human, is of such repute among humans' that they will defend one another to the death.[45] Brotherly love leads to great acts of courage and 'as for women', have women not helped in battle, saved husbands, countries and kings?[46]

This 'first fame among men' – 'premiere gloire entre les hommes' – transcends the variety of human forms and dispositions.[47] Love's presence makes humans (*hommes*) 'multiply, live together and perpetuate the world through the love and care they extend to their descendants'.[48] Apollo echoes the dignity-of-man and *Querelle* praise for human ingenuity when he argues that 'those who have invented something good for the advantage of all have been more esteemed than others'. Prometheus stole fire from Jupiter, Apollo asserts, out of 'the love he bore man'.[49] In Labé's *Debate* even the 'ordinary people' or *commun populaire* prize their experiences of love – a form of dignity attainable by all.[50] The male scholar, the professional or noble are not set apart from the rest of humankind as capable of a dignity unattainable by others.

Apollo, the advocate for Love, describes how the husband and wife in a marriage full of love bask in dignity, because who would not 'admit that married love is worthy (*di*[g]*ne*) of high esteem?' Love within marriage, not the institution of marriage itself, brings to man the 'companionship of a woman who faithfully manages his wealth; increases his pleasure; gently keeps him in check for fear he takes on too much for his health; protects him from troubles, even sometimes preventing them from happening; calms and soothes him; looks after him in sickness and in health'.[51] A version of the argument forwarded by the advocate Apollo could resurface in a real courtroom situation and by comparing its use there we can understand Labé's innovative rewriting of this typical *Querelle des*

45 Labé, *Débat de Folie et d'Amour*, in *Oeuvres complètes* ('*Oeuvres*'), pp. 68–9; Labé, *Debate of Folly and Love* ('*Debate*'), trans. Bourbon, pp. 72–5. My translations differ occasionally from Bourbon's, but the page references here are to her translation.

46 Labé, *Oeuvres*, p. 71; Labé, *Debate*, pp. 76–7.

47 Labé, *Oeuvres*, p. 68; Labé, *Debate*, pp. 72–3.

48 Labé, *Oeuvres*, p. 67; Labé, *Debate*, pp. 68–9.

49 Labé, *Oeuvres*, pp. 68–9; Labé, *Debate*, pp. 72–3.

50 Labé, *Oeuvres*, p. 70; Labé, *Debate*, pp. 74–5.

51 Labé, *Oeuvres*, p. 70; Labé, *Debate*, pp. 74–7.

femmes argument that woman in her role as wife served as a comfort and aid to her husband. This expectation could help encourage a bachelor to the altar, as we saw in Rabelais' *Tiers livre*.[52] Louis Servin, speaking as the *avocat général* and thus representing the interests of the king in a 1603 appeal before the Parlement de Paris, used the biblical equivalent to make a more traditional form of this argument, that 'marriage was ordered by the decree of God who created woman (*femme*) as an aid to man (*vne ayde à l'homme*)'.[53] In this legal appeal a wife wished to annul her marriage with a 'feeble-minded' (*debile d'esprit*) husband. The lawyers and the interrogation of the couple even raised questions about whether the husband could be considered a 'man' because he lacked reason and therefore the possibility of achieving the 'dignity' of man.[54] Servin argued in support of the indissoluble ties of marriage because the 'principal end of marriage' (*principal fin du mariage*) was so that 'the wife (*la femme*) was at the hand of the husband to help, console and comfort him in his labours, in order to be always ready to serve him. The more a man is weak and infirm, as is [the husband] Nicolas Gambert [in this case] the more such aid is necessary'.[55] The judicial decision by the Parlement de Paris in 1604 upheld the marriage.[56]

By contrast, in Labé's *Débat*, conjugal happiness does not come from God or from the institution of marriage, but from 'the love that sustains it'. Apollo continues and counters that in a marriage and household without love the 'wife never laughs', the couple is 'never at peace', they squander their wealth, the husband is driven out of his wits and eventually abandons his wife. As the advocate Apollo summarises: 'This is the unquestionable proof that only Love can bring to marriage the happiness, which they say can be found there'.[57] Worse than the

---

52 Juan Luis Vives, *L'Institution de la femme chrestienne. Tant en son enfance, que mariage, & viduité. Avec l'office du mary* (Paris: Denis Janot for Galiot du Pré, 1545), Bk IV, Ch. 1, *De l'office du mary*, fos 138v–139r; Sperone Speroni, *De la dignité des femmes*, in *De la cure famillere avec aucuns preceptes de mariage extraicts de Plutarque. Aussi un dialogue de la dignité des femmes* (Lyon: Jean de Tournes, 1546), p. 171; Jean de Marconville, *De l'heur et malheur de marriage, ensemble les loix connubiales de Plutarque traduictes en françois* (Paris: Jean Dallier, 1571), fo. 33r, Marconville is copying Vives; Rabelais, *Le Tiers livre des faicts et dicts héroïques du bon Pantagruel*, in *Œuvres complètes*, pp. 400–401.

53 Louis Servin, *Plaidoyez de Mre Loys Servin conseiller du roy en son Conseil d'Estat & advocat general en sa cour de Parlement. A la fin desquels les arrests intervenus sur iceuls*, 2 vols (Paris: Jean de Heuqueville, 1603–1605), vol. II, p. 34.

54 Ibid., vol. II, pp. 15–16.

55 Ibid., vol. II, p. 34: 'Au demeurant la principale fin du mariage a esté ordonnée par le decret de Dieu, lequel a crée la femme pour vne ayde à l'homme … cela a esté faict à ce que la femme fust en la main du mary pour le secourir, consoler, & soulager en ses trauauls, à fin d'estre tousjours preste pour le seruir: plus vn homme est foible & infirme, comme l'est Nicolas Gambert, plus vn tel secours luy est necessaire …'.

56 Ibid., vol. II, pp. 12, 36.

57 Labé, *Oeuvres*, p. 70; Labé, *Debate*, pp. 76–7.

wretched married couples are the Misanthropes 'buried in their own eccentricities' who 'do not care to love'. Even more pitiful is the loner who eats 'slovenly, alone', lives in a 'disorderly' house in fear, stinginess and ignorance. 'Yet it is worthwhile to say a word about them, in order to know how unpleasant and miserable are the lives of those who have chosen to live without Love'.[58]

Apollo explains the transforming power of love. Men and women try to improve and raise themselves to excellence for their lovers through philosophy, music, poetry and fashion. The detractors of women in the *Querelle des femmes* often protest about the 'artifice' used by women to trick men, but Labé demonstrates that this human folly is common to both sexes. Men wear 'tight and well-fitting hose, showing the movements of a well-proportioned body'. Women raise their breasts to the best angle and if her body is a perfect one, the woman wears a tight dress. If not, she covers her imperfections in 'ample folds'.[59]

Love is the source of 'glory, honour, benefit and pleasure' so that humans cannot live 'properly' without its pleasure and well-being.[60] With several skilful strokes of her pen, Labé moves beyond the *Querelle des femmes* as well as the dignity of man to redefine human excellence. It is 'love' or care, not a physical male image nor contemplation and wisdom, that lends dignity to humans. Labé sets the stage for her praise of Folly. When Apollo, as the advocate of Love, completes his pleading, the gods are ready to condemn Folly, but Jupiter announces that Mercury will present Folly's case. Folly had chosen the god of eloquence to represent her because she was certain he would not 'leave out anything that might serve my case'.[61] Mercury asks the gods to recall that, 'as soon as man was placed on earth, he began his life with Folly' so that since the beginning of humankind 'no Lady in the world has ever enjoyed such a good reputation'.[62]

Labé mocks the *hommes illustres* tradition when Mercury asks, 'what men (*hommes*) are more honoured than fools'? Alexander could not hide his thirst for wine and yet made himself adored like a god. Mercury asks the gods to imagine placing a wise man and a fool in the world to observe which of the two would gain the most esteem. 'Mr Wiseman' would wait to be summoned for help, 'remain all alone with his wisdom' and still have the leisure time to 'plant his cabbages'. The fool would hover around, come and go in haste, hustle and bustle with apparent importance, until he met someone of the same foolish streak to help him be regarded as a 'great man.' 'He will be esteemed, praised, valued and followed by everybody' and be 'praised to the heavens'. Like the Democritic in Tahureau's *Dialogues*, Rabelais in the *Fourth Book of Gargantua and Pantagruel* and Nicole Estienne's lament in her *Miseries of the Married Woman*, the advocate Mercury

---

[58] Labé, *Oeuvres*, p. 72; Labé, *Debate*, pp. 78–9.

[59] Labé, *Oeuvres*, pp. 74–5; Labé, *Debate*, pp. 82–3.

[60] Labé, *Oeuvres*, p. 77; Labé, *Debate*, pp. 86–7.

[61] Labé, *Oeuvres*, p. 60; Labé, *Debate*, pp. 52–3; François Rigolot, *Louise Labé lyonnaise, ou la Renaissance au feminin* (Paris, 1997), p. 208.

[62] Labé, *Oeuvres*, p. 85; Labé, *Debate*, pp. 100–101.

calculates that for each true wise man who becomes known in the world there are 10,000 fools in the minds and eyes of the people.[63] Moreover, Folly permits the inequity of laws, allowing the masses of people to follow one set of laws while the powerful 'adopt other laws for themselves'.[64] If the world was without Folly, who would enter into marriage, who would brave the seas, who would need lawyers or judges?[65] Love needs Folly as his companion, Mercury tells the gods, because what 'power and renown would [Love] have if he was close to wisdom'?[66]

When Mercury ends his praise of Folly, Jupiter realises that the gods have been 'diversely' moved and persuaded by the advocates. With the use of a completely fictional setting, Labé retains the openness of the dialogue as Jupiter pronounces 'a provisional decree' that the judgment will be suspended for a virtual eternity. 'In view of the difficulty and importance of your differences, and the diversity of opinions, we have postponed your case for three times seven times nine centuries'. Until that time Folly 'will serve as a guide to blind Love'.[67]

The pleadings on behalf of Love and Folly play with and invert the familiar dignity- and misery-of-man commonplaces. Man and woman share in the dignity of love or experience the misery of a life without any love. Even the ordinary people or *commun populaire* are allowed to bask in the glow of dignity when they love and are loved. And yet, the debate is not so simple that love represents dignity while folly leads to misery. Rather, Folly prevents total misery among humankind. 'In short, without this good Lady, man would shrivel up, and become dull, cheerless and broody'.[68] Labé's *Débat* recognises that diverse and contrary opinions may not be reconciled.

Both Tahureau and Labé satirise the dignity of man and demonstrate the abundance of human folly. For Tahureau and Labé, women are targets of derision alongside men while nobles receive their fair share of barbs along with the 'common people'. In dignity-of-man accounts, man was created as the king of the world, Lord of all creation. This excellence was by definition available only to a few, to an elite, through education, rank and fortune, whereas for Tahureau, Bruès and Labé differences in moral conduct determine human excellence or misery. In these dialogues, virtue or vice matter more than 'accidental' or fortune-based differences such as rank or sex. Moreover, each of these dialogues offers a

---

63 Labé, *Oeuvres*, pp. 86–7; Labé, *Debate*, pp. 102–5; [Nicole Estienne] Madame Liebault, *Les misères de la femme mariée, où se peuvent voir les peines et tourmens qu'elle reçoit durant sa vie. Mis en forme de stances* (Paris: Pierre Menier, no date), sig. B ij^r.

64 Labé, *Oeuvres*, p. 86, Labé, *Debate*, pp. 102–3.

65 Labé, *Oeuvres*, p. 88; Labé, *Debate*, pp. 106–7.

66 Labé, *Oeuvres*, p. 101; Labé, *Debate*, pp. 128–9.

67 Labé, *Oeuvres*, p. 103; Labé, *Debate*, pp. 132–3; Floyd Gray, *Gender, Rhetoric and Print Culture in French Renaissance Writing* (Cambridge, 2000), pp. 91, 104; Julie Campbell, *Literary Circles and Gender in Early Modern Europe: A Cross-Cultural Approach* (Aldershot, 2006), pp. 113, 120.

68 Labé, *Oeuvres*, p. 91; Labé, *Debate*, pp. 110–11.

civilisation story as an alternative to the creation story. In the mid- to late sixteenth century, the popular dialogue format allowed for moments of openness where more than one perspective could be explored. In Tahureau's dialogue human folly could be mocked and alternatives to the dignity of man could be explored, but the worldly Democritic led the naïve Cosmophile to a truth. By leaving out the Christian framework, Labé helps to keep her dialogue open.[69] Like the lawyers who argued on behalf of their clients before the Parlement, Apollo and Mercury deliberate the 'pour' and the 'contre' in the *Debate of Folly and Love*, but Labé suspends the judgment of Jupiter and his jury of gods. Labé's *Débat* used the backdrop of the pagan setting, the law, and elements of performance to rewrite and weave in many of the ideas of human dignity and misery as well as the *Querelle des femmes*.

Lawyers and the Interest in the *Querelle des femmes*

The humanist lawyer and historian Étienne Pasquier, a contemporary of Labé, Tahureau and Bruès, would enjoy a long literary and legal career through to the early 1600s. As discussed in the Introduction, Pasquier attended sessions of the sovereign courts in the Palais de Justice, listened to the advocates and followed the procedures from the time of his reception as a lawyer at the Parlement de Paris in November 1549. Throughout his decades as a lawyer in the Parlement de Paris and later a judicial officeholder, Pasquier corresponded and commented on the changing social and political situation of those in service of the king and state through the civil wars and beyond into the 1600s.

Pasquier's *Monophile* represents more of the status quo of the *Querelle des femmes* in the 1550s than the innovative shift evident in Labé's *Débat* or even Tahureau's *Dialogues*. As we saw in the opening section of this chapter, Pasquier's writing talents lay in transforming historical practice in his *Recherches de la France*, which he revised throughout his lifetime. The *Recherches* demonstrate the interest in reflecting on and exploring a variety of topics across a collection of chapters or essays, as will be examined in the writings of Mexia, Marconville and Montaigne in chapter six. The *Monophile*, however, is worth examining because of Pasquier's connection to the legal profession. Pasquier did not use the courtroom format as many previous medieval *Querelle* writers such as Pierre Michault, Martin Le Franc or even as Gratien Dupont did in the 1530s *Requeste du Sexe Masculin*. Instead Pasquier followed the more contemporary trend of setting the dialogue in a garden or as a gathering of gentleman and ladies.[70]

69 Smarr, *Joining the Conversation*, pp. 167, 170. In Speroni's dialogue considering 'natural and moral philosophy' Jupiter also defers judgment indefinitely.

70 Helen Swift, *Gender, Writing, Performance: Men Defending Women in Late Medieval France, 1440–1538* (Oxford, 2008), pp. 100, 106, 131, 145; Cox, *Renaissance Dialogue*, pp. 110–11; Kushner, 'Renaissance Dialogue', pp. 229–30.

The *Monophile* displays some of Pasquier's early training in rhetoric as well as his preparation for his profession as a lawyer. The *Palais libraire* Vincent Sertenas obtained the first ten-year privilege for Pasquier's *Monophile* in November 1553. In the mid-1550s Sertenas shared the second edition with other Palais libraires Jean Longis and the rue Neuve Nôtre Dame printer Estienne Groulleau, the same booksellers involved in producing and distributing Mexia's *Diverse leçons* in 1552 and through the following decade. From 1555 Charles L'Angelier also sold an edition of the *Monophile* from his boutique at the 'first pillar of the Grand'Salle in front of the chapel of the presiding judges'.[71] In 1557 Pasquier married a widow for whom he had won a case in the Parlement de Paris, and whom he described affectionately as a 'real virago' (*vraie viragine*) when reflecting on his life many years later.[72] A 1566 edition of the *Monophile* followed, reissued in 1567, and in March 1578, when Pasquier had built a reputation as a formidable advocate, Charles L'Angelier's nephew Abel obtained a ten-year privilege for this dialogue of Pasquier's youth and sold it from his stall at the first pillar of the Grand'Salle.[73] Less than a decade later Abel L'Angelier published the first edition of Pasquier's series of observations on the family, state and politics in his *Letters*, 1586.[74]

In the *Monophile*, Pasquier crafts a fictional dialogue in which several gentlemen returning from a military campaign relax by gathering to talk about the courage of their king and the 'fragility of human life' before settling into a more drawn-out discussion of women, love and marriage.[75] Pasquier features as one of the participants when his character chances upon the pastoral scene and engages in banter with the gathering of gentlemen and one lady. In the *Monophile* the group considers marriage customs such as the polygamy allowed by the followers of Mahommed, the sharing of wives by the Massagethes, the dissolution of marriage in ancient cultures, the best age to marry and whether it is better to marry for love or for the dowry.[76] 'Seigneur Pasquier' wandering nearby happens to hear the exchange and then joins the group, weighing whether to marry for love and

---

[71] On the *Monophile* see Pasquier's letter c. 1582–83 published in his *Lettres* at the boutique of Abel L'Angelier in 1586: 'A Monsieur Pitou, Seigneur de Savoye, Procureur General du Roy en la Chambre de Justice de Guyenne', in Étienne Pasquier, *Lettres familières*, ed. Dorothy Thickett (Geneva, 1974), VII:1, pp. 125–33.

[72] James Dahlinger, *Étienne Pasquier on Ethics and History* (New York, 2007), p. 25; Étienne Pasquier, 'A Monsieur Cossard, Conseiller du Roy, & Auditeur en la Chambre des Comptes à Paris', in *Les Œuvres d'Étienne Pasquier*, 2 vols (Amsterdam, 1723), vol. II, XXII:12, col. 683.

[73] Jean Balsamo and Michel Simonin, *Abel L'Angelier et Françoise de Louvain (1574–1620). Suivi du catalogue des ouvrages publiés par Abel L'Angelier (1574–1610) et la Veuve L'Angelier (1610–1620)* (Geneva, 2002), pp. 153–4.

[74] See Chapter 1, pp. 15–16.

[75] Étienne Pasquier, 'Le premier livre du Monophile', in *Œuvres*, vol. II, col. 699.

[76] Pasquier, *Monophile*, in *Les Œuvres*, vol. II, cols 704A, 706A, 714C–D, 715–16, 716A.

without consent of parents, which in the early 1550s was still legally possible, or whether the couple perfected and consummated their love by the communication of [their bodies].[77] The character Monophile speaks for monogamous love, while Philopole 'wants to [spread his] love in several places'.[78] At times, the writer Pasquier underlines the ambiguity of the dialogue, especially with some of the outrageous statements made by Philopole, who spoke either 'in earnest' (*a bon escient*) or 'in jest' (*en jeu*) and with such 'naïve gaiety' that one never knew whether he 'spoke only for pleasure or whether that was how he saw things'.[79] The character Glaphire takes the 'middle path (*moyenne voie*) in imitation of lawyers on the most contentious things'.[80]

The conversation follows the vagaries of love, and similar to Labé's *Débat* the speakers ponder the pros and cons of love, and ways of loving within marriage as well as the types of love beyond conjugal love. The character Pasquier summarises the extremes of happiness and torment in human life. The 'extreme love' experienced as a parent makes them 'forget' the 'torment and sadness' that children cause. But those things from which we receive the 'extreme contentment' sometimes also cause 'great pains and bitterness'. It would almost be to wish that 'man was not born' because having entered the world he endures 'infinite and intolerable miseries', along with extremes of 'felicity'.[81]

After listening to the men's speeches and occasionally laughing or smiling, the female speaker Charilée, a maiden, is angered to hear Philopole reflecting on whether fidelity (*loyauté*) is as required of a man as of a woman. Philopole asserts briefly ('ce ne sera point long') that men are permitted to do many things women are not because the 'same degree of liberty was not bestowed' upon women as men. Women are thus prevented from bearing arms or exercising any administration of republics and political office because women are 'incapable' (*inhabiles*) and 'not sufficient' (*non suffisantes*).[82] In a short outburst Philopole outlines some well-worn *Querelle des femmes* examples against the 'fragile' and 'lascivious' (*lubrique*) female sex and his statements provide a platform for the female character Charilée to participate more fully in the discussion.[83] Charilée comes to the defence of her sex, although Pasquier has the female character diminish her role because as she

---

77 Ibid., vol. II, col. 734.

78 Ibid., vol. II, cols 719–20.

79 Ibid., vol. II, cols 707–8, 712B.

80 Ibid., vol. II, col. 719; Eva Kushner, *Le Dialogue à la Renaissance: histoire et poétique* (Geneva, 2004), p. 29.

81 Pasquier, *Monophile*, in *Les Œuvres*, vol. II, col. 760A.

82 Ibid., vol. II, col. 737.

83 Virginia Cox, 'Seen but not Heard: The Role of Women Speakers in Cinquecento Literary Dialogue', in Letizia Panizza (ed.), *Women in Italian Renaissance Culture and Society* (Oxford, 2000), pp. 390–91, 393–4.

notes the 'validity of the case' in favour of women 'defends itself without an orator or advocate'.[84]

Pasquier's Charilée outlines a series of examples of female political leadership, military roles, women of learning, and the literary achievements of Sappho as well as the contemporary Marguerite de Navarre. Charilée protests that Philopole misrepresents 'worldly opinions' as 'the true and only nature' using an argument about female capabilities stunted though male tyranny that was very familiar to *Querelle* readers. Charilée points out that Socrates and Lycurgus granted military 'and other exercises' considered 'virile' to women. And taking a page from Erasmus's rhetorical advice in the *De copia*, she asks: 'What if I show you that in Lycia in times past man exercised all the acts that today are considered feminine, such an example would it not suffice to let you know such [a] thing consists only of worldly opinion'?[85] Laws imposed by men compound male perceptions of what is 'natural' in woman.

The character Charilée complains that men print their opinions about the female's fragile *esprit*, and then create laws to prevent wives from controlling their property because they cannot act without their husbands' consent to make gifts (*donations*) or in the 'alienation' of our [own] goods' (*alienations de nos biens*). And yet the husband was free to squander even the community of goods held between husband and wife. Charilée speaks against the men who prevent women from 'speeches and the administration of political estates'. Meanwhile great nations decline into ruin because of 'the stupidity and prodigality of men'. Charilée repeats the theme of numerous marriage treatises when she parallels the management of the household and the state because the 'order of a republic fraternises with that of a household' (*ordre d'une Republique fraternise avecques celuy d'une maison*). She asserts that the growth and maintenance of nations stems 'from the good husbandry and wisdom of women' (*du bon mesnage et sagesse des femmes*). This parallel between household governance and the state leads her to think that, if it was 'lawful' for women to 'apply their minds to such affairs', then in the same wise and prudent manner that women run their households they 'could guide and direct the affairs of a city'.[86] In Pasquier's dialogue, the woman rises to the defence of her sex.

Between the 1550s and 1578, when the bookseller Abel L'Angelier began to sell his new edition of the *Monophile* in the Palais de Justice, Pasquier became an established lawyer in the Parlement de Paris. Like the character Philopole in the *Monophile*, Pasquier the lawyer knew all too well how to assemble the proofs about woman's fragile *esprit*, how her nature was more 'imbecile' than man's or

84 Pasquier, *Monophile*, in *Les Œuvres*, vol. II, col. 738.

85 Pasquier, *Monophile*, ed. Balmas, p. 136.

86 On Charilée see also Jean-Paul Desaive, 'The Ambiguities of Literature', in N.Z. Davis and Arlette Farge (eds), *A History of Women in the West*, 4 vols (Cambridge, MA, 1993), vol. III, pp. 276–8; Maria Prendergast, *Renaissance Fantasies: The Gendering of Aesthetics in Early Modern Fiction* (Kent, OH, 1999), pp. 56–63.

how the Romans kept women in perpetual tutelage. As a lawyer he could present arguments of female weakness to prevent a remarried mother from regaining custody of her daughter when representing the opposing party, the girl's tutor.[87] Pasquier, however, also knew how to use these negative characterisations of female weakness in the *Querelle des femmes* to advance the interests of a female client in the 1570s and empower her to keep the goods and property acquired from and with a husband during her second marriage.[88] More flexible still, Pasquier could also argue for the right of a daughter to keep the inheritance bequeathed to her by her widowed mother in accordance with the custom of the region, thus allowing a mother to exercise her customary privilege to run her household affairs as she wished and grant one daughter a greater share of inheritance than her siblings. Like Folly's reason for choosing Mercury as her advocate in Louise Labé's *Débat*, Pasquier – ever the lawyer – said of his client, 'I pleaded for her and I assure you that I forgot nothing that I thought [could] serve to favour my case'.[89] As we shall see more fully in chapter eight on lawyers' pleadings, and as we saw in this chapter in the comparison of Labé's *Débat* with the extracts from a speech of the *avocat général* Louis Servin in the early 1600s, the examples used by lawyers to move, to charm and persuade an audience of judges might be quite familiar to a reader of *Querelle des femmes* texts or dialogues on human nature.

Matinées and *Après-disnées*

When the Seigneur de Cholières published *Les Neuf matinées* in Paris in 1585 and 1586 his printer bookseller Jean Richer announced to the reader that these dialogues on sale at his boutique near the Sorbonne on rue St Jean de Latran were 'jolly and lusty'.[90] The 'mysterious' Seigneur de Cholières, who sometimes signed his sonnets with the anagram A. DIANE OV ANGE (for Jean Dagoneau) or signed

---

87 AN, X1a 9208, Grands Jours de Poitiers, 5 November 1579, fos 266v–267r. Jean Chenu, *Cent notables et singulieres qvestions de droict, décidées par arrests memorables des cours souueraines de France*, 2nd edn, 2 vols (Paris: Nicolas Buon, 1603), question 19, vol. II, pp. 195–6.

88 AN, X1a 5071, fo. 480r; see the details of Pasquier's pleading in Lyndan Warner, 'Widows, Widowers and the Problem of "Second Marriages" in Sixteenth-Century France', in Sandra Cavallo and Warner (eds), *Widowhood in Medieval and Early Modern Europe* (New York, 1999), pp. 97–8.

89 Pasquier, *Lettres familières*, ed. Thickett, p. 74: 'je plaidois pour elle, et vous asseure que je n'y oubliay rien de ce que je pensois servir à la faveur de ma cause'; Labé, *Oeuvres*, p. 60; Labé, *Debate*, pp. 52–3; Rigolot, *Louise Labé*, p. 208.

90 Cholières was threatened with arrest. See Hope Glidden, *The Storyteller as Humanist: The Serées of Guillaume Bouchet* (Lexington, KY, 1981), p. 62. For the controversy see P.L. Jacob, 'Notice', in Seigneur de Cholières [Jean Dagoneau], *Œuvres de Seigneur de Cholières: Les Matinées* [1585], *Les Après-disnées* [1587], ed. E. Tricotel, 2 vols (Geneva, 1969), vol. I, pp. x–xv.

his works I.D. S de Cholières, had at one point in his career been a lawyer, and thus was used to the task of arguing for or against a topic. As a lawyer, Dagoneau had written some opening pieces in praise of the *procureur* Philibert Boyer's works on *The Style of the Court of Parlement and the Way to Proceed in all the Sovereign Courts in the Kingdom of France.*[91] The title alluding to the *matinées* reminds the reader that these dialogues will have advocates for and against a topic because the matinées were the morning sessions of the Parlement de Paris when the lawyers made their pleadings. The *Après-disnées*, first published in 1587 and reprinted in 1588, continued the allusion to the afternoon sittings of Parlement.

The *Matinées* cover a variety of topics, opening with tales of gold and the Spanish voyages to the new world, law, medicine, eunuchs, the route to nobility through arms or letters and 'ugly or beautiful women'. Half the topics concern the relations between husband and wife such as jealousy in marriage or the ideal age difference between spouses. Female characters are present for some of the conversations.[92] In the *Matinées* debating whether 'it is better to be or not to be married' Alexandre tells the rest of his companions they should look at the first dialogue of *The War of Males Against Females* (*La Guerre des masles contre les femelles*) to learn more about the benefits of marriage for husbands.[93] The *War of Males Against Females: Representing in Three Dialogues the Prerogatives and Dignities of One and the Other Sex*, also written by Cholières, was published in 1588 and sold in the Palais de Justice. Without mentioning his own name, Cholières explicitly connects his book on the battle of the sexes with his collection of dialogues on a wide range of topics. Cholières opted to publish some of his dialogues separately in the *Querelle des femmes* tradition, while other dialogues on women, men, marriage and sexuality were incorporated into his collections of miscellanies and diverse topics, the *Matinées* and *Après-disnées*.

In *La Guerre des masles contre les femelles*, as the participants stake out their positions – both in praise and vituperation of women – they remind the reader of the practice of speaking on both sides of a question. Cholières' character Nicogène, whose name loosely translates from Greek as 'victor over women', disdains satirical tongues and pens but regards flattery as even worse. Praise encourages

[91] Louis Loviot, 'Le mystérieux Seigneur de Cholières', *Revue des livres anciens* 1 (1913): 37–49; Philibert Boyer, *Le Stile de la Cour de Parlement & forme de proceder en toutes les cours souveraines du royaume de France* (Paris, 1602), sig. ã vj^{r}.

[92] Madamoiselle Euthelie, for example, is present for the discussion on marital authority (*De la puissance maritale*) and *De l'arbre de vie* in Cholières, *Matinées*, in *Œuvres*, vol. I; Cox, 'Seen but not Heard', p. 390.

[93] Cholières sends readers to his other works, *Œuvres*, vol. I, pp. 82, 89. For the attacks on woman's 'natural' lasciviousness and a husband's fear of becoming a cuckold, see *Œuvres*, vol. I, pp. 72, 76–7, 78–9; for Alexandre's defence see *Œuvres*, vol. I, pp. 80–82, 87, 89.

vice in women as in all others.[94] The character Ginécophile, or 'woman-lover' in Greek, protests that Nicogène would only retract his anti-woman comments when he had 'shown that white is black'.[95]

Ginécophile and his ally Boniface demonstrate cases of gynecocracy or female rule and Boniface questions the family-state model where the husband rules over wife and family as the king rules over his subjects.[96] Ginécophile questions why Nicogène ignores the value of the mother and her maternity, and points to cases of women's public roles in government. He questions the inequity of laws of inheritance including the Salic law and proposes in their place a matrilineal framework.[97] Boniface concludes his participation in the discussion by confessing that, while there are more imperfections among women than would be desirable, 'we [men] are hardly perfect'.[98] The conclusion of the third dialogue reminds the reader that the speakers have created the debate. Boniface brings the third dialogue to a close because if he pursued every avenue of praise for woman the possibilities would be limitless. Ginécophile adds a parting shot that Nicogène should at least cherish his mother and Nicogène graciously acknowledges that some women 'do marvels', but he praises God that one of his 'principal parties is appeased ... you have acquitted me the victory'. Cholières' dialogues frolic playfully through the debate on the sexes, but he combined his interest in the *Querelle des femmes* with a wide variety of topics such as nobility, the beard and the new world. In Cholières' dialogues these comparisons to other cultures, and questioning of laws and customs, deserve attention for raising questions in the minds of readers, but his dialogues were still 'closed' in the sense that the winner supported the status quo.

Plural Voices in Dialogue

Labé borrowed from a long tradition of using advocates and a courtroom atmosphere in *Querelle des femmes* trials with 'inconclusive outcomes' or 'deferred verdicts' as part of her *Débat*,[99] but her innovative use of the pagan gods allowed

---

[94] Sieur de Cholières [Jean Dagoneau], *La Guerre des masles contre les femelles: représentant en trois dialogues les prérogatives et dignitez tant de l'un que de l'autre sexe. Avec les meslanges poétiques du sieur de Cholieres* (Paris: Pierre Chevillot, 1588), fo. 8r.

[95] Cholières, *Guerre*, fo. 17v: 'Quant vous auriez à monstrer que le blanc est noir'.

[96] Ibid., fo. 37r. For Cholières on natural law and social practice, see Constance Jordan, *Renaissance Feminism: Literary Texts and Political Models* (Ithaca, NY, 1990), pp. 207–9.

[97] Cholières, *Guerre*, fos 59v–60v; on female inheritance, see fo. 88v. Ginécophile demands of his misogynist adversary Nicogène: 'Venez au point & me rendés raison pourquoy les legislateurs ont ainsi rébroué les femmes, que ne les ont ils balancé à mesme contrepoids que les hommes?' – see fos 48r–v.

[98] Ibid., fo. 90v.

[99] Swift, *Gender, Writing, Performance*, p. 145.

her to redefine human excellence and play with the ideas of human dignity and misery. The dialogues of Tahureau and Bruès explored a wide range of subjects and Bruès in particular pushed the relativism of each culture to the fore before arriving at a predetermined conclusion.[100] Pasquier and Cholières, active in the legal profession, used legal and political arguments as well as examples drawn from a variety of customs and cultures in their dialogues. Each of these writers published on a variety of topics in prose or in verse, from Pasquier's *Recherches de la France* to Labé or Tahureau's poetry.

As history books began to abandon the biblical timeline in favour of stories about the founding of civilisations, the writing on man and woman seems to have undergone a gradual shift too. The Christian framework gave sway to Nature or to debates about what was 'natural' and what was 'opinion' by comparing customs and civilisations. Of course, Nature could be used in the way God and his creation story had been used. Pasquier, for instance, revives and rewrites old commonplaces in his *Monophile* when one of the gentlemen suggests that 'Nature created woman with her eyes lowered … and man with his eyes raised'. By this point there had been so many variations of this commonplace in dignity- and misery-of-man as well as *Querelle des femmes* texts that the reader could have completed the thought in countless ways.[101]

The dialogue provided a useful platform to explore a range of social customs and a variety of practices across civilisations. Some of the writing we have seen in this chapter, such as sections of Tahureau's dialogues, Cholières' *Guerre des masles et femelles* promoted in his *Matinées*, or even Pasquier's *Monophile*, could be packaged and marketed as *Querelle des femmes* texts. But this theme of the nature of woman was also interwoven, embedded and sold in dialogues on multiple themes. Both the *Querelle des femmes* as well as the debate on the dignity and misery of man became subjects to explore, imitate and rework among the many topics of conversation in these sixteenth-century dialogues. Labé's *Débat de Folie et d'Amour* was the only debate or dialogue among the writings of her male contemporaries Bruès, Pasquier and Tahureau writing in the 1550s, or even the later works of Cholières, to remain 'open', defer the verdict or suspend judgment. Labé's substitution of a pagan setting of gods allowed for much more leeway in defining human excellence and folly than the usual Christian creation story or fictional gatherings of friends.

The next chapter pursues the opposing and plural voices of these dialogues in two ways. It examines a new genre, the essay, which developed to sustain the opportunity to reflect and question when the dialogue format became too limited or closed. And it continues the theme of how writers, printers and merchant booksellers packaged or promoted variety through a series of topics in chapters, moral lessons and essays.

---

[100] Kushner, *Le Dialogue*, pp. 77, 80.

[101] Pasquier, *Monophile*, in *Les Œuvres*, vol. II, col. 717C; see Chapter 3 above, pp. 61–2, 64–6.

Chapter 6

Diversity, Citation and the Invention of the Essay

The conversations, plural voices and variety of topics explored in the popular sixteenth-century dialogue could be found in other formats that allowed for multiple perspectives. Collections of diverse lessons allowed a writer to muse or to consider many perspectives and ambiguities of a topic without always arriving at a judgment. By drawing on, imitating and compiling from diverse sources, the process of musing, reasoning or even digressing became perhaps more important than arriving at a truth.[1] Emblem books, with both image and verse, might explore the *pro* and *contra* of the nature of man and woman or of virtues and their related vices. Travel books, 'cosmographies', collections of customs, morals, habits and nations exposed the reader to conflicting laws, customs, practices, religious beliefs and culture. This chapter examines early anthologies or miscellanies such as Pero Mexia's *Diverse lessons* (1552), which covered a variety of 'lessons' on the excellence of painting, on marriage customs, on cruelty, on the inventions of writing and paper, among other topics. Jean de Marconville also covered a range of topics in his writings, from collections of prodigious tales and strange cases to the positive and negative aspects of marriage and women to the institutions of governments and the law, and this chapter traces how he collected and imitated his examples. By the end of the century, the questions on man, woman and human nature resurface among musings and explorations of diverse topics known as the 'essay' after Michel de Montaigne's collection of *Essais*, first published in Bordeaux in 1580.

François Rigolot has characterised Montaigne's *Essais* as an inner dialogue. In the *Essais* Rigolot sees the 'gradual "inward turn" of the dialogical mode' and he suggests that Montaigne continued debate within the essays 'by bringing together contradictory opinions, and making them wrestle with each other'.[2] It is clear that Montaigne's peers recognised the genre as a new approach. In his *Bibliothèque* published by Abel L'Angelier in 1584, François de la Croix du Maine collects, categorises and assesses the books and the writers of his time. He praises Montaigne's 'great learning' and his 'diverse lessons, or variety of authors that he had read', but La Croix du Maine pauses to 'explain the title of this book, that

[1] Virginia Cox, *The Renaissance Dialogue* (Cambridge, 1992), p. 113.

[2] François Rigolot, 'Problematizing Renaissance Exemplarity: The Inward Turn of Dialogue from Petrarch to Montaigne', in Dorothea Heitsch and Jean-François Vallée (eds), *Printed Voices: The Renaissance Culture of Dialogue* (Toronto, 2004), pp. 13–14.

[Montaigne] calls Essays … If the word Essays means an attempt (*coup d'Essay*) or learning (*apprentissage*) then it is very humble and debased and does not feel at all haughty or arrogant'. The title could also mean 'Essays or experiences, that is to say, discourse to conform himself unto another', and it is equally suited to the book, which contains 'an ample declaration of the life of the said Sieur de Montaigne'.[3] Despite its novelty, the essay struck a chord because so many aspects were familiar. To underline the diversity of the human experience Montaigne often reflected on a citation gathered from a classical source or used a quotation to evoke a sentiment. He gathered these citations using the rhetorical technique of *inventio* (invention) to consider one side of an argument then another and to expose the contradictions, inconsistencies or weaknesses of both perspectives.

The juxtaposition of ideas on man and woman, vices and virtues, and the diverse customs, laws and morals of ancient and modern peoples did not begin in the printer's workshop. It began with reading and the practice of compilation as writers gathered their proofs and examples to imitate and put to use in a new dialogue, paradox, lesson, essay or argument *in utramque partem*. This practice known as *inventio* or the assembly of proofs was inextricably linked with how writers might deploy these examples in new writing and speeches or 'discovering the "places" in which suitable arguments can be found with a view to presenting them in the most persuasive style'.[4]

Erasmus Instructs How to Argue on Both Sides of the Question … of Man and of Woman

In order to understand how or why a writer might employ examples of women or men, or examples of rank, status or nation, we need to return briefly to Erasmus's instructions to his pupil in the *On the Abundance of Words and Ideas* (*De duplici copia verborum ac rerum*) of 1512 explored in the Introduction.[5] While Quintilian and Cicero acknowledged the importance of *inventio*, or the finding of proofs and examples, as one of the five parts of rhetoric, the persuasive orator needed to master *elocutio* in order to impose his personal style on the sources of arguments.[6] Erasmus adapted this rhetorical advice for the Renaissance world of writing

[3] François de La Croix du Maine, *La Bibliothèque du sieur de la Croix-du-Maine* (Paris: Abel L'Angelier, 1584), pp. 328–30, in Olivier Millet, *La première réception des Essais de Montaigne, 1580–1640* (Paris, 1995), pp. 52–4.

[4] Quentin Skinner, *Reason and Rhetoric in the Philosophy of Thomas Hobbes* (Cambridge, 1996), p. 47. *Dispositio* received less attention from classical rhetoricians and Quintilian, for example, included it within his account of *inventio*.

[5] Introduction, pp. 13–15.

[6] Marc Fumaroli, 'Rhetoric, Politics and Society: from Italian Ciceronianism to French Classicism', in James Murphy (ed.), *Renaissance Eloquence: Studies in the Theory and Practice of Renaissance Rhetoric* (Berkeley, CA, 1983), p. 264.

and print in the *De copia*, where he outlined the commonplace book method of assembling proofs and examples as well as how to deploy them to speak on both sides of an argument.[7] By the end of the sixteenth century, Erasmus's methods had triumphed and the 'rhetoric of citation' permeated the highest sovereign courts in France in remonstrances and lawyers' pleadings, as will be shown in chapter eight.[8]

To capture the vividness of a scene, sketch a 'mental picture' and to demonstrate one's ingenuity, Erasmus' rhetorical manual the *De copia* recommends the writer pays attention to the details of place, events, nation, social customs and habits.[9] 'Or we may take sex as a basis, and depict man on the one hand as firm, woman on the other as talkative, fickle, and superstitious'.[10] And then Erasmus taught his pupil how to dismantle an argument or how to argue on both sides of a question.[11] How does the writer or orator assess which are the appropriate examples to employ in each context? He must first learn or anticipate the composition of his audience. Erasmus echoes the textbooks of classical rhetoric when he tells his Renaissance reader that '[p]eople are most impressed, however, by examples that are ancient, splendid, national, and domestic'. The *De copia* repeats the idea that it is easiest to convince people of an idea if it is conveyed to them in their own language with familiar reference points. Erasmus assumes that the reader will be male. 'In fact in each nation, each class of person prefers what is his own, or else something that makes him feel superior, such as anecdotes about women, children, slaves, and barbarians'.[12] The *De copia* furnishes the hypothetical example of a father in grief over the death of his son and advises the schoolboy to 'confront him with women in the pagan tradition' brave at the death of several sons.[13] Erasmus compares the grieving father's experience initially on the basis of sex alone: 'Can you, a grown man, not bear what a feeble woman could? She overcame both her sex and her feelings as a parent; will you be defeated by one of these alone?' To further the comparison he suggests an example of a woman past the age of reproduction. 'She had no hope of repairing her loss, being of an age past-childbearing; you have a fertile wife, and are still healthy and virile yourself'. Erasmus enlarges the

---

7 Skinner, *Reason and Rhetoric*, pp. 111, 115.

8 Marc Fumaroli, *L'âge de l'éloquence: Rhétorique et 'res literaria' de la Renaissance au seuil de l'époque classique*, 2nd edn (Paris, 1994); Catherine Holmès, *L'éloquence judiciaire de 1620 à 1660: reflet de problèmes sociaux, religieux et politiques de l'époque* (Paris, 1967), p. 32; see Chapter 8, pp. 188–95.

9 Desiderius Erasmus, '*Copia*: Foundations of the abundant style' [*De duplici copia verborum ac rerum commentarii duo*], ed. Craig R. Thompson, *Collected Works of Erasmus*, 86 vols (Toronto, 1974), vol. XXIV, pp. 574–7.

10 Ibid., p. 583.

11 Thomas Sloane, 'Schoolbooks and Rhetoric: Erasmus's *Copia*', *Rhetorica* 9:2 (1991): 116–17, 119.

12 Erasmus, *De copia*, p. 608; Skinner, *Rhetoric and Reason*, pp. 129–30.

13 Erasmus, *De copia*, p. 619.

field of comparison to their status and education: 'Can you, a Roman and a man, not evince the qualities that a weak barbarian woman could? She was ignorant of learning and yet she could scorn something that shatters you in spite of your education and your great profession of philosophy'. Here Erasmus uses the sex, status, age, nation, religion, customs, lack of learning and inferior social status of the woman to push the comparison with the Roman father to its extreme. He elaborates on all the 'circumstances' to render his argument more persuasive.[14] Erasmus plays on the 'received' opinion among his assumed male readership and he counsels the writer or orator to play on the lesser expectations of the female sex, while like the defenders of women in the *Querelle* the writer proves female actions to surpass men's. The sixteenth-century writers examined in this chapter learned their schoolboy lessons well.[15]

Reading, Imitation, Compilation and Packaging in Mexia and Marconville

At mid-century the French version of Pero Mexia's *Diverses leçons* went on sale translated by Claude Gruget as he finished his translation of Speroni's *Dialogues*. The Palais de Justice bookseller Vincent Sertenas obtained the privilege and Estienne Groulleau printed Gruget's translation in October 1552, to share, as they often did, between the trio of Groulleau, Jean Longis and Sertenas.[16] These booksellers on the Île de la Cité in Paris reprinted Mexia's lessons in 1554, 1556, and Gruget added a new section of translation in 1560. Mexia's collection of lessons plays on the idea that variety delights humans.

Mexia's lessons span ancient and modern times, some prodigious, some moral, some historical, some 'scientific' or occult. '[P]illaged and imitated' by Boaistuau and Montaigne, the topics of Mexia's collection range from the ages of man to the question of whether men from a low estate (*basse condition*) should 'make themselves illustrious'.[17] Several of Mexia's lessons concern parallel lives of vice and virtue, as Erasmus counselled in the *De copia* as a means of demonstrating praise or blame.[18] He contrasts the cruelty, virtue and military discipline of King Tamburlaine with the less worthy life of the Roman emperor Heliogabalus.[19]

---

14 On maxims and or 'sayings' as further examples see ibid., p. 620.

15 For a nuanced understanding of the uses of male and female exemplarity by male and female writers, see Pollie Bromilow, *Models of Women in Sixteenth-Century French Literature: Female Exemplarity in the* Histoires tragiques *(1559) and the* Heptaméron *(1559)* (Lewiston, NY, 2007), pp. 10–19.

16 Pero Mexia, *Les Diverses leçons*, trans. Claude Gruget (Paris: Estienne Groulleau, 1552).

17 Pierre Villey, *Les sources et l'évolution des Essais de Montaigne*, 2 vols (Paris, 1908), vol. II, p. 29.

18 Erasmus, *De copia*, pp. 624–5.

19 Mexia, *Diverses leçons*, 1552 edn, fo. 136r.

Mexia juxtaposes the life of the papess Joan, who disguised herself as a man to become pope, with the empress Theodosia, who governed as a woman in 'peace and prosperity' without the 'aid' of father, husband or brother. Mexia considers whether Alexander or Scipio demonstrated more excellence in the virtue of moderation (*continence*).[20]

According to Mexia some men take pleasure in belittling the 'perfection of women' and accuse women of 'fickleness, weakness and many other imperfections', although men have many more 'defectuosities'. For Mexia women 'surpass men in all sorts of virtues' and 'yield to [men] in nothing' because women are equal or superior 'in love, in loyalty, in charity, in devotion, in pity, gentleness, temperance, mercy, and all other virtues'. Mexia differentiates men from women on one criterion – the call to arms – but he proves that even this category has exceptions. Mexia argues that man is superior to woman in the military arts alone because a skilled warrior needs 'pride, cruelty and many other [types of] wickedness' in which women are reluctant to engage. But he sets up his point, knowing he will demolish it because he could not possibly 'recite' all the 'praiseworthy stories' of female military skills such as the 'very valiant' Amazons who conquered large armies and brought nations under their 'sovereignty' and 'power'.[21] One could always find an example contrary to the common opinion. In Mexia's diverse lessons woman is man's constant companion. Female exempla accompany male exempla throughout the chapters remarking on human life, the world and the universe.

In 1564, Jean Dallier, the bookseller on the Pont St Michel who had sold François de Billon's *Fort inexpugnable de l'honneur feminin*, brought out three works by Jean de Marconville: a treatise on the *Goodness and Badness of Women*, another on the *Happiness and Unhappiness of Marriage*, and a collection of prodigious tales entitled the *Memorable Collection of Some Marvellous Cases* [*that*] *Happened in Our Age and Some Strange and Monstrous Things* [*that*] *Came to Pass in Centuries Past*. Marconville had the sixteenth-century habit of imitating and compiling whole sections from other texts. The *Recueil memorable*, written in July 1563, opens with reflections on the civil war caused by the 'discordant variety of opinions among men', and reproduces large slices of Boaistuau's *Théâtre du monde* concerning the misery of man, outlining the misery of soldiers, judicial officers and those in each estate.[22] Marconville's works on women, marriage and 'strange cases' reveal how the packaging of ideas began with finding the examples that, as Erasmus encouraged and Mexia demonstrated above, could be used to argue for or against any point.

In the *De la bonté et mauvaistié des femmes*, 1564, Jean de Marconville tells his reader that neither the 'Misogynists, enemies of the feminine sex', nor 'all the

---

20 Ibid., fos 14v–15v, 140r.

21 Ibid., fos 16r–v.

22 Jean de Marconville, *Recueil memorable d'aucuns cas merveilleux advenuz de noz ans, et d'aucunes choses estranges & monstrueuses advenües ès siècles passez* (Paris: Jean Dallier, 1564), fos 2v–14r.

Greek and Latin rhetoric in the world' could induce him to believe in the 'badness' of women.[23] Like the many 'learned pens' before him, he carefully attributes the 'misogynist' claims to another writer.[24] Marconville's works reveal the widening of sources for writers participating in the *Querelle des femmes* and one we have already investigated in chapter five in the dialogues of Tahureau, Bruès, Pasquier and Cholières. The creation story and usual proofs offered up in the *Querelle des femmes* were expanded by looking to new disciplines as possible sources of evidence. Jean de Marconville draws on travel literature and observations of morals, customs and laws from some acknowledged sources such as 'the great vessel of erudition' Pierre Boaistuau, Sebastien Munster's *Cosmography*, the *Singularities of Antarctic France* by the royal cosmographer André Thevet, as well as other unacknowledged sources such as Pero Mexia's *Diverse lessons* or the collection of ancient customs, laws and ceremonies known as the *Recueil de diverses histories* printed and sold throughout the 1540s by Jean de Tournes and a number of the Paris booksellers.[25] By juxtaposing observations of ancient, contemporary and new world cultures, Marconville questions the conventional notions of what was natural for women in his society. Marconville repackaged this variety of material in the form of an argument *in utramque partem* on the 'goodness and badness, virtues and vices, perfections & imperfections of women', and then he turned his attention to the 'benefits and inconveniences, delights and thorns of marriage'.[26] Dallier obtained and displayed the joint privilege for the *pro et contra* treatises on marriage and on woman and sold these two 1564 texts with Marconville's translation of Plutarch's precepts, although later the books on women and marriage were reprinted and sold separately in Paris, Rouen and Lyon.[27]

When Marconville set out to praise love and friendship within marriage, he could have found many precedents in *Querelle* texts such as Rabelais' *Tiers livre*, Erasmus' *Declamation on the Praises of Marriage*, 1525, or Vives' *Instruction of the Christian Wife*. He chose instead to adapt Mexia's *Diverses leçons* yet pretend

[23] Jean de Marconville, *De la bonté et mauvaistié des femmes*, ed. Richard Carr (Paris, 2000), p. 128.

[24] Ibid., pp. 134–5.

[25] Carr, 'Introduction', in ibid., pp. 10–11, 119; for Boaistuau, see pp. 184, 191, for Munster see pp. 63, 170. The cosmographer André Thevet recommended both Marconville's *Recueil memorable* and the *De l'heur et malheur de mariage*: ibid., pp. 85–6, 147–8, 195.

[26] Jean de Marconville, *De l'heur et malheur de marriage ... ensemble les loix connubiales de Plutarque traduictes en François* (Paris: Jean Dallier, 1571), fo. 1r.

[27] In the Bibliothèque nationale, the 1564 *De l'heur et malheur de mariage* and *De la bonté et mauvaisité des femmes* are paginated separately but bound together with the joint *Extraict du privilege du roy* on the last folio verso. The *De la bonté et mauvaistié des femmes* was published in Paris at Jean Dallier in 1564 and 1571, in Rouen in 1573, in Lyon in 1586, and reprinted into the early 1600s. The *De l'heur et malheur de mariage, ensemble les loix connubiales de Plutarque* was printed in Paris in 1564 and 1571, in Rouen in 1573, and reprinted into the early 1600s.

his source was Plutarch.[28] In the opening sonnet to the book on the happiness and unhappiness of marriage, François Gruget commends to the reader the wisdom Marconville has assembled from Plato, Plutarch and Vives, but omits the *Diverses leçons* as a key source, despite the fact his brother Claude had translated Mexia into French.[29] Marconville conceals Mexia as a source, juggles the order of Mexia's three linked chapters on marriage and leaves his reader with a false impression of his source material.[30] Marconville borrowed and compiled from Mexia's *Diverses leçons*, but more importantly he changed the meaning and context of the examples. Marconville transformed Mexia's writings on variety and diversity into an argument for monogamous Christian marriage.

Marconville begins his chapter on the 'diverse ceremonies that several nations have practised in contracting and celebrating marriage' with a paragraph that follows Mexia's opening paragraph almost word for word.[31] Marconville's added

---

28 Erasmus, *Déclamation des louenges de mariage*, trans. Louis de Berquin [attribution to Paris: Simon Dubois, 1525], facs. edn E.V. Telle (Geneva, 1976), sigs c iii^{r}–c iii^{v}, c iiii^{v}; Juan Luis Vives, *L'Institution de la femme chrestienne*, trans. Pierre de Changy (Paris: Denis Janot for Galiot du Pré, 1545), Bk II, ch. 3; Marconville, *De l'heur*, 1571 edn, fos 5r, 6r–v; Mexia, *Les Diverses leçons de Pierre Messie ... mises de castillan en françois, par Claude Gruget, Parisien* (Rouen: Jean Roger, 1626), pp. 288, 290–91.

29 François Gruget, 'Au lecteur ... Sonnet', in Marconville, *De l'heur et malheur de marriage ... ensemble les loix connubiales de Plutarque traduictes en françois* (Paris: Jean Dallier, 1564), sig. a iiij^{r}.

30 Marconville's second chapter, the *Exemple d'amitié conjugale, tant d'hommes que de femmes*, draws heavily on Mexia's Bk II, ch. 14, the *De la cordiale amytié de mariage, avec aucuns exemples de l'amour des mariez*. Then Marconville adds several chapters on punishment in marriage and heretical acts before he copies his sixth chapter *Des diverses ceremonies desquelles plusieurs nations on usé en contractant & celebrant le mariage* from Mexia's Bk II, ch. 15, *Des diverses coustumes que tenoient les anciens aux mariages*. Finally Marconville adds the *De l'aage en laquelle il convient se marier*, copying the idea from Mexia's Bk II, ch. 13, *Du quel estat & quel aage se doivent marier l'homme & la femme*.

31

PERO MEXIA – *Les diverses leçons*	MARCONVILLE – *De l'heur et malheur de mariage*
Des diverses coustumes que tenoient les anciens aux mariages, Bk II ch. 15.	Des diverses ceremonies desquelles plusieurs nations on usé en contractant & celebrant le mariage, ch. 6.
Le mariage se contracte avec le seul consenment [sic] de l'homme, & de la femme: mais à fin que ce consentement soit mieux authorisé, est requis de le monstrer par paroles, & signes exterieurs, pour ce que le Seigneur Dieu seul cognoit & penetre les cœurs. De là vient que les homes ont institué	Le mariage se faict, & est contracté par le mutuel consentement de l'homme & de la femme, mais afin qu'il soit plus authorisé & plus solonel il est requis de le monstrer par parolles & signes exterieurs, car Dieu seul void & cognoist les cueurs des personnes, qui est la cause pour laquelle les hommes ont introduict plusieurs &

words are shown here in square brackets, whereas Mexia's variations are shown in parentheses. 'Marriage is [made and] contracted with the [mutual] consent of man and of woman (alone) but so that this consent is given more authority [and done more publicly] it is required to demonstrate it with words and outward signs because only (the Lord) God [sees and] knows (and penetrates) the hearts [of people]'. Gruget would have been translating the work in the early 1550s before the Council of Trent decrees of 1563 on clandestine marriage and before the French royal edict of 1556/57. Marconville's work first published in 1564 echoes Mexia and copies his phrases, but alters them slightly to emphasise the more formal requirements of the public ceremonies required for a legitimate marriage. For Mexia, the consent alone (*seul consenment*) of the couple suffices, helped along by ceremonies. For Marconville a more public (*solonnel*) arrangement is required to demonstrate this consent that he emphasises as 'mutual'.

At this point, Mexia and Marconville's messages diverge. Mexia is less concerned with telling his reader about Christian traditions than with relating the unfamiliar and indulging the reader's interest in diversity: 'As for [the traditions] of Christians, they are well known, therefore I shall only treat some of the customs the barbarian nations and the Romans had in their marriages, whereupon (maybe) the diversity could provide pleasure'.[32] Marconville, however, opens and concludes his chapter with a focus on the Christian realm because a marriage must be '[made] publicly in the Church', and he reinforces how the ecclesiastical authorities ordered the 'blessing of these marriages' to minimise the risk of clandestine marriages and popular superstitions.[33]

One proof used by Mexia and Marconville considers the remarriage of a widow and widower in ancient Rome. The bride and groom in this remarriage had each survived at least twenty spouses and so there was great speculation in their community about which spouse would outlive the other. Mexia and Marconville reproduce this same tale of serial remarriage in completely separate contexts. The commonplace notebook practice of collecting examples, tales and precepts leads Mexia to place this tale of serial marriages within a series of 'strange cases' in his book of diverse lessons, while Marconville's treatise on marriage reproduces the tale of the remarrying widow and widower almost word for word in a chapter on heretics and heretical opinions about marriage. Marconville declares that his example had been compiled from a contemporary sixteenth-century writer in Latin who had copied it from St Jerome, but Marconville's most probable source was Claude Gruget's French translation of Mexia's *Diverses leçons*.

---

plusieurs ceremonies, & paroles solomnelles (Rouen edn, p. 292). diverses ceremonies en la celebration d'iceluy (1571 edn, fo. 18v).

32 Mexia, *Diverses leçons*, 1552 edn, fols 112r–v.

33 Marconville, *De l'heur*, 1571 edn, fols 18v–19r.

Pero Mexia – *Les diverses leçons* (1552)	Marconville – *De l'heur et malheur de marriage* (1564)
D'une femme qui fut mariée beaucoup de fois: & d'un homme qui avoit eu plusieurs femmes, lesquels à la fin se marierent ensemble: & de l'incontinence d'une autre femme. Bk II, ch. 24.	Des lourdes opinions d'aucuns here-tiques contempteurs de mariage, ch. 5.
Il [St Jerome] dit, qu'au temps du Pape Damase, il vid & cogneut à Rome une femme qui avoit esté legitimement mariée avec 22. hommes: & qu'elle estant vefue du vingt-deuxiesme, il se trouva un homme qui avoit aussi eu 20. femmes & estoit alors veuf de la derniere: & ainsi se trouvans tous deux libres, estans egaux en estat, & de basse condition, ils contracterent mariage ensemble, qui fut chose fort notable, & qui rendit un chacun de Rome tres-desireux de voir lequel des deux mourroit le premier: ce qui advint finalement à la femme: aux obseques de laquelle, tout le peuple Romain courut, & pour congratuler le mary, comme victorieux d'une grande bataille, luy mirent une couronne de Laurier sur la teste, le faisant aller apres le corps de sa femme tenant une Palme en la main, en signe de victoire, & une infinité de peuple l'accompagna en son triomphe. [Rouen edn, p. 197]	Et qu'ainsi soit, Rhodigin en ses antiques leçons recite un exemple pris de S. Hierosme qui dict qu'au tems du Pape Damase duquel il estoit secretaire qu'il veid en Rome une femme qui avoit esté legitimement mariée avec vingt & deux hommes, & qu'elle estant veufve du vingt-deuxiesme, il se trouva aussi un homme qui avoit eu vingt femmes & estoit lors veuf de la derniere, & ainsi se trouvans tous deux libres, egaux, & de basse condition, ils se marierent ensemble, qui fut chose fort notable, & qui rendit chacun fort desireux de sçavoir lequel des deux enterreroit l'autre, mais finalement advint que la femme mourut la premiere: aux obseques de laquelle tout le peuple Romain courut pour congratuler le mary comme victorieux d'une grande bataille, lequel ils couronnerent d'une couronne de l'aurier, tenant un rameau de Palme en la main en signe de sa victoire, & fut accompaigné d'un grand nombre de peuple en son triomphe. Que pourront dire les heretiques contre cest exemple de S.Hierosme? [1571 edn, fo. 18r][34]

Travel books, geography, classical literature and collections of morals and customs, sometimes disguised as the works of the Church Fathers of late antiquity, might provide examples for *Querelle des femmes* writers such as Marconville or Cholières in the second half of the sixteenth century. These writers were not restricting their readings or their writing. Jean de Marconville wrote on the goodness and badness of women, in favour of and against marriage, but also

[34] Mexia prepares the story by telling the reader of St Jerome's holiness and reliability as a witness to history, Rouen edn, pp. 196–7.

on strange and prodigious stories in his *Collection of some Marvellous Cases* (*Recueil d'aucuns cas merveilleux*), 1564, with its chapters on the civil wars in France and in Germany, on floods and comets, on the nature of human speech and words, on monstrous pregnancies, illness, contagion and death. Marconville had already published a work on law and the officeholders who upheld justice: *In The Manner of Policing the Christian Republic (according to God, Reason and Virtue), Containing the Estate and Office of Magistrates, together with the Source and Origin of Lawsuits and the Detestation of These, to Which is joined the Mal and Miseries that Come From Bad Neighbours*. Marconville reminds the reader that lawyers are necessary, but that lawsuits bring misery. Lawyers should avoid ambition and coveting honours, while officeholding judges and magistrates should cultivate an impeccable reputation of avoiding vice and seeking virtue.[35] Like many other sixteenth-century authors throughout this book, such as Gratien Dupont, Pasquier or Montaigne, Jean de Marconville crossed over from the law to literary endeavours and back again.

In his works, Marconville builds his arguments just as tangibly as Christine de Pisan and François de Billon constructed their fortified cities for the defence of women. Marconville even speaks in these terms of construction and fabrication; the detractors of the female sex are 'architects of laughter' and 'artisans of lies'.[36] Like Mexia, Jean de Marconville also knew how to dismantle an argument as Erasmus had carefully instructed his schoolboy. Writers immersed in this culture of commonplace books, of the assembly of proofs, paradoxes and presenting both sides of an argument, reflect the 'rhetoric of citation' with 'samples of diverse Authors' (*eschantillons de divers Autheurs*) developing in the law courts of France.[37] Understanding how to view a question from more than one perspective was a mental habit in early modern France. Knowing how to use examples and proofs to argue for and against the 'common opinion' was a desirable skill in literature and in the law courts, and Montaigne developed this talent in a new form in the *Essais*.

Montaigne, *exempla*, and the 'Rhetoric of Citation'

Montaigne's writing style in the *Essais* is important for two reasons. First of all, in reflecting on the human experience he touches on many of the familiar themes in the *Querelle des femmes*: the superiority or inferiority of woman's nature, as

[35] Jean de Marconville, *La Manière de bien policer la république chrestienne (selon Dieu, raison et vertu), contenant l'estat et office des magistrats, ensemble la source et origine des procès et détestation d'iceluy, auquel est indissolublement conjoinct le mal et misère qui procède des mauvais voisins* (Paris: Jean Dallier, 1562), fos 23r–32v, 61r–76v.

[36] Marconville, *De la bonté*, ed. Carr, pp. 17, 132.

[37] Étienne Pasquier, *Des recherches de la France*, in *Les Œuvres d'Étienne Pasquier*, 2 vols (Amsterdam, 1723), vol. I, col. 423.

well as the ideas of the dignity and misery of man – human excellence as well as human fragility. Both male and female exempla populate the pages of the *Essais*, but rather than write a simple dispute or a *pro et contra* format or even a dialogue, Montaigne's essays presented a new manner of sifting through the ideas of man and woman. *Querelle des femmes* titles and dignity- and misery-of-man titles continued to be published and sold, of course, even by Montaigne's Parisian bookseller, but the essay was a new way of looking at both sides of an argument and opening up the theme. In the essay, the process of reasoning, of suspending judgment, was as and possibly more important than arriving at a truth or conclusion.

Like many of the texts of the sixteenth century, such as the works of Mexia and Marconville examined in this chapter, the *Essais* are filled with proofs – borrowed citations and imitated passages from Seneca, Plutarch, Ovid, Plato, Virgil, Martial, as well as contemporary writers such as Mexia, travel writers and cosmographers.[38] Montaigne annotated the books in his tower library such as his 1563 copy of Lucretius' *On the Nature of Things* (*De rerum nature libri sex*) or his 1562 copy of Nicole Gilles' *Annales et croniques de France* and although he mocked his own undisciplined reading habits, Montaigne's writing style and his extensive use of citations belie an avid reader. In his essay on the education of children, dedicated to Diane de Foix, as published in the 1580 edition Montaigne laments the 'indiscreet writers of our age' who 'intermingle and wrest in whole sentences taken from ancient Authors supposing by such filching-theft to purchase honour and reputation to themselves', when instead these authors merely show the mediocrity of their own compositions. Writing in the margins of his copy of the 1588 *Essais*, Montaigne admitted to his own 'filchings' (*larrecins*). 'To reprove mine own faults in others, seems to me no more insufferable than to reprehend (as I do often) those of others in my self' and Montaigne hopes that he 'may perhaps be able to blear the eyes of the Judges from discerning' his own borrowings.[39] He had a taste for sayings or sentences, famously painted on the beams in his tower retreat. And he used examples to weigh an argument, considering one side then the other with a digression or two along the way.[40]

From the opening pages of the *Essais* – like his predecessors Mexia, Bruès, Pasquier, Tahureau and Labé – Montaigne addresses the masculine and feminine in the roles of men and women. The first essay, entitled *By divers means men come to a like end*, contrasts the act of surrender with Stoic constancy to prove that by opposite means one can realise the same end. In an example compiled from Jean Bodin's *Method for an Easy Comprehension of History* (*Methodus ad facilem historiarum cognitionem*) Montaigne narrates the outcome of a siege in which the

---

38 Pierre Villey, 'Catalogue des livres de Montaigne', in Montaigne, *Essais*, pp. xli–lxvi.

39 Montaigne, *Essais*, I:26, 'De l'institution des enfants', p. 147; Montaigne, *Essays*, vol. I. pp. 151; Montaigne Project, at http://artfl.uchicago.edu/images/montaigne/0054.jpg, accessed 8 November 2010.

40 Floyd Gray, *Gender, Rhetoric and Print Culture in French Renaissance Writing* (Cambridge, 2000), pp. 117–19.

victor would not deign to offer any conciliation to the conquered people apart from allowing the noble women to leave with honour intact and whatever possessions they could carry on their persons. These women 'with an unrelenting courage (*d'un cœur magnanime*)' had the inspired idea to load upon their shoulders their husbands, their children and their conquered Duke. The victorious Emperor was so impressed by their 'courage' and 'took so great pleasure at it, that he wept for joy' and he swallowed his hostility to the Duke and thereafter treated the besieged people with 'all favour and courtesy (*humainement*)'.[41] As he wrote in the late 1570s, Montaigne reflected on human reactions: whether a victor might respond to cowardly supplication or to brave constancy. Notwithstanding his example of courageous noblewomen, Montaigne suggests that the 'weakest natures (*natures plus foibles*)' such as 'women, children and the vulgar sort' yield out of 'tenderness and meekness', whereas the opposite attitude – which disdains tears and prayers, and which reveres 'the sacred image of virtue (*la saincte image de la vertu*)' – results from the 'effect of a courageous and imployable mind, holding a masculine and constant vigour, in honour and affection'.[42] By the 1588 edition Montaigne amended his essays to add a story about Alexander 'the hardiest among men and so gracious to the vanquished' that was 'directly against my first examples'. When Alexander saw the proud and obstinate silence of his vanquished enemy at Gaza it 'turned his anger into rage'.[43] Expanding and amplifying this example in the late 1580s or early 1590s, Montaigne reflected upon Alexander's vengeance at Thebes when he slaughtered more than 6,000, of whom 'not one was seen, either to run away or beg for grace'. This virtue evoked no pity from Alexander.[44] From the opening pages of the *Essais* in the 1580 edition, Montaigne shows how 'man (*l'homme*) is a wonderful, vain, divers, and wavering subject, [thus] it is very hard to ground any directly constant and uniform judgment upon him'.[45] Women, among the 'weakest natures', might display great feats of courage, while by 1588 and in subsequent versions one of the 'hardiest among men' lost his masculine self-control to rage and massacre. The contrasts, the opposites, the examples of masculine and feminine, of vice and virtue were developed by Montaigne from the outset and then heightened throughout the various phases of his writing, and the last amendments he crammed into the margins of the 1588 copy of the *Essais*.

From the 1580 edition of the *Essais* onwards, Montaigne told the reader of the essay on human presumption, a favourite theme of misery-of-man writers, that there are two parts to presumption: 'for a man to esteem himself overmuch' and

---

41 Montaigne, *Essais*, I:1 – 'Par divers moyens on arrive a pareille fin', p. 12A; Montaigne, *Essays*, vol. I, p. 18; Villey, *Les sources*, vol. I, pp. 322–3, 328–9.

42 Montaigne, *Essays*, vol. I, p. 18; Montaigne, *Essais*, p. 8A: 'effect d'une ame forte et imployable, ayant en affection et en honneur une vigueur masle et obstinée'.

43 Montaigne, *Essays*, vol. I, p. 20; Montaigne, *Essais*, p. 9B.

44 Montaigne, *Essays*, vol. I, p. 21; Montaigne, *Essais*, p. 10C; Montaigne Project, at http://artfl.uchicago.edu/images/montaigne/0002v.jpg, accessed 8 November 2010.

45 Montaigne, *Essays*, vol. I, p. 19; Montaigne, *Essais*, p. 9A.

'not sufficiently to esteem others'. About a decade later, Montaigne elaborated on this tendency by writing in the margins of his printed 1588 essays how he lessened 'the just value of those things which I possess' and enhanced 'the worth of things', deemed 'strange, absent and not mine own'. He acknowledged how the 'prerogative' of male 'authority' breeds a contempt 'wherewith husbands look upon their own wives with a vicious disdain and many fathers upon their children. So do I and between two like works I would ever weigh against mine'.[46] Montaigne reveals the uncertainty of his own judgment in order to undermine the presumption of others who deem themselves adequate judges. 'In sum, (to return to myself) the only matter for which I might make some account of myself is that wherein no man did think himself defective. My recommendation is vulgar, common and popular: For who ever thought he lacked wit?' Montaigne identifies himself with the common lot because any village man or woman places great faith in his or her own judgment. So he continues. 'There was never so base a porter, nor so silly a woman, but thought he had sufficient wit for his provision. We recognise easily in others, the advantage of courage, of bodily strength, of experience, of disposition and of beauty, but we never yield the advantage of judgment to anybody'.[47] Some scholars have assumed that Montaigne's introduction of the self excludes women, whereas the private and domestic concerns of his *Essais*, musing on his feelings, weaknesses, experiences, household concerns, servants, body, health and aging regularly bring women into the picture.[48]

The designated reader of the *Apologie de Raimond Sebond* is widely understood to be Marguerite de Valois, daughter of a king, sister of three kings and the eventual wife of a king, although François Rigolot suggests that the *Apologie* may be directed to the princess without naming her because Montaigne seeks a

[46] Montaigne, *Essays*, vol. II, p. 357; Montaigne, *Essais*, pp. 633A–634C: 'la prerogative de l'authorité faict que les maris regardent les femmes propres d'un vitieux desdain, et plusieurs peres leurs enfants'; at Montaigne Project, http://artfl.uchicago.edu/images/montaigne/0279.jpg, accessed 8 November 2010.

[47] Montaigne, *Essays*, vol. II, pp. 391–2; Montaigne, *Essais*, p. 656A: 'Somme pour revenir à moy, ce seul par où je m'estime quelque chose, c'est ce en quoy jamais homme ne s'estima deffaillant; ma recommandation est vulgaire, commune et populaire, car qui a jamais cuidé avoir faute de sens? … Il ne fut jamais crocheteur ny femmelette qui ne pensast avoir assez de sens pour sa provision. Nous reconnoissons ayséement és autres l'advantage du courage, de la force corporelle, de l'experience, de la disposition, de la beauté; mais l'advantage du jugement, nous ne le cedons à personne'.

[48] Cathleen Bauschatz was one of the first scholars to recognise the importance of female readership – see '"Leur plus universelle qualité, c'est la diversité": Women as Ideal Readers in Montaigne's *Essais*', *Journal of Medieval and Renaissance Studies* 19:1 (1989): 83–101; more recently see Bromilow, *Models of Women*, pp. 31–4, 46–50; by contrast other critics ignore female exempla: Timothy Hampton, *Writing from History: The Rhetoric of Exemplarity in Renaissance Literature* (Ithaca, NY, 1990); Zachary Schiffman, *On the Threshold of Modernity: Relativism in the French Renaissance* (London, 1991); Frederick Rider, *The Dialectic of Selfhood in Montaigne* (Stanford, CA, 1973).

broader 'female public'.[49] As Montaigne explains in the *Apologie*, it would be too easy to target the folly of the ordinary man – *l'homme en sa commune façon* – so he considers the 'small number of excellent men' who have taken humanity to 'the highest pitch of wisdom it may possibly reach'.[50] In this essay, as Rigolot quite rightly indicates, all of Montaigne's examples of excellence are men.[51] To crush male presumption, he compares these great men to animals, to women, and to each other. Like Agrippa, Bruès, Tahureau, Labé and Nicole Estienne, Montaigne demonstrates the confusion and contradictory opinions that the greatest human intellects have produced. He finds it ridiculous that such a 'miserable and wretched creature' who could not even claim to be 'master of himself' should be paraded as the 'Master' and 'Emperor' of the Universe.[52] As Montaigne developed the *Essais*, he added the experiences of the everyday – his valet, servants and the village peasants – and juxtaposed their lives with the absurdities of the so-called wise, eminent men of dignity. When he wished to belittle the so-called superiority of learned men, Montaigne often contrasted their achievements with the lives of simple folk. The *Apologie* revives the story, discussed in chapter three (Figure 3.3), in Gilles Corrozet's emblems and Jacques Tahureau's *Dialogues* about the wise man who looks to the heavens but tumbles into a hole because he fails to see what is under his very nose.[53] In Montaigne's version a girl seeing the philosopher Thalès always in contemplation with his eyes raised to the heavens 'laid something in his way to make him stumble' in order to warn him that he should not become too preoccupied with the 'matters above the clouds'. Thalès should 'look to himself' rather than gaze up at the heavens (*regarder plustost à soy qu'au ciel*)'.[54]

On Some Verses of Virgil was first published as part of the third book of the 1588 edition. Montaigne famously jests that this essay would get him into the *cabinets* or 'private rooms' of his female readers because he focused specifically

---

[49] François Rigolot, 'D'une théologie "Pour les dames" à une apologie "per le donne"?', in Claude Blum (ed.), *Montaigne: Apologie de Raimond Sebond De la theologia à la Théologie* (Paris, 1990), pp. 264, 267, 268, 271 and 273. Rigolot raises the important issue as to whether *homme* represents the general term *homme-homo* or specifically masculine as *homme-vir*. He finds 28 occurrences of the word *femme*, while there are 240 occurrences of the word *homme*.

[50] Montaigne, *Essays*, vol. II, p. 203; Montaigne, *Essais*, pp. 501–2A: 'petit nombre d'hommes excellens'; 'au plus haut point (C) de sagesse (A) où elle puisse atteindre'; 'loge' within them 'la hauteur extreme de l'humaine nature'.

[51] In other essays women served as examples of 'la grandeur de ces hommes': Montaigne, *Essais*, II:32, 'Defence de Seneque et de Plutarque', pp. 723A–724C.

[52] Montaigne, *Essays*, vol. II, p. 139; Montaigne, *Essais*, p. 450A.

[53] See Chapter 3, pp. 64–6.

[54] Montaigne, *Essays*, vol. II, p. 251; Montaigne, *Essais*, II:12, p. 538A; Rigolot, 'D'une théologie', p. 270; for other examples in the *Essais* contrasting women and simple folk with learned men, see II:12, p. 510A; III:8, 'De l'art de conferer', p. 926B; I:26, 'De l'institution des enfans', p. 169A.

on woman's nature, male and female sexuality, the institution of marriage and how women are shaped by their education and training. Montaigne confesses his likes and dislikes, discusses the effects of aging, before abruptly announcing, 'And now to our theme', as he reworks a borrowing from the *De officiis* (*On Duties*), not mentioning Cicero by name, nor setting the passage apart. 'Why was the act of generation (*action genitale aux hommes*) so natural, so necessary, and so just seeing we fear to speak of it without shame? … we pronounce boldly kill, rob, betray; and this we only dare to mutter through our teeth'.[55] Montaigne draws attention to the public discomfort with the most intimate, 'necessary' and private act in human life. He pursued the theme in the late 1580s or early 1590s, replacing words to make rhythmic sentences and adding passages to contrast the conditions that create a human life or take a life away. 'Everyone flees the sight of childbirth, but all run hastily to see a man die'. On his 1588 copy, Montaigne had written: 'To destroy a human being we seek a spacious field in broad daylight; to make one, we hide ourselves in some dark corner. It is our duty to conceal ourselves and blush in making [a human being], but glory to unmake one'.[56] Although fundamental to human preservation, the act of sex was associated with shame, whereas the act of murder brought honour as a display of military prowess on the battlefield.

Using Virgil's portrayal of an 'alluring, all naked, quick and panting Venus' in the *Aeneid* – never has a wife been so desirable – Montaigne finds her as 'somewhat stirring for a marital Venus' because a man 'does not marry for himself … but as much or more for his posterity and family. The use and interest of marriage concerns our offspring, a great way beyond us'.[57] Montaigne re-examines the most intimate details of married life, but not in the early *Querelle des femmes* sense of encouraging bachelors to the altar or warning them about the miseries of married life; nor in the way the voices defending women encouraged

[55] Montaigne, *Essays*, vol. III, p. 70; Montaigne, *Essais*, p. 847B: 'Qu'a faict l'action genitale aux hommes, si naturelle, si necessaire, et si juste, pour n'en oser parler sans vergogne et pour exclurre des propos serieux et reglez? Nous prononcons hardiment: tuer, desrobir et trahir; et cela, nous n'oserions qu'entre les dents?' See Cicero, *De officiis*, trans. Walter Miller (London, 1913), I.xxxv.128: '[The Cynics] censure and ridicule us for holding that the mere mention of actions that are not immoral is shameful, while other things that are immoral we call by their real names. Robbery, fraud, and adultery for example, are immoral in deed but it is not indecent to name them. To beget children in wedlock is in deed morally right; to speak of it is indecent'. See also Guy de Bruès, *Dialogues de Guy de Brués contre les Nouveaux Academiciens*, ed. Panos Morphos (Baltimore, MD, 1953), pp. 194, 196; Villey, *Les sources*, vol. I, pp. 88–9, 247.

[56] Montaigne, *Essais*, p. 878: '(B) 'Chacun fuit à le voir naistre, chacun suit à le voir mourir (C) Pour le destruire, on cerche un champ spacieux en pleine lumiere; pour le construire, on se musse dans un creux tenebreux et contraint. (B) C'est le devoir de se cacher et rougir pour le faire; et c'est gloire, et naissent plusieurs vertus, de le sçavoir deffaire'; Montaigne Project, at http://artfl.uchicago.edu/images/montaigne/0393.jpg, accessed 8 November 2010.

[57] Montaigne, *Essays*, vol. III, p. 72; Montaigne, *Essais*, pp. 849–850B.

conjugal love and promoted the institution of marriage using essentialist notions about wives as sources of comfort as discussed in chapters three, four and five.[58] Montaigne reflected on the practice of training girls for love while expecting them to commit to a life of modesty and chastity in the marriage contract.[59] Among the tales of adulterous wives and famous cuckolds, Montaigne acknowledged the effects of male authority. Like Agrippa, Pasquier's female character Charilée, Nicole Estienne's lamentation on the woes of the wife, and numerous *Querelle* defenders of women, Montaigne writing in the 1580s suggested that: 'Women are not altogether in the wrong, when they refuse the rules of life prescribed to the world, since men alone have established them without their consent'.[60]

Montaigne reworked, compiled examples and imitated topics, which were, as Floyd Gray suggests, 'thematically ubiquitous, exploring and reviewing what others have written'. On themes of the dignity and misery of man, women's nature and the fragility of the human condition, Montaigne, like his predecessors, was still 'weighing their opposing arguments'.[61] Cox and Rigolot have noted the shift from dialogue to the essay as a place to weigh and reflect upon ideas.[62] Montaigne was not trying to reach a foregone conclusion; rather he praises, he blames, and he questions and stresses the ambiguities, the inconsistencies and the impossibility of judgment.

Montaigne's extensive use of citations compares to the contemporary practices of lawyers in the Parlements and lower courts across France, who formed a significant portion of his reading audience. Hoffman has even suggested that Montaigne may have dictated the early *Essais* to secretaries, and if this is correct it may possibly explain why some of the passages from Virgil or Martial read like a pleading as the lawyer tries to heighten the sentiment of wrongdoing or promote the idea of heroism or virtue on behalf of a client.[63] Lawyers gathered proofs and evidence from far and wide for their pleadings before the law courts and chapter eight focuses on the 'rhetoric of citation' that pervaded lawyers' pleadings in the Parlements in the latter half of the sixteenth century. As we have seen in chapters four and five, writers such as Gratien Dupont, Louise Labé, Étienne Pasquier, the

---

58 See Chapter 3, pp. 51, 89; Chapter 4, pp. 115–16; Chapter 5, pp. 131–2. Symphorien Champier, *La Nef des dames vertueuses* (Paris: Jehan de la Garde, 1515), Bk II, ch. 2; Vives, *Institution de la femme chrestienne*, Bk IV, ch. 1, *De l'office du mary*, fos 138v–139r; Sperone Speroni, *De la dignité des femmes*, in *De la cure famillere avec aucuns preceptes de mariage extraicts de Plutarque. Aussi un dialogue de la dignité des femmes* (Lyon: Jean de Tournes, 1546), p. 171; Marconville, *De l'heur*, 1571 edn, fo. 33r.

59 Montaigne, *Essays*, vol. III, p. 80.

60 Ibid., vol. III, pp. 77–8; Montaigne, *Essais*, p. 854B: 'Les femmes n'ont pas tort du tout quand elles refusent les reigles de vie qui sont introduites au monde, d'autant que ce sont les hommes qui les ont faictes sans elles'.

61 Gray, *Gender, Rhetoric*, p. 13.

62 Cox, *Renaissance Dialogue*, p. 113, Rigolot, 'Problematizing', pp. 13–14.

63 George Hoffman, *Montaigne's Career* (Oxford, 1998), pp. 40–44.

Seigneur de Cholières [Jean Dagoneau] borrowed from the discipline of law to set the scene or to provide examples within their literary works. The gathering of proofs, evidence and commonplaces might be a two-way street as lawyers in the Parlements turned their attentions to writing on human nature and to a range of literary examples to set the tone for a pleading before the court, to persuade and capture the attention of the judges.

Montaigne's Career and the Uncertainty of Judgment

Montaigne took up his office as a *conseiller* in the Cour des Aides in the region of Périgueux in 1557 through a connection to his uncle Pierre Eyquem. Shortly thereafter he moved to the fourth *Chambre des requêtes* in Bordeaux as a *conseiller*, and when the chamber was dissolved in 1561 he became an officeholding *conseiller* (judge) in the Parlement of Bordeaux until 1570 when he sold his office.[64] His uncle Raymond Eyquem de Montaigne had been a *conseiller* in the Grand'Chambre and Montaigne's cousins and in-laws were also part of this milieu. When he married Françoise de la Chassaigne in 1565, her father and grandfather had served as *présidents* (presiding judges) in the Parlement de Bordeaux. Later his brother-in-law held a post as *président* in the first chamber in the Parlement de Bordeaux.[65] Montaigne's service as a magistrate in the 1560s, as the mayor of Bordeaux in the early 1580s, and an envoy between kings and parties of the civil wars in the mid- to late 1580s, meant that he was familiar with the need for eloquence in political, legal and diplomatic discourse. As a magistrate or *conseiller* who reported on cases and had a caseload assigned to him when the court was in session in Bordeaux, Montaigne was aware of the art of written persuasion as well as the back-and-forth tussle of lawyers' pleadings, their assembly of proofs and reasoning, and how the *conseillers* and presiding judges arrived at their decisions.[66] He was alert to the difficulties of judgment, a theme that recurs throughout the *Essais*.[67]

---

64 Fleury Vindry, *Les parlementaires français au XVIe siècle*, 2 vols (Paris, 1910–12), vol. II, pp. 27, 100; Katherine Almquist, 'Writing Pluralist Biography of Montaigne's Legal Career', *EMF: Studies in Early Modern France* 9 (2004): 63; Hoffman, *Montaigne's Career*, p. 30.

65 Philippe Desan, 'Combien gagnait Montaigne au Parlement de Bordeaux (un reçu de 27 août 1576)', *Montaigne Studies* 16 (2004): 41–4; Vindry, *Les parlementaires*, vol. II, pp. 8, 9, 15, 22, 40, 60.

66 Alain Legros, 'Montaigne "rapporteur": dix arrêts du Parlement de Bordeaux, premiers témoins de sa pratique du français écrit', *Journal de la Renaissance* 6 (2008): 293–303; Katherine Almquist, 'Montaigne Judging with Henri de Mesmes (May–June 1565)', *Montaigne Studies* 16 (2004): 39; Almquist, 'Writing … Montaigne's Legal Career', pp. 66–7, 70.

67 Hoffman, *Montaigne's Career*, p. 152.

The lawyers Étienne Pasquier and Antoine Loisel, whose social circle and background were discussed in the Introduction, and again for Pasquier in chapter five, were the Parisian acquaintances of Montaigne.[68] Each of these three legally trained humanists recognised the bewildering variety of customs and laws within the borders of France and beyond to the morals and habits of ancient civilisations and religions across Asia Minor and the new world from deflowering rituals, wives in common, family inheritance, burial practices, circumcision, breastfeeding, urinating and incest.[69] This diversity had been of curious interest in the earlier writings of Boemus' *Recueil de diverses histoires* and Mexia's *Diverses leçons*. To illustrate the problems of customs and judgment, Pasquier, Loisel and Montaigne each compiled the same proof derived from Herodotus of whether when one's father died 'the worthiest and most honorable sepulchre' might be to bury, to burn or to eat him 'as a testimony of piety and good affection'.[70] What might be horrifying in one culture could be honourable in another.

Mulling over this diversity in the *Essais*, Montaigne highlighted the ambiguities and the inconsistencies of man, woman and the human experience. The 'inconsistency' of argument became a virtue rather than a limitation as writers veered from one side to the other in an attempt to explore the possibilities of truth, having recognised that unassailable positions were all but impossible. Even Montaigne's numerous amendments and incessant editing and rewriting of his *Essais* until his death reinforced the continual shift of opinion and uncertainty of judgment. Neither the reflections on the nature of man and woman, nor the development of arguments on one side and then the other, nor the imitation and 'rhetoric of citation' were particularly new, but the essay with its 'inner dialogue', circling back and digressions had strayed from the familiar formats of the medieval disputes, Renaissance dialogues and paradoxes. Scholars interested in the evolution of the *Querelle des femmes* over the sixteenth century need to extend the scope of their studies beyond the traditional champions and enemies of the feminine sex. In the late 1500s and early 1600s writers gathered and assembled their examples of women from a range of sources and then reworked and

---

[68] On Pasquier, see Chapter 1, pp. 12–13, 16–17 and Chapter 5, pp. 122, 135–6; on Loisel see Chapter 1, pp. 12, 16n61.

[69] Montaigne, *Essais*, I:23 'De la coustume et de ne changer aisément une loy receüe', pp. 111–17; Montaigne Project, at http://artfl.uchicago.edu/images/montaigne/0039v.jpg, accessed 8 November 2010.

[70] Montaigne, *Essays*, vol. II, pp. 298–9, and vol. I, p. 115; Montaigne, *Essais*, II:12, 'Apologie de Raymond Sebond', p. 581A, and I:23, 'De la coustume et de ne changer aisément une loy receüe', p. 116A; Montaigne Project, at http://artfl.uchicago.edu/images/montaigne/0040v.jpg, accessed 8 November 2010; Etienne Pasquier, 'De la communauté des biens meubles, & conquests immeubles qui est en nostre France entre le mary & la femme', in *Recherches*, Bk 4, ch. XXI, in *Œuvres*, vol. I, cols 411–14; Jotham Parsons, 'The Political Vision of Antoine Loisel', *Sixteenth Century Journal*, 27:2 (1996): 473–4.

intertwined these deliberations with reflections on man in collections, anthologies and essays emphasising the diversity of the human experience.

Chapter 7
Books in the Palais de Justice and their Readers in the Late 1500s to Early 1600s

A sixteenth-century traveller wandering the crowded streets on the Île de la Cité would have been drawn to the thronging marketplace of the Palais de Justice and its stalls offering luxury items from lace to art and books. The residents of Paris and especially the attorneys, lawyers and magistrates who made their living from the royal and judicial administration would have been regular visitors to this market. This chapter examines the books sold from the stalls in the Palais de Justice in the late 1500s and early 1600s, and the Parisian households where some of these purchases could be found. Some of the titles and authors will already be familiar. As we saw in chapter six, by the mid- to late sixteenth century miscellanies such as Mexia's *Diverse lessons*, Marconville's works on women, marriage or 'strange cases', Montaigne's *Essais* focused on the human experience by drawing on examples from men and women, diverse customs and nations, ancient cultures and the new world, as well as the everyday practices and 'common opinions' of contemporary France.

Particular attention needs to be paid to the men who read for their work as lawyers, attorneys, judges or notaries and how this rapidly growing 'professional' readership annotated, took notes and collected commonplaces for their work in the Palais de Justice, royal or civic administration. Among these professional readers, the lawyers' book collections and note-taking practices are of special interest because the next chapter demonstrates how these advocates constructed their pleadings before the Parlement de Paris and what types of commonplaces they might use to persuade or move the judges and win a case.

Most of these lawyers and officeholders had wives and daughters or – earlier in life – mothers and sisters who shared a household with books. Montaigne disdained legal books and 'rhetoric' as superfluous to female needs, but he did recommend the reading of poetry and his own favourite subjects, history and moral philosophy, to allow women 'to temper the rashness of their own desires, to husband their liberty: lengthen the delights of life, gently to bear the inconstancy of a servant, the peevishness or rudeness of a husband, the importunity of years … and such like mind-troubling accidents'.[1] Alongside the civil law and royal ordinances,

[1] Montaigne, *Essais*, III:3, 'De trois commerces', pp. 822–3B; Montaigne, *Essays*, vol. III, pp. 42–3; Richard Sayce, *Essays of Montaigne: A Critical Exploration* (London, 1972), p. 125; Robert Cottrell, 'Gender Imprinting in Montaigne's Essais', *L'Esprit Créateur* 30 (1990): 92–3.

the staple items for the library of an officeholder or lawyer, the Palais de Justice booksellers stocked plenty of poetry, history or moral philosophy in French such as Guillaume du Bartas' *La Sepmaine* or Montaigne's *Essais*. The evidence of reading by women in the sixteenth and early seventeenth centuries presents more of a challenge to the researcher, and this chapter attempts to discern what we can learn from probate inventories about the books women had an interest in or had access to in their households. Women may have had fewer opportunities to study, and no chance at one of the legal professions or offices, but as wives, mothers and widows they shared many of the hopes and anxieties of their husbands and trained their children to prosper in dignity while preparing them for adversity. The sources are frustratingly limited, yet to ignore them is to risk suggesting that only men contributed to shaping this early modern culture. It does matter if literate daughters and mothers read and wondered about human excellence when they were mired in the misery of civil war, if they read the debates about women's nature and the expectations of a wife, or if they had access to the bewildering variety of customs unleashed by Montaigne in the *Essais*.

The Palais de Justice Marketplace for Books in the Late 1500s

The Parisian bookseller Abel L'Angelier, whose father, uncle, mother, stepfather, half-brother and wife all worked in the book trade within the Palais de Justice, began to distribute steady sellers such as *The New Style and Protocol Manual of the Chancellerie of France, Which Follows the Methods and Forms Practised Today* from an early point in his career in the 1570s in order to supply the cash flow needed to publish new literary works. He continued to sell these types of 'new and improved' versions of the legal and administrative guidebooks into the early 1600s. Denis Janot and Arnoul and Charles L'Angelier had shown the profitability of this combination of offerings sold to the lawyers, notaries, judges and attorneys from the 1530s through to the 1560s.[2] When L'Angelier acquired the royal privilege to print Montaigne's revised edition of the *Essais* expanded by 'six hundred additions' and 13 new essays, he chose to produce a handsome in-quarto edition in 1588 as well as a more compact, cheaper version.[3] Montaigne's *Essais*

[2] *Nouveau stile et prothocole de la Chancellerie de France, suivant la forme et maniere que lon use pour le iourd'huy* (Paris: Abel L'Angelier, 1577), privilege of 10 December 1576 without date limit, fo. title page verso. Denis Janot printed his *Stile et prothocole* in 1535. Jean Balsamo and Michel Simonin, *Abel L'Angelier et Françoise de Louvain (1574–1620). Suivi du catalogue des ouvrages publiés par Abel L'Angelier (1574–1610) et la Veuve L'Angelier (1610–1620)*, (Geneva, 2002), cat. no. 21.

[3] George Hoffman, *Montaigne's Career* (Oxford, 1998), pp. 104, 106, 112; Michel Simonin, 'Le Périgourdin au Palais: sur le voyage des *Essais* de Bordeaux à Paris', in M. Tetel and G. Mallary Masters (eds), *Le Parcours des Essais: Montaigne 1588–1988* (Paris, 1989), pp. 21–4.

had already made the leap from Bordeaux to Paris, because a version had been in circulation since 1587 from the boutique of Jean Richer, an occasional colleague of L'Angelier's, who was also busy in the late 1580s distributing the *Matinées* and *Après-disnées* dialogues of the Sieur de Cholières.[4]

When Montaigne's *Essais* came to market in 1588 the political crisis of the religious civil war loomed in the background; a crisis that became even more acute after the assassination of Henri III in 1589 and the problems Henri IV faced in asserting his claim to the French throne. The civil war divided the royalists and the Catholic League as each vied for control of Paris. Many of the usual clients of the marketplace in the Palais de Justice – the *parlementaires*, officeholders and lawyers – moved out of Paris to Tours or Melun. Although the booksellers went too, book production in these years was drastically reduced.[5] The *Essais*, especially with the stoic emphasis of the early essays, was one of the few *nouveautés* produced by L'Angelier in the crisis years of the late 1580s before the near shutdown of the business and recession of the early 1590s.

Reflecting on the crisis, the officeholder Vincent Gelée explained: 'Reader friend, during the calamitous times of the year 1590, to distract my mind from its oppressing worries, I devoted myself to the reading of a few books, among others the *General Guide of Finances*, treating the affairs of my vocation'. Gelée, a controller of accounts (*conseiller et correcteur ordinaire*) in the Chambre des comptes, had been studying a financial guidebook available from L'Angelier's boutique and under his privilege from 1585.[6] Gelée apparently spotted some errors and omissions in Jean Hennequin's *Le Guydon general des financiers* and so he had amended the text hoping the author would take it 'in stride' (*en bonne part*). Once the political crisis was over and as royalists and *politiques* began to return to Paris, Gelée turned to L'Angelier to publish his *Annotations*.[7] Among the other books Gelée could have read for distraction during the siege, was the in-quarto edition of Du Bartas' *Sepmaine*, a title under privilege to L'Angelier from 1582 and available from L'Angelier's boutique (Figure 3.2), Fontanon's two-volume edition of French ordinances, Plutarch's letters, Bodin's *Republic* and almost 160 volumes in packets. The bookseller taking the inventory of his library after his death in 1603 also found Gelée's copy of the *Guidon general des financiers*

---

4 See Chapter 5, pp. 139–41.

5 Henri-Jean Martin, *Livre, pouvoirs et société à Paris au XVIIe siècle (1598–1701)*, 2 vols (Geneva, 1969), vol. I, pp. 346–8; Denis Pallier, *Recherches sur l'imprimerie à Paris pendant la Ligue 1585–1594* (Geneva, 1975), p. 129.

6 Balsamo and Simonin, *Abel L'Angelier*, cat. no. 144.

7 Vincent Gelée, 'Au Lecteur', in *Annotations de Vincent Gelee conseiller du roy & correcteur ordinaire en sa Chambre des comptes. Sur le guidon general des finances* (Paris: Abel L'Angelier, 1594), pp. 2–3; Jean Hennequin, *Le Guydon general des financiers* (Paris: Abel L'Angelier, 1585). L'Angelier published the *Guidon* again in 1593: Balsamo and Simonin, *Abel L'Angelier*, cat. no. 231.

bound in vellum with gold and valued at 15 sols tournois.[8] With the location of his boutique by the first pillar of the Grand'Salle and his editorial choices in a career spanning over three decades, L'Angelier's target market was the Palais de Justice crowd of royal and civic officeholders, as well as the lawyers, attorneys (*procureurs*) and notaries practising their professions. Their wives, daughters and sisters who might come to the Palais de Justice marketplace to stroll along the stalls of luxury goods were also in his sights.

The humanist lawyer and eventual royal officeholder Étienne Pasquier recalled 'flipping through some books at L'Angelier's bookstall'.[9] His peers and colleagues Gelée, Loisel, Du Vair, Claude Expilly visiting from Grenoble, or even Montaigne visiting from Bordeaux, were probably all L'Angelier customers who became L'Angelier authors. And sometimes a bookseller became a friend. In 1594 Étienne Pasquier, still in Melun, wrote to L'Angelier back in Paris and even asked the publisher to greet – 'kiss their hands on my behalf' – their mutual friends Antoine Loisel and Pierre Pithou.[10] The lawyers, clerks and attorneys of the Palais de Justice and the workers at the market stalls might come to know each other in even more intimate circumstances. The widow of the merchant bookseller Jean Richer almost took a lawyer at Parlement to court over the illegitimate child that resulted from their 'carnal copulation', until he agreed to pay for the child's food and needs.[11]

By the second half of the century, some lawyers and indeed some enterprising printers and merchant booksellers began to see the market for the publication of lawyers' pleadings. When Pierre Ayrault, a lawyer at the Parlement de Paris, left the Palais de Justice for a post in Angers, he supposedly asked a printer to pack up and forward his books. The printer was carrying out this task when a bundle of papers in Ayrault's handwriting 'fell into his hands'. In sorting through these papers and in consulting some of Ayrault's 'own friends' the printer Martin le Jeune found them to be '*mémoires* written and edited by the Author containing a pure and simple narration of the cases and matters which occurred and how [Ayrault] debated them in the Court of Parlement according to the form and style of pleading common today, that is, half Latin, half French'. In presenting 21 of Ayrault's pleadings the printer chose 'the most notable cases' and claimed,

---

8 Archives nationales, Paris, Minutier central des notaires de Paris [hereafter AN, MC], post-mortem inventory of Vincent Gelée, *conseiller du roi* and controller (*correcteur*) in the Chambre des comptes, 7 October 1603, XXIV, 142; on Du Bartas, see Balsamo and Simonin, *Abel L'Angelier*, pp. 76–7, 120, cat. no. 83.

9 Étienne Pasquier, 'A Monsieur Buisson, Advocat en Parlement', in *Choix de lettres sur la littérature, la langue et la traduction*, ed. Dorothy Thickett (Geneva, 1956), VI:4, pp. 11–12; Étienne Pasquier, *Les Œuvres d'Étienne Pasquier*, 2 vols (Amsterdam, 1723), vol. II, VI:4, pp. 157–8.

10 Étienne Pasquier, 'Au Seigneur Abel L'Angelier, libraire', in *Lettres familières*, ed. Dorothy Thickett (Geneva, 1974), XV:10, p. 245.

11 Jérôme Pichon and Georges Vicaire, 'Documents pour servir à l'histoire des libraires des Paris, 1486–1600', *Bulletin du bibliophile* (1894): 353.

preserving Ayrault's modesty, that he decided to publish them without Ayrault's knowledge because of their 'public utility'.[12]

Book Collections, 'Professional' Reading and Note-taking

Typically a sixteenth-century lawyer in the Parlement might own the *Corpus juris civilis* and commentaries on Roman law as well as books of royal ordinances and an array of books of customary law.[13] Before his death in 1581, for example, the lawyer Jehan Bautru possessed an 'old' *coutumier* of France, the *coutumiers* of Orléans and Normandy, two *coutumiers* of Brittany, Charles Du Moulin's commentary on the customs of Paris, and several other *coutumiers* with commentaries for the regions of Bordeaux, Blois and Poitou. The lawyer Bautru could also go to his study to consult several works of 'decisions' or judgments including Jean de Coras' 'commentary on the Martin Guerre sentence' and an octavo edition of Pierre Ayrault's pleadings.[14]

By the 1590s and into the early seventeenth century it became much more common to print collections of *arrêts* or judgments that were often preceded by the pleadings of the case or the 'conclusions' of the *procureur général* or *avocat du roi* speaking on behalf of the interests of the king and the 'public good'.[15] These collections of 'notable decisions' begin to appear in the libraries in the households of lawyers and judicial officeholders in the early decades of the seventeenth century. When François Courtin died in September 1609 his widow asked the booksellers Jehan Houze and Pierre Febvrier to assess the worth of her husband's substantial library.[16] Courtin had been received as a lawyer in the Parlement de Paris, and occupied a position as a *greffier* or clerk of the Hôtel de Ville in Paris. He owned some of the same legal reference books as the lawyer Bautru who had died nearly three decades earlier, such as Charles Du Moulin's commentary on the customs of Paris and a 'Stille de la chancelerie'. Courtin was certainly familiar with the bookstall of Abel L'Angelier at the first pillar in the Grand'Salle of the

[12] 'L'imprimeur aux lecteurs', in Pierre Ayrault, *XXI Pledoiers faict en la cour de Parlement de Paris et arrests sur ce intervenuz* (Paris: Martin le Jeune, 1568), pp. 3–6.

[13] AN, MC, post-mortem inventory of Laurent de Croisettes, sieur de St. Mesme, lawyer at the Parlement de Paris, 28 January 1577, XXXIII, 187.

[14] AN, MC, post-mortem inventory of Jehan Bautru, lawyer at the Parlement de Paris, 14 August 1581, XXXIII, 194.

[15] Claude-Joseph de Ferrière (ed.), *Dictionnaire de droit et de pratique contenant l'explication des termes de droit, d'ordonnances, de coutumes et de pratique*, 2 vols (Paris: Veuve Brunet, 1769), vol. I, p. 143, and vol. II, pp. 362–3; Félix Aubert, 'Recherches sur l'organisation du Parlement de Paris au XVIe siècle (1515–1589)', *Nouvelle revue historique de droit français et étranger* 36 (1912): 179–201.

[16] AN, MC, post-mortem inventory of François Courtin, lawyer at the Parlement de Paris and *greffier*, 2–6 September 1609, III, 487.

Palais de Justice because he owned several distinctive works under privilege to the bookseller. The first edition of the pleadings of Claude Expilly, the *avocat général* in the Parlement of Grenoble, made it from the printing press and into L'Angelier's stock in August 1608 so Courtin had obtained his copy in the year before his death.[17] Courtin owned L'Angelier's five-volume in-octavo collective edition of Guillaume du Vair's works containing some accounts of the notable decisions of the Parlement in Aix-en-Provence as well as Du Vair's writings of moral philosophy, published in 1606 and 1607.[18] Courtin also owned a copy of the *Nouveau stile et prothocolle de la chancellerie* in the octavo format sold by Abel L'Angelier from 1588. The folio edition of Jean Bacquet's 'discours' in Courtin's home could have been one of Bacquet's works under privilege to L'Angelier and published by him in 1601, 1603 or 1608. For leisure Courtin owned an octavo edition of Montaigne's *Essays* available from L'Angelier in that format in 1600, 1602 and 1604 editions. Other books in Courtin's library, such as Jean Papon's collection of *arrêts* or Pasquier's *Recherches de la France*, could have been purchased at a number of booksellers from the 1560s onwards. Courtin's library included several works by Louis Le Caron such as his *Pandectes ou Digestes du droict françois* and *Les Responses ou decisions du droict françois*, but L'Angelier only shared the privilege for Le Caron's commentary on the custom of Paris owned by Courtin. The lawyer and clerk also possessed three volumes of the pleadings of Louis Servin, the *avocat général du roi* in the Parlement de Paris.[19]

The 'professional' reader such as a lawyer, attorney, clerk or judge could update his knowledge of the various types of cases through the circulation of manuscript copies of certain 'famous' pleadings, or by purchasing the print versions that became available towards the end of the sixteenth century. In addition to the printed books of their private libraries, lawyers often had little tables in their studies to stack and sort 'papers'.[20] Robert Descimon has detailed how, in the early modern period, attorneys (*procureurs*) at the Parlement and the Châtelet de Paris sold their offices or positions, but they also recognised the monetary value of their 'pratiques' or files of working papers and the background information gathered in preparation for cases.[21] Although printed versions of famous cases became more readily available, lawyers and attorneys also kept notes and manuscript copies of

---

[17] Balsamo and Simonin, *Abel L'Angelier*, cat. no. 465.

[18] AN, MC, Courtin inventory, 1609; Balsamo and Simonin, *Abel L'Angelier*, cat. nos. 427–31, 446–50.

[19] AN, MC, Courtin inventory, 1609; Balsamo and Simonin, *Abel L'Angelier*, cat. nos. 352, 379, 462.

[20] AN, MC, inventory of the [marital] community of goods, [Malingre, Bobie], 20 February 1590, XXIII, 134.

[21] Robert Descimon, 'Les auxiliaires de justice du Châtelet de Paris: aperçus sur l'économie du monde des offices ministériels (XVIe–XVIIIe siècle)', in Claire Dolan (ed.), *Entre justice et justiciables: les auxiliaires de la justice du Moyen Age au XXe siècle* (Québec, 2005), pp. 308, 310.

factums or legal briefs, consultations and pleadings copied out from the records of the court. Around the time that François Pithou was received as a lawyer in the Parlement de Paris in the late 1570s he recorded a series of *arrêts* to further his studies and took notes on his reading of civil and canon law and regional customs.[22] Gilles Le Maistre, a lawyer in the Parlement then *avocat général* and later *premier président* or the chief justice, copied out extracts of the Parlement de Paris *registres* and organised them according to topics such as 'bastards' and the 'community [of goods] between husband and wife'.[23] Four years after his death in 1562, Le Maistre's series of 'notable decisions' of the Parlement appeared in print. In a letter to the *avocat général du roi* Jacques Faye, Sieur d'Espesse, Étienne Pasquier mentions how he was content to 'unload' the pleadings and instruments used and to 'disburden' his memory of all the 'particularities' on a case once the *arrêt* was announced. Nevertheless, at Faye's 'request', Pasquier sent the *avocat général* a handwritten copy of a pleading from an infamous murder trial in 1571.[24]

Pierre Dupuy and his brother Jacques were both lawyers in the Parlement de Paris, although it seems that Pierre only pleaded once in 1607.[25] Their father Claude had been a *conseiller du roi* or officeholding judge in the Parlement de Paris from September 1575 until his death in 1594.[26] In a collection of papers, factums and *mémoires* now in the Bibliothèque nationale compiled by Pierre Dupuy and with his signature on the title page, Pierre kept his own manuscript notes and annotations on many remarkable legal cases of his era or sometimes arranged to have copies made. He evidently followed the pleadings of many famous lawyers such as Étienne Pasquier, Barnabé Brisson, Anne Robert and Antoine Arnauld. The Dupuy 115 manuscript also records the pleadings of Arnauld's father-in-law Simon Marion as well as Louis Servin in their capacities as *avocats du roi* speaking on behalf of the *procureur général du roi*.[27] Comments in the margins

22 BN, MS, Collection Dupuy [hereafter BN, MS Dupuy] 426, 'Notes et extraits de divers ouvrages d'histoire et de droit par François Pithou, autographe', fos 18r–21v, 29r–v, 39r, 40r, 55r; Suzanne Solente, 'Les manuscrits des Dupuy à la Bibliothèque nationale', *Bibliothèque de l'École des chartes* 88 (1927): 203–4.

23 BN, MS Dupuy 385, 'Extraict des registres du Parlement de Paris, rangés suivant l'ordre alphabétique des matières par Gilles Le Maistre, avocat du roi, puis premier président audit Parlement'. The date 1560 has been added to the title page of volume I in a different ink; *Nouvelle biographie générale depuis les temps les plus reculés jusqu'à 1850–60*, 46 vols (Copenhagen, 1968), volumes XXXIX–XL, col. 565.

24 Pasquier, *Les Œuvres*, vol. II, XII:1, cols 311–12; Roland Delachenal, *Histoire des avocats au Parlement de Paris 1300–1600* (Paris, 1885), p. 97.

25 Jérôme Delatour, 'De l'art de plaider doctement: Les notes de lecture de Pierre Dupuy, jeune avocat (1605–6)', *Bibliothèque de l'École des chartes* 153 (1995): 411.

26 Solente, 'Les manuscripts des Dupuy', pp. 179–80, 183; Delatour, 'De l'art de plaider', p. 391; Jérôme Delatour, *Les livres de Claude Dupuy: Une bibliothèque humaniste au temps des guerres de religion* (Paris, 1998).

27 BN, MS Dupuy 115, 'Recueil de plaidoiries, factums, arrêts et consultations des XVIe et XVIIe siècles'. The Dupuy 115 collection includes a 'célèbre' or 'famous pleading

highlighted the main points of each case, such as 'against clandestine marriages', and allowed the user to quickly find the legal points he needed to consult or to add some rhetorical flourish to a pleading with some references to 'love' or to 'woman'.[28] Some of the cases and notes appear to date back to the 1560s, but the manuscript collection of pleadings and factums continued into the early 1600s. As he compiled these handwritten copies of lawyers' pleadings Pierre Dupuy had access to copies of Jean Chenu's collection of famous cases first published in 1602 because he has noted in the margin 'See Chenu in his Questions'.[29] On another occasion, notes in the margin indicate that a case can be found in the third volume of Servin's books of pleadings.[30] At least twice, a reader has noted on the manuscript copy of a pleading in Dupuy 115 that 'Monsieur le Bret' had published the same pleading and noted where it could be found in Cardin Le Bret's printed collection.[31] Le Bret's *Recueil d'aucuns plaidoyez* was first published in 1597. L'Angelier sold it in an expanded in-octavo edition in 1602, the year after Le Bret had been named to the post of *avocat général*, and reprinted it in 1604 and 1609. The Veuve L'Angelier tried to protect Le Bret's published pleadings from piracy and obtained an extension of the privilege from the Parlement after 1610.[32]

The men consulting and marking up their working papers sometimes carried this habit over into the margins of their printed books. Annotations show how the early readers of the *Essais* seem to have enjoyed identifying the sources of Montaigne's citations. Claude Expilly, the lawyer in the Parlement de Grenoble

---

of Maistre Anthoine Arnauld', fo. 170r, as well as several separate folio sheets noting: 'Two pleadings of M. Ant. Arnaud'.

28 Ibid., fos 116r, 170r.

29 The marginal note about Chenu appears with reference to the question 'Si on peut estre releve de deception de moitie de juste prix', in ibid., fo. 118r; Jean Chenu, *Cent notables et singulières qvestions de droict, décidées par arrests mémorables des cours souueraines de France, partie d'iceux prononcez en robbes rouges: contenans les moyens et raisons décisives*, 2nd edn (Paris: Nicolas Buon, 1603). I owe a large debt to Jérôme Delatour not only for his generosity in responding to questions about Pierre Dupuy's handwriting but also for going out of his way to examine the Dupuy 115 manuscript in the BN Manuscripts room. He suggests that Dupuy probably annotated these pleadings when he was preparing for a career as a lawyer in the early 1600s. Private correspondence, 11 November 2005.

30 See BN, MS Dupuy 115, fo. 156r and on fo. 166r in the margin of a case: '22 Janvier 1600 Sr de Guinefolle accuse d'un meurtre faict en 77. Information en 89. Poursuitte … en 1599. Non recevables en la poursuitte tant ciuile que criminelle. Moreau. De Villiers. v. Servin tom. 3. plaid 23, plaid de dollé'.

31 Ibid.: 'Monsr Le Bret plaida son plaidoier est imprimé tout le 1er', fo. 215r, and 'Le plaid de Mr le Bret sur ceste cause est Imprimé le 25', fo. 222v.

32 Jean Bacquet, *Les Oevvres de Jehan Bacquet advocat dv roy en la Chambre dv thresor* (Paris: Veuve L'Angelier, 1611), sigs ˜e iv^{r-v}. In February 1610, the Veuve L'Angelier requested that Parlement extend privileges for several works including 'The Recueil des Plaidoyez de l'Aduocat le Bret' and 'le recueil d'Arrest par le feu Conseilller Loüet': Balsamo and Simonin, *Abel L'Angelier*, cat. no. 512, and p. 481.

and later a royal officeholder – whose pleadings published by L'Angelier in 1608 were owned, as we have just seen, by the lawyer and clerk François Courtin before his death in 1609 – possessed L'Angelier's 1588 in-quarto edition of the *Essais*. Expilly annotated his copy of the *Essais* by naming the sources of Montaigne's quotations and inscribed it with an autograph sonnet to the 'essais of messire Michel de Montagnes'.[33] Bernard Automne, who began practising as a lawyer in the late 1590s, included long citations from the 1595 edition of the *Essais* to illuminate the editions of his legal work *La Conférence du droict françois auec le droict romain*, first published in 1610.[34]

From the examples of lawyers-in-training, royal officeholders and clerks, such as Dupuy, Gelée and Courtin, we open a window onto these men at work, reading, taking notes, annotating their books and collections of paper, their professional needs supplied in part by a Palais de Justice bookseller.[35] Their reading practices will be essential to keep in mind in the next chapter on lawyers' pleadings in the Parlement de Paris because L'Angelier also supplied the books these men read for work and pleasure: classical authors, books of moral philosophy and history or works of contemporary French literature stuffed with the ideas and examples of man and woman. From these 'books of the humanities', as we shall see in the next chapter, lawyers could also collect sayings, maxims and proofs to delight, move or persuade a judge and win a lawsuit for a client. L'Angelier and the Palais de Justice booksellers clearly had much to offer the 'professional' male reader, but what might be of interest to these men seeking respite from their legal or administrative work or to the women in these households?

Stocking Titles for Contemplation and Leisure in the Palais de Justice

The Palais de Justice bookseller Abel L'Angelier offered many titles of French literature, moral philosophy and history from the late 1570s to the early 1600s. In 1584 Guillaume du Vair obtained an office as a judge (*conseiller*) in the Parlement de Paris, and he was the type of customer frequently seen at the bookstall of Abel

33 Alessandra Preda, '"Les siècles à venir te loueront à bon droit": Montaigne et Claude Expilly', *Montaigne Studies* 13 (2001): 192–3, 202–3, 205.

34 Michel Simonin, 'Bernard Automne (1564–après 1628) témoin et lecteur de Montaigne', *Montaigne Studies* 13 (2001), 322–3, 341–50; Catherine Magnien, 'Étienne Pasquier "familier" de Montaigne?', *Montaigne Studies* 13 (2001): 277–313; Jean Balsamo, 'Les *Essais* de Montaigne et leurs premiers lecteurs: exemplaires annotés (1580–1598)', *Montaigne Studies* 16 (2004): 144, 146.

35 For excellent in-depth studies of reading and book collecting in this milieu based on probate inventories, see Delatour, *Les livres*; Florence Greffe and José Lothe (eds), *La vie, les livres, et les lectures de Pierre de L'Estoille* (Paris, 2004).

L'Angelier.[36] As Du Vair later recalled: 'I saw a little book *Des saines affections* (*On the Healthy Passions*) that pleased me a lot for it was full of beautiful and solemn sayings to strengthen our spirits in such an age as this. It made me want to re-read the Stoics and look for consolation there'.[37] The anonymous little commonplace book called *Des saines affections* was published under L'Angelier's privilege at least three times.[38] The *Saines affections*, which inspired Du Vair, were

---

[36] Du Vair stayed in Paris throughout the siege, but eventually moved to the Parlement of Aix as *premier président* (1596) and later became Bishop of Lisieux: see Fleury Vindry, *Les parlementaires français au XVIe siècle*, 2 vols (Paris, 1910–12), vol. I, pp. 21–2; see the unparalleled sketch of Du Vair's life and family in Robert Descimon, 'Guillaume Du Vair (1556–1621): les enseignements d'une biographie sociale. La construction symbolique d'un grand homme et l'échec d'un lignage', in B. Petey-Girard and A. Tarrête (eds), *Guillaume du Vair: parlementaire et écrivain (1556–1621)* (Geneva, 2005), pp. 17–77.

[37] 'Au Lecteur', in Guillaume Du Vair, *Le Manuel d'Epictète* (Paris: Abel L'Angelier, 1591), sig. Aij^r or p. 2; René Radouant, *Guillaume Du Vair L'homme et l'orateur jusqu'à la fin des troubles de la Ligue 1556–1596* (Paris, 1907), p. 145, n, 3: 'J'ay veu vn petit liure des saines affections, qui m'a bien pleu, pour estre plein de belles & graues sentences, pour affermir noz esprits en vn tel temps que cestui-cy. Il m'a faict enuie de repasser sur les liures des Stoïques, & y cercher quelque consolation'.

[38] Since the 1990s there has been a flurry of research on the publication history of *Des saines affections* and its probable author Madeleine de L'Aubespine (1546–96). Madeleine de L'Aubespine was the daughter of a secretary of state serving the king, and was married in her teens to Nicolas de Villeroy, Sieur de Neufville, who succeeded his father-in-law and served several kings in the same role. For many years *Des saines affections* was attributed to Marie de Gournay or Marie Le Gendre (in part because the moral *discours* published in the early 1590s were combined in 1595 with further essays on similar themes under the title *Cabinet des saines affections* and the name Marie Le Gendre, Dame de Rivery. See Louis Loviot, 'Cabinet des saines affections 1595', *Revue de livres anciens* 2 (1916): 274–82; Evelyne Berriot-Salvadore, 'Marie le Gendre et Marie de Gournay, à la manière de …', in Ilana Zinguer, (ed.), *Le lecteur, l'auteur et l'écrivain, Montaigne 1492–1592–1992. Actes du colloque international de Haïfa* (Paris, 1993), pp. 237–51. Initial research on the publication history of the *Saines affections* separated the identity of Marie le Gendre from the author of the *Saines affections* and pointed to Madeleine de L'Aubespine as the probable author: see Lyndan Warner, 'Marie Le Gendre, the *Saines affections* and Moral Thought in the Late Sixteenth Century', in P. Ford and G. Jondorf (eds), *Women Writers in the French Renaissance: Proceedings of the Fifth Cambridge French Colloquium* (Cambridge, 1999), pp. 221–38. Jean Balsamo made precisions about the publication dates of the *Saines affections*, establishing with Michel Simonin the first edition as 1591 (with Abel L'Angelier as the unnamed but probable publisher), further L'Angelier editions in 1593, 1594, and another in 1600 as the *Parfaictes affections*: see Jean Balsamo, 'Abel L'Angelier et ses dames: les Dames des Roches, Madeleine de L'Aubespine, Marie le Gendre, Marie de Gournay', in D. de Courcelles and Carmen Val Julián (eds), *Des femmes et des livres: France and Espagnes, XIVe–XVIIe siècle* (Paris, 1999), pp. 117–36; Balsamo and Simonin, *Abel L'Angelier*, cat. nos. 223, 229, 239, 343. Colette Winn published a critical edition of *Des saines affections* under the title *Cabinet des saines affections*, borrowed from the 1595 edition that led to the confusion in modern scholarship about the identity of the author

18 *discours* on topics such as vanity, prosperity, adversity, sadness, friendship, on how to govern one's life, how to cope with one's children or the inability to have children, and how to understand that each person whether rich or poor, noble or of humble rank, is a 'prisoner of fortune'.[39] These meditations on the dignity and misery of the human condition, examined in the Introduction and chapter three, are attributed to Madeleine de L'Aubespine, a salon hostess in Paris who was the daughter of Claude de L'Aubespine, Secretary of State under Henri II, and the wife of Nicolas de Neufville, Sieur de Villeroy, the Secretary of State under Charles IX and Henri III before he experienced a spectacular fall from grace in 1588, only to rise again in the service of Henri IV.[40] During the crisis years of the siege of Paris, L'Angelier produced two books in 1590, four in 1591 (including Du Vair's stoic manual of Epictetus with its letter to the reader about a little book, the *Saines affections*), two in 1592 and four in 1593, a dramatic decline in production when compared to the 31 books the Palais de Justice bookseller published in the year 1584. The anonymous *Saines affections* was published in 1591, during these years of hardship when so few books were produced at all, and preceded L'Angelier editions in 1593, 1594 and 1600 under the title *Parfaictes affections*.

Other L'Angelier productions leading into this era included Étienne Pasquier's letters published in 1586, examined in the Introduction and chapter three, which contained letters of advice on marriage, letters addressed to female friends, letters about the clash of dignity and fortune, ambition, the choice of vocation, political

because it combined the 18 anonymous *discours* of the *Saines affections* (now attributed to Madeleine de L'Aubespine) with the works of Marie Le Gendre, Dame de Rivery. See [Madeleine de L'Aubespine], *Cabinet des saines affections*, ed. Colette Winn (Paris, 2001), and the separate publication, Marie Le Gendre, *L'exercice de l'âme vertueuse*, ed. Colette Winn (Paris, 2001).

Isabelle de Conihout (working with Pascal de Ract-Madoux) has been conducting fascinating research on the personal library of Madeleine de L'Aubespine at the Conflans estate she shared with her husband Nicolas de Villeroy: see Isabelle de Conihout and Pascal Ract-Madoux, 'Ni Grolier, Ni Mahieu, Laubespine', *Bulletin du bibliophile* (2004): 63–88; Isabelle de Conihout, 'La "belle librarie" évanouie de Nicolas de Villeroy retrouvée', in I. de Conihout, *et al.* (eds), *Henri III mécène: des arts, des sciences et des lettres* (Paris, 2006), pp. 318–29. Anna Klosowska has edited and translated her poetry and brought to light more information about her relationships with poets of her time such as Ronsard and Desportes: see Madeleine de L'Aubespine, *Selected Poems and Translations: A Bilingual Edition*, ed. and trans. Anna Klosowska (Chicago, IL, 2007); Anna Klosowska, 'Madeleine de l'Aubespine: Life, Works, and Auto-Mythography: An Exchange with Ronsard, ca. 1570–80', *French Forum* 32:1–2 (2007): 19–38. Jean Balsamo has further analysed *Des saines affections* to underline the influence of Plutarch and Seneca as sources of the collection: see '*Des saines affections* (1591) et le syncrétisme philosophique dans la culture de cour sous Henri III et Henri IV', *Journal de la Renaissance* 6 (2008): 23–36.

39 [Madeleine de L'Aubespine], *Des saines affections* (Paris: Abel L'Angelier, 1593), sigs Dij^{r-v}, Ciij^{r-v}.

40 Anna Klosowska, 'Introduction', in L'Aubespine, *Selected Poems*, p. 7.

events, royal edicts and the consequences of the conduct of widows.[41] Pasquier confessed to his lawyer friend Loisel that the title *Les Lettres d'Estienne Pasquier* might not please everyone because some might think this mix of topics 'not suitable for missives' or that he wrote too boldly 'of the age, of the State, of households'.[42] Madeleine and Catherine des Roches of Poitiers' printed collection of *Missives* appeared only five or six weeks after Pasquier's *Lettres* left the press, and he shared his delight with Loisel about L'Angelier's near simultaneous 'publication of our letters'.[43] Loisel and Pasquier had visited the salon of this mother and daughter during the *Grands Jours* when a delegation of lawyers, judges and clerks from the Parlement de Paris spent the autumn of 1579 at Poitiers to clear up a backlog of court cases and appeals caused by the civil wars. Pasquier, Catherine des Roches and other contributors produced a series of poems on *The Flea*, later published by L'Angelier, using the occasion of a flea landing on Catherine's breast as a starting point.[44] The works of Du Bartas, the Dames des Roches, Du Vair, Pasquier's *Lettres*, Montaigne's *Essais* and the anonymous *Saines affections* were among the *nouveautés* or contemporary works of literature and moral philosophy in the 1580s and early 1590s that complemented the legal manuals and financial guidebooks meant for the professional readers. These titles were valuable enough to his business that in November 1593 L'Angelier petitioned the Parlement de Paris to have Lyon printers respect his privileges for Montaigne's *Essais*, Pasquier's *Lettres* and translations by Guillaume du Vair. The court ordered the confiscation of the counterfeit copies.[45]

In 1594, as book production began to recover from the siege of Paris, L'Angelier published – apart from Gelée's *Annotations*, speeches by Antoine Loisel and a new issue of the *Saines affections* – a new title in the *Querelle des femmes*: the *Defensive Paradox Where it is Faithfully Demonstrated that Woman is a lot more Perfect than Man in all Virtuous Action.* Alexandre de Pontaymeri dedicated this *Paradoxe apologique* to Catherine de Clermont, the Maréchale de Retz and prominent hostess of a literary salon that Madeleine de L'Aubespine as well as

[41] Étienne Pasquier, *Les Lettres d'Estienne Pasquier conseiller et advocat general du roy en la Chambre des comptes de Paris* (Paris: Abel L'Angelier, 1586), fos 54v–55r, 60v–62v; see Introduction, pp. 12–13, 16–17, and Chapter 3, p. 53.

[42] Etienne Pasquier, 'A Monsieur Loisel, Advocat en Parlement', in *Lettres familières*, ed. Thickett , X:12, p. 184.

[43] For an introduction to and translation of the des Roches' *Missives*, see Madeleine and Catherine des Roches, *From a Mother and Daughter: Poems, Dialogues and Letters of Les Dames des Roches*, ed. and trans. Anne Larsen (Chicago, IL, 2006), pp. 243–71.

[44] Kendall Tarte, *Writing Places: Sixteenth-Century City Culture and the Des Roches Salon* (Newark, DE, 2007), pp. 17–19, 26–36. On the Grands Jours de Poitiers and *La Puce* see Madeleine and Catherine des Roches, *Les Secondes Œuvres*, ed. Anne Larsen (Geneva, 1998), pp. 16–24, 108–22, 334.

[45] Pallier, *Recherches*, p. 515, document no. 207, 12 November 1599.

Pasquier attended on occasion.[46] Moreover, L'Angelier printed and distributed for the first time the *Walk* [*with*] *M. de Montaigne* (*Proumenoir de M. de Montaigne*) by the young Marie de Gournay, who had been one of the first readers to respond so enthusiastically to Montaigne's *Essais*.[47] In 1595, alongside another series of imprints on custom, law, finance and a reprint of the *Proumenoir*, the *Essais* of M. de Montaigne appeared again on the shelves of L'Angelier's boutique, this time in the posthumous version edited with a preface by Marie de Gournay. All these 1594–95 titles – the paradox on the female sex, Gournay's *Proumenoir* and Montaigne's *Essais* – were successful enough to merit several reprints and the renewal of privileges by L'Angelier to ensure his exclusivity. Another edition of the *Paradoxe apologique* on the female sex followed in 1596. In 1600 a further L'Angelier edition of L'Aubespine's *discours* on the human condition complemented yet another dialogue in the *Querelle des femmes* under his privilege: the *Discourse in Favour of Ladies against the Reproachers (Mesdisants). Disputed between two Ladies, Cleophile and Clorinde and a Gentleman named the Sieur Cloridan.*[48]

It is significant that new titles in the traditional *Querelle des femmes* format of arguing for and against the female sex and dialogues continued to appear for sale at booksellers' stalls. Yet more and more works musing on a variety of topics, mixing commonplaces and exempla, such as Montaigne's *Essais* or *Pasquier's Lettres*, or the *Saines affections*, began to take their places comfortably and repeatedly in the bookseller's stock and in the households of his customers. These titles adopted the approaches identified in chapters five and six of incorporating female exempla and reflections on woman and marriage to illuminate discussions of human nature across an expanding array of topics. In turn, these wide-ranging discussions of human excellence and folly, and governing one's conduct in facing adversity and overcoming vice, reflected woman's experience as well as man's.

---

46 L. Clark Keating, *Studies on the Literary Salon in France, 1550–1615* (Cambridge, MA, 1941), pp. 103–25, esp. 109–11; Étienne Pasquier, 'A Monsieur Airault, de Tours 1591' and 'A Madame de Rez', in *Œuvres*, vol. II, XV:2, cols 435–8; Alexandre de Pontaymeri, *Paradoxe apologique ou il est fidèllement demonstré que la Femme est beaucoup plus parfaicte que l'Homme en toute action de vertu* (Paris: Abel L'Angelier, 1594). On Retz's literary circle see Julie Campbell, *Literary Circles and Gender in Early Modern Europe: A Cross-Cultural Approach* (Aldershot, 2006), pp. 73–96.

47 Unfortunately, there is no room here to do justice to Marie de Gournay, her writing, the scholarship on her relationship to Montaigne or her influence on the posthumous edition of the *Essais*. For the best-rounded understanding of her life and works see Marie de Gournay, *Œuvres complètes*, eds J-C. Arnould, *et al.*, 2 vols (Paris, 2002).

48 *Discours en la faveur des dames, contre les mesdisans, disputé entre deux dames, Cleophile & Clorinde & un gentilhomme nommé le sieur Cloridan* (Paris: Abel L'Angelier, 1600). There is a ten-year privilege dated 6 May to L'Angelier. See P. Renouard MS, L'Angelier no. 259; Balsamo and Simonin, *Abel L'Angelier*, cat. no. 336. The 1594 copy of the *Paradoxe apologique* in the Bibliothèque de l'Arsenal is bound with this *Discours*.

Tracing the Female Reader in the Late Sixteenth Century

All four of the personal dedications in the *Essais* were addressed to women and, as discussed in chapter six, the longest of all essays, the *Apologie for Raimond Sebond*, is directed to a female reader.[49] Even as he concluded the 1580 edition, Montaigne expected that for Mme Duras the companionship of his book might be a substitute for his company, and when the memories of their visit together faded she could refresh her memory of him by reading the *Essais*.[50] Montaigne later sent a copy of his *Essais* as a gift to Mademoiselle Paulmier.[51] He expected his *Essais* to be read by women as well as men. By the time he wrote the third book of the *Essais*, Montaigne was aware of his female audience and played on it.

Locating and understanding the reading experiences of potential female readers of titles such as the *Essais* is exceedingly difficult. Susan Broomhall has used correspondence between sisters, husbands and wives and between female friends to document women's exchange of books and access to reading material. Jane Couchman has shown how the noblewoman Louise de Coligny was an avid reader of letters, but in her extensive correspondence she never mentions the many texts to which she had access in the library of the Orange-Nassau family and reveals only a few times the title of books or authors to which she was exposed.[52] Tracing women's book-reading practices in letter-writing and following book purchases and requests for titles becomes more promising for women as one approaches the eighteenth century.[53] Pollie Bromilow and Cathleen Bauschatz have explored

---

49 Cathleen Bauschatz, '"Leur plus universelle qualité, c'est la diversité": Women as Ideal Readers in Montaigne's *Essais*', *Journal of Medieval and Renaissance Studies* 19:1 (1989): 83–101; François Rigolot, 'D'une théologie "Pour les dames" à une apologie "per le donne"?', in Claude Blum (ed.), *Montaigne: Apologie de Raimond Sebond De la theologia à la Théologie* (Paris, 1990), pp. 261–90; N.Z. Davis, 'A Renaissance Text to the Historian's Eye: The Gifts of Montaigne', *Journal of Medieval and Renaissance Studies* 15 (1985): 47–56; Cottrell, 'Gender', pp. 85–96; see Chapter 6, pp. 155–6.

50 Montaigne, *Essais*, II:37 'De la ressemblance des enfans aux peres', p. 763A; Steven Rendall, *Distinguo: Reading Montaigne Differently* (Oxford, 1992), pp. 92–4.

51 Montaigne, *Œuvres*, Lettre XXXII, 'A Mademoiselle Paulmier', p. 1396. In the very short letter Montaigne mentions her husband twice, to acknowledge the debt and service Montaigne owes to him, but his book is intended for Mlle Paulmier.

52 Susan Broomhall, *Women and the Book Trade in Sixteenth-Century France* (Aldershot, 2002), pp. 28–30; Jane Couchman, 'La lecture et le lectorat dans la correspondance de Louise de Coligny', in Isabelle Brouard-Arends (ed.), *Lectrices d'Ancien Régime* (Rennes, 2003), pp. 400–401. We must resist the temptation to fabricate 'Definite Library Holdings' from the sources of a female author, which mars an otherwise fascinating account of reading in and readers of Hélisenne de Crenne's works: Diane Wood, *Hélisenne de Crenne: At the Crossroads of Renaissance Humanism and Feminism* (London, 2000), pp. 24–5.

53 Madeleine van Strien-Chardonneau, 'Une lectrice du XVIIIe siècle Belle de Zuylen / Isabelle de Charrière (1740–1805): Livres et pratiques de lecture à travers sa

representations of female readers in sixteenth-century fiction or in dedications as the imagined 'target public', but Bromilow and Bauschatz both acknowledge that these depictions of women reading in bed or in their cabinets – often written by male authors – do not substitute for the 'material reality of readership'. This is especially true given the expressed concerns to limit the range of available literature because according to the humanism of the era reading might influence women's actions just as it did for men.[54]

Daughters from literate households passed on humanist values, to their children as we saw in the Introduction when Madeleine de L'Hôpital urged her sons to pursue their studies with enthusiasm and rigour like their grandfather the former Chancellor.[55] Ironically we have the reading notes of the Chancellor Michel de l'Hôpital, carefully written in Latin and following Tacitus, Suetonius and Caesar page by page, interspersed with the occasional Greek, but there is no comparable source for the reading tastes and interests of his daughter.[56] Household accounts of noblewomen supply evidence of bookbinding, commissions for manuscripts, but also purchases of printed books.[57] Alternatively the inscriptions on a flyleaf indicate ownership of books by women from noble to humble trade backgrounds.[58] Nonetheless, the 'problem of identifying female book ownership' persists for historians of early modern book culture. As Cynthia Brown and Martha Driver attest, it is 'astonishing' that the 'accounts of the libraries of certain prominent female intellectuals, such as Marguerite de Navarre, have still not been recovered'.[59]

A variety of methods have been used to reconstruct the reading and book ownership of Madeleine de L'Aubespine, to whom the anonymous *Des Saines affections*, published at least three times by L'Angelier, is now attributed. A beauty and intellect celebrated by the poets Ronsard and Philippe Desportes, after 1570 she inherited some of the fine library of her brother, Claude III de L'Aubespine,

---

correspondance', in Brouard-Arends (ed.), *Lectrices*, pp. 177–86.

[54] Pollie Bromilow, 'Les femmes lectrices: de la fiction au seizième siècle: enjeux idéologiques d'un lieu commun', in Brouard-Arends (ed.), *Lectrices*, pp. 261, 263, 267; Cathleen Bauschatz, '"Le plaisir du texte" dans les *Dames Galantes* de Brantôme', in ibid., pp. 649–56.

[55] BN, MS Dupuy 194, letter 20, Madeleine de l'Hôpital to her sons, 5 May [no year].

[56] BN, MS Dupuy 491, 'Lettres, harangues, notes et minutes, en grande partie autographes, du chancelier Michel de l'Hospital', fos 83r–122v.

[57] Anne-Marie Legaré, 'Reassessing Women's Libraries in Late Medieval France: The Case of Jeanne de Laval', *Renaissance Studies* 10:2 (1996): 222.

[58] Broomhall, *Women*, pp. 36–40.

[59] Cynthia Brown and Martha Driver, 'Introduction: Women and Book Culture in Late Medieval and Early Modern France', *Journal of the Early Book Society for the Study of Manuscripts and Printing History. Special Focus: Women and Book Culture in Late Medieval and Early Modern France* 4 (2001): 2. This special issue contains a wealth of scholarship on female readers and book owners.

a secretary of state like her father and husband after his death. Isabelle Conihout and Pascal Ract-Madoux have been able to track many of Claude's purchases to the 1560s, though none later than 1569, and to the workshops of at least four bookbinders from 1565 to 1570.[60] The listing of books possessed at Madeleine de L'Aubespine's death in 1596 is missing, but the item numbers of the inventory were inscribed in brown ink on the books and Conihout has been able to trace about 90 of the at least 1,481 books known to have been in her possession through inheritance, gift or purchase. Madeleine's collection comprised mostly printed books (only five manuscripts are known so far) in the humanities and classics, architecture, medicine, history and geography, theology, Italian, architecture and literature, and she drew upon this vast library to compose her poetry and her advice on maintaining a tranquility of spirit when faced with the miseries of life. By 1617, when Madeleine's husband Nicolas de Villeroy died, their estate at Conflans housed an impressive library of 3,000 books, for which the inventory survives.[61]

Inventories are an imperfect source, but, as we have just reviewed, the types of evidence for female book ownership and women readers present a formidable challenge to the early modern researcher. Even for the libraries of 'professional' male readers, for whom we have notes, annotations and other types of evidence, the gaps in inventories are sometimes galling. For example, Du Bartas' *Première Sepmaine* and La Primaudaye's *French Academy* (*Académie françoise*) are two titles of the dignity- and misery-of-man literature dating from the 1580s owned by Claude Amelot, a Parlement de Paris lawyer when he died in the mid-1580s. Amelot had a sizeable library and although the inventory provides information about the author or title for about 124 of the volumes, a further 416 volumes are simply listed in 'packets' of 'diverse authors' or by format as big folio books or little 'in-octavo' and 'in-seize' pocket books.[62] This is where many of the titles of history, moral philosophy, poetry and literature might be lurking.[63]

Nevertheless, for the sixteenth century inventories survive for a wider social range of households than other types of sources for book ownership and they can be used to sample either this broad spectrum of households or to focus on a specific social band such as royal officeholders.[64] In some particular instances, inheritance,

---

60 Conihout and Ract-Madoux, 'Ni Grolier', p. 85; Conihout, 'La "belle librarie"', p. 324.

61 Conihout and Ract-Madoux, 'Ni Grolier', p. 77.

62 MC, AN, Paris, post-mortem inventory of Claude Amelot, lawyer, 20 January 1584, LXXXVII, 66.

63 Roger Doucet, *Les bibliothèques parisiennes au XVIe siècle* (Paris, 1956), p. 11.

64 Annie Charon, 'Les grandes collections du XVIe siècle', and Pierre Aquilon, 'Petites et moyennes bibliothèques (1530–1660)', in Claude Jolly (ed.), *Histoire des bibliothèques françaises*, vol. II, *Les bibliothèques sous l'Ancien Régime 1530–1789*, 4 vols (Paris, 1988–1992), vol. II, pp. 85–99, 180–205; Albert Labarre, *Le livre dans la vie amiénoise du seizième siècle: l'enseignement des inventaires après décès, 1503–1576* (Paris, 1971); A.H. Schutz, *Vernacular Books in Parisian Private Libraries in the Sixteenth Century According*

marital separation, the location of the books in the household or at a separate country property, allow us to access the titles that may have been available to wives and daughters, although again, it is hard to say anything definitive about men's and women's reading practices from the inventories.

Using a series of probate inventories from 1540 to 1610 gathered from notaries' offices (*études*) in Paris, I did a broad count looking for book ownership in over 750 households. Almost one in five Parisian households with sufficient means to warrant an inventory, from humble tailors to well-born hereditary nobles, possessed at least one book – a finding similar to the rates of early modern book ownership calculated by Roger Chartier and Albert Labarre.[65] Not surprisingly, a higher rate of at least 75 per cent of the households of *gens de justice* such as clerks, attorneys, notaries and lawyers, and all the way up the social scale to *noblesse de robe* officeholders, active in the area around the Palais de Justice, possessed books.

From these probate or post-mortem inventories, we only get occasional glimpses into the reading lives of early modern women. As we move beyond the mid-century, female signatures (as well as male signatures) on the inventories become more common as the practice of witnessing the inventory changed. One clue as to literacy is the signature of the 'parties' and the 'witnesses' to any contract, inventory or act drawn up by a notary. From 1560, notaries were required to have the parties and witnesses sign and to indicate if the parties could not sign. By 1579, the royal ordinance of Blois assumes that in the large towns and cities 'most probably one could have witnesses who know how to sign'. If there was a party unable to sign the notaries were required to find an additional witness to sign the act and to indicate the 'quality', residence and parish of the parties and witnesses to the act.[66] Of course, a female signature does not necessarily mean a female

---

to the Notarial Inventories (Chapel Hill, NC, 1955); Hélène Michaud, 'Les bibliothèques des secrétaires du roi au XVIe siècle', *Bibliothèque de l'Ecole des chartes* 126 (1968): 333–76; M. Connet and J. Megret. 'Inventaire de la bibliothèque des du Prat', *Bibliothèque d'Humanisme et Renaissance* 3 (1943): 72–128.

[65] See Labarre's admirable analysis of book ownership in sixteenth-century Amiens, *Le livre*; Roger Chartier, *Lecteurs & lectures dans la France d'Ancien Régime* (Paris, 1987). My research on 'private libraries in early modern Paris', based on probate inventories from the Minutier central des notaires de Paris in the AN, will be published separately. I sampled across a range of notarial *études*, then focused more closely on bookowners among the artisans and trades, the merchants and the bourgeois de Paris, the nobility, students and faculty, but especially the *gens de justice* and officeholders. I noted and then put aside the probate inventories of clergy and workers in the book trade.

[66] François A. Isambert (ed.), *Recueil général des anciennes lois françaises depuis l'an 420 jusqu'à la Révolution de 1789*, 29 vols (Paris, 1822–33), ordinance of Orléans, January 1560, article 83, vol. XIV, p. 85, and ordinance of Blois, May 1579, articles 165–7, vol. XIV, part II, pp. 420–21; Robert Descimon, 'Les notaires de Paris du XVIe au XVIIIe siècle: office, profession, archives', in Michael Cassan (ed.), *Offices et officiers 'moyens' en France à l'époque moderne* (Limoges, 2004), p. 36; Florence Greffe and Valérie Brousselle,

reader, although it is a clue to one kind of literacy. The inventories are instructive, but it is nevertheless difficult to prove in a 'systematic' way that a wife, mother or daughter had access to books in a household or the inclination to read them.[67] Nevertheless, a sketch of women at least as owners of books does begin to emerge in the details.

In chapters two, three and four we encountered the Châtelet de Paris notary Gilbert de Hodic and his wife Geneviève Bureau who were avid collectors of the literature of the *Querelle des femmes* and appear to have been regular visitors to the booksellers on the Île de la Cité in the early decades of the sixteenth century. In their Paris house Hodic owned over 400 volumes, while his wife had a separate collection of 50 volumes of French books that she 'declared to be for her use'. The marketplace of the Palais de Justice continued to be of interest among this social milieu. In the second half of the century, Ysabeau de la Fontaine, a 'noble' widow living on the rue de la Calendre, arranged for Galliot Corrozet from the well-known Palais de Justice book trade family to inventory and assess the worth of the books in the study of her recently deceased husband Guillaume Martin, a lawyer in the Parlement de Paris. Martin, with Étienne Pasquier and Antoine Loisel, had been part of the delegation from the Parlement de Paris that participated in the Grands Jours de Poitiers in the autumn of 1579.[68] By 1591 Martin's library had become so large it took Corrozet three afternoons to complete the assessment. Ysabeau de la Fontaine was clearly literate and even her daughter Geneviève, a minor, witnessed and signed the inventory while her son, also a minor, did not. Another son had held a position as a clerk in the Chambre des comptes but had predeceased his father, so his widow, La Fontaine's daughter-in-law, signed and witnessed the inventory on behalf of La Fontaine's granddaughter. In the Martin household, works of contemporary French literature and moral philosophy share the library with an extensive collection of legal books and the classics in Latin. Isabeau, her daughter Geneviève, and possibly her daughter-in-law or granddaughter had available to them many books sold by Abel L'Angelier such as Montaigne's *Essais*, the *Lettres* of Etienne Pasquier, or the poetry of Jacques Yver's playful *Printemps d'Yver* reflecting on woman's nature, one of the first books published by L'Angelier in 1572, and again in 1578.[69]

Some libraries in the sixteenth century seem to be located in a study or cabinet, a predominately male preserve, where one might find a 'harquebuse' or other

---

'Introduction', in F. Greffe and V. Brousselle (eds), *Documents du Minutier central des notaires de Paris: Inventaires après décès (1547–1560)* (Paris, 1997), p. 10.

[67] Mary C. Erler, *Women, Reading, and Piety in Late Medieval England* (Cambridge, 2002), p. 3; David McKitterick, 'Women and their Books in Seventeenth-Century England: The Case of Elizabeth Puckering', *The Library* 1 (2000): 363–4.

[68] AN, Grands Jours de Poitiers, Plaidoiries, X1a 9208, fos 202r–204v.

[69] AN, MC, post-mortem inventory of Guillaume Martin, lawyer at the Parlement de Paris, 10 June 1591, XXIII, 135.

weapons as well as maps of the world.[70] Sometimes, however, a devotional book or a book of hours can be found among the linens with scissors and sewing equipment or in a separate room; and from their placement in the inventory, we can infer that they might have belonged to the lady of the household.[71] More rarely, if a family was wealthy enough for mothers or daughters to have their own rooms separate from communal spaces, the inventory might reveal their reading interests. When Nicolas Luiller died, the inventory of the household listed 40 books in his daughter Anne's private sitting room and about a dozen books possessed by his wife Charlotte de Livres. As Barbara Diefendorf explains, both Luiller and his son had their own studies full of legal books, but apart from the mostly vernacular books read by the mother and daughter, Anne had 'her own copy of the Paris customary law' and Charlotte possessed 'two volumes of Ordinances of the city of Paris'.[72] In the household of Ysabeau Marron and her husband Jehan de la Robertière, a lawyer in the Parlement and also professor of law at the University of Paris, many familiar titles in French such as Du Bartas' *Première Sepmaine* and Mexia's *Diverse leçons* shared space with the law books in 1585. So many of the 158 titles were in French, about 50 per cent, that Pierre Aquilon has suggested they might represent the interests of this literate wife from a background of financial officeholders.[73]

When the *greffier* François de Courtin died in 1609, as we saw above, he owned many recent legal titles for which Abel L'Angelier held the privilege, and was a probable customer of the Palais de Justice bookseller. Courtin's widow Marie de Corde, who signed and witnessed the inventory, might have immersed herself in the octavo edition of Montaigne's *Essais* in her household. Although it is tempting to infer reading from the book ownership, the inventory reveals that Marie de Corde's husband left her with five children under the age of 5 – the youngest only three weeks old. We shall probably never know whether, with the help of servants and probably a wetnurse, Marie had the opportunity to be an engaged reader of the *Essais* in her possession.

The sisters Jane and Catherine de Mansencal describe to 'devout ladies' how, when faced with a similar situation, their mother, a widow with two toddlers, maintained the household after her husband, a presiding judge (*président*) of the

---

70 Chantal Turbide has studied the books needed for royal duties or management of noble properties in the exceptional case of the former Queen Regent: 'Les livres trouvé dans l'Hôtel de la Reine après le décès de Catherine de Médicis (1519–1589)', in Brouard-Arends (ed.), *Lectrices*, pp. 33–45.

71 AN, MC, post-mortem inventory of Damoiselle Renée Gesbert, widow of defunct Martin Berruyer notary and *sécretaire du roi*, 10 January 1571[2], VI, 77; AN, MC, post-mortem inventory of 'honourable' Anne Roussel, widow of Claude Henry, merchant and bourgeois de Paris, June 1585, III, 192.

72 Barbara Diefendorf, *Paris City Councillors in the Sixteenth Century: The Politics of Patrimony* (Princeton, NJ, 1983), p. 178.

73 Pierre Aquilon, 'La bibliothèque de Jean de la Rebertière', in Jean Céard (ed.), *Langage et vérité* (Geneva, 1993), pp. 213, 218–19, 221.

Parlement of Toulouse, Pierre de Mansencal, died in the early 1570s.[74] They claim that Gabrielle de Coignard 'during her widowhood having to rule her daughters and govern the household, knew so well how to manage (*mesnager*) the hours of the day, the gifts and intelligence she had received from the heavens that she made these Christian verses [as] witnesses to the virtuous thoughts she maintained in her mind and in her leisure'.[75] Gabrielle was the daughter of Jean Coignard, a judge (*conseiller*) at the Parlement de Toulouse and the *maître* of the *Jeux floraux* poetry contest from 1535 to 1555, years when Gratien Dupont, the Sieur de Drusac and author of the *Controversies of the Masculine and Feminine Sexes*, was active. From a social milieu of royal officeholders, Coignard's literacy seems to have been passed on to her daughters before she died in 1586 when they were still in their teens.[76]

High-ranking noble women such as Madeleine de L'Aubespine were active in the world of literary salons and had access to hundreds and sometimes thousands of books. A few such as L'Aubespine, the Dames des Roches, Gournay made the transition from the circulation of manuscripts to the printed page, all published by L'Angelier. Among this circle of birth nobles serving the king, or provincial nobles, or families achieving officeholder status, we have varied but firm evidence of female literacy with interests ranging from devotional works to moral philosophy, but a much sketchier idea of actual reading practices.

Access to Books on Human Nature in the Bourgeois to 'Noble' Household

In chapters two, three and four we reviewed the works of the *Querelle des femmes* and the dignity and misery of man of the first half of the sixteenth century and the types of households in which these texts could be found. For the evolving literature of the second half of the century, explored in chapters five and six, which began to combine male and female exempla in collections of dialogues, lessons, 'strange cases', *discours* and essays of moral philosophy, we need to turn to inventories of the late sixteenth and early seventeenth centuries. We have already seen in this chapter tracing the female reader and male 'professional' reading practices the many L'Angelier legal titles and new literary offerings such as Montaigne's *Essais* and Pasquier's *Letters* available in the households of royal officeholders as well as notaries and lawyers.

---

74 Vindry, *Les parlementaires*, vol. II, pp. 142, 144.

75 Jane and Catherine de Mansencal, 'Aux Dames Devotieuses', in Gabrielle de Coignard, *Œuvres chrestiennes* (Tournon: Jaques Faure, 1595): 'laquelle durant son veuvage ayant à commander des filles, & a gouverner sa maison sceut si bien mesnager, & les heures du iour, & les graces, d'entendement qu'elle avoit receu du ciel, qu'elle fit en ces vers Chrestiens tesmoins des vertueuses pensees dont elle entretenoit son esprit, & son loisir.'

76 Gabrielle de Coignard, *Spiritual Sonnets: A Bilingual Edition*, trans. Melanie Gregg (Chicago, IL, 2004), pp. 4–5.

The inventories of the late 1580s and early 1590s relating to the Parlement de Paris lawyer Jacques Malingre and his wife Anne Bobye provide a possible insight into the range of reading material available in households from varying degrees of social rank. Anne Bobye's father stemmed from a merchant background and her marriage to Jacques Malingre, designated as a 'noble homme', appears to reflect her family's aspiration for upward mobility. But there must have been some difficulties in the marriage because after about ten years and at least two living children, 'honnorable femme' Anne Bobye separated 'in goods' from Malingre.[77] The inventories of separate properties make it clear to us which books were available to Bobye and which books were for her husband's use and provide an excellent comparison of the type of reading available in the household of a lawyer and 'noble', in contrast with the types of books available in a household from a more 'bourgeois' background.

The inventory at Malingre's Parisian residence at Port St Landry reveals a rather cosy little study. The lawyer had an oak desk with drawers, a table for his 'papers', a shabby rug, a small desk, a mirror, five little bed ticks or mattresses, a Flemish-style trunk, two stools, and two maps including one of the 'universal world'. Malingre hung a portrait of himself on the wall, a little painting depicting the story of the chastity of Suzanne, as well as religious imagery of 'our Lady' and 'our Lord'.[78] In Malingre's book collection over 60 of 118 titles, such as the 'old and worn' six-volume set of civil law, relate to legal matters.[79] Malingre's interest in the *Treatise on the Dissolution of Marriage for Reasons of Impotence* is noteworthy considering his marital status, although it relates to a famous case before the Parlement de Paris when the lawyer Étienne Pasquier represented the wife in a request for dissolution of a marriage.[80] For leisure, and perhaps to embellish the odd pleading in Parlement, his taste ran to the classics in Latin and French. The inventory-takers note that Malingre's *Lives of Plutarch* was 'worn' and his Holy Bible in Latin was even more 'worn'. He owned Juvenal's *Satires* in Latin and French, and not only Erasmus' *Praise of Folly* but the *Adages* (*Chiliades*) in Latin

---

77 On the range of labels attached to each social status see Robert Descimon, "Un langage de la dignité. La qualification des personnes dans la société parisienne de l'époque moderne', in Fanny Cosandey (ed.), *Dire et vivre l'ordre social en France sous l'Ancien Régime* (Paris, 2005), pp. 69–123, esp. the table compiled by Laurence Croq and Descimon, reflecting how these social epithets changed over the early modern periods, pp. 66–7.

78 AN, MC, Post-mortem inventory of Jacques Malingre, lawyer at the Parlement de Paris, 27 February 1591, XXIII, 135.

79 Inventory [marital] community of goods, Jacques Malingre, lawyer at the Parlement de Paris, 20 February 1590, XXIII, 134; AN, MC, inventory, XXIII, 135, 27 February 1591.

80 Antoine Hotman, *Traicté sur la dissolution de mariage par l'impuissance et froideur de l'homme ou de la femme* (Paris: Mamert Patisson chez Robert Estienne, 1581); Paul Bouteiller, 'Étienne Pasquier avocat au Parlement de Paris (1549–1585)', *Bulletin de la Société de l'histoire de Paris et de l'Île de France* 117 (1990): 59–60.

as well. While he could consult Cicero's speeches in French, Malingre balanced his collection with Dolet's *De imitationis Ciceronianis*.

Despite the protestations of his wife, from whom he was separated 'in goods', Malingre arranged for another inventory of the property occupied by Anne Bobye with particular attention paid to her parents' possessions.[81] The inventories coincided with the death of Anne Bobye's mother Marie Maheut in 1590 and Anne Bobye was the sole heir of her parents. As a widow Marie would have had exclusive access to a modest collection of books, although we do not know by how long her husband, a merchant and *bourgeois de Paris*, had predeceased her. Anne protested the inventory as unnecessary because in her view the inheritance from her parents did not belong to the marital community of goods. Her husband, however, insisted and the inventory of Anne's inheritance was taken at her husband's expense as part of the inventories of the two properties. Both Malingre and Anne Bobye signed inventories of the two properties so we know that Bobye could write in a steady hand. Two female servants were instrumental in pointing out to the notaries the possessions from the estate of Bobye's parents.

In Anne's household the notaries found that some possessions had been rescued from the soldiers or 'gents de guerre' threatening the area around her parents' country house in Meudon during the civil wars. Among the articles listed in the inventory we find the 'Books of Pierre Bobye and Marie Maheut his wife, father and mother of the said Anne'. The two dozen titles owned by the Bobye family reveal a strong interest in questions of moral philosophy and included two illuminated manuscript books of hours. Apart from a huge tome of 'old ordinances' and some extremely popular titles such as Nicole Gilles' *Annales de France*, during the civil wars the Bobye family could read Jean de Marconville's *Recueil memorable d'aucuns cas merveilleux advenuz de noz ans, et d'aucunes choses estranges & monstrueuses advenües ès siècles passez*. Marconville's collection of strange or prodigious tales, which we discussed in chapter six, range from a discussion of human misery, the misery of civil war, the misery of each estate, to examples of good and bad women.[82] Marconville's treatises were sold by Jean Dallier on the Pont St Michel connecting the Île de la Cité to the university quarter in the 1560s and 1570s. Similarly, the Bobye family's copy of Jacques Tahureau's *Dialogues* on human nature, the nobility, the law, medicine and the 'woman question', which we examined in chapter five, might have provided some leisure reading from the 1560s onwards. The family also owned a bilingual Latin–French edition of Vives'

---

[81] AN, MC, inventory, XXIII, 134, 20 February 1590. The inventory does not indicate an address, but a Pierre Bobye, on rue des Marmouzets, rented a house to Gilles Corrozet in 1562: Pichon and Vicaire, *Bulletin du bibliophil*e (1894): 40. Malingre had property on the rue des Marmouzets at his death in 1591.

[82] Jean de Marconville, *Recueil memorable d'aucuns cas merveilleux advenuz de noz ans, avec autre sommaire recueil d'aucunes choses estranges & monstrueuses advenües ès siècles passez* (Paris: Jean Dallier, 1564).

dialogues.[83] Both Tahureau's and Vives' dialogues were available from the Paris bookseller Gabriel Buon in the 1560s and '70s or for sale in Antwerp. In 1568, a bookseller in Antwerp packaged Jean de Marconville's *De la bonté and mauvaistié des femmes* with Tahureau's *Dialogues*, evidently capitalising on the *Querelle des femmes* aspect of the Cosmophile and the Democritic's discussion. And one can forever wonder whether the copy of Tahureau's dialogues in the Bobye household might have been the Antwerp edition that combined it with Marconville's *De la bonté et mauvaistié des femmes*, given the presence of another Marconville title among the collection.[84] The biblical and emblem book of morals, the *Figures et quadrins historicques de la bible*, available from Jean de Tournes' press in Lyon might have provided solace and moral guidance in the troubled years of civil war. A recent purchase dating from the late 1580s, and one available from Abel L'Angelier in the Palais de Justice, was Guillaume du Vair's *Traicte de la saincte philosophie*. The inventory-takers clearly note that the book is by Du Vair although the work was first published anonymously.[85] Did someone in the Bobye family purchase Guillaume du Vair's stoic treatise from the Palais de Justice bookseller two to three years before Marie Maheut's death? Anne's signature to both of the inventories provides another clue to her level of literacy, but of course we cannot say for certain that she read the inherited books or purchased her own.

The female reader is far more challenging to trace than her male counterpart even within the upper reaches of society. Her access to books is much harder to prove than for the sons and husbands whose 'cabinets' or 'studies' are clearly indicated in many inventories and whose training in the commonplace book method of reading is well documented.[86] Even the reading interests, personal library, the poetry, translations, moral philosophy written by Madeleine de L'Aubespine, a daughter, sister and wife of secretaries of state and prominent salon hostess, are still under discovery. The male professional reader and the humanist are familiar creatures to us, with known interests in the classics, history, rhetorical and legal manuals and *nouveautés* or new titles in French literature. By studying their annotations on legal cases, their manuscript notes and reading practices, by tracing literary connections in humanist letters, by comparing the

---

83 Juan Luis Vives, *Les Dialogues de Jan loys Vives, traduits de latin en françois, pour l'exercice des deux langues, par Benjamin Jamin ... ausquels est ajoustée l'explication françoise des mots latins* (Paris: Gabriel Buon, 1573). Buon sold a small in-16 edition, but the work was also printed in Antwerp in 1571 and Nancy in 1573.

84 Sold in Antwerp in an in-16 format by Pierre Vibert from 1568, see Jacques Tahureau, *Les Dialogues: non moins profitables que facetieux* [1565], ed. Max Gauna (Geneva, 1981), p. lxi.

85 Abel L'Angelier published anonymous 1587 and 1588 editions: see Balsamo and Simonin, *Abel L'Angelier*, cat. nos. 173, 199; Guillaume du Vair, *De la sainte philosophie* (Paris, 1946), p. 115, n. 2.

86 Ann Moss, *Printed Commonplace-Books and the Structuring of Renaissance Thought* (Oxford, 1996).

detailed probate inventories with the catalogues of Palais de Justice booksellers, as we have done in this chapter, we can even determine some lawyers, clerks or officeholders as readers of books from and probable customers of Palais de Justice booksellers such as Abel L'Angelier. The female owners of books, particularly from a merchant or *bourgeois* background, such as Anne Bobye or her mother Marie Maheut, remain elusive and their reading practices even more so. Tracing the books from compilation practices of the writers (as we did in chapter six) to the editorial policies of the booksellers in the marketplace and into the households provides the opportunity to understand how owners collected their books through inheritance, purchase or gift and, where the evidence allows, how they might have read or understood them in the unstable social and political world of the late sixteenth century.

To continue on this theme in chapter eight, let us now turn back to the 'professional' reader, especially the lawyer, whom we encountered in the first half of this chapter and consider how he might put his reading practices to use in the courtroom.

Chapter 8
Rhetoric, Print and Lawyers' Pleadings in the Parlement de Paris

In the sixteenth century the courts of justice were filled with people who failed to live up to the ideals set out in royal edicts governing family and marriage or the ideals of the Renaissance man of dignity and the modest, chaste wife who was his companion. Lawyers in particular made a trade out of human misery, and their working papers, consultations and pleadings were reminders of the human propensity for vice. Pride, avarice, greed and lust could be found in abundance in lawsuits between siblings over a share of an inheritance, in cases pitting widows against their relatives or in appeals where an impotent husband failed to impose himself as master and head of household. This chapter focuses on both the court registers as well as the printed versions of lawyers' pleadings and judicial decisions to examine early modern rhetorical practices in the Parlement de Paris. Lawyers borrowed examples from moral philosophy, history, classical and patristic literature to captivate the interest of the judges and set the tone in a case, either by accentuating the virtues and actions of a client, or by magnifying the vices and misdeeds of the opposing party.

It is helpful to remember that early modern lawyers, jurists, officeholders and notaries were immersed in a culture of paradox. Lawyers in particular inhabited a world where they confronted both sides of an argument on a daily basis. They were hired to speak on one side and to know how to refute or respond to counter-arguments made by the lawyers for the opposing party. This way of thinking was familiar from the early modern paradoxes and dialogues and the art of speaking on both sides of an argument (*in utramque partem*) that we have examined in this book – exploring vice and virtue, dignity and misery, the superiority or inferiority of woman relative to man. Of course many of the writers in the *Querelle des femmes*, on the dignity and misery of man and on human nature, such as Gratien Dupont, the Seigneur de Cholières, Guillaume du Bartas, Étienne Pasquier, Guillaume du Vair, Michel de Montaigne, had experience as lawyers or judges.

The pleading strategies of lawyers in two appeals to the Parlement de Paris are scrutinised in detail in this chapter. The first appeal follows a noblewoman through four stages of life as a daughter, wife, widow and remarried woman. The second case involves a nobleman in his various roles as master of a household, as a companion or lover, as a father, husband and brother. Both cases hold up to the cold light of day the early modern ideals of the family and household as well as the virtues and vices explored in debates on the dignity and misery of man and in the *Querelle des femmes*. Oral pleadings by lawyers before the great sovereign courts such as the Parlement de Paris highlighted the performance of the lawyer before a panel of judges. The written summaries of pleadings in the court registers (*registres*) recorded the parties to the suit, their lawyers' names, the *procureur général du roi* or one of his deputies who spoke on behalf of the king to protect the state interests, as well as the eventual *arrêt* or judicial decision in the appeal. As we saw in chapter seven, versions of 'famous pleadings' and summaries of judicial decisions circulated in manuscript as well as in print and were annotated and marked up as working copies by royal officeholders, or by lawyers such as François Pithou or Pierre Dupuy.

This chapter compares the pleadings recorded by clerks in the court registers with the versions circulating in print because this juxtaposition allows us to understand how making the leap to print allowed for amplification of the pleadings. The printed versions of these oral pleadings often expanded the examples of vice and virtue by imitating and borrowing from classical literature, history, the *Querelle des femmes* texts or collections of lessons on human nature. Printing lawyers' speeches and judicial decisions was an emerging genre at the end of the sixteenth- and in the early seventeenth century. These printed pleadings with their 'rhetoric of citation' and practice of *inventio* became more and more like the literary titles of the *Querelle des femmes* and *nouveautés* on human nature also for sale at the bookstalls of the Palais de Justice.

Printing Lawyers' Pleadings and the 'Rhetoric of Citation'

In certain instances, the pleadings reproduced in print are virtually identical to the court registers of the Parlement de Paris and the reader can place more faith in the printed account if the editor has indicated 'extracted from the registers of Parlement'.[1] At times the court registers follow the long-winded lawyers, page after page, while the print version only presents the highlights.[2] The printed collections of the pleadings of a lawyer or king's attorney-general were often expanded and amplified more than the bare recording of the court registers, especially when

[1] Archives nationales de France [hereafter AN], Registres, Parlement de Paris, Civil, Plaidoiries, X1a 5071, 16 July 1577, fos 470v–489v; Jean Chenu, *Cent notables et singulières qvestions de droict, décidées par arrests mémorables des Cours souueraines de France, partie d'iceux prononcez en robbes rouges: contenans les moyens et raisons décisives*, 3rd edn (Paris: Robert Fouet, 1606), question 64, pp. 264–73.

[2] Jean Chenu, *Cent notables et singulières qvestions de droict, décidées par arrests mémorables des cours souueraines de France, partie d'iceux prononcez en robbes rouges: contenans les moyens et raisons décisives*, 2nd edn (Paris: Nicolas Buon, 1603), question 24, pp. 234–44; AN, Registres, Parlement de Paris, Civil, Plaidoiries 'Matinées', X1a 5032, 17 May 1571 and 31 May 1571 fos 224r–256r, 346r–362v.

the orator or author of the printed version wished to display his talents.[3] While the court registers might record, for example, 'Ayrault for the appellant and Poussemothe for the defendant were heard together', Pierre Ayrault's published collection provided his pleading for the reader, but he was also careful to present parts of the speech of the opposing lawyer Pierre Poussemothe.[4]

The ability to persuade – as an orator or a writer – depended on rhetorical 'invention' or the assembly of proofs, evidence, examples and commonplaces, and then on how these proofs were arranged and presented to an audience.[5] The appeals before the Parlement could be presented through written documents (a process aided by the attorneys) or through oral pleadings. For the lawyers, the prestige of the performance on the parquet before the Parlement de Paris, as well as their university training, separated them as a profession from the attorneys, although some lawyers such as Pithou worked only with written evidence.[6] The orator was a man of the moment. He persuaded through his delivery of the speech, by modulating his voice, through gesture and by charming his audience.[7] The lawyer usually only had one or two opportunities to persuade the judges before whom he appeared on behalf of his clients – the pleading and then a rejoinder (*duplique*) or reply (*replique*). Once written down and circulated in manuscript, the lawyer's speech became a model and a treasury for other lawyers, attorneys, and jurists. If the same speech was printed, legal professionals could return to it at their leisure for repeated readings and as a reference work to consult in future cases, as we saw in the personal library of Francois Courtin and others in chapter seven.[8] The printed collections of notable cases were tools for consultation and tended to cross-reference cases and point out the pleading strategies and legal principles employed by lawyers in similar cases.[9] The rhetorical training was the same, but the delivery – from the lawyer's voice, rhythm, actions and gestures – shifted once the speech made it onto the printed page. As we shall see, the printed pleadings

---

[3] Marie Houllemare, 'Un avocat parisien entre art oratoire et promotion de soi (fin XVIe siècle)', *Revue historique* 306:2 (2004): 296.

[4] AN, Registres, Parlement de Paris, Civil, Plaidoiries, 'Matinées', X1a 5015, 14 July 1567, fo. 79v; Pierre Ayrault, *XXI Pledoiers faict en la cour de Parlement de Paris et arrests sur ce intervenuz* (Paris: Martin le Jeune, 1568), pp. 188–98.

[5] Quentin Skinner, *Reason and Rhetoric in the Philosophy of Thomas Hobbes* (Cambridge, 1996), pp. 111–12.

[6] Sara Beam, *Laughing Matters: Farce and the Making of Absolutism in France* (Ithaca, NY, 2007), p. 85.

[7] Brian Vickers, *In Defence of Rhetoric* (Oxford, 1988), p. 65; Cicero, *De oratore*, trans. E.W. Sutton, 2 vols (London, 1942), I. xxxi, 142–3.

[8] See Chapter 7, pp. 167–71.

[9] Ayrault, *XXI Pledoiers*, pp. 195–6; Chenu points out how lawyers disputing a sister's renunciation of her portion of the inheritance used the same legal points as the appeal involving Isabeau d'Anglure, Dame de Pavant, argued in the Parlement de Paris four years earlier and which we shall examine below – see Chenu, *Cent notables*, 1603 edn, p. 241.

and books of 'notable decisions' often altered the emphasis and the presentation of speeches in the court registers and allowed for amplification. Ayrault confided to the reader that in a pleading before the court he did not pause to relate Julius Cæsar's comments on the morals of the ancient Gauls and those of 'other authors' on the Roman laws concerning the 'community and society between husband and wife', because these observations were 'too common (*vulgaire*)'. Nevertheless, Ayrault did not refrain from adding it to the printed version of his pleading and including details on book six of Caesar's *De bello gallico* along with the names of the 'other authors' Dionysius of Halicarnassus and Plutarch conveniently placed in the margin.[10] Étienne Pasquier recalled complaining to his friend the former *procureur-général du roi* Jacques Faye, Sieur d'Espesse, about the developing habit in the Parlement of adding 'samples of diverse authors' to speeches, a fashion for which Faye was partly responsible. Faye's 'harangues' published after his death, Pasquier revealed, were 'more pleasing to read, by the way', than they were to listen to when Faye delivered them.[11]

Elizabeth Brown notes how, at the end of the fifteenth century, the accounts of the pleadings recorded by the clerks of the civil court (*greffe civil*) of the Parlement de Paris become 'incomparably more detailed because the greffier uses copies of the pleadings, supplied by the advocates, to amend the notes that he or his colleagues had taken'. By the end of the sixteenth century the summaries of proceedings in the court registers became brief once again as the practice of printing the pleadings spread.[12] Lawyers had the opportunity, if not the duty, to correct the record as written down by the clerks, before three days had passed. Pleadings as they appear in the court registers, then, are said to be résumés or summaries.[13] In some instances an *arrêt* or decree had a broader impact than the simple settlement of a dispute between two parties. For example, in the private dispute between a remarried widow and her stepchildren, the *arrêt* of 1578, pronounced 'solemnly' in the red robes of judicial office, had the effect of amending the 1560 royal edict of second marriages and extending the law from widows to widowers.[14] Such

---

10 Ayrault, *XXI Pledoiers*, p. 72.

11 Étienne Pasquier, *Des recherches de la France*, in *Les Œuvres d'Étienne Pasquier*, 2 vols (Amsterdam, 1723), vol. I, Bk 4, ch. XXVII, cols 423–4: 'plus belles paraventure, à lire, qu'elles n'avoient estés à prononcer'.

12 Elizabeth Brown, 'Le greffe civil du Parlement de Paris au XVIe siècle: Jean du Tillet et les registres des plaidoiries', *Bibliothèque de l'École des chartes* 153 (1995): 328; Roland Delachenal, *Histoire des avocats au Parlement de Paris 1300–1600* (Paris, 1885), pp. 229–30.

13 Delachenal, *Histoire des avocats*, p. 104; Alexis François, 'Origine et déclin du "bel usage" parlementaire', *Revue d'histoire littéraire de la France* 25 (1918): 206–7.

14 See Lyndan Warner, 'Widows, Widowers and the Problem of "Second Marriages" in Sixteenth-Century France', in Sandra Cavallo and L. Warner (eds), *Widowhood in Medieval and Early Modern Europe* (New York, 1999), pp. 84–107; AN, Registres, Parlement de Paris, Civil, Conseil, X1a1659, 16 May 1578, fos 289r–v.

famous cases certainly appeared in print, but many more *arrêts* and pleadings in print were banal private matters. The collections of *arrêts* were simply intended as guidebooks and manuals on how to plead or approach a type of case.[15] The reader of these guidebooks was not privy to the deliberation process of the presiding judge and at least ten *conseillers* or judges, which took place behind closed doors.[16]

To praise or to blame a woman in the *Querelle des femmes*, authors gathered exemplars of virtue and vice in commonplaces such as the chastity of Penelope or the cruelty of Medea. In a similar manner, a lawyer at the Parlement might explain the circumstances of his client or besmirch the reputation of an appellant by using these exemplars of virtue to paint a positive moral portrait of his client or to call into question the character of his opponent.[17] When a husband had abandoned his wife for several years, a lawyer might remark that she should have followed 'the example of the chaste Penelope who ... waited for her Ulysses for twenty years'. Although sought after in marriage by several suitors, Penelope 'excused herself with a courteous and crafty invention that everyone knows'.[18] In naming Penelope, a lawyer or a writer could quickly evoke the virtues of chastity and fidelity in a wife.[19] We find precisely this type of example collected by a humanist in his careful reading of the works of Pico della Mirandola, Quintilian's *Institutio oratorio*, Caesar's commentaries on the wars of Gaul, as well as the *Opuscules of Plutarch* in the translation of Jacques Amyot. In a handwritten notebook, under the margin heading 'Against cuckolds', a carefully copied extract from the reading of Plutarch relates how Penelope graciously outwitted her suitors to the delight of her husband Ulysses.[20]

The demonstrative or epideictic rhetoric found in the debate on the dignity and misery of man or in the *Querelle des femmes* addresses the character, sex, rank, age and circumstances and actions of a person through *laus* or praise and *vituperatio* or blame. Deliberative rhetoric, used in the political realm, advises a course of action to persuade or dissuade. Forensic or judicial rhetoric used in the courtroom seeks a just verdict through means of proof and refutation, and the lawyers listed

---

15 François Olivier-Martin, *Histoire du droit français des origines à la Révolution* (Paris, 1992), pp. 538–9; Pasquier, *Les Œuvres*, vol. II, col. 578; John Dawson, *The Oracles of the Law* (Ann Arbor, MI, 1968), pp. 313–14.

16 Édouard Maugis, *Histoire du Parlement de Paris: de l'avènement des rois à la mort d'Henri III*, 3 vols (New York, 1913–16), vol. I, pp. 286–91.

17 François Rigolot, 'The Renaissance Crisis of Exemplarity', *Journal of the History of Ideas* 59:4 (1998): 558.

18 Chenu, *Cent notables*, 1603 edn, question 14, p. 169.

19 For other examples of the use of Penelope in lawyers' pleadings, see BN, MS, Collection Dupuy [hereafter BN, MS Dupuy] 115, 'Recueil de plaidoiries, arrêts et consultations des XVIe et XVIIe siècles', fo. 203v; Chenu, *Cent notables*, 1603 edn, question 15, p. 173.

20 BN, MS Dupuy 896, 'Recueil d'extraits relatifs à divers sujets de la main d'Augustin Dupuy(?)', fo. 89r.

'moyens' or the principal points of proof in both their written submissions and in their oral pleadings. Describing the *Querelle des femmes* as a 'rhetorical exercise' suggests that the epideictic rhetoric of praise and blame can be separated from deliberative rhetoric, which persuades or dissuades from an action, and from the forensic rhetoric employed by lawyers in their pleadings to prove or disprove.[21] Yet in order to persuade or dissuade from a course of action, as in deliberative oratory, or in order to prove or disprove, as in judicial speech, there is inevitably some overlap of the genres of rhetoric. Brian Vickers notes that the praise and blame of epideictic became the 'dominant mode' of rhetoric in the Renaissance as 'forensic and deliberative eloquence' declined.[22] Cicero sent the reader of his section on epideictic oratory in the *De inventione* back to his descriptions of the 'attributes of persons' in judicial rhetoric where the prosecuting lawyer tries to discredit the defendant in court by describing the 'circumstances', past actions and the 'attributes of persons'.[23] Cicero suggested that there is a general store of arguments about the name, nature or sex, family and age, manner of life, fortune, 'habit', character or disposition, achievements and so on that can be employed in forensic rhetoric, political rhetoric and the rhetoric of praise and blame.[24] Aristotle, Cicero, Quintilian and the author of the *Rhetorica ad Herennium* acknowledged that the epideictic rhetoric of praise and blame could be used to persuasive ends in other contexts such as politics or in the courtroom.[25] Each genre of rhetoric addressed certain topics and subtopics, but the orator could use the general store of arguments in all.[26] So a lawyer representing his client before the Parlement at times resorted to the same techniques used in the epideictic rhetoric of the *Querelle des femmes* and the dignity and misery of man to exalt or to humble a man or a woman. The models of classical rhetoric provided by Aristotle, Quintilian and Cicero allowed for an overlapping of rhetorical categories, and the Renaissance commonplace book method outlined by Erasmus in the *De copia* blurred the rhetorical categories even further because it emphasised gathering examples from a wide array of sources. The eloquence of the courtroom or the town hall that used

---

21 Marc Angenot, *Les Champions des femmes: examen du discours sur la supériorité des femmes 1400–1800* (Montréal, 1977), pp. 152, 160; E.V. Telle, *L'Œuvre de Marguerite d'Angoulême Reine de Navarre et la querelle des femmes* (Toulouse, 1937), pp. 36–7; Madeleine Lazard, *Images littéraires de la femme à la Renaissance* (Paris, 1985), p. 11.

22 Vickers, *In Defence*, p. 285.

23 Cicero, *De inventione*, trans. H.M. Hubbell (London, 1949), II.x.32–4, I.xxiv.34.

24 Ibid., II.lviii.177; Vickers, *In Defence*, p. 54; Brian Vickers, 'Rhetoric and Poetics', in Charles Schmitt and Quentin Skinner (eds), *The Cambridge History of Renaissance Philosophy* (Cambridge, 1988), p. 744.

25 Vickers, *In Defence*, pp. 55–6.

26 Marc Fumaroli, 'Rhetoric, Politics and Society: From Italian Ciceronianism to French Classicism', in James Murphy (ed.), *Renaissance Eloquence: Studies in the Theory and Practice of Renaissance Rhetoric* (Berkeley, CA, 1983), pp. 257–8, 262–4.

the energy and emotion of the moment to persuade an audience gave way to an emphasis on the ability to move the solitary reader at home in the study.[27]

In a printed format these examples could be conveniently placed in the margins of the text to quickly summarise an argument. To facilitate the reading of Pierre Ayrault's pleadings before the Parlement in the late 1560s, for example, the printer explained to the reader how 'allegations' within the speech had been highlighted in the margins – 'les allegations, qui estoyent parmy le contexte, nous les auons rejectees en la marge'.[28] Lawyers and officeholders such as Étienne Pasquier recognised that the emphasis on *inventio* resulted from the lawyers' attempts to please the judges in the Parlement de Paris, especially Christophe de Thou, who was the *premier président* from 1562 to 1582. Marc Fumaroli notes that the development of a 'rhetoric of citation' created a type of eloquence, which emphasised the 'invention of the orator, the treasures of his memory, that a Ciceronian style would mask'.[29] While the classical orator may have delivered his pleading in a seamless fashion, the early modern lawyers' pleadings appearing in sixteenth- and early seventeenth-century printed editions display an Erasmian emphasis on *inventio* or the assembly of proofs such as commonplaces. The techniques of compilation adopted in the moral philosophy of Boaistuau, Mexia, Marconville or Montaigne worked well in print. A number of authors have commented on how extensive citation resulted in 'puffed up' or 'pompous' speeches and led the legal profession into a crisis by the 1620s; and the printed versions of pleadings and commentaries on judicial decisions certainly contributed to this malaise.[30] Pasquier chided his friend Antoine Loisel about two speeches he had given in the early 1580s as part of a judicial delegation to Western France that were later published. '[W]hat you [Loisel] esteem to be the most rich' Pasquier considered 'the most poor' because of the many 'Greek and Latin passages' that 'grace your speech'. Pasquier complained that 'in this new genre of eloquence … we must not only name the authors from whom we borrow, but moreover, we set down their passages in writing at length'. When the orators borrowed 'undigested pieces' or citations from the Greeks and Romans, Pasquier commented that they did not actually follow the classical style.[31] Loisel also sent these speeches to Montaigne, who reciprocated with his admiration and a dedicated copy of the *Essais*, full

27 Vickers, *In Defence*, pp. 276, 282, 285–6.

28 'L'imprimeur aux lecteurs', in Ayrault, *XXI Pledoiers*, pp. 3–6.

29 Marc Fumaroli, *L'âge de l'éloquence: Rhétorique et 'res literaria' de la Renaissance au seuil de l'époque classique* (Paris, 1994), pp. 444–5 and n. 36; Étienne Pasquier, *Lettres familières*, ed. Dorothy Thickett (Geneva, 1974), VII:12, p. 101; Brown, 'Greffe civil', p. 369.

30 Jérôme Delatour, 'De l'art de plaider doctement: Les notes de lecture de Pierre Dupuy, jeune avocat (1605–6)', *Bibliothèque de l'École des chartes* 153 (1995): 412; Alexis, 'Origine', p. 210; Catherine Holmès, *L'éloquence judiciaire de 1620 à 1600: reflet de problèmes sociaux, religieux et politiques de l'époque* (Paris, 1967), p. 32.

31 Pasquier, *Lettres familières*, pp. 99–100.

of his own reflections on Latin and some Greek passages.[32] Jacques Faye, the Sieur d'Espesse, tried to imitate the smooth style of the 'ancient orators' in one of his *harangues* opening a session of Parlement, but the *procureur général* later admitted to Pasquier that it required three times as much effort as one 'patched together with several passages'.[33]

The printed pleadings of the *avocats généraux* Claude Expilly or Louis Servin provide evidence of the adoption of a 'rhetoric of citation' by the 1590s, and as we saw in chapter seven, the lawyer and clerk Francois Courtin owned both in the early seventeenth century.[34] Claude Expilly became a lawyer at the Parlement of Grenoble in 1583 and later acquired a series of offices, culminating in his appointment as *avocat général* in 1604 and Conseiller d'État in 1608.[35] As we saw in chapter seven, Expilly identified the sources of Montaigne's citations in his 1588 L'Angelier edition of the *Essais* produced with margins wide enough to allow for annotation. Expilly's reading practices call attention to the style of his pleadings, which follow a 'rhetoric of citation'.[36]

From 1596 L'Angelier stocked Expilly's collection of poetry and a little over a decade later he sold Expilly's pleadings and the judgments of the Parlement of Grenoble from the first pillar of the Grande'Salle in the Palais de Justice in Paris.[37] Expilly commented that 'civil actions' are often 'wearisome' or 'tedious' and so both the judges and the parties to the lawsuits need to seek some respite as Achilles did when he played the lyre to calm his soul upon returning from battle.[38] Expilly combines the commonplace-book reading practices lawyers brought to their pleadings as 'artificial proofs' with the 'given proofs' based on legal reasoning, consultations of the body of civil law, canon law, previous *arrêts* and any relevant customary law. His printed speeches are full of male and female examples of

---

32 Michel Reulos, 'L'importance des practiciens dans l'humanisme juridique', in *Pédagogues et juristes* (Paris, 1963), p. 123; Jean Balsamo and Michel Simonin, *Abel L'Angelier et Françoise de Louvain (1574–1620). Suivi du catalogue des ouvrages publiés par Abel L'Angelier (1574–1610) et la Veuve L'Angelier (1610–1620)* (Geneva, 2002), pp. 262, 619; Montaigne, *Essais de Michel de Montaigne*, ed. J.V. Le Clerc, 4 vols (Paris, 1856), vol. IV, pp. 271–2, 'Lettre de Antoine Loisel à Montaigne, 1 novembre 1582', and vol. IV, p. 262, 'Dedicace manuscrite d'un exemplaire des *Essais* à Antoine Loisel'.

33 Pasquier, *Les Recherches*, in *Les Œuvres*, vol. I, Bk 4, ch. XXVII, cols 423–4.

34 Louis Servin, *Plaidoyez de Mre Loys Servin conseiller du roy en son Conseil d'Estat & advocat general en sa cour de Parlement. A la fin desquels les arrests intervenus sur iceuls*, 2 vols (Paris: Jean de Heuqueville, 1603–1605).

35 *Dictionnaire de biographie française*, 20 vols (Paris, 1932–), vol. XIII, cols 324–5.

36 Alessandra Preda, '"Les siècles à venir te loueront à bon droit": Montaigne et Claude Expilly', *Montaigne Studies* 13 (2001): 205.

37 Claude Expilly, *Les Poèmes du Sieur d'Expilly. À Madame la marquise de Monceaux* (Paris: Abel L'Angelier, 1596), p. 216.

38 Claude Expilly, *Plaidoyez de M. Claude Expilly, conseiller du roy & son advocat general au Parlement de Grenoble. Auec quelques arrests & reglemens notables dudit Parlement* (Paris: Abel L'Angelier, 1608), pp. 121, 126.

virtue and vice, of classical tales of misfortune and other embellishments meant to charm and persuade.

Lawyers recognised the role of the passions in persuasion and the need to move the audience. In the courtroom, the lawyer had to persuade a presiding judge and his *conseillers*. More importantly, as Expilly reminded the reader, one of the purposes served by rhetorical ornaments in the courtroom might be to resuscitate the interest of a judge who had been at work since dawn. But when the oral pleading was transformed by printing, the reader became the judge, perhaps a fellow lawyer preparing his own consultations. And so we find a notable difference between oral pleadings as recorded in the court registers and the presentation of these pleadings in print by the lawyers who delivered them or by jurists presenting the cases as part of a series of 'notable decisions'. Print allowed for amplification, whether it was creating an image or a mental picture of the circumstances of a party to a lawsuit or using a citation to set a tone and reflect on an issue, strategies familiar to any reader of Montaigne's *Essais*.[39]

Printing the Dignity of the Men and Women of the Noble House of Anglure

An appeal to the Parlement de Paris in the late 1560s involving the noble house of Anglure illustrates the impact of printing upon the presentation of the argument in lawyers' pleadings. Probing this legal case also shows how the lawyers ascribed 'attributes of persons' such as the sex, age, family and rank to describe the 'circumstances' and past actions of the parties to the suit, and of their parents. Throughout this appeal, the lawyers debated the place of woman as daughter and wife as well as the reputation of a noble household (*maison*) and the importance of maintaining its dignity, status and role in the state while preserving it from ruin and misery.

Isabeau d'Anglure, the only child of Francois d'Anglure, Sieur and Vicomte d'Étoges, and Anne du Bec, was still a toddler when her mother died. Her widower father remarried and fathered six more children. When Isabeau reached the age of 19 or 20, her father François arranged for her to marry a 'gentilhomme' from Lorraine.[40] In the October 1539 negotiations for the match it was agreed that François would pay 10,000 *livres* to the couple upon consummation of the marriage, and on 6 November the sum was duly paid. Years later when François d'Anglure died, the conflicts about the significance of this payment began. According to the lawyers for Isabeau d'Anglure's surviving half-brother and the child of another

[39] Skinner, *Reason and Rhetoric*, pp. 182–5; Desiderius Erasmus, '*Copia:* Foundations of the Abundant Style' [*De duplici copia verborum ac rerum commentarii duo*], ed. Craig Thompson, *Collected Works of Erasmus*, 86 vols (Toronto, 1974–), vol. XXIV, pp. 574–7.

[40] François de Baldoche, écuyer, Sieur des Estangs. On the Anglure family see Maxence Hermant, 'La commande artistique en Champagne du Nord au XVIe siècle: les vicomtes d'Étoges et leurs tombeaux', *Etudes marnaises* (2006): 95–120.

half-brother, in accepting the 10,000 *livres* Isabeau and her husband thus renounced any claim to a paternal inheritance. Isabeau disagreed and presented two major demands through her lawyer: she wished to see her share of the movable and immovable goods left by her father, and desired a 'surrendering of account' and the 'remainder' of the value of the maternal goods. To this effect, she had obtained *lettres royaux* in August 1566 and wanted to execute this writ notwithstanding any renunciation or 'release' she may have made in the marriage contract. The *lettres* outlined five 'points' that affected the validity of the renunciation and the length of time it had taken her to come forward with her complaint. She had been a minor (*en bas aage*), owing 'honour and obedience' to her father and followed his wishes 'out of fear' of 'disobeying him' –'pour craincte qu'elle auoit de luy desobeyr'. She had been subject to 'deceit, fraud and inducement (*dol, fraude et induction*)' before making the renunciation, thus she had been 'deceived out of more than half of the value of her inheritance' – 'deceue doultre moictie de juste pris'.[41] Once married, she had been under the 'fear and power' of her husband and still could not act.[42] The Requêtes du Palais, a court of first instance, decided in Isabeau's favour.[43] As a minor and a daughter, she owed obedience to her father. As a wife, 'when her first husband was her master and lord', Isabeau was subject to marital authority.[44] Isabeau's half-brothers appealed the decision and so reopened the issue of whether she had been cheated out of her inheritance because she could not challenge her father's authority and later could not act independently of her husband. The *Querelle des femmes* writer Hélisenne de Crenne, in works published frequently during the years of Isabeau d'Anglure's unfolding drama, complained of the authority of fathers pressuring daughters into marriage ('ton pere te presse'). A daughter's legal 'condition' provided her with no power (*puissance*) because she could not act without a father's consent (*consentement*). Although Hélisenne defended matrimony, her *Familiar and Invective Letters* and her novel the *Angoisses douloureuses qui procèdent d'amour* also repeatedly pointed out the husband's authority over the wife.[45]

Was some of the wealth of Isabeau's mother diverted to her half-brothers? According to Jehan de Saint Meloir, the advocate for Isabeau d'Anglure, her

---

41 AN, Registres, Parlement de Paris, Civil, Plaidoiries 'Matinées', X1a 5014, 26 June 1567, fo. 446r, Jean Le Maistre pleading; C.J. de Ferrière (ed.), *Dictionnaire de droit et de pratique*, 2 vols (Paris: Veuve Brunet, 1769), vol. II, p. 135.

42 Chenu, *Cent notables*, 1603 edn, pp. 220–21.

43 AN, X1a 5014, fos 445r, 448v; Chenu, *Cent notables*, 1603 edn, p. 221.

44 The court register mentions only 'master', but Chenu's print version adds 'et seigneur', fo. 446v.

45 Hélisenne de Crenne, *Les Œuvres de ma dame Helisenne de Crenne. A sçavoir, les angoisses douloureuses qui procedent d'amours. Les Epistres familières et invectives & Le songe de ladicte dame. Le tout reveu & corrigé de nouveau par elle* (Paris: Etienne Groulleau, 1560), facs. edn (Geneva, 1977): on paternal authority see sigs Kiiij^{v}–Kv^{r}; on marital authority, see sigs Nvii^{r}–Nvii^{v}, Nviii^{v}–O, Lii^{r}, Iiij^{r}.

mother brought 'great riches' in movable property and real estate to the marriage with François d'Anglure. After her mother's death, Isabeau's father 'seized' these 'heritages' and used them for many years. Isabeau's lawyer explained that, 'out of fear and reverence for her father as well as other practices led by her [step]mother, who told this young gentlewoman that her father was making her a good match and that if she did not take it, he would be displeased about it and [Isabeau] would be ill-treated as much by him as by her stepmother'. By these 'inducements and persuasions', Isabeau d'Anglure consented.[46] In contracting Isabeau's marriage, her father arranged that for a single payment of 10,000 *livres* his daughter would renounce any future inheritance as well as the movable goods and revenue, but he did so 'without rendering account or showing any inventory to her' that as a minor 'her father was bound to convey to her'. As Saint Meloir suggests, her father thus nullified the agreement because she was a minor entitled to an account of a parent's administration.[47]

Her future husband promised to make her ratify the renunciation once their marriage had been consummated or face a penalty of damages and interest. She had 'solicited her husband several times' and despite 'speaking to him and entreating him', he 'flatly refused' to 'amend' the ratification and 'forbid' her to pursue the matter. 'And for these reasons [he] was mean to her' – 'luy monstroit mauuais visage' – 'saying to her and making her say that if she talked about it, he would be displeased and several other words of authority that a husband can use against his wife'. None of these details appear in the printed version of the pleadings apart from the mention of the 'fear and reverence' in which Isabeau held her father and later her husband.

Saint Meloir, Isabeau d'Anglure's lawyer, also downplayed the time limit on civil actions because 'out of fear of her father' she made this renunciation, and 'out of fear of her husband' she had been prevented from pursuing her fair portion during the marriage; and 'while the fear [and impression] lasts the time and statute of limitations does not run'.[48] Isabeau's fear of her husband only ended

---

[46] AN, X1a 5014, fo. 448v. The fear, the obedience, the one-off payment in exchange for renunciation and the forced marriage outlined by Anglure's lawyer and published by Chenu resurfaces in a 1674 case and how lawyers describe the experience of a daughter of a first marriage bed at the hands of a father and stepmother; see Sarah Hanley, 'The Family, the State, and the Law in Seventeenth- and Eighteenth-Century France: The Political Ideology of Male Right versus an Early Theory of Natural Rights', *The Journal of Modern History* 78 (2006): 289–332.

[47] AN, X1a 5014, fos 449r–v. According to customary law for Vitry, minors were entitled to an account of the administration of their property and the deduction of expenses once they came of age: Charles Bourdot de Richebourg (ed.), *Nouveau coutumier général: ou Corps des coutumes générales et particulières de France, et des provinces connues sous le nom des Gaules*, 4 vols (Paris, 1724), vol. IV, ch. IV, articles 63, 73, pp. 317–18.

[48] AN, X1a 5014, fos 449r–v, Chenu, *Cent notables*, 1603 edn, p. 230; F.A. Isambert, *Recueil général des anciennces lois françaises depuis l'an 420 jusqu'à la Révolution de 1789*, 29 vols (Paris, 1822–33), vol. XI, 'Ordonnance sur la réformation de la justice', Louis

with his death, and the printed version embellishes this thought with a citation from Martial: '*res est imperiosa timor*' – 'fear is an imperious thing'.[49] In case stressing fear and obedience did not work with the judges, Saint Meloir added a further point: Isabeau's 'foreign' husband took her to the Duchy of Lorraine, 'a distant country' where she lived outside of 'subjection to the king' and his laws for more than twenty years.[50] Perhaps Saint Meloir remembered Quintilian's archer from the *Institutio oratoria*, discussed in chapter four, whose rhetorical strategy of resorting to multiple arguments was employed by *Querelle des femmes* writers. An archer confident of hitting the target will be 'content with one shaft', but the archer who 'has no such confidence will do well to launch several and give fortune a chance to come to his assistance'.[51]

Thus Isabeau d'Anglure's lawyer suggests to the court that she was never able to defend her interests. She had to wait until widowhood and the recovery of her legal persona before she could even consider proceeding with her grievance. As Louis Le Caron underlined in his observations on French law, 'in France in regions of customary law (*pays coustumier*) and written law, as well as in several other provinces, the wife is so reduced under the authority of the husband, that without [his authority] she can not contract or indebt [herself], nor dispose of her patrimonial goods, nor appear [in court] to defend her interests, unless she is authorised by justice'.[52] She did, of course, have this one protection as a wife under French law: to seek the 'authority of justice'. Her lawyer never mentioned this possibility, but her opponents in the courtroom made certain that her failure to exercise this right did not escape the attention of the judges. Instead her lawyer informed the court that when her husband died about seven or eight years before, Isabeau d'Anglure had returned to France and later remarried Charles de Coustes, *chevalier de l'ordre du roi*, Sieur de Pavant and *lieutenant de la compagnie* of the Duke Charles III of Lorraine.[53] She did not begin the legal process to recover her inheritance as an independent widow, but only once she had the backing of a new and powerful husband.[54]

The lawyers for the heirs of François d'Anglure, the appellants in this case, presented a different interpretation of events to the Parlement de Paris. Jean Le

XII, Lyon, June 1510, art. 46, pp. 595–6; Isambert, *Recueil général*, vol. XII, 'Ordonnance sur le fait de la justice', Francis I, Villers-Cotterêts, 1539, art. 134, p. 628.

[49] Chenu, *Cent notables*, 1603 edn, p. 230; Martial, *Epigrams*, trans. Walter Ker, 2 vols (Cambridge, MA, 1968), vol. II, Bk XI, epigram LVIII, line 8.

[50] AN, X1a 5014, fo. 448v; Chenu, *Cent notables*, 1603 edn, p. 231.

[51] Quintilian, *Institutio oratoria*, ed. and trans. H.E. Butler, 4 vols (London, 1920–22), vol. II, p. 145, IV.v.13–17.

[52] Louis Le Caron, *Memorables ou Observations du droict françois rapporté av Romain ciuil & canonic*, 2nd edn (Paris: Iamet Mettayer & P. L'Hvillier, 1603), fo. 162v.

[53] M. le Baron d'Hannoncelles, *Metz ancien*, 2 vols (Metz, 1856), vol. I, p. 14.

[54] Tim Stretton, *Women Waging Law in Elizabethan England* (Cambridge, 1998), pp. 139–42.

Maistre appeared on behalf of Isabeau's half-brother Jacques d'Anglure, the heir to the title of Vicomte d'Étoges. Jean Cauchon represented Monseigneur le Maréchal Claude de la Châtre in his role as tutor to Anne d'Anglure, the only son and heir of Isabeau's half-brother René, who, as both Cauchon and Le Maistre reminded the court, had died in glory in 1562 in the service of the King on the battlefield at Dreux.[55]

Le Maistre's opening argument as it appears in the court register explained how 'ancient and modern' lawmakers had been careful to ensure that their subjects remained in 'peaceful enjoyment' of their possessions.[56] Louis XII's 1510 ordinance was based on the 'reason' that patrimony and inherited property should not be 'uncertain' or 'without security' because 'the state of the Kingdom' depended on the 'greatness' and 'preservation' of 'the great households and families of this Kingdom'.[57] To allow Isabeau d'Anglure and her second husband their 'purpose and intention' to 'return to an inheritance' placed the security of possession and the stability of families in peril. This 'intention' is as 'clear as day'.[58] To 'overthrow' the 'divisions' of property among 'household and family' had ramifications even beyond the 'noble and very ancient house of Anglure', among whose members can be counted 'several great and valiant persons who died in the service of the Kings of France'.[59] Cauchon's pleading went even further: 'Besides [giving] his own life' René d'Anglure, Isabeau's half-brother, 'used a good and great part of his goods' even to the point of selling and alienating some of his inheritance to support the war efforts of the king. Nevertheless, his half-sister and her husband wished to gain access to some of that inheritance.[60]

The Effect of Printing on the Lawyer's Pleading

Although Le Maistre and Cauchon point to the importance of this great family's service to the state, the versions of their pleadings in the court register pale in comparison to the printed case in Jean Chenu's collection of *Singulières questions de droict, décidées par arrests mémorables ... contenans les moyens et raisons decisives*, first published in 1602 with 64 questions, expanded in 1603 as a second edition of 100 questions, and with a fourth edition by 1611. Chenu's printed

55 AN, X1a 5014, fo. 445v, Le Maistre pleading; fo. 447^{v}, Cauchon pleading.

56 AN, X1a 5014, fo. 445r, Le Maistre pleading; Digest of Justinian [hereafter Digest] 41.3.1.

57 AN, X1a 5014, fos 445r–v; Isambert, *Recueil général*, 'Ordonnance sur la réformation de la justice', Louis XII, Lyon, June 1510, vol. XI, art. 46, pp. 595–6; Ibid., 'Ordonnance sur le fait de la Justice', Francis I, Villers-Cotterêts, 1539, vol. XII, art. 134, p. 628.

58 AN, X1a 5014, fo. 446v.

59 Ibid., fo. 445v.

60 Ibid., fo. 447v.

version did not distinguish between the pleadings of Le Maistre and Cauchon, and mixed elements from both. The resulting printed version is more explicit and long-winded on the conservation of great families and their underpinning of the state than either of the two court register pleadings recorded by the clerks. On each point, the print version amplified the argument. Where the clerk recorded Le Maistre as briefly citing the 'jurisconsult' on the law of usucaption, the print version adds the reference to Gaius in Justinian's *Digest* in the margin. Where the register briefly quoted a speech by Cicero, the print version reproduces the citation fully in order to remind the reader that '[a] man can inherit an estate from his father but a good title to the estate, that is freedom from anxiety and litigation, he inherits not from his father but from the law'.[61] The print version narrated from Sidonius Apollinaris on the introduction of a statute of limitations to France added the lapse of time established by Emperor Theodosius as 30 years, bringing 'profound peace for the human race', and further cited a variety of 'Authors, not only political, but also Ecclesiastical' who supported a time limit on civil actions.[62] Flowery praise compared the kings of France to Roman emperors: 'we can boast that the prudence of our Kings and their zeal for justice, the desire to shorten law suits surpassed the diligence [speed] of Roman Emperors', because they 'shortened and curtailed' the law even further.[63] To Louis XII's 'ordinance of ten years', the printed pleading adds the 1539 ordinance introduced by François I, under which minors had ten years beyond their age of majority to bring a suit against a tutor and therefore were without hope of restitution after the age of 35.[64] The printed pleading told the reader that these royal ordinances, which aimed to maintain the 'peace, ease, and tranquility of households', were the basis for denying the lawsuit. Extending the impact of the case from the noble household of Anglure to the state, the printed version explains that the case not only concerned the

> … private wealth of the appellants, but also the state of all noble houses in France, which would be greatly shaken up if such lawsuits were accepted and admitted and if the renunciations made by daughters in favour of males were not upheld and authorised, as they should be for the preservation of the splendour

---

[61] Digest 41. 3. 1; Cicero, *In Defence of A. Caecina*, in *The Speeches*, trans. H. Grose Hode (London, 1927), XXVI, 74, pp. 170–71.

[62] Chenu, *Cent notables*, 1603 edn, p. 222; Saint Sidonius Apollinaris, *Poems and Letters*, trans. W. Anderson, 2 vols (Cambridge: MA, 1965), vol. II, Bk VIII, letter VI, 7, pp. 424–5; *The Theodosian Code and Novels and the Sirmondian Constitutions*, trans. Clyde Pharr, *et al.* (New York, 1969), [Novels of Valentinian III], N Val 27.3, p. 538, and [Theodosian Code], 4.14.1, p. 95.

[63] Chenu, *Cent notables*, 1603 edn, p. 221.

[64] Isambert, *Recueil général*, vol. XII, art. 134, p. 628; Chenu, *Cent notables*, 1603 edn, p. 222.

> and dignity of households and families and the propagation of the names and arms of these [households] of which the males are the columns and pillars.[65]

The printed pleading repeats this sentiment in Greek, quoting Euripides that 'male children are the pillars of households'.[66] Neither the reference to Euripides, nor its indirect source, can be found in the court registers of Le Maistre's or Cauchon's pleadings, but the print version placed the Greek citation at the centre of the argument and added a marginal reference to attract the attention of the interested reader. Here the printed pleading for the appellants hit full stride. The 'strength and stability' of these noble families supports the 'flourishing State', the pleading claims, insisting on this 'masculine prerogative' or the need to favour males, as a truism or 'French axiom confirmed by several previous *arrêts* of the sovereign courts'. The print version stresses the possible consequences of allowing Isabeau d'Anglure to return to the paternal inheritance, 'not only' for the Anglure family, 'but [for] all the great households of France'.[67] The printed pleading underlines the connection between the governance of the family and household and the political foundations of the state, and alters the 'decisive reasons' – to borrow the phrase from the title of Chenu's collection of *Singular Questions of Law* – presented to the Parlement de Paris by the advocates. The notion of masculine prerogative never really arises in the court registers to the extent that it is emphasised in the printed record.

Moreover, the print version mutes Isabeau's complaints that her first husband refused to act on her behalf. He was a *sénéchal* in Lorraine and was thus familiar with the courts of justice. Chenu's printed account shortens the tale of coercion by Isabeau's father and stepmother, instead reiterating Le Maistre's claim that Isabeau did not demonstrate how her father 'threatened or intimidated her' into making the renunciations and 'quittances' or releases. Even male authority had its limits so the printed version emphasises Isabeau's choices by adding a phrase not found in the court registers – 'nor that her said husband had threatened, beaten or abused her'.[68] In the court registers Cauchon also challenged Isabeau's claims of 'fear and paternal reverence' by pointing out that her father had been dead for 22 years. During her marriage there was no 'force', no 'threats', and no 'impediment done to her'. After Le Maistre's complaints about lack of proof of paternal and marital fear, Cauchon pursued the point that lay beneath the entire lawsuit and that the print version embellished and expanded. In France 'women are not so subject

65 Chenu, *Cent notables*, 1603 edn, pp. 222–23.

66 The citation of Euripides is taken from Artemidoris of Daldis: see *Onirocriticon libri V*, ed. Roger Pack (Leipzig, 1963), Bk II, ch. 10, p. 116; Artemidoris of Daldis, *La clef des songes: Onirocriticon*, trans. A.J. Festugière (Paris, 1975), Bk II, ch. 10, p. 109: 'car les enfants mâles sont des piliers des maisons'.

67 Chenu, *Cent notables*, 1603 edn, p. 223.

68 AN, X1a 5014, fo. 447r, Le Maistre pleading; Chenu, *Cent notables*, 1603 edn, p. 225.

to their husbands that they can not become authorised by Justice in the defence of their rights … she had the proper redress and should protest before the Judge, or before the notary … and not having done so, she should blame herself for having let the time for restitution run out'.[69] Neither reverence for a father nor the fear of disobeying him were sufficient cause to break a contract, Le Maistre and Cauchon argued, although Louis Le Caron's *Observations on French Law* noted that renunciations must be 'free and voluntary' without 'constraint' or 'threats'.[70]

To be fair, some of the amplifications of the print version supported Saint Meloir in his rebuttal of the length of time that had elapsed before Isabeau d'Anglure sought her 'just portion'. In print Saint Meloir claimed that his opponents 'swelled' up 'to praise and extol' the time limits, but it was 'repugnant' to 'Christian charity' for a Christian man to seize the goods of another and then maintain his 'usurpation' because he had been in possession for many years.[71]

Without a doubt, Jean Chenu transformed the presentation of the pleadings in the Anglure case as he spliced together the pleadings of Le Maistre and Cauchon to bring 'male prerogative' to the fore. The printed versions of a pleading could enlarge and enrich the layers of case law, edicts, civil law, but the lawyers, judges and magistrates who read these printed versions would be interested in how the lawyers on the winning and losing sides had pleaded their cases. We must remember that Chenu was a lawyer, not a judge. While he could identify and emphasise the reasoning of the lawyers and reprint the *arrêts*, he had no access to the reasons behind notable decisions and could not 'reveal' which of the lawyers' arguments had actually been persuasive.[72] He could print the conclusion of the *procureur général du roi* or king's attorney-general who argued that it would be 'dangerous' to 'accept the facts posed by the defendants', but the attorney-general represented the 'public good' and the interests of the king. The *procureur général du roi* was not a judge and the decision did not always fall in the way he might hope.[73] To win the case, to sway the judges, a lawyer needed to intensify the emotion in the courtroom and to do this he incorporated the rhetoric of praise and blame, or 'demonstrative rhetoric', into his performance. As we shall see in this next section, the lawyers in the Anglure case regularly enhanced their pleadings by borrowing from literature.

---

69 AN, X1a 5014, fo. 448r, Cauchon pleading; Chenu, *Cent notables*, 1603 edn, p. 226: '[E]n France les femmes ne sont subjectes à leurs maris qu'elles ne se puissent faire authorizer en Iustice pour la defense de leurs droicts … elle auoit le remede conuenable, & deuoit protester ou pardeuant le Juge, ou pardeuant le Notaire … ce que n'ayant faict, elle se doit imputer la faute, d'auoir laissé couler le temps de restitution'.

70 Le Caron, *Memorables*, fo. 182v.

71 Chenu, *Cent notables*, 1603 edn, p. 229.

72 Sarah Hanley, '"The Jurisprudence of the Arrêts": Marital Union, Civil Society and State Formation in France, 1550–1650', *Law and History Review* 21:1 (2003): 14–15, 21–3.

73 AN, X1a 5014, fo. 449v; Chenu, *Cent notables*, 1603 edn, p. 232; Dawson, *Oracles*, pp. 323, 333–6.

Demonstrating Praise and Blame in Lawyers' Oral Pleadings and then in Print

A lawyer needed to set out the points of law by using 'given' proofs such as previous judgments and evidence, but he also had to please his audience in his delivery with what writers on rhetoric called 'artificial proofs' that could arouse the emotions of the judges enough to win them over to a client's case.[74] Lawyers incorporated moral dimensions into their pleadings with an abundant use of literary citations from classical and patristic sources to intensify the winning points of a case and if possible turn the judges against the opposing party. For Montaigne, the reasoning of the lawyers and the presentation of the cases in Parlement was the source of the dignity of the institution. The back and forth of opposing viewpoints, which allowed the parlementaires 'to treat of matters diversely', was 'as good and better than to treat them' in only one fashion because it allowed matters to be addressed 'more copiously and more profitably'. Montaigne admired, above all, the competence (*suffisance*) of the lawyers and officeholders in the Parlement that nourished its 'dignity' among the people: 'taking their glory (*beauté*), not by the judgment, which to them is routine (*quotidienne*), and is common to all judges', but from the 'pursuit of varied and opposing arguments which legal matters can so well accommodate'.[75] In crafting these arguments lawyers made extensive use of ornament and embellishment to set the tone and mood.

In the Anglure case, the 'moyens' or principal points of law concerned royal ordinances governing the time limits on a lawsuit and the accepted practices concerning a daughter's renunciation of a paternal or maternal inheritance at the time of her marriage. But the art of persuasion did not end with the points of law. The lawyer used his skills of oratory to teach (*docere*), to delight (*delectare*) and to move (*movere*) his audience.[76] To achieve this, a lawyer needed to embellish his pleading, as the *avocat général* Expilly acknowledged when he noted the need to pause in the courtroom to 'pick some flowers' because a 'mind always busy at work cannot last unless it relaxes'.[77] In the courtroom before an audience well schooled in the feats and misdeeds of ancient heroes and classical gods, lawyers cultivated

---

74 Erasmus, *De copia*, p. 605.

75 Montaigne, *Essais*, II:12, pp. 509–10C; Montaigne, *Essays*, vol. II, pp. 215–16; Montaigne Project, at http://artfl.uchicago.edu/images/montaigne/0221.jpg, accessed 10 November 2010: 'Les arrests font le point extreme du parler dogmatiste et resolutif: si est ce que ceux que nos parlemens presentent au peuple les plus exemplaires, propres à nourrir en luy la reverence qu'il doit à cette dignité, principalement par la suffisance des personnes qui l'exercent, prennent leur beauté non de la conclusion, qui est à eux quotidienne, et qui est commune à tout juge, tant comme de la disceptation et agitation des diverses et contraires ratiocinations que la matiere du droit souffre'.

76 Fumaroli, *L'âge de l'éloquence*, p. iii.

77 Expilly, *Plaidoyez*, pp. 122–3.

the praise of virtue and the blame of vice familiar from the ideas of the dignity and misery of man and woman circulating in the literary and philosophical titles.

Beyond the legal reasoning that we have examined, how could the lawyers for the Anglure men persuade the court that Isabeau's motives were dubious at best? In a passage worthy of any *Querelle des femmes* text, the pleading explained why the Vicomte d'Étoges and father of the Anglure siblings married his first wife, the mother of Isabeau. 'The Sieur d'Estoges chose the said du Bec, not for her goods but for her virtue, imitating the saying of the wise Bias, who asked what was "the best dowry for a married woman? – a chaste life"'. Le Maistre downplayed the wealth of Isabeau's mother, Anne du Bec, and instead emphasised the generosity of the Vicomte d'Étoges as a father on the eve of his daughter's wedding, noting the jewels, rings and the luxurious fabrics of 'crimson velvet coated with gold' that Isabeau wore upon leaving her father's house. The print version contrasts the questionable motives of Isabeau's claim with the conduct of her mother Anne du Bec – a woman rich in virtue but not in worldly goods according to the lawyers for Isabeau's opponents. The lawyer pleased the court and set the tone by reciting a passage from the *Odes* of Horace: 'Their only dowry, and a big one it is, is the upright character they have received from their parents, and the chastity that goes with an unbreakable compact and shies away from [another] husband'.[78] Underlining the fact that virtue brings its own rewards, the lawyer weighs the conduct of the parents against the actions of their daughter. As a remarried widow she had not maintained loyalty to her first husband but instead had listened to the seductive words of another. Moreover Isabeau was willing to bring dishonour to her family through her pursuit of her fair portion of inheritance. Whereas Le Maistre had used these examples to open his pleadings and set the emotional tone of his arguments, the print version reserves these characterisations for the closing arguments. In the courtroom and in print an example compiled from Plautus, in which a virtuous wife speaks quietly to her husband and his slave, guided the judge as well as the reader. 'Personally I do not feel that my dowry is that which people call a dowry, but purity and honour and self-control, fear of God, love of parents, and affection for my family, and being a dutiful wife to you, sir'.[79] The lawyer attempted to discredit Isabeau d'Anglure by contrasting her actions with the virtue of obedient daughters, who became compliant and faithful wives without concern for riches and property.

During his peroration, the brother's lawyer reminded the court that Roman law did not permit a child to challenge his father or accuse him of 'fraud'. Le Maistre suggested that Isabeau d'Anglure 'would have done better to keep quiet' and thus

[78] AN, X1a 5014, fo. 445v; Chenu, *Cent notables*, 1603 edn, p. 227; 'Sayings of the Seven Sages, Bias of Priène', in *Ausonius*, trans. H. Evelyn White, 2 vols (London, 1919), vol. II, pp. 272–3, my translation; or Horace, *Odes and Epodes*, trans. Niall Rudd (Cambridge, MA, 2004), Bk III, ode 24, pp. 198–9.

[79] Chenu, *Cent notables*, 1603 edn, p. 227; Plautus, *Amphitryon*, in *Plautus*, ed. Paul Nixon, 5 vols (Cambridge, MA, 1916–38), vol. I, act II, scene II, pp. 88–9.

follow the example of a famous woman of antiquity who did not challenge the testament of her parent and 'thought it better to honour her mother's will with patience rather than overturn it in court'.[80] The lawyer for Isabeau's brother lamented how Isabeau accused her father of 'deceit, fraud and inducement' long after her renunciation, whereas Afronia the illustrious woman in Valerius Maximus' story accepted her fate and 'chose not to go to law'.[81]

Even though this case centred on the circumstances of the first marriage of Isabeau d'Anglure, we must look elsewhere to understand the reality that inspired it. According to Isabeau's lawyer she was a fearful and obedient daughter, and then a wife who submitted to the authority of her husband in conformity with the ideals of woman in the *Querelle des femmes*. The two lawyers representing her brother and nephew painted a portrait of a self-serving woman who laid claim to an inheritance, without regard for the effect on the family honour or name. There were certainly a range of more negative 'attributes of persons' that could have been used against a woman in court. And lawyers did not hesitate to 'blacken the reputation' of an opponent when they thought it would further their case.[82]

Guillaume du Vair, the stoic philosopher and magistrate, published a series of notable decrees pronounced 'solemnly' or publicly in red robes in the Parlement de Provence. Du Vair's collected legal, literary and philosophical works were sold in at least three editions in the early 1600s by Abel L'Angelier in the Palais de Justice and owned in a five-volume set by the Parlement de Paris lawyer and clerk of the Bureau de Ville Francois Courtin, discussed in chapter seven.[83] In one of these cases a wife, described by the lawyer for the complainant as a 'domestic demon', could have walked off the pages of any *Querelle des femmes* text. According to the lawyer trying to discredit her, this wife at first used 'blandishments and caresses' to get her way, and when that did not work with her older husband she filled the house with 'shouts and tempests', so that instead of finding 'consolation and comfort' in this marriage, her husband experienced 'torments and troubles'. The lawyer echoes the numerous complaints against and anxieties about wives in works such as Dupont's *Controverses of the Masculine and Feminine Sexes* discussed in chapter four.[84] This wife entered her husband's home only 'to pillage it' – 'pour la butiner' – and 'not to bring the title and sweetness of a wife, but to

80 The court registers cite Aulus Gellius, but the printed version correctly cites Valerius Maximus: see Valerius Maximus, *Memorable Sayings and Doings*, trans. D.R. Shackleton Bailey, 2 vols (Cambridge, MA, 2000), Bk VII, 8, pp. 180–81.

81 AN, X1a 5014, fo. 447r; Chenu, *Cent notables*, 1603 edn, pp. 226–7.

82 Holmès, *L'éloquence judiciaire*, p. 118.

83 Guillaume du Vair, *Arrests sur quelques questions notables prononcez en robbe rouge au Parlement de Provence* (Paris: Abel L'Angelier, 1607); Balsamo and Simonin, *Abel L'Angelier*, cat. nos. 429 (1606), 447 (1607), 496 (1610); see Chapter 7 on Du Vair, pp. 171–4, and on Courtin's library, pp. 167–8, 181.

84 Gratien Dupont, *Controverses des sexes masculin et fœmenin* (Paris: Denis Janot, 1540), Bk II, fo. 101r–102v.

take away that of widow and heir'. She bullied and tormented her husband – 'le violente et tourmente' – then she 'besieged' and 'constrained' him into making her the sole heir because the husband lived 'in fear' of his wife.[85] The lawyer accused her of 'unruly appetites' for remarrying so soon after her husband's death and of governing herself badly – 'mauvaise gouuernement'.[86]

Isabeau d'Anglure's rank and her longstanding inaction meant that even the opposing lawyers fell short of accusing her of outright vice. She was just not as virtuous as she might have been had she remained silent. In following the timeline of events, it is evident that shortly after her remarriage her new husband Charles de Coustes, the Sieur de Pavant, supported the pursuit of her 'portion'. She claimed she was unable to act as a minor under the tutelage of her father, unable to convince her first husband, unwilling to act independently of her first husband and seek the authority of justice, but why did she not act once her husband died? She had been a widow for at least seven or eight years before her remarriage, but she did nothing.[87] We have seen how a printed version of a lawsuit might transform the lawyers' pleadings to favour a particular interpretation of a judicial decision, how lawyers might borrow commonplaces from the *Querelle des femmes* or the ethos of virtue and nobility to build up a picture of a wife, daughter, husband, brother or household. The irony of this case resides in the pivotal role of an absent figure. Isabeau's second husband was merely named as a party to the suit, though he was surely its catalyst. Beyond his status as *chevalier de l'ordre du roi* and *lieutenant de la compagnie* of the Duke of Lorraine, there is nary a word about him in the court registers or the printed version.

In the dispute between Isabeau d'Anglure and her brothers, the role and expectations of a woman as daughter, wife, widow and sister became central to the presentation of the case for both parties. The rhetoric of citation, with examples gathered from Valerius Maximus, Horace, Plautus, Euripides, Cicero, Sidonius and Martial, among others, assisted the lawyers in magnifying their characterisations of Isabeau and her circumstances either as a dutiful, obedient daughter and wife or as a greedy sister who should have remained modest and silent rather than sully the family name. Her male kin bearing the family name and moreover bearing arms and spilling their blood on the battlefield for the kings of France set out to defend the dignity of the noble household (*maison*) of Anglure against a potential change of fortune. They relied on the idea that families and households formed the foundation of the royal state so that the interests of the family should not be shaken by the individual demands of a daughter and sister.

---

[85] Guillaume du Vair, *Les Œuvres de Messire Guillaume du Vair* (Paris: S. Cramoisy, 1641), pp. 1028–9, 1037.

[86] Ibid., p. 1038.

[87] Isabeau d'Anglure and her husband lost the appeal in the *arrêt* of 26 June 1567 and the Parlement de Paris denied them the execution of their writ: AN, X1a 5014, fo. 449v; Chenu, *Cent notables*, 1603 edn, pp. 232–3.

If some cases and *arrêts* upheld the idea of the importance of family name and honour, the father governing the household, and a husband's authority over his wife, at other times judicial decisions could be more ambiguous.[88] Lawyers and judges knew all too well that the judicial system in sixteenth-century France was hardly consistent or systematic. Even if lawyers and jurists were 'actively building a French legal system', they constantly debated and positioned themselves with reference to aspects of Roman law or acknowledged the bewildering effects of hundreds of areas of French customary law where the custom of one area did not apply in another. Rather than standing 'firmly on legal grounds', the ground was always shifting in the late sixteenth century and early seventeenth century.[89] Lawyers and judges lived in a world of paradox: of pleadings for and against, of dignity and misery, of vice and virtue, of order as well as disorder. Lawyers were trained to speak on behalf of a client, even in difficult cases that might go against a prevailing ideology, and to be able to refute the arguments of the opposing lawyer. The competing systems of law – customary law, that is, both the old custom and the new custom reformed from the fifteenth through seventeenth centuries, canon law, Roman law, royal edicts – could be used to argue a point. Not just one or the other, but sometimes all of the above.

As Montaigne wrote in the 1580 edition of the *Essais* when discussing the astonishing range of opinions 'concerning vice and virtue':

> I have heard it reported of a judge, who when he met with any sharp conflict between Bartolus and Baldus, or any case admitting contrariety, was wont to write in the margin of his book, 'A question for a friend', which is to say that the truth was so entangled, and disputable, that in such a case he might favour which party he should think good ... To so infinite a science, depending on the authority of so many opinions, and of so arbitrary a subject, it cannot be, but that an exceeding confusion of judgments must arise. There are very few processes so clear, but the lawyers' advice upon them will be found to differ: What one company has judged, another will adjudge the contrary, and the very same will another time change opinion. Hence we see ordinary examples by this licence, which wonderfully blemish the authority and luster of our law, never to stay upon one sentence, but to run from one to another judge, to decide one same case.[90]

Pasquier concurred that if one were to try a case at the various Parlements it would win or lose according to the customs of the region. 'Transfer from the Parlement of

[88] Evelyne Berriot-Salvadore, *Les femmes dans la société française de la Renaissance* (Geneva, 1990), pp. 27, 32, 38–40.

[89] Hanley, 'Jurisprudence', p. 21. Hanley is closer to the mark since she acknowledged the 'volatility of the theory of male right' in 'The Family, the State', p. 289.

[90] Montaigne, *Essays*, II:12, vol. II, p. 306; Montaigne, *Essais*, p. 582A: 'de ne s'arrester aux arrests, et courir des uns aux autres juges pour decider d'une mesme cause'.

Dauphiné to that of Paris a case sent from one jurisdiction to another and it would lose. Send it back to from Paris to Grenoble and it would win there'.[91]

When Vice is More Evident than Virtue

A 1599 appeal before the Parlement de Paris pitted the widow of a nobleman against his brothers. The case was clouded by the dubious circumstances under which the nobleman had lived his life, fathering illegitimate children and marrying at the last possible moment before his death. It is useful to analyse this appeal because notions about family honour, the nobility, dignity and the governance of the household were at stake, and yet clearly the deceased gentleman had fallen far below the usual ideals of virtuous conduct. Lawyers in early modern France could be called upon to legitimate family practices that did not meet the ideals of self-governance – when vice was more evident than virtue, and the father, the husband or master did not govern the household as the conduct books would have wished. Lawyers employed a range of literary allusions and resorted to a wide array of competing systems of law, beyond royal edicts, to discuss the issues of dignity and rank and how they might apply in an irregular marital union between a man and a woman of unequal origins.

This appeal concerning the validity of the marriage between the nobleman and his former servant involved three famous *parlementaires* speaking as advocates – Anne Robert, Antoine Arnauld and Simon Marion. The advocates Antoine Arnauld and Anne Robert were held in such high esteem that Henri IV had once taken the visiting Duc de Savoie to the Parlement to hear them plead in a case where Arnauld's father-in-law, Simon Marion, acted as the *avocat du roi*.[92] By the 1630s, the printers and booksellers of the *avocat général du roi* Louis Servin's collection of pleadings, *arrêts* and notable decisions would even advertise the additional attraction of Robert and Arnauld's speeches.[93] Jean Chenu's collection of 'singular questions of law' printed versions of the pleadings of Robert and Arnauld as well as Marion acting as *procureur général du roi* in the 1599 appeal.

In Chenu's depiction of the case, the Sieur de la Brossardière had welcomed a farmer's daughter as his domestic servant in 1583 and 'employed [her] for the most base things' – 'aux choses plus viles'. He fell in love with her, that is, he was 'amoureux', 'seduced' her – 'la desbaucha' – and over a period of 15 years they had four children, two of whom survived. In June of 1597, ill and 'without

91 Pasquier, *Lettres familières*, p. 73: 'Evoquez du Parlement du Dauphiné à celuy de Paris une cause qui soit fondee en regrès, [that is, sent from one jurisdiction to another] elle s'y perdra. Renvoyez-là de Paris à Grenoble, elle s'y gaignera'.

92 Fumaroli, *L'âge de l'éloquence*, p. 442; *Dictionnaire de biographie française*, vol. III, p. 854.

93 Louis Servin, *Actions notables et plaidoyez de messire Louys Servin ... à la fin desquels sont les arrests intervenus sur iceux ... Ensemble les plaidoyers de M.A. Robert, Arnault et autres* (Paris: G. Alliot and C. Morlot, 1631).

hope of recovery', the Sieur de la Brossardière wrote his will and bequeathed some of his goods to his illegitimate children. The following evening, upon taking further advice, he was transported to the local parish church where his marriage was celebrated and blessed in the presence of a lawyer relative of his new wife as well as other witnesses. La Brossardière then revoked his will and recognised his children by Georgine Maillet as his legitimate offspring. He died the next day. After his death his brothers challenged the marriage before a court of first instance, but the marriage was declared 'good and valid' – 'bon et valable' – and the children legitimate.

At the heart of the resulting appeal lay questions about the dignity, nobility or the quality of the widow and her children. Were they 'fit to inherit'? Maillet was new to her nobility, yet the widow held the power of *garde noble*. According to the court registers a newly noble widow, possessing the right of *garde noble* or the privilege of guardianship of her children and usufruct of their lands, fought an action brought by her two brothers-in-law in 1597 and won the case, which the brothers then appealed from the presidial court of Angers to the Parlement in 1599.[94] As guardian and tutor of La Brossardière's children Georgine Maillet had control over and use of their property without any constraint over her government of the household, and this was precisely the objection of her in-laws. If the children's noble birthright was uncertain or sullied because of the nature of their parents' relationship, the children or their widowed mother needed to prove not only the children's legitimacy but also their 'noble' qualities or dignity and virtue through merit and training to 'live nobly'.[95]

While Chenu's version relates some of the colourful detail behind the legal proceedings, the court registers simply recorded the persons involved and the dates and 'sentences' of the case before it was appealed to the Parlement. From the court registers we learn little about the pleadings in the appeal beyond the identities of the lawyers: Robert on behalf of the brothers and Arnauld representing the widow. Chenu's printed version focuses on the validity of the marriage and the legitimacy of the children. The court registers, however, noted that the appeal was not in respect of the whole cause but only a challenge concerning the right of Sieur de la Brossardière's newly legitimated children to inherit 'tiltres', specifically the right of the eldest male to inherit the noble title to the family name and land.[96]

Chenu's printed version alleges many sordid details about the self-governance of the widow. 'Among other things' Robert, 'rebukes' Maillet for her lack of

---

94 Chenu's printed version records the sénéchaussée of Anjou as the court of first instance.

95 Three accounts of the case each report a different configuration of children: Chenu's printed version suggests a surviving boy and girl out of four children; the BN Dupuy 115 manuscript records two boys to the exclusion of girls, the court registers mention both 'children' and that La Brossardière's brothers had 'nephews'.

96 AN, Registres, Parlement de Paris, Civil, Plaidoiries, X1a 5205, 29 March 1599, fos 96r–v.

chastity and accuses her of 'prostituting herself' to others. The lawyer even goes so far as to suggest that a parish priest was her companion during the Sieur de la Brossardière's time as a prisoner of war. There was no reason to declare the marriage 'good and valid', according to Robert, because it was concluded by the 'allurements, enticements and persuasions' of Maillet and her lawyer cousin, who would have warned the deceased that bequests to 'bastard children' were 'null'.

To remind the court of Maillet's humble origins as a servant and unwed companion of her master, Robert juxtaposed the dignity of a wife within marriage with the disorderly life of a concubine. He announced to the court that 'the name of concubine' is a 'name of [illicit] sensuality' – *nomen est voluptatis* – while the 'name of wife' is a 'name of dignity' – *nomen est dignitatis*. While marriage 'brings the union together', concubinage stains or 'blemishes the blood ties'. A concubine 'brings forth [a child] against the vow', while a legitimate wife begets 'from within the vow'. While one 'announces her marriage', the other 'conceals her filth under a union'.[97] The conduct and self-governance of the Sieur de la Brossardière was not under scrutiny to the same extent as the tenant farmer's daughter, who had managed to transform herself from servant to companion to mother of La Brossardière's natural children to noble wife and finally widow with the guardianship of her former lord's children and control over their property. To underline how the concubine 'disguises herself as a legitimate wife' – 'se desguise en femme legitime' – in the printed version Robert's pleading cites a passage from 'the Poet': 'She calls it wedlock, gives her fault an honest name'. Readers would easily have been able to identify Virgil and his allusion to Dido's predicament in publicising her love with Aeneas.[98]

To please the judges and to move them to favour his client, the lawyer needed to use rhetorical ornaments and examples to persuade the judges of the essence of the case.[99] Like their literary counterparts such as Montaigne reflecting on human nature, Marconville debating the *Querelle des femmes* or Madeleine de L'Aubespine considering the dignity and misery of man in the second half of the sixteenth century, lawyers assembled proofs from sources well beyond the Bible and the creation story. The lawyers appearing before the Parlement drew on a wide variety of sources in their 'rhetoric of citation': previous *arrêts*, articles of customary law, a title of law from Justinian's *Digest*, canon law, ancient Greek tragedy or comedy, the Church Fathers, the Roman poets, tales of illustrious women, classical myths. The assortment of authorities summoned before the court can at times astonish.[100] Marie Houllemare has demonstrated how Anne Robert prepared notes and literary commonplaces ready to insert into a speech or

97 Chenu, *Cent notables*, 1603 edn, pp. 186–7.

98 Virgil, *The Fourth Book of Virgil's Æneid on the Loves of Dido and Æneas*, trans. Richard Fanshaw (Oxford, 1924), p. 33, line 172; Virgil, *Eclogues, Georgics, Æneid I–VI*, trans. H. Rushton Fairclough (Cambridge, MA, 1999), pp. 432–3, line 172.

99 Skinner, *Reason and Rhetoric*, p. 104.

100 Dawson, *Oracles*, pp. 318, 338.

a pleading.[101] Erasmus could not have asked for a better pupil in the *De copia*. On the subject of dowry Robert cited both Justinian's *Code* and the *Novels* before he turned to the Greek playwright Plautus to magnify his point. In the *Trinummus* or *Three Bob Day*, the impoverished Lesbonicus complains to his young Athenian friend Lysiteles that marrying his sister without a dowry would be like giving his 'own sister for a concubine, more than wife'.[102] On the inequalities of status and rank between the Sieur de la Brossardière and his 'servant', Robert once again considered Justinian's *Code* and the *Digest* before he intensified his pleading with examples from Apuleius and Ovid.[103] In the *Golden Ass* Venus disparages Psyche, who was pregnant with Cupid's child, for attempting to pose as his wife: 'Since as the marriage was made between unequal persons, in no town, without witnesses, and not by the consent of their parents, therefore the marriage is illegitimate, and the child (that shall be born) a bastard'.[104] Meanwhile in Ovid's *Heroides* humble Deianira complains to her powerful husband Hercules: 'As the ill-mated steer yoked miserably at the plough, so fares the wife who is less than her mighty [man]'.[105] The reader of Robert's pleading encounters this 'rhetoric of citation' with each turn of the page.

The margin of Robert's printed pleading gets straight to the point for the busy reader: 'If a contract is necessary in a marriage'. Using the rhetorical technique of *paradiastole* or redescription, Robert declares that without a marriage contract vice will be confused with virtue, purity with lechery, honour with dishonesty, bastards with legitimate children, 'which would be to extinguish entirely the dignity of the sacrament of marriage and to mar and alter the honour of honest [virtuous] families'.[106] Robert assembles a variety of church authorities in support of a public wedding and banns: Tertullian's *To His Wife*, Saint Ambrose, the canon law, articles from the Fourth Lateran Council and from the 24th session of the Council of Trent

[101] Houllemare, 'Un avocat parisien', pp. 287–9.

[102] Plautus, *Trinummus* or *Three Bob Day*, in *Plautus*, vol. V, 3.2.1, pp. 164–5, line 690. Louis Le Caron cites the same passage: *Memorables ou Observations du droict françois*, fo. 293v.

[103] Chenu, *Cent notables*, 1603 edn, p. 188.

[104] Lucius Apuleius, *The Golden Ass*, trans. W. Adlington [1566], (London, 1928), Bk VI, pp. 262–3.

[105] Ovid, *Heroides and Amores*, trans. G. Showerman (London, 1931), Bk IX, pp. 110–11, lines 29–30. The pleading substitutes *viro* for *minor*.

[106] Chenu, *Cent notables*, 1603 edn, p. 188: 'Car sans le contract l'on ne peut discerner la concubine de la femme legitime, & se faict vn meslange de vice & de la vertu, de la pudicité auec la paillardise, de l'honneur auec de la turpitude, des bastards auec les legitimes, qui seroit entierement esteindre la dignité du sacrement de mariage, & perdre & alterer l'honneur des honnestes familles'.

in 1563, in which the proclamation of banns on 'three successive feast' days is 'expressly recommended'.[107]

The French state had issued a royal edict in 1556/57 to prevent a young son or daughter from entering a clandestine marriage without parental consent, but what if the couple was already mature or no longer had parents to keep them in check? From 1579 the Ordinance of Blois began to regulate cases of unequal marriage involving adult children without parents through a requirement for banns on three separate holy days.[108] Saving this royal ordinance for the last weapon of his argument, Robert contends that in its attempt to 'preserve the dignity of marriage' the ordinance threatened to nullify a marriage unless it had observed the publication of banns and therefore the law would 'unmask the concubines who disguised themselves as honourable wives' – 'femmes d'honneur'.[109] Because Maillet had lived publicly and openly as a concubine, Robert suggested that she needed to make amends or 'expiate' her actions by the 'proclamation of banns' so that everyone would know she had become a legitimate wife.

In the debates of the dignity and misery of man, a man might aspire to master his vices and base appetites and to achieve a level of wisdom and dignity shared by the angels and other celestial beings. For a woman the highest honour was to achieve the dignity of a wife, to act as a comfort to her husband, control her appetites, and live in virtue in order that she be able to govern the household and her children and servants. The crux of the *Querelle des femmes* debates was an anxiety among husbands and fathers that a wife might fail to be a person of honour, chastity and modesty. At every opportunity, Robert reminded the court of Maillet's low station by birth, her disorderly past with the Sieur de la Brossardière (and he hinted at others without quite saying that La Brossardière was cuckolded or questioning paternity), and tried to downplay her newly honourable status as noble widow and guardian.

---

107 Tertullian, [*Ad uxorem*] *À son épouse*, ed. and trans. C. Munier (Paris, 1980), Bk II, p. 191; St Ambroise, lib. 9 epist. I; *Decretum Gratiani*, Part I in 2 volumes of *Corpus juris canonici emendatum et notis illustratum. Gregorii XIII. pont. max. iussu editum* (Rome, 1582), Causa XXX, questio V, cols 2069–78, accessed via the UCLA Digital Library Program *Corpus juris canonici (1582)*, at http://digital.library.ucla.edu/canonlaw, accessed 10 November 2010; Norman Tanner (ed.), *Decrees of the Ecumenical Councils*, 2 vols (London 1990), vol. I, p. 258, article 51: *De pœna contrabentium clandestina matrimonia* or 'On the punishment of those who contract clandestine marriages'; ibid., vol. II, Council of Trent, Session 24, 'Canons on the reform of marriage', pp. 755–6.

108 Isambert, *Recueil général*, vol. XIV, Henri III, May 1579, 'Ordonnance rendue sur les plaintes et doléances des états-généraux assemblés à Blois', art. 40, p. 391.

109 Chenu, *Cent notables*, 1603 edn, p. 188; Isambert, *Recueil général*, vol. XIV, Henri III, 1579, Blois, articles 40, 41, 42, pp. 391–2. The printed version of the pleading in Chenu cites the articles 41 and 42 that focus on the consent of fathers, mothers and tutors under pain of death; however, the words of Robert's speech clearly emphasise the publication of banns, which is article 40.

By the royal edict of 1629, the rules regarding marriage between persons of unequal rank become much more severe and families or accomplices had much to lose if a family member skipped the formalities of contract, banns and public ceremony and entered into a marriage without consultation of parents, brothers, tutors or relatives.[110] Despite the restrictions on families and marriages in place after 1579 and tightened again in 1629, however, James Farr has uncovered a pattern of 'lenient judgments' and '*de facto* decriminalization' in cases of clandestine marriage before the Burgundian courts.[111] The officeholders, lawyers, *procureurs* and notaries working to keep the legal system running knew all too well the distinction between the ideal and the real – between human dignity and misery. The contrast between the ideal of dignity embodied by the 'perfect magistrate' and the courtroom he inhabited did not escape notice. At the time of La Brossardière-Maillet's contested marriage there was still some room to manoeuvre, and the lawyers slipped and slid around the existing royal edicts, customary, canon and civil laws as best they could.

When the famous lawyer Antoine Arnauld strode onto the parquet to begin his representation of the widow Georgine Maillet, according to the print version of the pleading he derided his opponent for having wanted to 'batter the honour of the mother' – 'sugiller l'honneur de la mere'. Arnauld reminded the Parlement that in the original lawsuit – which his client had won – the judge had made his enquiries immediately after the death of the Sieur de la Brossardière, within recent 'memory' of the gentleman's history with Maillet and of their 'conduct' together (*desportements*).[112] Arnauld carefully rehabilitates the honour of Maillet as a mother and wife by reminding the court of the 'celebration' of the marriage in the 'holy Church', how the couple 'loved each other with marital affection'. Arnauld echoes canon and civil law principles when he refers to their 'mutual and reciprocal consent', much as we saw in chapter six in Jean de Marconville's treatment of the marriage bond and mutual consent in his 1564 paradox on the happiness and unhappiness of marriage.[113] The training of the heirs for their positions of nobility and dignity began under the governance of their father, Arnauld told the court, when La Brossardière supported his son at school from the age of ten 'with the highest stipend at the table of the schoolmaster' – 'à la plus haulte pension à la table du maistre'.[114]

---

110 Hanley, 'Jurisprudence', pp. 26–7.

111 James Farr, 'Parlementaires and the Paradox of Power: Sovereignty and Jurisprudence in *Rapt* Cases in Early Modern Burgundy', *European History Quarterly* 25 (1995): 345.

112 Chenu, *Cent notables*, 1603 edn, pp. 188–9.

113 *Decretum Gratiani*, in *Corpus juris canonici*, causa XXVII, questio 2, canon 2, cols 1995–6, 1989–90; Digest. 50. 17. 30, *Nuptias non concubitus, sed consensus facit*, or 'Agreement and not sleeping together makes the marriage'. See Chapter 6, p. 150.

114 Chenu, *Cent notables*, 1603 edn, p. 189.

Arnauld's pleading on behalf of the widow Maillet is a fabric of Roman and French legal references woven together with the decisions of contemporary lawsuits and embroidered with classical quotations. Arnauld suggested to the court that the Sieur de la Brossardière was quite clear in his intentions when he donned a garment of new satin, heard the Mass, received the sacrament and praised God that he was able to complete the marriage ceremony; Arnauld quoted from Seneca at length to strengthen his point:

> Yet we are never more careful in our giving, never do we wrestle more in making decisions than when, with all self-interest banished, only the ideal of good remains before our eyes; we are bad judges of our duties only so long as they are distorted by hope and fear and that most slothful of vices, pleasure. But when death has shut off all these, and has brought us to pronounce sentence as incorrupt judges, we search for those who are most worthy to inherit our possessions, and there is nothing that we arrange with more scrupulous care than this, which is of no concern to ourselves.[115]

Arnauld underlines the public nature of La Brossardière and Maillet's wedding ceremony with yet another citation in his conclusion. Tertullian explained that, in the marriage sacrament, 'the Church cements, and the oblation confirms, the benediction signs and seals; the angels carry back the news [to heaven], the Father holds for ratified'.[116]

For the humanist Pierre Dupuy, writing a brief account of the La Brossardière-Maillet appeal in the handwritten collection of pleadings, *factum* and legal consultations compiled in the early 1600s as he prepared for the legal profession, the main question concerned the legitimacy of the 'bastard' children and whether they were 'fit to inherit' because of the hasty circumstances of the marriage of their parents – a 'gentilhomme de bonne maison' and his 'concubine'.[117] Dupuy saw a connection 'on the subject of this case' with another lawsuit involving bastard children from the noble house of the Sieur de la Borde et de Néron, in which the lawyer Antoine Arnauld represented one of the parties and Louis Servin represented the king's interests for the attorney-general. Guy III d'Arbaleste, Sieur de la Borde et de Néron, fathered bastard children with a long-term female companion and he left these children a legacy in his will.[118] Each of these noble

115 Seneca, *On Benefits*, in *Moral Essays*, trans. John Basore, 3 vols (London, 1963), vol. III, pp. 226–7, IV. xi, 5: (some variation); Chenu, *Cent notables*, 1603 edn, p. 191.

116 Tertullian, *À son épouse*, Bk 2, VIII, 6, pp. 148–9: *Ecclesia concilauit, confirmauit oblatio, Angeli nunciarunt, & pater scilicet cœlestic, ratum habuit*, translated as 'que l'Église ménage, que confirme l'offrande, que scelle la bénédiction; les anges le proclament, le Père céleste le ratifie'; Chenu, *Cent notables*, 1603 edn, p. 192.

117 BN, MS Dupuy 115, fo. 227v.

118 Guy III Arbaleste, the brother of Charlotte Arbaleste, Mme de Mornay, never married but had two 'natural' sons, Isaac and Abraham Arbaleste. A.H. Taillandier, 'Notice

bastard bearers, as Pierre Dupuy commented in his annotations, were of an age and a lineage – 'parens et gens de marque' – that would suggest they should have been capable of governing a household. And yet in their families' eyes they were not able to govern themselves and their passions, and fell short of expectations of ideal fathers and masters of a household.[119]

In the La Brossardière–Maillet appeal Arnauld argued in favour of the widow and her children's right to their inheritance, whereas in the Sieur de la Borde case he rejected the right of bastard children to claim the bequest their natural father left them in his will. Arnauld invoked the customary law in the region of Melun that prevented a bastard child inheriting from a parent unless the child had been legitimised through marriage.[120] Arnauld, one of the most talented lawyers of his generation, was fully at ease arguing for or against any topic, whether supporting children's claim to inheritance against a deceased nobleman's brothers in one appeal, or rejecting the right of 'natural' children to claim under a will in another. Throughout the sixteenth century, ordinances, legal handbooks and remonstrances by the king's attorneys reminded lawyers of their duty to represent only the causes they knew to be just and the clients in whom they believed. They were reminded to be honest and 'communicate', or share all the pertinent documents in a case and not withhold items from opponents.[121] Colin Kaiser has documented how the officeholders at the top of the social and professional pyramid were subject to a 'moralizing pressure' and regulation through 'mercurial' tribunals, and systematic checks of the 'moral and religious qualities' of new judges. Even the *avocats généraux* as the king's servants exhorted their fellow parlementaires to live up to this ideal. Although lawyers did not hold venal or purchased offices, they were nevertheless subject to a pressure to maintain their dignity.[122] Writing in the early seventeenth century, Bernard de La Roche Flavin reminded the lawyer that 'probity and virtue' would build his credibility in the eyes of the judges. 'Trust and authority is the power of persuasion, indeed it is persuasion itself'. Lawyers

historique sur le château et les seigneurs de La Borde-le-Vicomte', *Revue archaéologique* 13 (1856): 113–18.

119 BN, MS Dupuy 115, 25 February 1601, fos 227v, 228v. Guy III Arbaleste, Sieur de la Borde et de Néron complained in his will that his brothers had prevented him from marrying.

120 Bourdot de Richebourg (ed.), *Nouveau coutumier général*, vol. III, ch. XXI, arts 297, 298, p. 454.

121 Isambert, *Recueil général,* vol. XIV, Charles IX, 1560, 'De la justice et de la police', esp. art 58, p. 80; Bernard de La Roche Flavin, *Treize livres des Parlemens de France esquels est amplement traicté de leur origine et institution* (Geneva: Matthieu Berjon, 1621), pp. 310–12, 346–7; Fumaroli, *L'âge de l'éloquence*, pp. 436–7.

122 Colin Kaiser, 'Les Cours souveraines au XVIe siècle: morale et Contre-Réforme', *Annales-économies, sociétés, civilisations* 37 (1982): 18–19, 21; Fumaroli, *L'âge de l'éloquence:*, pp. 436–7; Miriam Yardeni, 'L'ordre des avocats et la grève du Barreau parisien en 1602', *Revue d'histoire économique et sociale* 44 (1966): 484, 491–2.

needed to persuade the judges that they were 'men of their word' – 'gens de bien & veritables'.[123]

The Range of Possibilities on Both Sides of an Argument

Hanley argues that '[c]ollecting and printing notable *arrêts* (past and present), [jurists] built a body of case law and advanced a legal theory of binding precedents – notable *arrêts* treated as law – based on it'.[124] Both Robert and Arnauld called the attention of the Parlement to the judicial decisions of similar cases at the level of first instance such as the *sénéchaussée* or presidial court as well as precedents in the Parlement de Paris, but, as one might expect, courtroom opponents did not concur in their interpretations of these *arrêts*. Arnauld rebuked Robert's interpretation of contemporary judicial decisions on the validity of marriages, which 'could not be adapted to [fit] the facts'.[125] When Anne Robert published his own series of pleadings and comments on judicial decisions, the *Rerum Judicatarum* in 1596, he gave a copy to Étienne Pasquier. In his response Pasquier admired the diligence of jurists such as Louis Le Caron, Choppin, Chenu, Loüet and Robert himself for their publication of collections of *arrêts* as well as outlining the 'pour' and the 'contre' of the parties to the lawsuits. These collections were 'rich' as guides to legal practice. However, Pasquier questioned whether the *arrêts* or judicial decisions 'should be reputed [to be] Laws for all of France'. He reminded Robert that, whenever a lawyer alleged an *arrêt* from a similar case before the Parlement, the *premier président* or chief justice Christophe de Thou would scoff, 'good for him' – 'bon pour luy' – and ask the lawyer to 'defend his case' for 'good and valid [*valables*] reasons'.[126]

In his printed collection of pleadings, Pierre Ayrault presented both his pleadings and some of the points of the opposing counsel. In one case a widowed mother declared that she did not want to accept the nomination by the relatives to become *tutrice* and *curatice* of her children, but when a local judge ordered that she take the oath she appealed the verdict of the sénéchal of Auvergne to the Parlement de Paris.[127] Ayrault, who represented her, demonstrated to the reader how to argue for a widow who did not want guardianship of her child. He used

---

123 La Roche-Flavin, *Treize livres des Parlemens*, pp. 302–3: 'La creance & l'authorité est le nerf de la persuasion, voire c'est la persuasion mesme'.

124 Hanley, 'Jurisprudence', pp. 21–3; Sarah Hanley, 'Social Sites of Political Practice in France: Lawsuits, Civil Rights, and the Separation of Powers in Domestic and State Government, 1500–1800', *American Historical Review* 102:1 (1997): 32–6.

125 See Pierre Pithou, *Coustumes du bailliage de Troyes en Champagne conférées au coustumes de France* (Paris: Cardin Besongne, 1630), 1st edn 1598, article 108, p. 298; Chenu, *Cent notables*, 1603 edn, pp. 191–2.

126 Pasquier, 'A Monsieur Robert, Advocat en la Cour de Parlement de Paris', in *Les Œuvres*, Bk XIX, Letter XV, col. 578.

127 See Ayrault, XII *Pledoiers*, pp. 188–98; AN, X1a 5015, 14 July 1567, fo. 79v.

the practices of the Romans 'considered the equal of a dozen nations', which kept women in perpetual tutelage, not because they lacked 'judgment', but because the office would take the mother too much into the public realm. For flourish he added the Greek playwright Menander, a favourite source for the attackers of women in the *Querelle des femmes*, before using the old customary law of Auvergne as well as the new reformed customary law both of which allowed the mother to become *tutrice* 'if she wishes'.[128] But Ayrault was anxious to show the complexity of the issue and included several perspectives. He explained how the opposing lawyer argued that it was a mother's 'duty (*devoir*)' to accept the post especially because guardianships were 'dative' in France, granted in the presence of a judge who had taken advice from relatives, neighbours or friends.[129] Not only did Ayrault give a brief account of both sides of the case, he cross-referenced another case he had pleaded for a widow. In this instance the widow had lost her guardianship of the children when she remarried. After the remarriage ended in a second widowhood, and with no children from the second marriage bed, the mother attempted to recover custody of her children from the first marriage and Ayrault advocated for her.[130] Neither mother represented by Ayrault ended up with the guardianship of her child. In one case this was the desired outcome of the mother, in the other it was not. But Ayrault presented the reader of his collection of pleadings with three variations on a legal topic. And the reader learned that considering the opposite case might help one to gather examples and proofs to present the most persuasive argument before a judge in order to win.

John Dawson demonstrated that secrecy about judicial decisions diminished in the late sixteenth- and early seventeenth century in publications such as Georges Loüet's *Recueil d'aucuns notables arrests donnez en la cour du Parlement de Paris*, sold by Abel L'Angelier and later his widow in the Palais de Justice in editions appearing in quick succession in 1609, 1610, 1611, 1612, 1613, 1614, 1616 and 1620.[131] Loüet, unlike many of the other compilers of *arrêts*, was actually a judge, not a lawyer. But Dawson found 'no developed theory as to the binding force of judicial decisions'. Although lawyers like Robert or Arnauld in the LaBrossardière–Maillet appeal might refer to the judgments of previous cases, they

---

128 Dupont, *Controverses*, Janot 1540 edn, fos 94v–95v or sigs MMvi^{v}–MMvii^{v}.

129 In a different appeal to the Parlement, a lawyer made a similar rejoinder that the French 'are not ruled by Roman law, that we are in a French monarchy, ruled and governed on other terms than Rome whose law recognized three sorts of guardianship *scilicet testamentariam, legitimam, & daiuam*: in France they are all dative because they are given and appointed by a judge at the nomination of the relatives' – see Chenu, *Cent notables*, 1603 edn, question XXI, vol. II, pp. 215–16.

130 See Ayrault, *XII Pledoiers*, esp. pp. 195–6; AN, X1a 5014, 10 June 1567, fo. 352v.

131 Balsamo and Simonin, *Abel L'Angelier*, cat. nos. 486 (1609), 501 (1610), 518 (1611), 530 (1612), 536 (1613), 543 (1614), 563 (1616), 589 (1620); Georges Loüet, *Recueil d'aucuns notables arrests donnez en la cour du Parlement de Paris* (Paris: Abel L'Angelier, 1609).

did so blindly and without knowledge of the judges' reasons for those decisions.[132] Lawyers used whatever other 'persuasive' means of proof might 'favour' the case of their client, whether customary law, Justinian's *Digest* or a passage from Ovid or Virgil. As we saw in chapter five, Pasquier had pleaded on behalf of a female client whose mother had left her a bequest larger than her siblings' portions as permitted under the customs of the region. The opposing lawyers' stressed the need for equality between the children: 'I pleaded for her and I assure you that I forgot nothing that I thought might favour my case … I had the customary law [on my side], with the explicit will of the mother, but I didn't have the good opinion (*air*) of the judges for me'.[133]

The lawyers might refer to *arrêts* or royal edicts, but never to the exclusion of other competing authorities – even canon law – when it might prove useful to their case. Lawyers knew how to dip into the ideology of the family as the foundation of the French state – that governing one's vices and virtues led to good household government and that these households provided the pillars, columns and foundations of the royal state. Some judges, lawyers, notaries, attorneys and royal officeholders may have tried to promote or protect the idea that a father governed his family and household the way a king had the power to govern and rule the state. Lawyers, however, had clients who were human and as prone to inferiority, vice and misery as they were to striving for virtue to achieve the level of wisdom or the performance of public duty outlined in the 'dignity of man' treatises. The books of notable decisions are full of examples in which mothers, fathers, sons and daughters failed to behave according to ideals of virtue and dignity outlined in the books of moral philosophy. Maxims of self, household and state governance, while admirable and often alluded to as examples of virtue, had to yield to courtroom reality. Both the Sieur de la Brossardière and the Sieur de la Borde and de Néron had maintained 'concubines', fathered children with them, apparently against the wishes of their families, and lived outside of the permitted boundaries of conduct and marriage.

Speaking as a servant of the king in his role as *avocat du roi* Simon Marion summarised the main points of the dispute between the brothers of the Sieur de la Brossardière and his widow. Marion was the father-in-law of the lawyer Antoine Arnauld who represented La Brossardière's widow and had thus tried to persuade the court of the validity of the marriage and the legitimacy of the children. Marion's speech laments the sordid nature of the marriage and its 'imperfect' start. The king's attorney-general reminded the court that the 'origin and institution of marriage comes from God and no other', which was intended to demonstrate 'the excellence and greatness of marriage'. 'At the point of death' and under the cloak

---

[132] Dawson, *Oracles*, pp. 323–4, 338.

[133] Pasquier, *Lettres familières*, p. 74: [J]e plaidois pour elle, et vous asseure que je n'y oubliay rien de ce que je pensois servir à la faveur de ma cause'; Barbara Diefendorf, *Paris City Councillors in the Sixteenth Century: The Politics of Patrimony* (Princeton, NJ, 1983), pp. 267–8.

of 'clandestinity', the Sieur de la Brossardière entered a marriage without a 'civil contract' to outline the marital 'community of goods' and without provisions for a dowry or dower; an arrangement far from the 'noble and perfect' ideal. Nonetheless, Marion told the court that, if one or both of the spouses acted in 'good faith', then the children born of the union were legitimate, even if the circumstances of the marriage gave rise to the 'disputes' that would follow. Marion picked up on a point in his son-in-law Arnauld's pleading and noted that the brothers of the Sieur de la Brossardière had acknowledged Maillet in writing as their 'sister-in-law' and the children as their 'nephews'. The 'pretext' and 'idea' of marriage in terms of the legitimacy of the children had the same 'virtue' or merit and the same 'effects' as a 'just, true and perfect' marriage.[134] In both the printed version and the court registers Marion refers to the scholastic doctrine of the 'trois biens' or three goods of marriage – *bonum prolis, sacramentum, bonum fidei* – that is the intent to have children, to submit to the sacrament and to be faithful to it and to one's partner.[135] While the king's attorney-general may have preferred an ideal household with virtue on display and vices held in check, the reality was all too evident. The court found in favour of Maillet as widow of the Sieur de la Brossardière and mother of his children despite the imperfections of their relationship, the lack of marriage contract and the missing banns.

This father and 'come lately' husband had achieved his dying wish of ensuring the future of his children; and in this sense, paternal authority was confirmed despite its imperfect start. On appeal, the judicial decision had upheld the marriage for a second time and allowed La Brossardière's widow and the mother of his children to protect her eldest son's title to family name and property from encroachment by his noble uncles. While there may have been an ideological push to present the family as a miniature model of the royal state, in which a wife or daughter submitted to the benevolent governance of her husband or father as the head of household, some cases were much more ambiguous. Lawyers and judges were not systematic in their interpretation of paternal and marital authority, nor were they consistent in the application of the law.[136] The ideology of the governance of self, household and state was certainly available to the royal and civic officeholders,

---

[134] AN, X1a 5205, fos 96r–v; Chenu, *Cent notables*, 1603 edn, pp. 192–3: 'La couleur & l'opinion du mariage quant à faire les enfans legitimes ayant la mesme vertu & les mesmes effects que le iuste, vray & parfaict mariage'.

[135] Peter Lombard, *The Sentences* [*Sententiæ in IV libris distinctæ*], trans. Giulio Silano (Toronto, 2007), Distinctio XXXI, Cap. 182 (1), *De tribus bonis coniugii.*

[136] Jacques Corbin, *Decisions de droict et de practique iugees par arrets des cours souveraines de France* (Paris: Jean Millot, 1611), chapters LXVII, CXIX and CXXXIII; Warner, 'Widows, Widowers'; AN, X1a, 1659, fos 289r–v. On the Sieur de la Borde, BN, MS Dupuy 115, fo. 227v; Berriot-Salvadore, *Les femmes*, pp. 27, 32, 38–40; Barbara Diefendorf, 'Give Us Back Our Children: Patriarchal Authority and Parental Consent to Religious Vocations in Early Counter-Reformation France', *Journal of Modern History* 68 (1996): pp. 267–8, 272–4; Farr, 'Parlementaires', p. 345; for a later period see Julie

lawyers and notaries.[137] They may even have promoted it. But in a Renaissance culture of paradox, which explored both the dignity of man and its underbelly the misery of man, notaries, attorneys, lawyers and their wives knew all too well the circumstances and the households that did not live up to this ideal.

Hardwick, 'Between State and Street: Witnesses and the Family Politics of Litigation in Early Modern France', in Desan and Merrick, (eds), *Family, Gender*, pp. 127–8.

[137] Hanley, 'Social Sites', p. 30; Hanley, 'Jurisprudence', pp. 4, 11–12.

Chapter 9
Conclusion

This book has charted the circulation of French ideas about man and woman from the late 1400s to the early 1600s, exploring in depth for the first time the fundamental connections between the *Querelle des femmes* on the nature of woman and the Renaissance debate on the dignity and misery of man. By examining the Renaissance ideas of man and woman side by side we discover the extent to which many of the commonplaces of the early sixteenth-century *Querelle des femmes* originated in the discussion of the dignity and misery of man. There is more crossover and overlap than distinction or separation. Moreover, the traffic was not simply one way. Writers on human nature complaining of the vanity or follies of man often borrowed and incorporated extensive examples of the virtuous deeds of women to underline the weaknesses of man.

This comparison of the literature on the nature of man and woman shifts our understanding because it divulges early modern concerns about the conduct of husbands and wives. It reveals anxieties about rank and social mobility as bourgeois and professional households concentrated resources on the purchase of offices serving the royal state, which conferred dignity and noble status. Even hereditary nobles worried about strategic marital alliances and the possibility of a loss of fortune – a father's actions or a son's placement might have consequences for the dignity of the household. At all social levels a wife's honour and her role in setting a virtuous, chaste, moderate example helped preserve the status of the household and keep ruin at bay. Some of these social tensions are echoed in lawyers' pleadings where concerns – about marriages between those of unequal rank, about disorder and reputation, about title to property, about the conduct of wives and daughters and their obedience to male authority, about the importance of upholding the place of the noble household in the royal state while preserving it from downfall – were exposed to the full glare of the courtroom.

This book questions the notion that the ideas circulating in these moral discussions were merely rhetorical. Early modern society weighed diverse commonplaces, considered examples and counterexamples as a means to understand their topsy-turvy world and perhaps determine a neglected truth along the way. An obvious example is the reading practices of lawyers, and the gathering of commonplaces in notebooks ready for use in a speech to persuade the judges on behalf of a client. The 'rhetoric of citation' became prevalent in lawyers' pleadings in the Parlement de Paris during the latter half of the sixteenth century and early 1600s because lawyers knew judges might be swayed by moral argument as much as by any combination of customary laws, royal edicts, Roman law or even canon law they could bring to bear on each legal question. Many of the commonplaces of praise and blame, of man and of woman as husbands and wives or as sons and daughters, resurfaced when lawyers needed to characterise the conduct of clients and opposing parties. In the courtroom the virtues and vices of the *Querelle des femmes* and the dignity- and misery-of-man literature had a practical application – to win the case. The concluding chapters confirm the connection between the rhetoric of praise and blame found in the *Querelle des femmes* and writing on human nature and the forensic rhetoric employed by advocates in their pleadings before the Parlement de Paris. Once spoken, lawyers' pleadings were often further embellished and developed if they made the transition into print, and were sold in the marketplace of the Palais de Justice in Paris alongside the volumes of moral philosophy, classics and history that had provided many of the original citations and *exempla* used to set the tone and move the audience of judges.

Initially the *Querelle des femmes* continued a medieval debate as early printers and booksellers transformed manuscripts such as Martin Le Franc's *Champion des dames* into printed bestsellers. But the *Querelle des femmes* was not static. As it shifted from manuscript to print it also began to change from the medieval dispute to the Renaissance dialogue, and eventually to chapters and *exempla* strewn throughout collections of diverse lessons, *discours* or essays reflecting on the human condition. The literature of the dignity and misery of man transformed from a genre that had its origin in the creation story of Genesis to a more varied account of human civilisations in the new world and among ancient cultures near and far that introduced a new moral relativity. These wide-ranging collections about the morals, customs and habits of peoples throughout history and across the world shared a fascination with the virtuous and the vicious, the potential for greatness or weakness that characterised the dignity- and misery-of-man literature. Despite this evolution of the genre, readers in the late 1590s and early 1600s could still wander the bookstalls in the Palais de Justice and the Île de la Cité and purchase a traditional style of *Querelle des femmes* text in defence of the female sex or a work on human dignity and misery. Or these customers could choose the new manner of musing on these longstanding questions about human nature in Montaigne's *Essais*.

The chapters on the book trade reveal how booksellers helped to perpetuate these debates and promote the sales of their stock, adapting to the interests of their clientèle. The editorial policies of the printers and merchant booksellers, who pursued the royal privileges allowing them to bring these titles to market, provide further proof of the juncture between the history of ideas and the print culture of early modern France. We have traced how booksellers targeted and marketed their wares, sometimes offering potential customers the works of authors such as Speroni, Marconville or Tahureau packaged specifically as *Querelle des femmes* texts, sometimes selling these works as collections, miscellanies or as a series of dialogues on diverse topics. These writers compiled and recycled from their own works – and those of others – moving examples from one genre to another, such as Boaistuau's praise of woman and marriage copied from his 'advice for princes' book and inserted into his treatise on the misery of man. Following these ideas in print from the distribution networks of booksellers in Paris and Lyon to the potential readers and personal libraries of the customers who purchased these titles gives insight into the connections so obvious to Renaissance writers and readers, yet overlooked by modern scholars in the pursuit of separate academic fields and disciplines.

Without question, women as daughters, wives and mothers experienced a legal and political condition inferior to their male counterparts in the early modern period and had fewer educational and occupational opportunities. However, to argue, as Gratien Dupont did in the 1530s, against marriage and wives and for the inferiority of woman without allowing a Champion to come to her defence required daring, humour and skills of persuasion, for two reasons. First of all, the value of a good wife was obvious to the large swathes of the population who married despite all the warnings of inevitable misery that a *Querelle des femmes* writer such as Dupont or Desportes could muster. The economic support of a wife's labour, her dowry, the value of her social networks and the potential of the children she raised, the promise of her 'comfort' and 'aid' – all of her contributions formed parts of the widespread and 'common opinion' recognising the necessity and importance of a wife and mother in order for a household to prosper in early modern France. Secondly, considering the opposite and contrary point of view was an integral part of the Renaissance outlook. By examining the Renaissance rhetorical practice of arguing *in utramque partem* – that is, on both sides of an argument – we move beyond the dismissal of ideas on the nature of woman as just a 'literary game' and the assumption that only the voices of women writers defending their sex could be 'sincere' or 'feminist'. The *Querelle des femme*s was more than a struggle between the forces of misogyny and feminism. It must be understood with reference to both Renaissance rhetorical practices of exploring opposing voices, contradictory opinions and neglected truths, and the social importance of marriage and household rank. Similarly we cannot simply relegate the dignity of man to Adam's condition in the Garden of Eden and the misery of man to the human condition after the Fall. Paradox, ambiguity and inconsistency shaped the early modern mental world. Not one, nor the other. Sometimes both, sometimes many.

The pull to address the opposite view to a question was strong. So strong that Gratien Dupont, one of the only French authors to argue exclusively for the inferiority of woman without having a Champion rise to her defence, could not resist the need to add a defence against his detractors in the form of a legal petition in all subsequent editions of his book – an enterprise aided and abetted by the publishers of the new version. From the second edition onwards Masculine Sex was the complainant against Feminine Sex in a case to be heard before Lady Reason, with lawyers speaking on behalf of both parties. Some sixteenth-century dialogues were 'closed', but they allowed a conversation of competing voices and aired some neglected truths before reaching a conclusion. Contradiction was a mental habit. Louise Labé's magisterial refashioning of the themes of human misery and dignity in the form of a hearing between the advocates for Love and Folly was unusual for a sixteenth-century dialogue, because Jupiter and a jury of gods deferred the verdict and left the reader to reflect on the possible outcome. Montaigne preferred to consider subjects 'diversely' and found 'beauty' in the 'varied and opposing arguments' of lawyers' pleadings in the Parlements. His *Essais* lack closure, digress, suspend judgment, circle around the topic and back again, but the theme always relates to the 'wonderful, vain, divers and wavering subject' that was man (*l'homme*). And yet it is clear that Renaissance man had a constant companion in woman because man and woman 'are cast in the same mould; education and custom excepted, there is no great difference between them'.[1] For Renaissance writers and readers, the practice of filtering through contradictions and bringing together diverse examples was an essential part of understanding the range of possible truths about the human experience.

[1] Montaigne, *Essays*, vol. I, p. 19, vol. III, p. 128; Montaigne, *Essais*, pp. 9A, 897B: 'sont jettez en mesme moule; sauf l'institution et l'usage, la difference n'y est pas grande'.

Bibliography

Manuscript Sources

Archives nationales, Paris

Registres, Série X, Parlement de Paris
Parlement Civil, Conseil
X1a 1659, 3 April 1578 – 14 June 1578
Parlement Civil, Plaidoiries 'Matinées'
X1a 5014, 3 April 1567 – 3 July 1567
X1a 5015, 3 July 1567 – 4 November 1567
X1a 5032, 19 April 1571 – 22 June 1571
Parlement Civil, Plaidoiries
X1a 5071, 3 June 1577 – 23 July 1577
X1a 5076, 22 February 1578 – 24 March 1578
X1a 5205, 24 March 1599 – 27 April 1599
X1a 5226, 31 January 1601 – 26 February 1601
X1a 5261, 1 June 1604 – 30 June 1604
Grands Jours de Poitiers, Plaidoiries
X1a 9208, 25 September 1579–19 December 1579

Minutier central des notaires de Paris
Études
[1537–47] CXXII, 1085–6
[1539–43] LXXXVI, 89
[1540–50] III, 117–19
[1544–46] VI, 67–8
[1546] LXXXVI, 92
[1548–52] XIX, 272–3
[1549] III, 300–301
[1556] III, 306–7
[1560–61] XIX, 281–2
[1560–64] VI, 74–5
[1562–65] LIX, 25
[1564–70] VI, 76
[1564–71] CXXII, 126–7
[1566–68] III, 317–19
[1567, 1580–81] VIII, 424–6
[1568–72] III, 329

[1571–73] VI, 77
[1572–77] XXXIII, 187
[1574–79] VI, 78–9
[1575] LIV, 85
[1578–85] XXXIII, 194
[1581–85] III, 348–50
[1581] XCI, 129
[1582–98] XLIX, 215
[1584–85] LXXXVII, 66
[1584–85] III, 191–2
[1584–86] IX, 285–6
[1585–87] III, 193–4
[1589–1600] LXXXVIII, 123
[1589–90] XXIII, 134
[1591] XXIII, 135
[1595–1600] XLIX, 182
[1600–1604] XXIV, 142
[1601] III, 467–8
[1600–1606] XI, 114
[1609] III, 487

Bibliotheque nationale de France, Manuscripts

Collection Dupuy
115, Recueil de plaidoiries, arrêts et consultations des XVIe et XVIIe siècles
194, Meslanges de lettres de divers grands personnages
385, Extraict des registres du Parlement de Paris, rangés suivant l'ordre alphabétique des matières par Gilles Le Maistre, avocat du Roi, puis premier président audit Parlement
426, Notes et extraits de divers ouvrages d'histoire et de droit par François Pithou, autographe
491, Lettres, harangues, notes et minutes, en grande partie autographes, du chancelier Michel de l'Hospital
896, Recueil d'extraits relatifs à divers sujets – de la main d'Augustin Dupuy(?)

Réserve
Renouard, Philippe. Imprimeurs et libraires parisiens: L'Angelier
Renouard, Philippe. Imprimeurs et libraires parisiens: Denis Janot
Renouard, Philippe. Imprimeurs et libraires parisiens: Jeanne de Marnef [Veuve Janot]

Unpublished Material

Rawles, Stephen. 'Denis Janot Parisian printer and bookseller, 1529–1544. A bibliographical study', 3 vols, PhD thesis, University of Warwick (1976).

Renouard, Jacques. 'L'Officine des L'Angelier, libraires parisiens 1536–1562', Mémoire présentée par Jacques Renouard candidat au diplôme supérieur, University of Paris (1916).

Printed Primary Sources

Agrippa, Henricus Cornelius. *De la noblesse & preexcellence du sexe fœminin* (Paris: Denis Janot, c. 1535).

Agrippa, Henricus Cornelius. *Trois livres de la philosophie occulte ou magie*, trans. Jean Servier, 3 vols (Paris: Berg, 1981–82).

Agrippa, Henricus Cornelius. *De nobilitate et præcellentia fœminei sexus* [1529], eds R. Antonioli, *et al.* (Geneva: Droz, 1990).

Agrippa, Henricus Cornelius. *De occulta philosophia libri tres*, ed. V. Perrone Compagni (Leiden: Brill, 1992).

Agrippa, Henricus Cornelius. *Declamation on the Nobility and Preeminence of the Female Sex*, trans. and ed. Albert Rabil (University of Chicago Press, 1996).

Alexis, Guillaume. *Œuvres poétiques*, 3 vols (Paris: SATF, 1896–1908).

Apuleius. *The Golden Ass*, trans. W. Adlington [1566], Loeb Classical Library (London: Heinemann, 1928).

Artemidoris of Daldis [Artemidori Daldiani]. *Onirocriticon libri V*, ed. Roger Pack (Leipzig: Teubner, 1963).

Artemidoris of Daldis. *La clef des songes: Onirocriticon*, trans. A.J. Festugière (Paris: Vrin, 1975).

Aurigny, Gilles d'. *Le livre de police humaine contenant briefve decription de plusieurs choses dignes de memoire ... maintes belles sentences d'historiens & philosophes divers propos & faictz d'hommes prudens. Qui est une œuvre veritablement beau noble & excellent fort necesaire à toutes gens* (Paris: Charles L'Angelier, 1544).

Ausonius. *Ausonius*, trans. H. Evelyn White, Loeb Classical Library, 2 vols (London: Heinemann, 1919).

Ayrault, Pierre. *XXI Pledoiers faict en la cour de Parlement de Paris et arrests sur ce intervenuz* (Paris: Martin le Jeune, 1568).

Bacquet, Jean. *Les Oevvres de Jehan Bacquet advocat dv roy en la Chambre dv thresor ... Reveves, corrigees et avgmentees de plusieurs arrests, & decisions notables* (Paris: Veuve L'Angelier, 1611).

Baduel, Claude. *Traicté trèsutile et fructueux de la dignité de mariage et de l'honneste conversation des gens doctes, & lettrez*, trans. Guy de la Garde (Paris: Arnoul L'Angelier, 1548).

Belleforest, Francois de. *L'histoire universelle du monde: contenant l'entière description & situation des quatre parties de la terre, la division estendue d'une chacune region & provinces d'icelles: Ensemble l'origine & particulières moeurs, loix, coustumes, religion, & ceremonies de toutes les nations, et peuples par qui elles sont habitués. Divisée en quatre livres* (Paris: G. Mallot, 1570).

Billon, François de. *Le Fort inexpugnable de l'honneur du sexe feminin* (Paris: Jean Dallier, 1555), facsimile edn Michael Screech (New York: Johnson Reprint Corporation, 1970).

Blasons anatomiques du corps feminin (Paris: Charles L'Angelier, 1543).

Boaistuau, Pierre. *Institution du royaume chrestien, extraictes de plusieurs fameux autheurs Grecz et Latins, sacrés & prophanes, mise en langue francoise, Par P. du Boaistuau, surnommé Launay, gentilhomme francois* (Paris: [Gilles Robinot], 1559).

Boaistuau, Pierre. *Histoires tragiques* [1559], ed. Richard Carr (Paris: Société des Textes Français Modernes, 1977).

Boaistuau, Pierre. *Bref discours de l'excellence et dignité de l'homme* [1558], ed. M. Simonin (Geneva: Droz, 1982).

Boaistuau, Pierre. *Le Théâtre du monde où il est faict un ample discours des misères humaines* [1558], ed. M. Simonin (Geneva: Droz, 1982).

Boccaccio, Giovanni. *Le Livre de Jehan Bocasse de la louenge et vertu des nobles et cleres dames, translaté et imprimé novellement à Paris* (Paris: Antoine Vérard, 1493).

Boccaccio, Giovanni. *Le plaisant livre de noble homme Jehan Bocace, poète florentin, auquel il traicte des faictz et gestes des illustres et cleres dames, traduict de latin en françois* (Paris: Arnoul and Charles L'Angelier, 1538).

Boemus, Johann. *Recueil de diverses histoires touchant les situations de toutes régions et pays contenuz es trois parties du monde, avec les particulières moeurs, loix et cérémonies de toutes nations et peuples y habitans* (Paris: Denis Janot, 1542).

Boemus, Johann. *Recueil de diverses histoires, touchant les situations de toutes regions & pais, contenus es trois parties du monde: avec les particulières mœurs, loix, & ceremonies de toute nations & peuples y habitants. Reveu & verifié jouxte le vray exemplaire Latin* (Lyon: Jean de Tournes, 1544).

Bouchet, Jean. *Le Jugement poetic de l'honneur femenin & sejour des illustres claires & honestes dames* (Poitiers: A l'enseigne du Pelican davant le Palais [Marnef brothers], 1536).

Bourdot de Richebourg, Charles (ed.). *Nouveau coutumier général: ou Corps des coutumes générales et particulières de France, et des provinces connues sous le nom des Gaules*, 4 vols (Paris: Chez Claude Robustel, 1724).

Bovelles, Charles de. *Liber de sapiente / Le livre du sage*, ed. P. Magnard (Paris: Vrin, 1982).

Bovelles, Charles de. [Bovillus, Carolus.] *Que hoc volumine continentur: Liber de intellectu; Liber de sensu; Liber de nichilo; Ars oppositorum insuper mathematicum opus quadripartitum: De numeris perfecti* (Paris: Henri Estienne, 1511).

Boyer, Philibert. *Le Stile de la cour de Parlement & forme de proceder en toutes les cours souveraines du royaume de France* (Paris: Claude de Monstr'oeil, 1602).

Brachart, Charlotte de. *Harengue faicte par damoiselle Charlotte de Brachart surnommée Arétuze qui s'adrese aux hommes qui veuillent deffendre la science aux femmes* (Chalon-sur-Saône: Jean Des Preyz, 1604).

Bruès, Guy de. *Dialogues de Guy de Brués contre les Nouveaux Academiciens*, ed. Panos Morphos (Baltimore, MD: John Hopkins Press, 1953).

Calvin, Jean. *Institution de la religion chrestienne* (Geneva: François Perrin, 1566).

Calvin, Jean. *Institutes of the Christian Religion* [1559], ed. John McNeill (London: SCM Press, 1960).

Champier, Symphorien. *La Nef des dames vertueuses* (Paris: Jehan de la Garde, 1515).

Champier, Symphorien [and Robert de Balsac]. *La Nef des princes et de batailles de noblesse avec aultres enseignemens utilz et profitables a toutes manieres de gens pour cognoistre bien vivre et mourir* (Lyon: Guillaume Balsarin, 1502).

Champier, Symphorien [and Robert de Balsac]. *La Nef des princes et des batailles de noblesse ... et aultres enseignemens utilz et proffitables à toutes manières de gens pour congnoistre à bien vivre et mourir ... Le régime d'ung jeune prince et les proverbes des prïnces et aultres petitz livres très utilz et proffitables* (Paris: Le Noir, 1525).

Chenu, Jean. *Cent notables et singulières questions de droict, décidées par arrests mémorables des cours souueraines de France, partie d'iceux prononcez en robbes rouges: contenans les moyens et raisons décisives*, in *Recueil de règlemens notables ... donnez entre ... juges, magistrats et autres officiers royaux ... pour l'exercice de leurs offices*, 2nd edn, 2 vols (Paris: Nicolas Buon, 1603).

Chenu, Jean. *Cent notables et singulières questions de droict, décidées par arrests mémorables des cours souueraines de France, partie d'iceux prononcez en robbes rouges: contenans les moyens et raisons décisives*, in *Recueil de règlemens notables ... donnez entre ... juges, magistrats et autres officiers royaux ... pour l'exercice de leurs offices*, 3rd edn, 2 vols (Paris: Robert Fouet, 1606).

Cholières, Sieur de [Jean Dagoneau]. *La Guerre des masles contre les femelles: représentant en trois dialogues les prérogatives et dignitez tant de l'un que de l'autre sexe. Avec les meslanges poëtiques du sieur de Cholières* (Paris: Pierre Chevillot, 1588).

Cholières Seigneur de [Jean Dagoneau]. *Œuvres de Seigneur de Cholières*: *Les Matinées* [1585], *Les Après-disnées* [1587], ed. E. Tricotel, 2 vols (Geneva: Slatkine Reprints, 1969).

Cicero. *De officiis*, trans. Walter Miller, Loeb Classical Library (London: Heinemann, 1913).
Cicero. *In Defence of A. Caecina*, in *The Speeches*, trans. H. Grose Hode, Loeb Classical Library (London: Heinemann, 1927).
Cicero. *De oratore*, trans. E.W. Sutton, Loeb Classical Library, 2 vols (London: Heinemann, 1942).
Cicero. *De inventione*, trans. H.M. Hubbell, Loeb Classical Library (London: Heinemann, 1949).
Coignard, Gabrielle de. *Œuvres chrestiennes* (Tournon: Jaques Faure, 1595).
Coignard, Gabrielle de. *Spiritual Sonnets: A Bilingual Edition*, trans. Melanie Gregg (University of Chicago Press, 2004).
Coquillart, Guillaume. *Les droitz nouveaulx, avec le débat des dames et des armes* (Paris: Veufve Jehan Trepperell, c. 1499).
Corbin, Jacques. *Decisions de droict et de practique iugees par arrets des cours souveraines de France* (Paris: Jean Millot, 1611).
Corpus juris canonici emendatum et notis illustratum. Gregorii XIII. pont. max. iussu editum (Rome, 1582), UCLA Digital Library Program, *Corpus Juris Canonici* (1582), at http://digital.library.ucla.edu/canonlaw, accessed 17 November 2010.
Corrozet, Gilles. *Hecatomgraphie: C'est a dire les descriptions de cent figures & hystoires, contenantes plusieurs appophtegmes, proverbes, sentences, & dictz tant des anciens que des modernes* (Paris: Denis Janot, 1540); 'French Emblems at Glasgow' website, University of Glasgow, at http://www.emblems.arts.gla.ac.uk/french/index.php.
Corrozet, Gilles. *Second livre des fables d'Ésope* [1548], ed. Paola Cifarelli (Geneva: Slatkine, 1992).
Cotgrave, Randle. *A Dictionarie of the French and English Tongues* (London: Adam Islip, 1611), facsimile edn William Woods (Columbia, SC: University of South Carolina Press, 1950).
Crenne, Hélisenne de. *Les Œuvres de ma Dame Helisenne de Crenne. A sçavoir, les angoisses douloureuses qui procedent d'amours. Les Epistres familières et invectives & Le songe de ladicte dame. Le tout reveu & corrigé de nouveau par elle* (Paris: Estienne Groulleau, 1560), facsimile edn (Geneva: Slatkine, 1977).
Crenne, Hélisenne de. *A Renaissance Woman: Helisenne's Personal and Invective Letters*, trans. and eds Marianna Mustacchi and Paul Archambault (Syracuse University Press, 1986).
Dampmartin, Pierre de. *De la Conoissance et merveilles du monde et de l'homme* (Paris: Thomas Perier, 1585).
Des Roches, Madeleine and Catherine. *Les Œuvres de Mes Dames des Roches de Poitiers, mere et fille* (Paris: Abel L'Angelier, 1578).
Des Roches, Madeleine and Catherine. *Les Œuvres de Mes Dames des Roches de Poetiers, mere et fille, seconde edition* (Paris: Abel L'Angelier, 1579).

Des Roches, Madeleine and Catherine. *Les Œuvres* [1578], ed. Anne Larsen (Geneva: Droz, 1993).

Des Roches, Madeleine and Catherine. *Les Secondes Œuvres*, ed. Anne Larsen (Geneva: Droz, 1998).

Des Roches, Madeleine and Catherine. *From a Mother and Daughter: Poems, Dialogues and Letters of Les Dames des Roches*, ed. and trans. Anne Larsen (University of Chicago Press, 2006).

Deschamps, Eustache. *Œuvres complètes*, 11 vols (Paris: Firmin Didot, 1878–1903).

Desportes, Philippe. *Les premières œuvres* (Paris: Robert Estienne, 1573).

Dialogue apologétique excusant ou deffendant le dévot sexe fémenin, introduict par deulx personnaiges, l'un a nom Bouche maldisant, l'autre Femme deffendant, auquel pour excuser ou deffendre le dict sexe est alleguée la saincte escripture: les docteurs de l'Eglise comme sainct Jherosme, sainct Ambroise, sainct Gregoire, sainct Augustin, sainct Bernard et plusieurs auctorités des philosophes (Paris: [attributed to Frédéric d'Egmont], 1516).

Discours en la faveur des dames, contre les mesdisans, disputé entre deux dames, Cleophile & Clorinde & un gentilhomme nommé le sieur Cloridan (Paris: Abel L'Angelier, 1600).

Dolet, Étienne. *Correspondance: Répertoire analytique et chronologique suivi du texte de ses lettres latines*, ed. Claude Longeon (Geneva: Droz, 1982).

Du Bartas, Guillaume de Saluste. *Commentaires & annotations sur la sepmaine de la creation du monde de Guillaume de Saluste, seigneur du Bartas* (Paris: Abel L'Angelier, 1583).

Du Bartas, Guillaume de Saluste. *Les Œuvres de Guillaume de Saluste, Seigneur du Bartas* (Paris: Michel Gadouleau, 1583).

Du Bartas, Guillaume de Saluste. *La sepmaine* [1581], ed. Yvonne Bellenger, 2 vols (Paris: Nizet, 1981).

Du Guillet, Pernette. *Les Rithmes et poesies de gentile, et vertueuse dame D. Pernette du Guillet Lyonnoise. Avecq'le triumphe des Muses sur Amour: et autres nouvelles compositions* (Paris: De l'imprimerie de Jeanne de Marnef, 1546).

Du Saix, Antoine. *L'Esperon de discipline pour inciter les humains aux bonnes lettres ... en laquelle est traicté de la nourriture et instruction des enfans* (Paris: Denis Janot, 1538).

Du Vair, Guillaume. *Le Manuel d'Epictète* (Paris: Abel L'Angelier, 1591).

Du Vair, Guillaume. *Arrests sur quelques questions notables prononcez en robbe rouge au Parlement de Provence* (Paris: Abel L'Angelier, 1607).

Du Vair, Guillaume. *Les Œuvres de Messire Guillaume du Vair* (Paris: S. Cramoisy, 1641).

Du Vair, Guillaume. *De la sainte philosophie / Philosophie morale des stoïques*, ed. G. Michaut (Paris: Vrin, 1946).

Dufour, Anthoine. *Les Vies des femmes célèbres* (1504), ed. G. Jeanneau (Geneva: Droz, 1970).

Dupont, Gratien. *Les Controversses des sexes masculin et femenin* (Toulouse: Jacques Colomiés, 1534).

Dupont, Gratien. *Controverses des sexes masculin et femenin* (no place, 1536).

Dupont, Gratien. *Controverses des sexes masculin et femenin* (no place, 1537).

Dupont, Gratien. *Controverses des sexes masculin et fœmenin* (Paris: Denis Janot, 1538).

Dupont, Gratien. *Controverses des sexes masculin et fœmenin* (Paris: Denis Janot, 1540).

Dupont, Gratien. *Controverses des sexes masculin et fœmenin* (Paris: Alain Lotrian, 1541).

Dupont, Gratien. *Controverses des sexes masculin et fœmenin* (Paris: Jehan du Pré, 1541).

Erasmus, Desiderius. *Complainte de la paix*, trans. Louis de Berquin (Lyon: P. de Vingle, c. 1531).

Erasmus, Desiderius. '*Copia*: Foundations of the Abundant Style' [*De duplici copia verborum ac rerum commentarii duo*], in *Collected Works of Erasmus*, ed. Craig R. Thompson, 86 vols (University of Toronto Press, 1974–), vol. XXIV, pp. 279–658.

Erasmus, Desiderius. *Déclamation des louenges de mariage*, trans. Louis de Berquin [attribution to Paris: Simon Dubois, 1525], facsimile edn E.V. Telle (Geneva: Droz, 1976).

Estienne, Charles. *Paradoxes ce sont propos contre la commune opinion: debats, en forme de declamations forenses: pour exerciter les ieunes advocats en causes difficiles* (Poitiers: Jean de Marnef, 1553).

Estienne, Charles. *Paradoxes*, ed. Trevor Peach (Geneva: Droz, 1998).

[Estienne, Nicole], Madame Liebault. *Les misères de la femme mariée, où se peuvent voir les peines et tourmens qu'elle reçoit durant sa vie. Mis en forme de stances* (Paris: Pierre Menier, no date).

Expilly, Claude. *Les Poèmes du Sieur d'Expilly. À Madame la marquise de Monceaux* (Paris: Abel L'Angelier, 1596).

Expilly, Claude. *Plaidoyez de M. Claude Expilly, conseiller du roy & son advocat general au Parlement de Grenoble. Auec quelques arrests & reglemens notables dudit Parlement* (Paris: Abel L'Angelier, 1608).

Firenzuola, Agnolo. *Discours de la beauté des dames*, trans. Jean Pallet (Paris: Abel L'Angelier, 1578).

Fontaine, Charles. *Figures du Nouveau testament* (Lyon: Jean de Tournes, 1556).

Gelée, Vincent. *Annotations de Vincent Gelee conseiller du roy & correcteur ordinaire en sa Chambre des comptes. Sur le Guidon general des finances* (Paris: Abel L'Angelier, 1594).

Gournay, Marie de. *Œuvres complètes*, eds Jean-Claude Arnould, *et al.*, 2 vols (Paris: Champion, 2002).

Grosnet, Pierre. *Les Motz dorez de Cathon, en françoys et en latin, avecques bons et très utiles enseignemens, proverbes, adages, auctoritez et ditz moraulx des saiges, prouffitables à ung chascun* (Paris: Jean Longis, 1531).

Habert, Pierre. *Le Miroir de vertu et chemin de bien vivre, contenant plusieurs belles histoires par quatrains et distiques moraux, le tout par alphabet, avec le stile de composer toutes sortes de lettres missives, quittances et promesses, la punctuation et acens de la langue françoise, l'instruction et secrets de l'art d'escriture, reveu et augmenté de nouveau par l'auteur* (Paris: Claude Micard, 1571–72).

Hennequin, Jean. *Le Guydon général des financiers. Contenant la conservation & interpretation des droits sacrez & inalienables du domaine du roy & couronne de France* (Paris: Abel L'Angelier, 1585).

Horace. *Odes and Epodes*, trans. Niall Rudd, Loeb Classical Library (Cambridge, MA: Harvard University Press, 2004).

Hotman, Antoine. *Traicté sur la dissolution de mariage par l'impuissance et froideur de l'homme ou de la femme* (Paris: Mamert Patisson chez Robert Estienne, 1581).

Innocent III [Lotario dei Segni], *De miseria condicionis humane*, ed. Robert Lewis (Athens, GA: University of Georgia Press, 1978).

Isambert, François A (ed.). *Recueil général des anciennes lois françaises depuis l'an 420 jusqu'à la Révolution de 1789*, 29 vols (Paris: Belin-Leprieur, 1822–33).

[Justinian]. *The Digest of Justinian*, eds Theodor Mommsen, Paul Krueger and Alan Watson, 4 vols (Philadelphia, PA: University of Pennsylvania Press, 1985).

[L'Aubespine, Madeleine de]. *Des saines affections* (Paris: Abel L'Angelier, 1593),

[L'Aubespine, Madeleine de]. *Cabinet des saines affections*, ed. Colette Winn (Paris: Champion, 2001).

L'Aubespine, Madeleine de. *Selected Poems and Translations: A Bilingual Edition*, ed. and trans. Anna Klosowska (University of Chicago Press, 2007).

La Louenge des femmes, Invention extraite du commentaire de Pantagruel, sus L'Androgyne de Platon (Lyon: Jean de Tournes, 1551), facsimile edn Ruth Calder (New York: Johnson Reprint, 1967).

La Marche, Olivier de. *La Source d'honneur, pour maintenir la corporelle élégance des dames en vigueur fleurissant et pris inextimable, avec une belle épistre d'une noble dame à son seigneur et amy* (Lyon: Romain Morin, 1531).

La Perrière, Guillaume de. *La Morosophie de Guillaume de la Perrière, Tolosain, contenant cent emblèmes moraux* (Lyon: Macé Bonhomme, 1553).

La Perrière, Guillaume de. *Le Théâtre des bons engins & La Morosophie*, facsimile edn Alison Saunders (Aldershot: Scolar Press, 1993).

La Perrière, Guillaume de. *Le Théâtre des bons engins* (Paris: Denis Janot, 1544).

La Primaudaye, Pierre de. *Academie françoise, en laquelle il est traité de l'institution des moeurs et de ce qui concerne le bien & heureusement viure en tous estats & conditions: Par les preceptes de la doctrine & les exemples de la vie des anciens sages, & hommes illustres*, 4th edn (Lyon: Jean Veirat, 1591).

La Requeste faicte et baillée par les Dames de la ville de Tholose (1555), eds Jean-François Courouau and Philippe Gardy (Toulouse: Presses Universitaires du Mirail, 2003).

La Roche Flavin, Bernard de. *Treize livres des Parlemens de France esquels est amplement traicté de leur origine et institution* (Geneva: Matthieu Berjon, 1621).

Labé, Louise. *Oeuvres complètes*, ed. François Rigolot (Paris: Gallimard, 1986).

Labé, Louise. *Debate of Folly and Love: A New English Translation with the Original French Text*, trans. Anne-Marie Bourbon (New York: Lang, 2000).

Le Caron, Louis. *Memorables ou Observations du droict françois rapporté av Romain ciuil & canonic*, 2nd edn (Paris: Iamet Mettayer & P. L'Hvillier, 1603).

Le Fournier, Andre. *La décoration d'humaine nature, et aornement des dames. Compile et extraict des tres excellens docteurs et plus expers medecins* (Paris: Jehan Sainct Denys and Jehan Longis, 1530).

Le Franc, Martin. *Le Champion des dames. Livre plaisant copieux & habondant en sentences. Contenant la deffence des dames contre Malebouche & ses consors, & victoire d'icelles. Compose par Martin Franc, secretaire du feu pape Felix V & nouvellement imprimé à Paris* (Paris: Galiot du Pré, 1530).

Le Franc, Martin. *Le Champion des dames* [c. 1440], ed. Arthur Piaget (Lausanne: Payot, 1968).

Le Franc, Martin. *Le Champion des dames*, ed. Robert Deschaux, 5 vols (Paris: Champion, 1999).

Le Gendre, Marie. *L'exercice de l'âme vertueuse*, ed. Colette Winn (Paris: Champion, 2001).

Lemaire de Belges, Jean. *Les Illustrations de Gaule et singularitez de Troye* (Lyon: Jean de Tournes, 1549).

Lesnauderie, Pierre de. *La Louange du mariage ou Recueil des histoires des vertueuses et illustres femmes* (Paris: Denis Janot, no date).

Lesnauderie, Pierre de. *La Louenge de mariage et recueil des hystoires des bonnes, vertueuses et illustres femmes* (Paris: Pierre Sergent, 1523).

Loisel, Antoine. *Pasquier ou dialogue des advocats*, in M. Dupin (ed.), *Lettres sur la profession d'avocat et bibliothèque choisie des livres de droit qu'il est plus utile d'acquérir et de connaître*, 4th edn, 2 vols (Paris: Waré, 1818), vol. I, pp. 183–336.

Lombard, Peter. *The Sentences* [*Sententiæ in IV libris distinctæ*], trans. Giulio Silano (Toronto: Pontifical Institute of Mediaeval Studies, 2007).

Loüet, Georges. *Recueil d'aucuns notables arrests donnez en la cour du Parlement de Paris* (Paris: Abel L'Angelier, 1609).

Marconville, Jean de. *La Manière de bien policer la république chrestienne (selon Dieu, raison et vertu), contenant l'estat et office des magistrats, ensemble la source et origine des procès et détestation d'iceluy, auquel est indissolublement conjoinct le mal et misère qui procède des mauvais voisins* (Paris: Jean Dallier, 1562).

Marconville, Jean de. *Traicté enseignant d'ou procede la diversité des opinions des hommes. Ensemble l'excellence de la loy chrestienne par sus toutes les autres* (Paris: Jean Dallier, 1563).
Marconville, Jean de. *De l'heur et malheur de mariage* (Paris: Jean Dallier, 1564).
Marconville, Jean de. *De la bonté et mauvaistié des femmes, ensemble les loix connubiales de Plutarque traduictes en françois* (Paris: Jean Dallier, 1564).
Marconville, Jean de. *De l'heur et malheur de marriage, ensemble les loix connubiales de Plutarque traduictes en françois* (Paris: Jean Dallier, 1571).
Marconville, Jean de. *Recueil memorable d'aucuns cas merveilleux advenuz de noz ans, et d'aucunes choses estranges & monstrueuses advenües ès siècles passez* (Paris: Jean Dallier, 1564).
Marconville, Jean de. *De la bonté et mauvaistié des femmes*, ed. Richard Carr (Paris: Champion, 2000).
Martial, *Epigrams*, trans. Walter Ker, Loeb Classical Library, 2 vols (Cambridge, MA: Harvard University Press, 1968).
[Maugin, Jean]. *Les Figures de l'Apocalypse de Saint Ian apostre et dernier evangeliste exposées en latin et vers francoys* (Paris: De l'imprimerie d'Estienne Groulleau, 1547).
Mexia, Pero. *Les Diverses leçons*, trans. Claude Gruget (Paris: Estienne Groulleau, 1552).
Mexia, Pero. *Les Diverses leçons*, trans. Claude Gruget (Paris: Vincent Sertenas, 1552).
Mexia, Pero. *Les Diverses leçons de Pierre Messie, gentil-homme de Sevil. Mises de castillan en françois, par Claude Gruget, Parisien* (Rouen: Jean Roger, 1626).
Mirandola, Pico della. *On the Dignity of Man*, trans. Charles Glenn Wallis (New York: Macmillan, 1985).
Montaigne, Michel de. *Essais de Michel de Montaigne*, ed. J.V. Le Clerc, 4 vols (Paris: Garnier, 1856).
Montaigne, Michel de. *The Essayes of Michael Lord of Montaigne* [1603], trans. John Florio, 3 vols (London: J.M. Dent Everyman's Library, 1910).
Montaigne, Michel de. *Œuvres complètes*, eds Albert Thibaudet and Maurice Rat (Paris: Gallimard, 1962).
Montaigne, Michel de. *The Complete Essays*, trans. Michael Screech (Harmondsworth: Penguin, 1991).
Montaigne, Michel Eyquem de. *Les Essais de Michel de Montaigne* [1595], eds Pierre Villey and V.L. Saulnier (Paris: PUF, 1965).
[Navarre, Marguerite de]. *Histoires des amans fortunez. Dediées à trèsillustre Princesse Madame Marguerite de Bourbon Duchesse de Nivernois*, ed. Pierre Boaistuau (Paris: Vincent Sertenas and Gilles Robinot, 1558).
Nouveau stile et prothocole de la Chancellerie de France, suivant la forme et maniere que l'on use pour le iourd'huy (Paris: Abel L'Angelier, 1577).
Ovid. *Heroides and Amores*, trans. G. Showerman (London: Heinemann, 1931).

Ovid. *Metamorphoses*, trans. and ed. Mary Innes (Harmondsworth: Penguin, 1986).

Paradin, Claude. *Quadrins historiques de la Bible. Revuz, & augmentez d'un grand nombre de figures* (Lyon: Jean de Tournes, 1555).

Parmentier, Jean. *Œuvres poétiques* [1531], ed. Françoise Ferrand (Geneva: Droz, 1971).

Pasquier, Étienne. *Recherches de la France / Pourparler du Prince* (Paris: Jean Longis and Robert Mangier, 1560)

Pasquier, Étienne. *Des recherches de la France, livre premier et second* (Paris: Gilles Robinot, 1581).

Pasquier, Étienne. *Les Lettres d'Estienne Pasquier conseiller et advocat general du roy en la Chambre des comptes de Paris* (Paris: Abel L'Angelier, 1586).

Pasquier, Étienne. *Les Œuvres d'Étienne Pasquier*, 2 vols (Amsterdam: Compagnie des Libraires Associez, 1723).

Pasquier, Étienne. *Choix de lettres sur la littérature, la langue et la traduction*, ed. Dorothy Thickett (Geneva: Droz, 1956).

Pasquier, Étienne. *Le Monophile* [1554], ed. E.H. Balmas (Milan: Cisalpino, 1957).

Pasquier, Étienne. *Lettres familières*, ed. Dorothy Thickett (Geneva: Droz, 1974).

Philostratus. *Les Images ou tableaux de platte peinture des deux Philostrates sophistes grecs et des statues de Callistrate* (Paris: Veuve Abel L'Angelier and Veuve M. Guillemot, 1615).

Pisan, Christine de. *Le Trésor de la cité des dames, selon dame Christine de la cité de Pise, livre tresutile & prouffitable pour l'introduction des roynes, dames, princesses, & autres femmes de tous estatz, auquel elles pourront veoir la grande & saine richesse de toute prudence, saigesse, honeur, & dignité dedans contenues* (Paris: Denis Janot for Jehan André, 1536).

Pithou, Pierre. *Coustumes du bailliage de Troyes en Champagne conférées au coustumes de France* (Paris: Cardin Besongne, 1630).

Plautus. *Plautus*, ed. Paul Nixon, Loeb Classical Library, 5 vols (Cambridge, MA: Harvard University Press, 1916–38).

Plutarch. *Plutarche de Cheroné, grec, ancien philosophe et historiographe, traictant entierement du gouvernement en mariage* (Paris: Denis Janot, 1536).

Plutarch. *Le liure de Plutarche de l'education & nourriture des enfans, traduyct de latin en francoys* (Paris: Vincent Sertenas, [1537]).

Plutarch. *Cinq opuscules de Plutarque Cheronne* (Paris: Jeanne de Marnef, 1546).

Plutarch. *Opuscules de Plutarque, des vertueux et illustres faitz des anciennes femmes* (Paris: Jeanne de Marnef, 1546).

Pontaymeri, Alexandre de. *Paradoxe apologique, où il est fidèllement demonstré que la Femme est beaucoup plus parfaicte que l'Homme en toute action de vertu* (Paris: Abel L'Angelier, 1594).

Quintilian. *Institutio oratoria*, ed. and trans. H.E. Butler, Loeb Classical Library, 4 vols (London: Heinemann, 1920–22).

Rabelais, François. *Œuvres complètes*, ed. Guy Demerson (Paris: Seuil, 1973).
Rigoley de Juvigny, Jean-Antoine (ed.). *Les Bibliothèques françoises de La Croix du Maine et de Du Verdier*, 6 vols (Paris: Saillant and Nyon, 1772–73).
Romieu, Marie de. *Les Premieres œuvres poetiques de Mademoiselle Marie de Romieu Viuaroise contentant un brief discours, que l'excellence de la femme surpasse celle de l'homme non moins récreatif que plein de beaux exemples* (Paris: Lucas Breyer, 1581).
Romieu, Marie de. *Les Premières œuvres poétiques*, ed. Andre Winandy (Geneva: Droz, 1972).
Sainte-Marthe, Charles de. *La Poésie francoise de Charles de Saincte Marthe* (Lyon: Le Prince, 1540).
Scève, Maurice. *Microcosme*, ed. Enzo Guidici (Paris: Vrin, 1976).
Seneca. *On Benefits*, in *Moral Essays*, trans. John Basore, Loeb Classical Library, 3 vols (London: Heinemann, 1963).
Servin, Louis. *Plaidoyez de Mre Loys Servin conseiller du roy en son Conseil d'Estat & advocat general en sa cour de Parlement. A la fin desquels les arrests intervenus sur iceuls*, 2 vols (Paris: Jean de Heuqueville, 1603–1605).
Servin, Louis. *Actions notables et plaidoyez de messire Louys Servin ... à la fin desquels sont les arrests intervenus sur iceux. Dernière édition ... Ensemble les plaidoyers de M. A. Robert, Arnault et autres* (Paris: G. Alliot and C. Morlot, 1631).
Sforza, Isabella. *De la vraye tranquilité de l'esprit* (Lyon: Jean de Tournes, 1546).
Sidonius Apollinaris, Saint. *Poems and Letters*, trans. W. Anderson, 2 vols (Cambridge: MA: Harvard University Press, 1965).
Speroni, Sperone. *De la cure famillere avec aucuns preceptes de mariage extraicts de Plutarque, aussi un dialogue de la dignité des femmes* (Lyon: Jean de Tournes, 1546).
Speroni, Sperone. *Les Dialogues de Messire Speron Sperone Italien, traduitz en françoys, par Claude Gruget, Parisien* (Paris: Vincent Sertenas, 1551).
Stanton, Domna (ed.). *French Feminist Poems from the Middle Ages to the Present: A Bilingual Anthology* (New York: Feminist Press, 1985).
Tabourot, Étienne. *Les Bigarrures dv Seigneur des Accordz* (Paris: Jean Richer, 1583).
Tahureau, Jacques. *Les Dialogues ... non moins profitables que facetieux, ou les vices d'vn chacun sont repris fort aprement pour nous animer dauantage à les fuir, & suiure la vertu* (Paris: Gabriel Buon, 1570).
Tahureau, Jacques. *Les Dialogues: non moins profitables que facetieux* [1565], ed. Max Gauna (Geneva: Droz, 1981).
Tanner, Norman (ed.). *Decrees of the Ecumenical Councils*, 2 vols (London: Sheed and Ward, 1990).
Tardif, Guillaume. *Le livre intitulé l'art de bien vivre et de bien mourir* (Paris: for Antoine Verard, 1496).

Tertullian. [*Ad uxorem*] *À son épouse*, ed. and trans. C. Munier (Paris: Cerf, 1980).

The Montaigne Project, University of Chicago, at http://www.lib.uchicago.edu/efts/ARTFL/projects/montaigne

The Theodosian Code and Novels and the Sirmondian Constitutions, trans. Clyde Pharr, *et al.* (New York: Greenwood Press, 1969).

[Tournes, Jean de]. 'L'Imprimeur au lecteur', in Johann Boemus, *Recueil de diverses histoires ... Reveu & verifié jouxte le vray exemplaire Latin* (Lyon: Jean de Tournes, 1544).

[Tournes, Jean de]. 'L'Imprimeur aux imprimeurs', in Bonaventure des Periers, *Recueil des œuvres de feu Bonaventure des Periers* (Lyon: Jean de Tournes, 1544), sig. n 3v.

[Tournes, Jean de]. 'L'Imprimeur au lecteur benivole salut … De Lyon ce 28. de Iuin, M.DXXXXVI', in Isabella Sforza, *De la vraye tranquilité de l'esprit* (Lyon: Jean de Tournes, 1546), pp. 2–4.

[Tournes, Jean de]. 'L'Imprimeur au lecteur salut … de Lyon ce quatriesme de Septembre MD.XLIX', in Jean Lemaire de Belges, *Les Illustrations de Gaule et singularitez de Troye* (Lyon: Jean de Tournes, 1549).

Tournes, Jean de. 'L'Imprimeur au lecteur … De Lyon ce IIII. Avril 1552', in *Opuscules de divers autheurs Medecins* (Lyon: Jean de Tournes, 1552), pp. 3–5.

Tournes, Jean de. 'L'Imprimeur au lecteur', in Claude Paradin, *Quadrins historiques de la Bible. Revuz, & augmentez d'un grand nombre de figures* (Lyon: Jean de Tournes, 1555).

Tournes, Jean de. 'L'imprimeur au lecteur', in Suetonius, *De la Vie des XII Césars traduit par George de la Boutière, Autunois* (Lyon: Jean de Tournes, 1556).

Tournes, Jean de. 'L'imprimeur aux lecteurs salut', in Charles Fontaine, *Figures du Nouveau testament* (Lyon: Jean de Tournes, 1556).

Tournes, Jean de. 'L'imprimeur a tout benivole lecteur S.', in Pontus de Tyard, *Mantice ou Discours de la verité de Divination par Astrologie* (Lyon: Jean de Tournes and Guillaume Gazeau, 1558).

Valerius Maximus, *Memorable Sayings and Doings*, trans. D.R. Shackleton Bailey, 2 vols (Cambridge, MA: Harvard University Press, 2000).

Virgil. *The Fourth Book of Virgil's Æneid on the Loves of Dido and Æneas*, trans. Richard Fanshaw (Oxford: Blackwell, 1924).

Virgil. *Eclogues, Georgics, Æneid I–VI*, trans. H. Rushton Fairclough (Cambridge, MA: Harvard University Press, 1999).

Vives, Juan Luis. *L'Institution de la femme chrestienne*, trans. Pierre de Changy (Paris: Jean Kerver, 1542), [Geneva: Slatkine, 1970].

Vives, Juan Luis. *L'Institution de la femme chrestienne. Tant en son enfance, que mariage, & viduité. Avec l'office du mary. Le tout composé en latin, par Loys Vives. Et nouuellement traduict en langue françoyse, par Pierre de Changy* (Paris: Denis Janot for Galiot du Pré, 1545).

Vives, Juan Luis. *Les Dialogues de Jan loys Vives, traduits de latin en françois, pour l'exercice des deux langues ... ausquels est ajoustée l'explication françoise des mots latins* (Paris: Gabriel Buon, 1573).
Xenophon. *Science pour s'enrichir honnestement et facilement, intitulee Leconomic Xenophon* (Paris: Geoffroy Tory, 1531).

Secondary Sources

Abelard, Jacques. *Les Illustrations de Gaule et singularitez de Troye de Jean Lemaire de Belges* (Geneva: Droz, 1976).
Adams, Alison, Stephen Rawles and Alison Saunders (eds). *A Bibliography of French Emblem Books of the Sixteenth and Seventeenth Centuries*, Travaux d'Humanisme et Renaissance 331 and 362, 2 vols (Geneva: Droz, 1999–2002).
Albistur, Maïté and Daniel Armogathe. *Histoire du féminisme français du moyen âge à nos jours* (Paris: Éditions des femmes, 1977).
Allen, Prudence. *The Concept of Woman*, 2 vols (Grand Rapids, MI: Eerdmans, 1997–2002).
Almquist, Katherine. 'Montaigne Judging with Henri de Mesmes (May–June 1565)', *Montaigne Studies* 16 (2004): 37–40.
Almquist, Katherine. 'Writing Pluralist Biography of Montaigne's Legal Career', *EMF: Studies in Early Modern France* 9 (2004): 58–76.
Angenot, Marc. *Les Champions des femmes: examen du discours sur la supériorité des femmes 1400–1800* (Montréal: Presses de L'Université de Québec, 1977).
Aquilon, Pierre. 'Petites et moyennes bibliothèques (1530–1660)', in Claude Jolly (ed.), *Histoire des bibliothèques françaises*, vol. II, *Les bibliothèques sous l'Ancien Régime 1530–1789*, 4 vols (Paris, 1988–92), vol. II, pp. 180–205.
Aquilon, Pierre. 'La bibliothèque de Jean de la Rebertière', in Jean Céard (ed.), *Langage et vérité* (Geneva: Droz, 1993).
Armstrong, Elizabeth. *Before Copyright: The French Book Privilege System 1498–1526* (Cambridge University Press, 1990).
Ascoli, Georges. 'Essai sur l'histoire des idées féministes en France: du XVIe siècle à la Révolution', *Revue de synthèse historique* 13 (1906): 25–42.
Aubert, Félix. 'Le Parlement de Paris au XVIe siècle', *Nouvelle revue historique de droit français et étranger* 29 (1905): 737–90, and 30 (1906): 58–83, 179–209.
Aubert, Félix. 'Recherches sur l'organisation du Parlement de Paris au XVIe siècle (1515–1589)', *Nouvelle revue historique de droit français et étranger* 36 (1912): 52–132, 178–242, 309–69.
Aulotte, Robert. *Amyot et Plutarque: La tradition des moralia au XVIe siècle* (Geneva: Droz, 1965).
Balsamo, Jean. 'Abel L'Angelier et ses dames: les Dames des Roches, Madeleleine de L'Aubespine, Marie le Gendre, Marie de Gournay', in D. de Courcelles

and Carmen Val Julián (eds), *Des femmes et des livres: France and Espagnes, XIVe–XVIIe siècle* (Paris: École nationale des chartes, 1999), pp. 117–36.

Balsamo, Jean. 'Les *Essais* de Montaigne et leurs premiers lecteurs: exemplaires annotés (1580–1598)', *Montaigne Studies* 16 (2004): 143–50.

Balsamo, Jean. '*Des saines affections* (1591) et le syncrétisme philosophique dans la culture de cour sous Henri III et Henri IV', *Journal de la Renaissance* 6 (2008): 23–36.

Balsamo, Jean and Michel Simonin. *Abel L'Angelier et Françoise de Louvain (1574–1620). Suivi du catalogue des ouvrages publiés par Abel L'Angelier (1574–1610) et la Veuve L'Angelier (1610–1620)* (Geneva: Droz, 2002).

Bauschatz, Cathleen. '"Leur plus universelle qualité, c'est la diversité": Women as Ideal Readers in Montaigne's *Essais*', *Journal of Medieval and Renaissance Studies* 19:1 (1989): 83–101.

Bauschatz, Cathleen. '"Le plaisir du texte" dans les *Dames Galantes* de Brantôme', in Isabelle Brouard-Arends (ed.), *Lectrices d'Ancien Régime* (Presses Universitaires de Rennes, 2003), pp. 649–56.

Beam, Sara. 'The "basoche" and the "bourgeoisie seconde": Careerists at the Parlement of Paris during the League', *French History* 17:4 (2003): 367–87.

Beam, Sara. *Laughing Matters: Farce and the Making of Absolutism in France* (Ithaca, NY: Cornell University Press, 2007).

Benson, Pamela Joseph. *The Invention of the Renaissance Woman: The Challenge of Female Independence in the Literature and Thought of Italy and England* (University Park, PA: Penn State Press, 1992).

Berriot, François. 'Pierre de Dampmartin vu à travers sa *Conoissance et merveilles du monde et de l'homme* entre Plutarque et Montaigne', in *Prose et prosateurs de la Renaissance* (Paris: Sedes, 1988), pp. 279–89.

Berriot-Salvadore, Evelyne. *Les femmes dans la société française de la Renaissance* (Geneva: Droz, 1990).

Berriot-Salvadore, Evelyne. 'Les héritières de Louise Labé', in Guy Demerson (ed.), *Louise Labé, les voix du lyrisme* (Lyon: Éditions du CNRS, 1991), pp. 93–105.

Berriot-Salvadore, Evelyne. 'Marie le Gendre et Marie de Gournay, à la manière de …', in Ilana Zinguer (ed.), *Le lecteur, l'auteur et l'écrivain, Montaigne 1492–1592–1992. Actes du colloque international de Haïfa* (Paris: Champion, 1993), pp. 237–51.

Bloch, Howard. *Medieval Misogyny and the Invention of Western Romantic Love* (University of Chicago Press, 1991).

Bock, Gisela. 'Women's History and Gender History: Aspects of an International Debate', *Gender and History* 1:1 (1989): 7–30.

Bock, Gisela. *Women in European History* (Oxford: Blackwell, 2002).

Bock, Gisela and Margarete Zimmermann. 'The European *Querelle des femmes*', *Disputatio: An International Journal of the Late Middle Ages* 5 (2002): 127–56.

Bouchereaux, S.M. 'Recherches bibliographiques sur Gilles Corrozet', *Bulletin du bibliophile* (1948): 204–20, 291–301, 324–37, 393–411, 470–78, 532–8, 584–96, and (1949): 35–47, 93–107, 134–51, 147–54, 196–202.

Bouteiller, Paul. 'Étienne Pasquier avocat au Parlement de Paris (1549–1585)', *Bulletin de la Société de l'histoire de Paris et de l'Île de France* 117 (1990): 45–65.

Bowen, B.C. 'Cornelius Agrippa's *De vanitate*: Polemic or Paradox?', *Bibliothèque d'Humanisme et Renaissance* 34:2 (1972): 249–65.

Bowen, Barbara. 'Jacques Tahureau Revisited', *French Studies* 30:1 (1976): 19–27.

Bromilow, Pollie. 'Les femmes lectrices de la fiction au seizième siècle: enjeux idéologiques d'un lieu commun', in Isabelle Brouard-Arends (ed.), *Lectrices d'Ancien Régime* (Presses Universitaires de Rennes, 2003), pp. 261–8.

Bromilow, Pollie. *Models of Women in Sixteenth-Century French Literature: Female Exemplarity in the* Histoires tragiques *(1559) and the* Heptaméron *(1559)* (Lewiston, NY: Edwin Mellen, 2007).

Broomhall, Susan. *Women and the Book Trade in Sixteenth-Century France* (Aldershot: Ashgate, 2002).

Brouard-Arends, Isabelle (ed.). *Lectrices d'Ancien Régime* (Presses Universitaires de Rennes, 2003).

Brown, Cynthia and Martha Driver (eds), *Journal of the Early Book Society for the Study of Manuscripts and Printing History. Special Focus: Women and Book Culture in Late Medieval and Early Modern France* 4 (2001).

Brown, Elizabeth. 'Le greffe civil du Parlement de Paris au XVIe siècle: Jean du Tillet et les registres des plaidoiries', *Bibliothèque de l'École des chartes* 153 (1995): 325–71.

Brucker, Gene. 'The Italian Renaissance', in Guido Ruggiero (ed.), *A Companion to the Worlds of the Renaissance* (Oxford: Blackwell, 2002), pp. 23–38.

Butler, Judith. *Gender Trouble: Feminism and the Subversion of Identity*, 2nd edn (London: Routledge, 1999).

Campbell, Julie. *Literary Circles and Gender in Early Modern Europe: A Cross-Cultural Approach* (Aldershot: Ashgate, 2006).

Carr, Richard. *Pierre Boaistuau's* Histoires tragiques*: A Study of the Narrative Form and Tragic Vision* (Chapel Hill, NC: North Carolina University Press, 1979).

Carr, Richard. 'The Resolution of a Paradox: Alexandre de Pontaymeri's Response to the *Querelle des femmes*', *Renaissance Studies* 17:2 (2003): 246–56.

Carron, Jean-Claude. 'The Persuasive Seduction: Dialogue in Sixteenth-Century France', in M. Logan and P. Rudnytsky (eds), *Contending Kingdoms: Historical, Psychological, and Feminist Approaches to the Literature of Sixteenth-Century England and France* (Detroit, MI: Wayne State University Press, 1991), pp. 89–106.

Carron, Jean-Claude. 'Dialogical Argument: Scripting Rhetoric (The Case of Guy de Bruès's *Dialogues*)', *South Central Review* 10:2 (1993): 20–31.

Cartier, A. and Adolphe Chennevière. 'Bibliographie d'Antoine du Moulin', *Revue d'histoire littéraire de la France* 4 (1895): 469–90, and (1896): 90–106.

Cartier, A., *et al.* (eds). *Bibliographie des éditions des de Tournes, imprimeurs lyonnais*, 2 vols (Paris: Editions des Bibliothèques Nationales, 1937–38).

Cave, Terence. *The Cornucopian Text: Problems of Writing in the French Renaissance* (Oxford: Clarendon, 1979).

Cazauran, Nicole. 'Boaistuau et Gruget éditeurs de l'*Heptaméron*: à chacun sa part', *Travaux de littérature* 14 (2001): 149–69.

Cazès, Hélène. 'Nicole Estienne à ses miroirs: les "félicitéz" de mariage et les *Misères de la femme mariée*', in J. Lecointe *et al.* (eds), *Devis d'amitié, Mélanges en l'honneur de Nicole Cazauran* (Paris: Champion, 2002), pp. 747–66.

Céard, Jean. *La nature et les prodiges* (Geneva: Droz, 1977).

Charon, Annie [Parent]. *Les métiers du livre à Paris au XVIe siècle (1535–1560)* (Geneva: Droz, 1974).

Charon, Annie. 'Le monde de l'imprimerie humaniste: Paris', in Roger Chartier and Henri-Jean Martin (eds), *Histoire de l'édition française*, 4 vols (Paris: Promodis, 1984), vol. I, *Le livre conquérant*, pp. 237–53.

Charon, Annie. 'Les grandes collections du XVIe siècle', in Claude Jolly (ed.), *Histoire des bibliothèques françaises*, vol. II, *Les bibliothèques sous l'Ancien Régime 1530–1789*, 4 vols (Paris: Promodis, 1988–92), pp. 85–102.

Charon, Annie. 'A propos des femmes et des métiers du livre dans le Paris de la Renaissance', in D. de Courcelles and Carmen Val Julián (eds), *Des femmes et des livres: France and Espagnes, XIVe–XVIIe siècle* (Paris: École nationale des chartes, 1999), pp. 137–48.

Chartier, Roger. *Lecteurs & lectures dans la France d'Ancien Régime* (Paris: Seuil, 1987).

Chartier, Roger and Henri-Jean Martin (eds). *Histoire de l'édition française*, 4 vols (Paris: Promodis, 1984), vol. I, *Le livre conquérant*.

Chassaigne, Marc. *Étienne Dolet: portraits et documents inédits* (Paris: Albin Michel, 1930).

Chavy, Paul. *Traducteurs d'autrefois: Moyen Âge et Renaissance*, 2 vols (Paris: Champion, 1988).

Christie, Richard Copley. *The Martyr of the Renaissance: A Biography* (London: Macmillan, 1880).

Colie, Rosalie. *Paradoxia Epidemica: The Renaissance Tradition of Paradox* (Princeton University Press, 1966).

Collins, James. 'The Economic Role of Women in Seventeenth-Century France', *French Historical Studies* 16:2 (1989): 436–70.

Conihout, Isabelle de. 'La "belle librarie" évanouie de Nicolas de Villeroy retrouvée', in Isabelle de Conihout, *et al.* (eds), *Henri III mécène: des arts, des sciences et des lettres* (Paris: Presses de l'Université Paris-Sorbonne, 2006), pp. 318–29.

Conihout, Isabelle de and Pascal Ract-Madoux, 'Ni Grolier, Ni Mahieu, Laubespine', *Bulletin du bibliophile* (2004): 63–88.

Connet, M. and J. Megret. 'Inventaire de la bibliothèque des du Prat', *Bibliothèque d'Humanisme et Renaissance* 3 (1943): 72–128.

Constant, Jean-Marie. *Les Français pendant les guerres de religion* (Paris: Hachette, 2002).

Cottrell, Robert. 'Gender Imprinting in Montaigne's *Essais*', *L'Esprit Créateur* 30 (1990): 85–96.

Couchman, Jane. 'La lecture et le lectorat dans la correspondance de Louise de Coligny', in Isabelle Brouard-Arends (ed.), *Lectrices d'Ancien Régime* (Presses Universitaires de Rennes, 2003), pp. 399–408.

Cox, Virginia. *The Renaissance Dialogue* (Cambridge University Press, 1992).

Cox, Virginia. 'Seen but not Heard: The Role of Women Speakers in Cinquecento Literary Dialogue', in Letizia Panizza (ed.), *Women in Italian Renaissance Culture and Society* (Oxford: Legenda, 2000), pp. 385–400.

Daenens, Francine. 'Isabella Sforza: Beyond the Stereotype', in Letizia Panizza (ed.), *Women in Italian Renaissance Culture and Society* (Oxford: Legenda, 2000), pp. 35–56.

Dahlinger, James. *Étienne Pasquier on Ethics and History* (New York: Lang, 2007).

Darmon, Pierre. *Mythologie de la femme dans l'Ancienne France* (Paris: Seuil, 1983).

Daubresse, Sylvie. *Le Parlement de Paris ou 'la voix de la raison' (1559–1589)* (Geneva: Droz, 2005).

Davis, N.Z. *Society and Culture in Early Modern France* (Stanford University Press, 1975).

Davis, N.Z. 'Ghosts, Kin and Progeny: Some Features of Family Life in Early Modern France', *Dædalus* 106 (1977): 87–114.

Davis, N.Z. 'Beyond the Market: Books as Gifts in Sixteenth-Century France', *Transactions of the Royal Historical Society* 33 (1983): 69–89.

Davis, N.Z. 'Le monde de l'imprimerie humaniste: Lyon', in Roger Chartier and Henri-Jean Martin (eds), *Histoire de l'édition française*, 4 vols (Paris: Promodis, 1984), vol. I, *Le livre conquérant*, pp. 255–77.

Davis, N.Z. 'A Renaissance Text to the Historian's Eye: The Gifts of Montaigne', *Journal of Medieval and Renaissance Studies* 15 (1985): 47–56.

Davis, N.Z. 'Boundaries and the Sense of Self in Sixteenth-Century France', in Thomas Heller, *et al.* (eds), *Reconstructing Individualism: Autonomy, Individuality, and the Self in Western Thought* (Stanford University Press, 1986), pp. 53–63.

Dawson, J.C. *Toulouse in the Renaissance: The Floral Games, University and Student Life, Étienne Dolet (1532–34)* (New York: Columbia University Press, 1923).

Dawson, John. *The Oracles of the Law* (Ann Arbor, MI: University of Michigan Law School, 1968).

Delachenal, Roland. *Histoire des avocats au Parlement de Paris 1300–1600* (Paris: Plon, 1885).

Delatour, Jérôme. 'De l'art de plaider doctement: Les notes de lecture de Pierre Dupuy, jeune avocat (1605–6)', *Bibliothèque de l'École des chartes* 153 (1995): 391–412.

Delatour, Jérôme. *Les livres de Claude Dupuy: Une bibliothèque humaniste au temps des guerres de religion* (Paris: Éditions de l'Enssib, 1998).

Demonet, Marie-Luce (ed.). *Montaigne et la question de l'homme* (Paris: PUF, 1999).

Desaive, Jean-Paul. 'The Ambiguities of Literature', in N.Z. Davis and Arlette Farge (eds), *A History of Women in the West*, 4 vols (Cambridge, MA: Harvard University Press, 1993), vol. III, *Renaissance and Enlightenment Paradoxes*, pp. 261–94.

Desan, Philippe. 'Combien gagnait Montaigne au Parlement de Bordeaux (un reçu de 27 août 1576)', *Montaigne Studies* 16 (2004): 41–4.

Desan, Suzanne and Jeffrey Merrick (eds). *Family, Gender and Law in Early Modern France* (University Park, PA: Penn State Press, 2009).

Descimon, Robert. 'Élites parisiennes entre le XVe et XVIIe siècle: du bon usage du Cabinet des titres', *Bibliothèque de l'École des chartes* 155 (1997): 607–44.

Descimon, Robert. 'The Birth of the Nobility of the Robe: Dignity versus Privilege in the Parlement de Paris, 1500–1700', in Michael Wolfe (ed.), *Changing Identities in Early Modern France* (Durham, NC: Duke University Press, 1997), pp. 95–123.

Descimon, Robert. 'The "bourgeoise seconde": Social Differentiation in the Parisian Municipal Oligarchy in the Sixteenth Century, 1500–1610', *French History* 17:4 (2003): 388–424.

Descimon, Robert. 'Les notaires de Paris du XVIe au XVIIe siècle: office, profession, archives', in Michel Cassan (ed.), *Offices et officiers 'moyens' en France à l'époque moderne: Profession, culture* (Presses Universitaires de Limoges, 2004), pp. 15–42.

Descimon, Robert. 'Guillaume Du Vair (1556–1621): les enseignements d'une biographie sociale. La construction symbolique d'un grand homme et l'échec d'un lignage', in B. Petey-Girard and A. Tarrête (eds), *Guillaume du Vair: parlementaire et écrivain (1556–1621)* (Geneva: Droz, 2005), pp. 17–77.

Descimon, Robert. 'Les auxiliaires de justice du Châtelet de Paris: aperçus sur l'économie du monde des offices ministériels (XVIe–XVIIIe siècle)', in Claire Dolan (ed.), *Entre justice et justiciables: les auxiliaires de la justice du Moyen Age au XXe siècle* (Québec: Presses de l'Université Laval, 2005), pp. 301–25.

Descimon, Robert. 'Un langage de la dignité. La qualification des personnes dans la société parisienne de l'époque moderne', in Fanny Cosandey (ed.), *Dire et vivre l'ordre social en France sous l'Ancien Régime* (Paris, Éd. de l'EHESS, 2005), pp. 69–123.

Dewald, Jonathan. *The Formation of a Provincial Nobility: The Magistrates of the Parlement de Rouen 1499–*1610 (Princeton University Press, 1980).

Diefendorf, Barbara. *Paris City Councillors in the Sixteenth Century: The Politics of Patrimony* (Princeton University Press, 1983).

Diefendorf, Barbara. 'Give Us Back Our Children: Patriarchal Authority and Parental Consent to Religious Vocations in Early Counter-Reformation France', *Journal of Modern History* 68 (1996): 265–307.

Doucet, Roger. *Les bibliothèques parisiennes au XVIe siècle* (Paris: Picard, 1956).

Erler, Mary. *Women, Reading, and Piety in Late Medieval England* (Cambridge University Press, 2002).

Evain, Aurore, *et al.* (eds). *Théâtre de femmes de l'Ancien Régime: XVIe siècle* (Publications de l'Université de Saint-Étienne, 2006)

Farr, James. 'Parlementaires and the Paradox of Power: Sovereignty and Jurisprudence in *Rapt* Cases in Early Modern Burgundy', *European History Quarterly* 25 (1995): 325–51.

Faye, Emmanuel. 'De la dignité de l'homme selon Charles de Bovelles', in Pierre Magnard (ed.), *La dignité de l'homme* (Paris: Champion, 1995), pp. 125–42.

Ford, Philip and Paul White (eds). *Masculinities in Sixteenth-Century France: Proceedings of the Eighth Cambridge French Renaissance Colloquium 5–7 July 2003* (Cambridge: Cambridge French Colloquia, 2006).

Foyster, Elizabeth. *Manhood in Early Modern England: Honour, Sex, and Marriage* (London: Longman, 1999).

François, Alexis. 'Origine et déclin du "bel usage" parlementaire', *Revue d'histoire littéraire de la France* 25 (1918): 201–10.

Franklin, Margaret. *Boccaccio's Heroines: Power and Virtue in Renaissance Society* (Aldershot: Ashgate, 2006).

Fumaroli, Marc. 'Rhetoric, Politics and Society: From Italian Ciceronianism to French Classicism', in James Murphy (ed.), *Renaissance Eloquence: Studies in the Theory and Practice of Renaissance Rhetoric* (Berkeley, CA: University of California Press, 1983), pp. 257–64.

Fumaroli, Marc. *L'âge de l'éloquence: Rhétorique et 'res literaria' de la Renaissance au seuil de l'époque classique*, 2nd edn (Paris: Albin Michel, 1994).

Glidden, Hope. *The Storyteller as Humanist: The* Serées *of Guillaume Bouchet* (Lexington, KY: French Forum, 1981).

Goursolas-Marcy, Céline. '"Controverses", "Jugement", "Requête" et *Querelle des femmes* (1534–55): Du droit de réponse dans un débat institué par les hommes', *Textuel* 49 (2006): 189–203.

Grafton, Anthony. *What was History? The Art of History in Early Modern Europe* (Cambridge University Press, 2007).

Grafton, Anthony and Lisa Jardine. *From Humanism to the Humanities: Education and the Liberal Arts in Fifteenth and Sixteenth-Century Europe* (London: Duckworth, 1986).

Gray, Floyd. *Gender, Rhetoric and Print Culture in French Renaissance Writing* (Cambridge University Press, 2000).

Greenwood, Thomas. 'Guy de Bruès', *Bibliothèque d'Humanisme et Renaissance* 13 (1951): 173–86, 266–9.

Greffe, Florence and Valérie Brousselle (eds), *Documents du Minutier central des notaires de Paris: Inventaires après décès (1547–1560)* (Paris: Archives nationales, 1997).

Greffe, Florence and José Lothe (eds), *La vie, les livres, et les lectures de Pierre de L'Estoille* (Paris: Champion, 2004).

Guillerm, Luce, *et al.* (eds). *Le miroir des femmes*, 2 vols (Presses Universitaires de Lille, 1983–84).

Hampton, Timothy. *Writing from History: The Rhetoric of Exemplarity in Renaissance Literature* (Ithaca, NY: Cornell University Press, 1990).

Hanley, Sarah. 'Family and State in Early Modern France: The Marriage Pact', in Marilyn Boxer and Jean Quataert (eds), *Connecting Spheres: Women in the Western World, 1500 to the Present* (Oxford University Press, 1987), pp. 53–63.

Hanley, Sarah. 'Engendering the State: Family Formation and State Building in Early Modern France', *French Historical Studies* 16 (1989): 4–27.

Hanley, Sarah. 'Social Sites of Political Practice in France: Lawsuits, Civil Rights, and the Separation of Powers in Domestic and State Government, 1500–1800', *American Historical Review* 102:1 (1997): 27–52.

Hanley, Sarah. '"The Jurisprudence of the Arrêts": Marital Union, Civil Society and State Formation in France, 1550–1650', *Law and History Review* 21:1 (2003): 1–40.

Hanley, Sarah. 'The Family, the State, and the Law in Seventeenth- and Eighteenth-Century France: The Political Ideology of Male Right versus an Early Theory of Natural Rights', *The Journal of Modern History* 78 (2006): 289–332.

Hannoncelles, M. le Baron d'. *Metz ancien*, 2 vols (Metz: Rousseau-Pallez, 1856).

Hardwick, Julie. *The Practice of Patriarchy: Gender and the Politics of Household Authority in Early Modern France* (University Park, PA: Penn State Press, 1998).

Hardwick, Julie. 'Between State and Street: Witnesses and the Family Politics of Litigation in Early Modern France', in Suzanne Desan and Jeffrey Merrick (eds), *Family, Gender and Law in Early Modern France* (University Park, PA: Penn State Press, 2009), pp. 101–36.

Haydn, Hiram. *The Counter-Renaissance* (New York: Harcourt, 1967).

Hermant, Maxence. 'La commande artistique en Champagne du Nord au XVIe siècle: les vicomtes d'Étoges et leurs tombeaux', *Etudes marnaises* (2006): 95–120.

Hodges, Elizabeth. 'Representing Place in Gilles Corrozet's *Antiquitez de Paris*', *French Studies* 62:2 (2008): 135–49.

Hoffman, George. *Montaigne's Career* (Oxford: Clarendon, 1998).

Holmès, Catherine. *L'éloquence judiciaire de 1620 à 1660: reflet de problèmes sociaux, religieux et politiques de l'époque* (Paris: Nizet, 1967).

Holt, Mack P. *The French Wars of Religion, 1562–1629*, 2nd edn (Cambridge University Press, 2005).

Horowitz, Maryanne. 'The Image of God in Man: Is Woman Included?', *The Harvard Theological Review* 72 (1979): 175–206.

Horowitz, Maryanne. 'The Woman Question in Renaissance Texts', *History of European Ideas* 8 (1987): 587–95.

Houllemare, Marie. 'Un avocat parisien entre art oratoire et promotion de soi (fin XVIe siècle)', *Revue historique* 306:2 (2004): 283–302.

Huppert, George. *The Idea of Perfect History: Historical Erudition and Historical Philosophy in Renaissance France* (Urbana, IL: University of Illinois Press, 1970).

Huppert, George. *Les bourgeois gentilhommes: An Essay on the Definition of Elites in Renaissance France* (University of Chicago Press, 1977).

Huppert, George. *Public Schools in Renaissance France* (Urbana, IL: University of Illinois Press, 1984).

Jolly, Claude (ed.). *Histoire des bibliothèques françaises*, vol. 2, *Les bibliothèques sous l'Ancien Régime 1530–1789*, 4 vols (Paris: Promodis, 1988–92).

Jones, Ann Rosalind. *The Currency of Eros: Women's Love Lyric in Europe, 1540–1620* (New Haven, CT: Yale University Press, 1990).

Jordan, Constance. *Renaissance Feminism: Literary Texts and Political Models* (Ithaca, NY: Cornell University Press, 1990).

Kahn, Victoria. *Rhetoric, Prudence and Skepticism in the Renaissance* (Ithaca, NY: Cornell University Press, 1985).

Kaiser, Colin. 'Les Cours souveraines au XVIe siècle: morale et Contre-Réforme', *Annales-économies, sociétés, civilisations* 37 (1982): 15–31.

Keating, L. Clark. *Studies on the Literary Salon in France, 1550–1615* (Cambridge, MA: Harvard University Press, 1941).

Kelley, Donald. *Foundations of Modern Historical Scholarship: Language, Law and History in the French Renaissance* (New York: Columbia University Press, 1970).

Kelly, Joan. *Women, History and Theory: The Essays of Joan Kelly* (University of Chicago Press, 1984).

Kelso, Ruth. *Doctrine for the Lady of the Renaissance* (Urbana, IL: University of Illinois Press, 1956).

Klosowska, Anna. 'Madeleine de l'Aubespine: Life, Works, and Auto-Mythography: An Exchange with Ronsard, ca. 1570–80', *French Forum* 32:1–2 (2007): 19–38.

Kraye, Jill. 'Moral Philosophy', in Charles Schmitt and Quentin Skinner (eds), *The Cambridge History of Renaissance Philosophy* (Cambridge University Press, 1988), pp. 303–86.

Kristeller, Paul. *Renaissance Thought: The Classic, Scholastic and Humanist Strains* (New York: Harper & Row, 1961).

Kritzman, Lawrence. *The Rhetoric of Sexuality and the Literature of the French Renaissance* (Cambridge University Press, 1991).

Kushner, Eva. *Le dialogue à la Renaissance: histoire et poétique* (Geneva: Droz, 2004).

Kushner, Eva. 'Renaissance Dialogue and Subjectivity', in Dorothea Heitsch and Jean-François Vallée (eds), *Printed Voices: The Renaissance Culture of Dialogue* (University of Toronto Press, 2004), pp. 229–42.

Labarre, Albert. *Le livre dans la vie amiénoise du seizième siècle: l'enseignement des inventaires après décès, 1503–1576* (Paris: Nauwelaerts, 1971).

Larsen, Anne. 'Paradox and the Praise of Women: From Ortensio Lando and Charles Estienne to Marie de Romieu', *Sixteenth Century Journal* 28:3 (1997): 759–74.

Lauvergnat-Gagnière, Christiane. 'La rhétorique dans le *Débat de Folie et Amour*', in Guy Demerson (ed.), *Louise Labé, les voix du lyrisme* (Lyon: Editions du CNRS, 1991), pp. 53–67.

Lazard, Madeleine. *Images littéraires de la femme à la Renaissance* (Paris: PUF, 1985).

Lazard, Madeleine. 'Protestations et revendications féminines dans la littérature française du XVIe siècle', *Revue d'Histoire Littéraire de la France* 6 (1991): 859–77.

Lazard, Madeleine. *Les avenues de Fémynie: les femmes à la Renaissance* (Paris: Fayard, 2001).

Le Roy Ladurie, Emmanuel. *The Royal French State 1460–1610* (Oxford: Blackwell, 1994).

Lefranc, Abel. 'Le Tiers Livre de Pantagruel et la querelle des femmes', in *Rabelais, Étude sur Gargantua, Pantagruel, Le Tiers Livre* (Paris: Albin Michel, 1953), pp. 263–315.

Legaré, Anne-Marie. 'Reassessing Women's Libraries in Late Medieval France: The Case of Jeanne de Laval', *Renaissance Studies* 10:2 (1996): 209–29.

Legros, Alain. 'Montaigne "rapporteur": dix arrêts du Parlement de Bordeaux, premiers témoins de sa pratique du français écrit', *Journal de la Renaissance* 6 (2008): 293–303.

Lepreux, Georges. *Gallia typographica*, 5 vols (Paris: Champion, 1909–1914).

Loüet, Georges. *Recueil d'aucuns notables arrests donnez en la cour du Parlement de Paris* (Paris: Abel L'Angelier, 1609).

Loviot, Louis. 'Le mystérieux Seigneur de Cholières', *Revue des livres anciens* 1 (1913): 37–49.

Loviot, Louis. 'Cabinet des saines affections 1595', *Revue des livres anciens* 2 (1916): 274–82.

Lyons, John. *Exemplum: The Rhetoric of Example in Early Modern France and Italy* (Princeton University Press, 1989).

McKitterick, David. 'Women and their Books in Seventeenth-Century England: The Case of Elizabeth Puckering', *The Library* 1 (2000): 359–80.

Maclean, Ian. *Woman Triumphant: Feminism in French Literature 1610–1652* (Oxford: Clarendon, 1977).

Maclean, Ian. *The Renaissance Notion of Woman* (Cambridge University Press, 1980).
Magnard, Pierre (ed.). *La dignité de l'homme: actes du colloque tenu à la Sorbonne-Paris IV, en novembre 1992* (Paris: Champion, 1995).
Magnien, Catherine. 'Étienne Pasquier "familier" de Montaigne?', *Montaigne Studies* 13 (2001): 277–313.
Martin, Henri-Jean. *Livre, pouvoirs et société à Paris au XVIIe siècle (1598–1701)*, 2 vols (Geneva: Droz, 1969).
Martin, Henri-Jean (ed.). *Le livre dans l'Europe de la Renaissance: Actes du XXVIIe colloque international d'études humanistes de Tours* (Paris: Promodis, 1988).
Martinet, Jean-Luc. *Montaigne et la dignité humaine: contribution à une histoire du discours de la dignité humaine* (Paris: Eurédit, 2007).
Maugis, Édouard. *Histoire du Parlement de Paris*, 3 vols (Paris: Picard, 1913–16), facsimile reprint (New York: Franklin, 1967).
Mazzocco, Angelo. *Interpretations of Renaissance Humanism* (Leiden: Brill, 2006).
Michaud, Hélène. *La Grande chancellerie et les écritures royales au seizième siècle (1515–1589)* (Paris: PUF, 1967).
Michaud, Hélène. 'Les bibliothèques des secrétaires du roi au XVIe siècle', *Bibliothèque de l'Ecole des chartes* 126 (1968): 333–76.
Migiel, Marilyn. 'The Dignity of Man: A Feminist Perspective', in M. Migiel and Juliana Schiesari (eds), *Refiguring Woman: Perspectives on Gender and the Italian Renaissance* (Ithaca, NY: Cornell University Press, 1991), pp. 211–32.
Millet, Olivier. *La première réception des Essais de Montaigne, 1580–1640* (Paris: Honoré Champion, 1995).
Mohl, Ruth. *The Three Estates in Medieval and Renaissance Literature* (New York: Columbia University Press, 1933).
Moss, Ann. *Printed Commonplace-Books and the Structuring of Renaissance Thought* (Oxford: Clarendon, 1996).
Mousnier, Roland. *La Venalité des offices sous Henri IV et Louis XIII*, 2nd edn (Paris: PUF, 1971).
Nash, Jerry. 'The Christian–Humanist Meditation on Man: Denisot, Montaigne, Rabelais Ronsard, Scève', *Bibliothèque d'Humanisme et Renaissance* 54:2 (1992): 353–71.
Nash, Jerry. 'Renaissance Misogyny, Biblical Feminism, and Hélisenne de Crenne's *Epistres familieres et invectives*', *Renaissance Quarterly* 50:2 (1997): 379–410.
Nauert, Charles. *Agrippa and the Crisis of Renaissance Thought* (Urbana, IL: University of Illinois Press, 1965).
Nauert, Charles. *Humanism and the Culture of Renaissance Europe*, 2nd edn (Cambridge University Press, 2006).

Nyström, Urban. *Poèmes français sur les biens d'un ménage depuis* L'Oustillement au villain *du XIIIe siècle jusqu'aux* Controverses *de Gratien Du Pont* (Helsinki: Annales Academiæ scientarium fennicæ, 1940).

O'Brien, John. 'État présent: Are We Reading what Montaigne Wrote?', *French Studies* 58:4 (2004): 527–32.

Offen, Karen. 'History of Women', in Bonnie Smith (ed.), *The Oxford Encyclopedia of Women in World History*, 4 vols (Oxford University Press, 2008), vol. II, pp. 463–71.

Olivier-Martin, François. *Histoire du droit français des origines à la Révolution* (Paris: CNRS, 1992).

Omont, Henri. *Catalogue des éditions françaises de Denys Janot, libraire parisien (1529–45)* (Paris: Société de l'histoire de Paris, 1899).

Oulmont, Charles. 'Gratian du Pont Sieur de Drusac et les femmes', *Revue des études rabelaisiennes* 4 (1906): 1–28, and 5 (1907): 135–53.

Pallier, Denis. *Recherches sur l'imprimerie à Paris pendant la Ligue 1585–1594* (Geneva: Droz, 1975).

Parent, Annie. *Les Métiers du livre à Paris au XVIe siècle (1535–1560)* (Geneva: Droz, 1974).

Parsons, Jotham. 'The Political Vision of Antoine Loisel', *Sixteenth Century Journal* 27:2 (1996): 453–76.

Patrides, C.A. *Premises and Motifs in Renaissance Thought and Literature* (Princeton University Press, 1982).

Peach, Trevor. 'Une source négligé de l'antifeminisme au XVIe siècle: le "Contra Amores" de Platina et les "Dialogues" de Jacques Tahureau', *Studi francesi* 19 (1975): 201–13.

Peach, Trevor. 'Another View of *Les Dialogues* of Jacques Tahureau', *French Studies* 33:3 (1979): 272–87.

Peach, Trevor. *Nature and Reason: étude critique des Dialogues de Jacques Tahureau* (Geneva: Slatkine, 1986).

Pérouse, Gabriel. *Nouvelles françaises du XVIe siècle: Images de la vie du temps*, Travaux d'Humanisme et Renaissance 154 (Geneva: Droz, 1977).

Pichon, Jérôme and Georges Vicaire. *Documents pour servir à l'histoire des libraires de Paris, 1486–1600* (Paris: Techener, 1895).

Pichon, Jérôme and Georges Vicaire. 'Documents pour servir à l'histoire des libraires de Paris, 1486–1600', *Bulletin du bibliophile* (1894).

Postel-Lecocq, Sylvie. 'Femmes et presses à Paris au XVIe siècle: quelques exemples', in Pierre Aquilon and H.J. Martin (eds), *Le livre dans l'Europe de la Renaissance: Actes du XXVIIe colloque international d'études humanistes de Tours* (Paris: Promodis, 1988), pp. 253–63.

Pottinger, David. *The French Book Trade in the Ancien Regime, 1500–1791* (Cambridge, MA: Harvard University Press, 1958).

Preda, Alessandra. '"Les siècles à venir te loueront à bon droit": Montaigne et Claude Expilly', *Montaigne Studies* 13 (2001): 187–205.

Prendergast, Maria. *Renaissance Fantasies: The Gendering of Aesthetics in Early Modern Fiction* (Kent, OH: Kent State University Press, 1999).

Radouant, René. *Guillaume Du Vair L'homme et l'orateur jusqu'à la fin des troubles de la Ligue 1556–1596* (Paris: Société Française d'Imprimerie, 1907).

Rawles, Stephen. 'Corrozet's *Hecatomgraphie*: Where Did the Woodcuts Come From and Where Did They Go?', *Emblematica* 3:1 (1988): 31–64.

Ray, Meredith K. 'Textual Collaboration and Spiritual Partnership in Sixteenth-Century Italy: The Case of Ortensio Lando and Lucrezia Gonzaga', *Renaissance Quarterly* 62:3 (2009): 694–747.

Rendall, Steven. *Distinguo: Reading Montaigne Differently* (Oxford: Clarendon, 1992).

Renouard, Philippe. *Imprimeurs parisiens, libraires, fondeurs de caractères et correcteurs d'imprimerie: Depuis l'introduction de l'imprimerie à Paris (1470) jusqu'à la fin du XVIe siècle* (Paris: Claudin, 1898).

Renouard, Philippe. *Documents sur les imprimeurs, libraires ... ayant exercé à Paris de 1450–1600* (Paris: Société de l'Histoire de Paris et de l'Île de France, 1901).

Renouard, Philippe. *Imprimeurs et libraires parisiens du XVIe siècle. Fascicule Breyer* (Paris: Bibliothèque nationale, 1982).

Renouard, Philippe. *Imprimeurs et libraires parisiens du XVIe siècle. Fascicule Cavellat, Marnef, Cavellat* (Paris: Bibliothèque nationale, 1986).

Renouard, Philippe and Brigitte Moreau (eds). *Inventaire chronologique des éditions parisiennes*, 5 vols (Paris: Bibliothèque nationale, 1972–).

Reeser, Todd. *Moderating Masculinity in Early Modern Culture* (Chapel Hill, NC: University of North Carolina Press, 2006).

Reulos, Michel. 'L'importance des practiciens dans l'humanisme juridique', in *Pédagogues et juristes: congrès du Centre d'études supérieures de la Renaissance de Tours: été 1960* (Paris: Vrin, 1963), pp. 119–33.

Rice, Eugene. 'The Renaissance Idea of Christian Antiquity: Humanist Patristic Scholarship', in Albert Rabil (ed.), *Renaissance Humanism: Foundations, Forms, and Legacy,* 3 vols (Philadelphia, PA: University of Pennsylvania Press, 1988), vol. I, pp. 17–28.

Rice, Eugene. *The Renaissance Idea of Wisdom* (Cambridge, MA: Harvard University Press, 1958).

Richardson, Lula McDowell. *The Forerunners of Feminism in French Literature of the Renaissance from Christine de Pisa to Marie de Gournay* (Baltimore, MD: John Hopkins University Press, 1929).

Rider, Frederick. *The Dialectic of Selfhood in Montaigne* (Stanford University Press, 1973).

Rigolot, François. '1493, The Rhétoriqueurs', in Denis Hollier (ed.), *A New History of French Literature* (Cambridge, MA: Harvard University Press, 1989).

Rigolot, François. 'D'une théologie "Pour les dames" à une apologie "per le donne"?', in Claude Blum (ed.), *Montaigne: Apologie de Raimond Sebond De la theologia à la Théologie* (Paris: Champion, 1990), pp. 261–90.

Rigolot, François. 'Rabelais, Misogyny, and Christian Charity: Biblical Intertextuality and the Renaissance Crisis of Exemplarity', *Publications of the Modern Language Association of America* 109 (1994): 225–37.

Rigolot, François. *Louise Labé lyonnaise, ou la Renaissance au feminin* (Paris: Champion, 1997).

Rigolot, François. 'The Renaissance Crisis of Exemplarity', *Journal of the History of Ideas* 59:4 (1998): 557–63.

Rigolot, François. 'Problematizing Renaissance Exemplarity: The Inward Turn of Dialogue from Petrarch to Montaigne', in Dorothea Heitsch and Jean-François Vallée (eds), *Printed Voices: The Renaissance Culture of Dialogue* (University of Toronto Press, 2004), pp. 3–24.

Roelker, Nancy Lyman. *One King, One Faith: The Parlement of Paris and the Religious Reformations of the Sixteenth Century* (Berkeley, CA: University of California Press, 1996).

Rouget, François. 'Quelques éléments nouveaux sur les éditions anciennes de Du Bartas', *Bibliothèque d'Humanisme et Renaissance* 66 (2004): 133–49.

Salmon, J.H.M. *Society in Crisis: France in the Sixteenth Century* (London: Methuen, 1979).

Saulnier, V.L. *Maurice Scève*, 2 vols (Paris, 1948–49).

Saunders, Alison. *The Sixteenth-Century Blason Poétique* (Bern: Lang, 1981).

Saunders, Alison. *The Sixteenth Century French Emblem Book: A Decorative and Useful Genre*, Travaux d'Humanisme et Renaissance 224 (Geneva: Droz, 1988).

Saunders, Alison. 'Paris to Lyon and Back Again: Trends in Emblem Publishing in Mid-Sixteenth Century France', in Philip Ford and Gillian Jondorf (eds), *Intellectual Life in Renaissance Lyon: Proceedings of the Cambridge Lyon Colloquium 14–16 April 1991* (Cambridge: Cambridge French Colloquia, 1993), pp. 63–79.

Sayce, Richard. *Essays of Montaigne: A Critical Exploration* (London: Weidenfield & Nicolson, 1972).

Sayhi-Périgot, Béatrice. 'À l'arrière-plan des *Recherches* I et II: le *Pourparler du Prince*', in *Étienne Pasquier et ses Recherches de la France* (Paris: Presses de l'École Normale Supérieure, 1991), pp. 63–77.

Schiffman, Zachary. 'Montaigne and the Rise of Skepticism in Early Modern Europe: A Reappraisal', *Journal of the History of Ideas* 45:4 (1984): 499–516.

Schiffman, Zachary. *On the Threshold of Modernity: Relativism in the French Renaissance* (London: John Hopkins University Press, 1991).

Schutz, A.H. *Vernacular Books in Parisian Private Libraries in the Sixteenth Century According to the Notarial Inventories* (Chapel Hill, NC: University of North Carolina Press, 1955).

Screech, M.A. 'Rabelais, de Billon and Erasmus: A Re-examination of Rabelais's Attitude to Women', *Bibliothèque d'Humanisme et Renaissance* 13 (1951): 241–65.

Seifert, Lewis. *Manning the Margins: Masculinity and Writing in Seventeenth-Century France* (Ann Arbor, MI: University of Michigan Press, 2009).

Servadio, Gaia. *Renaissance Woman* (London: Taurus, 2005).

Shennan, J.H. *The Parlement of Paris* (London: Eyre & Spottiswoode, 1968).

Shepard, Alexandra. *Meanings of Manhood in Early Modern England* (Oxford University Press, 2003).

Simonin, Michel. 'Notes sur Pierre Boaistuau', *Bibliothèque d'Humanisme et Renaissance* 38:2 (1976): 323–33.

Simonin, Michel. 'Peut-on parler de politique éditoriale au XVIe siècle: le cas de Vincent Sertenas libraire parisien', in Pierre Aquilon and H.-J. Martin (eds), *Le livre dans l'Europe de la Renaissance: Actes du XXVIIe colloque international d'études humanistes de Tours* (Paris: Promodis, 1988), pp. 264–81.

Simonin, Michel. 'Le Périgourdin au Palais: sur le voyage des *Essais* de Bordeaux à Paris', in M. Tetel and G. Mallary Masters (eds), *Le Parcours des Essais: Montaigne 1588–1988* (Paris: Amateurs de livres, 1989), pp. 17–30.

Simonin, Michel. 'Abel L'Angelier: Le politique du Palais', in *Politique et littérature en France au XVIe et XVIIe siècles: actes du colloque international Monopoli ... 1995* (Paris: Didier, 1997), pp. 53–86.

Simonin, Michel. 'Trois femmes en librairie: Françoise de Louvain, Marie L'Angelier, Françoise Patelé (1571–1645)', in D. de Courcelles and Carmen Val Julián (eds), *Des femmes et des livres: France and Espagnes, XIVe–XVIIe siècle* (Paris: École nationale des chartes, 1999), pp. 149–61.

Simonin, Michel. 'Bernard Automne (1564–après 1628) témoin et lecteur de Montaigne', *Montaigne Studies* 13 (2001): 315–60.

Skinner, Quentin. *The Foundations of Modern Political Thought*, 2 vols (Cambridge University Press, 1978).

Skinner, Quentin. 'Thomas Hobbes: Rhetoric and the Construction of Morality', *Proceedings of the British Academy* 76 (1991): 1–61.

Skinner, Quentin. *Reason and Rhetoric in the Philosophy of Thomas Hobbes* (Cambridge University Press, 1996).

Sloane, Thomas. 'Schoolbooks and Rhetoric: Erasmus's *Copia*', *Rhetorica* 9:2 (1991): 113–29.

Smarr, Janet. *Joining the Conversation: Dialogues by Renaissance Women* (Ann Arbor, MI: University of Michigan Press, 2005).

Solente, Suzanne. 'Les manuscrits des Dupuy à la Bibliothèque nationale', *Bibliothèque de l'École des chartes* 88 (1927): 177–250.

Sozzi, Lionello. 'La "dignitas hominis" dans la littérature de la Renaissance française', in A.H.T. Levi (ed.), *Humanism in France at the End of the Middle Ages and in the Early Renaissance* (Manchester University Press, 1970), pp. 176–98.

Sozzi, Lionello. 'Boccaccio in Francia nel cinquecento', in Carlo Pellegrini (ed.), *Boccaccio nella cultura francese* (Florence: Olschki, 1971).

Sozzi, Lionello. 'La "dignitas hominis" chez les auteurs lyonnais du XVIe siècle', in *Actes du colloques sur l'humanisme lyonnais au XVIe siècle* (Presses Universitaires de Grenoble, 1974), pp. 295–338.

Sozzi, Lionello. *La dignité de l'homme à la Renaissance* (Turin: Giappichelli, 1982).

Stretton, Tim. *Women Waging Law in Elizabethan England* (Cambridge University Press, 1998).

Strien-Chardonneau, Madeleine van. 'Une lectrice du XVIIIe siècle Belle de Zuylen / Isabelle de Charrière (1740–1805): Livres et pratiques de lecture à travers sa correspondance', in Isabelle Brouard-Arends (ed.), *Lectrices d'Ancien Régime* (Presses Universitaires de Rennes, 2003), pp. 177–86.

Supple, James. *Arms versus Letters: The Military and Literary Ideals in the 'Essais' of Montaigne* (Oxford: Clarendon, 1984).

Swift, Helen. *Gender, Writing, Performance: Men Defending Women in Late Medieval France, 1440–1538* (Oxford: Clarendon, 2008).

Taillandier, A.H. 'Notice historique sur le château et les seigneurs de La Borde-le-Vicomte', *Revue archéologique* 13 (1856): 113–18.

Tarte, Kendall. *Writing Places: Sixteenth-Century City Culture and the Des Roches Salon* (Newark, DE: University of Delaware Press, 2007).

Tchemerzine, Avenir. *Bibliographie d'éditions originales et rares d'auteurs francais des XVe, XVIe, XVIIe, et XVIIIe siècles*, 10 vols (Paris: Plée, 1927–33).

Telle, E.V. *L'Œuvre de Marguerite d'Angoulême Reine de Navarre et la querelle des femmes* (Université de Toulouse, 1937).

Timmermans, Linda. *L'accès des femmes à la culture (1598–1715): un débat d'idées de Saint François de Sales à la Marquise de Lambert* (Paris: Champion, 1993).

Trinkaus, Charles. *In Our Image and Likeness: Humanity and Divinity in Italian Humanist Thought*, 2 vols (London: Constable, 1970).

Trinkaus, Charles. *The Scope of Renaissance Humanism* (Ann Arbor, MI: University of Michigan Press, 1983).

Tosh, John. *Manliness and Masculinities in Nineteenth-Century Britain: Essays on Gender, Family, and Empire* (New York: Pearson, 2005).

Turbide, Chantal. 'Les livres trouvé dans l'Hôtel de la Reine après le décès de Catherine de Médicis (1519–1589)', in I. Brouard-Arends (ed.), *Lectrices d'Ancien Régime* (Presses Universitaires de Rennes, 2003), pp. 33–45.

Vickers, Brian. *In Defence of Rhetoric* (Oxford: Clarendon, 1988).

Vickers, Brian. 'Rhetoric and Poetics', in Charles Schmitt and Quentin Skinner (eds), *The Cambridge History of Renaissance Philosophy* (Cambridge University Press, 1988), pp. 715–45.

Vickers, Nancy J. 'The unauthored 1539 volume in which is printed the *Hecatomphile, The Flowers of French Poetry*, and *Other Soothing Things*', in Margreta de Grazia, *et al.* (eds), *Subject and Object in Renaissance Culture* (Cambridge University Press, 1996), pp. 166–88.

Victor, Joseph. *Charles de Bovelles, 1479–1553: An Intellectual Biography* (Geneva: Droz, 1978).

Viennot, Éliane. 'La diffusion du féminisme au temps de Louise de Labé', in Béatrice Alonso and É. Viennot (eds), *Louise Labé 2005* (Publications de l'Universite de Saint-Étienne, 2004), pp. 21–35.

Viennot, Éliane. *La France, les femmes et le pouvoir*, 2 vols (Paris: Perrin, 2006–2008).

Villey, Pierre. *Les sources et l'évolution des Essais de Montaigne*, 2 vols (Paris: Hachette, 1908).

Vindry, Fleury. *Les parlementaires français au XVIe siècle*, 2 vols (Paris: Champion, 1910–12).

Warner, Lyndan. 'Marie Le Gendre, the *Saines affections* and Moral Thought in the Late Sixteenth Century', in P. Ford and G. Jondorf (eds), *Women Writers in the French Renaissance: Proceedings of the Fifth Cambridge French Colloquium* (Cambridge: Cambridge French Colloquia, 1999), pp. 221–38.

Warner, Lyndan. 'Widows, Widowers and the Problem of "Second Marriages" in Sixteenth-Century France', in Sandra Cavallo and L. Warner (eds), *Widowhood in Medieval and Early Modern Europe* (New York: Longman, 1999), pp. 84–107.

Wilkin, Rebecca. *Women, Imagination and the Search for Truth in Early Modern Europe* (Aldershot: Ashgate, 2008)

Winn, Colette. 'La *dignitas mulieris*: les enjeux idéologiques d'une appropriation du XVe au XVIIe siècles', *Études Littéraires* 27 (1994): 11–24.

Wood, Diane. *Hélisenne de Crenne: At the Crossroads of Renaissance Humanism and Feminism* (London: AUP, 2000).

Yardeni, Miriam. 'L'ordre des avocats et la grève du Barreau parisien en 1602', *Revue d'histoire économique et sociale* 44 (1966): 481–507.

Zaercher, Véronique. 'Entre dispute et conciliation : stratégies et figures du "consensus" dans le dialogue de la seconde moitié du XVIe siècle', *Revue d'histoire littéraire de la France* 101 (2001): 1331–48.

Zimmermann, Margarete. 'Querelle des Femmes, querelles du livre', in D. de Courcelles and Carmen Val Julián (eds), *Des femmes et des livres: France and Espagnes, XIVe–XVIIe siècle* (Paris: École nationale des chartes, 1999), pp. 79–94.

Zimmermann, Margarete. 'The *Querelle des femmes* as Cultural Studies Paradigm', in Anne Jacobson Schutte, *et al.* (eds), *Time, Space and Women's Lives in Early Modern Europe* (Kirksville, MO: Truman State University Press, 2001), pp. 17–28.

Zimmermann, Margarete. '*The Old Quarrel*: More than Just Rhetoric', in Wolfram Aichinger, *et al.* (eds), *The* Querelle des Femmes *in the Romania* (Vienna: Turia und Kant, 2003), pp. 27–43.

Zinguer, Ilana. *Misères et grandeur de la femme au XVIe siècle* (Geneva: Slatkine, 1982).

Reference Works

Biographie universelle ancienne et moderne, ed. Louis-Gabriel Michaud, 52 vols (Paris: Michaud, 1811–28).

Dictionnaire de biographie française, 20 vols– (Paris: Letouzey et Ané, 1932–).

Dictionnaire de droit et de pratique contenant l'explication des termes de droit, d'ordonnances, de coutumes et de pratique, ed. C.J. de Ferrière, 2 vols (Paris: Veuve Brunet, 1769).

Nouvelle biographie générale depuis les temps les plus reculés jusqu'à 1850–60, 46 vols (Paris: Firmin-Didot, 1855–70), reprint (Copenhagen: Rosenkilde, 1968).

Index

For Product Safety Concerns and Information please contact our EU representative GPSR@taylorandfrancis.com
Taylor & Francis Verlag GmbH, Kaufingerstraße 24, 80331 München, Germany

www.ingramcontent.com/pod-product-compliance
Ingram Content Group UK Ltd.
Pitfield, Milton Keynes, MK11 3LW, UK
UKHW010957180926
475701UK00004B/424
9781138379701